Susan Steigerwald
223 Oakey Ave.
Greendale, IN  47025

# In a Far Country

# In a Far Country

*The True Story of
a Mission, a Marriage, a Murder, and the
Remarkable Reindeer Rescue
of 1898*

.

John Taliaferro

PublicAffairs · New York

Published in the United States by PublicAffairs™,
a member of the Perseus Books Group.

Public Affairs books are available at special discounts for bulk purchases in the U.S.
by corporations, institutions, and other organizations. For more information, please
contact the Special markets Department at the Perseus Books Group, 11 Cambridge
Center, Cambridge, MA 02142, call (617) 252-5298, or email
special.markets@perseusbooks.com.

*Set in Fairfield with Cloister Open Face display*
*Book design and Composition by Mark McGarry, Texas Type & Book Works*

Library of Congress Cataloging-in-Publication Data

Taliaferro, John, 1952-
    In a far country : the true story of a mission, a marriage, a murder, and the
remarkable reindeer rescue in 1898. — 1st ed.
        p. cm.
    Includes bibliographical references and index.
    ISBN-13: 978-1-58648-221-3
    ISBN-10: 1-58648-221-1
    1. Barrow, Point (Alaska)—History—19th century.  2. Whaling ships—Alaska—
Barrow, Point—History—19th century.  3. Overland Relief Expedition (1897-1898).
4. Bear (Ship).  5. Reindeer—Alaska—Barrow, Point—History—19th century.
6. Lopp, William Thomas, 1864-1939.  7. Lopp, Ellen Louise Kittredge, 1868-1947.
8. Missionaries—Alaska—Prince of Wales, Cape—Biography.  9. Prince of Wales,
Cape (Alaska)—Biography.  10. Eskimos—Alaska—Prince of Wales, Cape—
History—19th century.  I. Title.

    F912.B2T35 2006
    979.8'02—dc22                                                    2006009159

FIRST EDITION
10 9 8 7 6 5 4 3 2 1

*For Jane*

The man who turns his back upon the comforts of an elder civilization, to face the savage youth, the primordial simplicity of the North, may estimate success at an inverse ratio to the quantity and quality of his hopelessly fixed habits. He will soon discover, if he be a fit candidate, that the material habits are the less important. The exchange of such things as a dainty menu for rough fare, of the stiff leather shoe for the soft, shapeless moccasin, of the feather bed for a couch in the snow, is after all a very easy matter. But his pinch will come in learning properly to shape his mind's attitude toward all things, and especially toward his fellow man. For the courtesies of ordinary life, he must substitute unselfishness, forbearance, and tolerance. Thus, and thus only, can he gain that pearl of great price,—true comradeship. He must not say "Thank you"; he must mean it without opening his mouth, and prove it by responding in kind. In short, he must substitute the deed for the word, the spirit for the letter.

·

—JACK LONDON, "IN A FAR COUNTRY" (1899)

# Contents

# In a Far Country

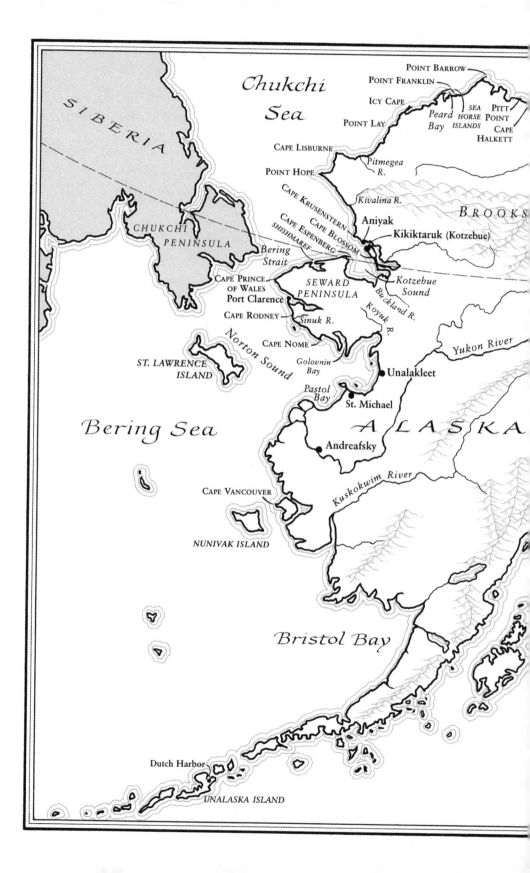

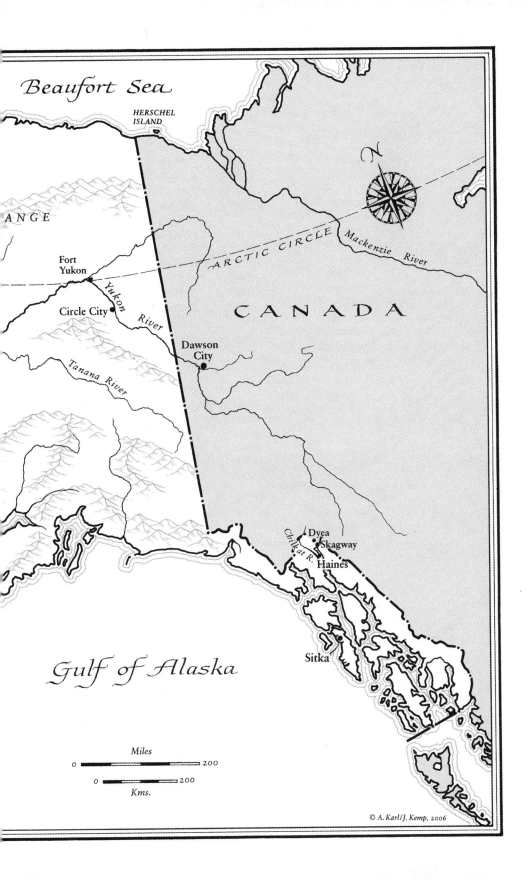

Beaufort Sea

HERSCHEL
ISLAND

ANGE

ARCTIC CIRCLE

Mackenzie River

Fort
Yukon

Circle City

Yukon River

CANADA

Dawson
City

Tanana River

Dyea
Skagway
Chilkat R. Haines

Gulf of Alaska

Sitka

Miles
0 ——————— 200

0 ——————— 200
Kms.

© A. Karl/J. Kemp, 2006

# Introduction

TOM AND ELLEN LOPP had long since accustomed the natives to knock before entering. Yet the rap on the outer door was decidedly sharper than the polite thump that they might expect from one of the villagers. On the twenty-fourth of January, with the temperature at thirty below, an Eskimo would have kept his mitten on, softening the blow. This sound was more imperative, more official, definitely not Eskimo.

The Lopps had not seen another white man since September, when the revenue cutter had dropped anchor briefly at the end of its annual Arctic patrol and put a boat ashore to share news and collect mail. In previous years, the Lopps would have caught sight of a dozen or more ships passing through the Bering Strait, bound for San Francisco from the whaling grounds of the Beaufort and Chukchi seas. At Cape Prince of Wales, where the Lopps lived, the strait is at its most narrow, the Russian shore only fifty-five miles away. On clear days, the headlands of East Cape, Siberia, are a sturdy seam stitched across the western horizon.

This past fall, however, the Lopps had observed no sails or plumes of coal smoke, and they had noticed only one set of lights in the boreal darkness. "So perhaps some were frozen or wrecked up north," Ellen Lopp wrote to her family in Minnesota, accepting that her letter would not reach them until the following year. By now the sea was choked with ice, and any ships still in Arctic waters would be icebound or worse. This time of year even the overland link between the Cape and the nearest white outpost, the government reindeer station and Lutheran mission at Port Clarence, sixty miles around the coastline of Seward Peninsula, was treacherous and reluctantly traveled. The stranger at the door, then, was in dire need, on critical business, or both.

He certainly looked Eskimo. He wore a deerskin *atigi* trimmed with wolf fur and deerskin boots soled with the tough hide of bearded seal. The only anomaly was a woolen scarf to protect cheeks livid from harsh winter travel. Not until he gave his name did Tom Lopp recognize him. He was Lieutenant David H. Jarvis, second in command of the U.S. Revenue Cutter Service's *Bear*, the ship that had called at Cape Prince of Wales four months earlier and on numerous occasions before then. Almost as surprising as the presence of Jarvis was that of a second man, Charlie Antisarlook, an Eskimo whom Lopp knew better than he did the Revenue Cutter Service officer. Lopp had befriended Antisarlook not long after coming to the Cape, eight years earlier, and Lopp had been instrumental in persuading the government to entrust Antisarlook with his own herd of reindeer, which now grazed a hundred miles to the south, on Norton Sound. Lopp was certain that Antisarlook would not have traveled so far from his home on a whim. Nor, he suspected, could Jarvis have made it this far without Antisarlook. As Lopp sized up his two trail-stiff visitors, dozens of Cape villagers approached across the packed snow, inquisitive about the unexpected outsiders.

Never one to be thrown off balance for long, Lopp invited the two men indoors to warm and explain themselves. The Lopp house was far from roomy, barely big enough for the family, even less so since the birth of a fourth child in October. Lopp had built it himself. Lumber — anything milled, forged, or manufactured—had to come by ship from

Outside—more than two thousand miles to the south and reachable only three or four months of the year. For those living seventy miles below the Arctic Circle, the only available building materials were earth, animal skin, snow, ice—natives were masters of all of these—or Lopp's choice, driftwood logs, flung seaward by Alaska's muscular rivers and washed up on beaches many hundreds of miles from their origin. (While natives from Greenland to Siberia—known variously as Inuit, Inupiat, Yup'ik, and in Alaska also by the catch-all, Eskimo*—esteemed wood as a source of fuel, shelter, sleds, and boats, few of the Arctic's indigenous people had ever laid eyes on a living tree of any stature.)

The Lopp house was twenty feet by twenty-four, as proud and crude as any homestead on the American frontier. On either side of the tight entry hall was a storeroom and a small waiting room, where natives were welcome to warm themselves and linger over the boggling pictures in the Sears, Roebuck catalogue and the *Ladies' Home Journal*. Next came a combined kitchen and living room, and in the rear two tiny bedrooms where the family slept. In their first years at Cape Prince of Wales, Ellen Lopp had papered the walls with newspapers from home, providing insulation of two different sorts. Cast-iron stoves burned driftwood or coal, one hauled by sled, the other dearly freighted by ship in burlap sacks.

The Lopps knew Lieutenant Jarvis only slightly. Every year since Tom had arrived at the Cape in 1890, and Ellen two years later, the *Bear* had been a predictable and protective presence in their lives. With the purchase of Alaska from Russia in 1867, the job of patrolling its thirty thousand miles of wild coastline, the Aleutian archipelago, and the hunting grounds of the Bering, Chukchi, and Beaufort seas fell to the Revenue Cutter Service, an arm, in this case a very long arm, of the U.S. Treasury. The mission of the Revenue Cutter Service

---

* Today many regard "Eskimo" as a pejorative term, although it is still acceptable in Alaska. The author uses the term not out of disrespect but in keeping with common usage of the nineteenth and early twentieth centuries.

was primarily to protect Alaska's rich resources of walrus, seal, and salmon from foreign poachers and to prevent the sale of liquor and firearms to Alaskan natives, who, though scarcely related to the restive and only recently suppressed Indians of the American plains, were nonetheless measured, and on occasion threatened, with the same yardstick.

Over the years, the scope of the small fleet of revenue cutters had expanded considerably. If Alaska were draped across the lower forty-eight states, it would eclipse an area from the Atlantic Ocean to the Mississippi River and from Lake Michigan to the Gulf of Mexico. Even after the half-million-square-mile possession received a civil government of sorts in 1884, it could boast of little law and even less order. The few hundred daring souls who pressed their luck in this fantastically far-flung icebox clung to the southeastern-most harbors, such as Sitka, the former Russian outpost and seat of territorial government. A few had chanced as far as Dutch Harbor, on the Aleutian island of Unalaska, or St. Michael, near the mouth of the Yukon. But by January 1898, when Lieutenant Jarvis appeared at the Lopps' door, the number of white residents living north of latitude 64 north—the entire top half of Alaska, an expanse exceeding that of the original thirteen colonies—was fewer than three dozen. These intrepid outlanders could be delineated into two distinct and often antagonistic categories: missionaries and whalers, the latter group including the traders who tagged along with them.

It fell to the U.S. Revenue Cutter Service to abet the welfare of both. This entailed rescuing the shipwrecked and health-wracked; refereeing disputes between whalers and whalers, whalers and natives, whalers and missionaries, missionaries and natives; and ferrying men, families, and supplies between remote outposts such as Cape Prince of Wales and the relative safety of civilization. In the final decades of the nineteenth century, the Revenue Cutter Service *was* the Stars and Stripes in northern Alaska—not that they waved ubiquitously. Weather permitting, the *Bear* visited Cape Prince of Wales twice a year, once in July when the ice receded and once in September on the way home to San Francisco for the winter. Given the geographical enormity of its jurisdiction, the *Bear* never lingered at the Cape; it usually stayed for less than a day. The waters were dangerously shallow and the surf frequently forbidding. On a typical visit by the *Bear*, Tom Lopp would go aboard, perhaps staying the night and sharing a meal with the officers. If time allowed, some of the ship's crew might stretch their sea legs at the Cape for an hour or two. No matter what, by November the *Bear* was always safely berthed far to the south.

Tom and Ellen Lopp were missionaries. Each had chosen Cape Prince of Wales for its extremity, its opportunity, and its sheer adventure, although it is fair to say that neither had any advance notion of the extent to which circumstances would exceed their youthful expectations. He was from Indiana, thirty-three years old, and raised Presbyterian; she from Minnesota, four years younger, a Congregationalist. They met at the Cape in July 1892 and were married the following month. Both had previous experience teaching school in the States, and teaching was the first order of business at the Cape, after survival. Proselytizing came more slowly, as they learned the Eskimo language, Inupiaq, and the Eskimos learned theirs. With the Lopps, more so than with most missionaries, adjustment was a two-way street: Natives had as much to teach the Lopps as the Lopps had to teach the natives, whom the missionaries, to their credit, chose to regard as their hosts.

From the start, the Lopps had tried not to be holier-than-thou, instead seeking a more reasoned blend of piety and pragmatism. They grasped that if salvation and damnation hung in the balance from a spiritual standpoint, then the same was true from a temporal standpoint. The twentieth century was looming just beyond the horizon, a colossal temblor of technology, pathogens, and conceit powerful enough to upend anything in its path. Given this nearly tectonic inevitability, the Lopps felt that part of their duty was to educate and

Christianize the Eskimos, of course, but also to prepare them—not just for the next life, but for the new world as well, while at the same time not obliterating the old one entirely.

For as long as Eskimos have inhabited North America—ever since their forebears crossed the land bridge from Siberia many thousands of years ago—their survival had depended on their ability to kill walruses, seals, whales, and, not least of all, caribou. But in the latter half of the nineteenth century, the harpooners and gunners of the white man's ships had decimated the aquatic mammals, and now the caribou had become scarce, too. Scientists continue to dispute the cause of the caribou's disappearance from the Bering Strait. Some speculate that hunters armed with breech-loading rifles drove the herds into the hard-to-reach interior of Alaska. Others attribute the caribou exodus to a natural shift in migratory patterns. Either way, the dearth of caribou was of enormous concern to coastal Eskimos. No other animal's fur combined the warmth, comfort, and resilience of caribou. Ultimately the persistent absence of caribou from the northwest coast of Alaska made it harder for natives to clothe and feed themselves and obliged them to become more dependent on outsiders—particularly the Chukchi, their immediate neighbors across the Bering Strait.

Despite sharing a similar ethnic heritage, Alaskan Eskimos and Chukchi were rivals, with ancient battle scars to prove it. Yet they never stopped trading with each other; every summer their skin-covered *umiaks*, many large enough to hold thirty passengers and tons of goods, turned the Bering Strait into an Arctic Bosporus. Historically the exchange between the two groups was fairly even. Only lately had the balance begun to tip, and caribou were largely to blame. Whereas Alaskan Eskimos had hunted caribou for generations, natives throughout Siberia, including the Chukchi, had long ago seen the wisdom of breeding caribou into meeker, more manageable reindeer that could be herded, trained to pull sleds and carry packs, even milked. Caribou and reindeer remained close cousins, both *Rangifer tarandus*, and could interbreed. But reindeer had a thousand-year head start toward docility; caribou would always be caribou, not readily tamed. Consequently the Chukchi, who owned vast numbers of reindeer, had something that the Eskimos, who persisted in chasing the ever wild, increasingly elusive caribou, did not.

For Tom Lopp, who cared perhaps as much about saving lives as souls, the solution appeared straightforward: His flock badly needed a herd.

Caribou were the past, reindeer the future, and Lopp's superiors in Washington agreed. "[Reindeer] will do more than preserve life," vouched Sheldon Jackson, the general agent of education for Alaska. "[They] will advance the self-respect of the people and advance them in the scale of civilization." Even more than that, Jackson continued (now playing to the gallery of skeptics who wondered why Alaska was part of America at all), reindeer "will also utilize the hundreds of thousands of square miles of moss-covered tundra . . . and make those now useless barren wastes conducive to the wealth and prosperity of the United States."

With financial backing first from private donors and then from Congress, the revenue cutter *Bear* was dispatched to Siberia in 1891 to purchase reindeer. The *Bear* made similar trips nearly every summer over the next decade. The idea of establishing a reindeer station at Port Clarence, southeast of Cape Prince of Wales, was not Tom Lopp's originally, but he played an instrumental role in proving its efficacy. In 1893, the third year of the reindeer endeavor, Lopp took leave from his Cape mission and became superintendent of the station at Port Clarence.

A believer before, he was now an ardent apostle. The more he worked with reindeer, the more he became convinced of their suitability to Alaska. Acolytes followed. Above all, Lopp promoted an apprenticeship program whereby natives who learned to herd and stuck with it could eventually be rewarded with ownership of their

own animals. When he and Ellen—with one child already and another on the way—returned to Cape Prince of Wales after a year, they
drove a hundred reindeer with them. Their initiative was the next vital
step toward an "endless chain" of herds, linking and enriching every
native village in northern Alaska.

There was no better proof of Lopp's vision and his already measur-
able success than the appearance of Lieutenant Jarvis and Charlie
Antisarlook in January 1898. And yet there was nothing more ironic
than the purpose of their visit. Jarvis had come to requisition the Cape
Prince of Wales reindeer herd and drive it—no, he wanted Lopp to
drive it—to Point Barrow, at the northernmost tip of Alaska, where
eight whaling ships had tarried greedily in the fall and were now icebound, their crews facing likely starvation unless someone could bring
succor, which at this late date could come in only one form: reindeer
meat on the hoof. All this Jarvis spelled out as he and Antisarlook
thawed by the stove and devoured a hot meal. The rescue effort even
had an official name, the Overland Relief Expedition, and bore the
urgent blessing of no less than President William McKinley.

Tom Lopp was on the spot. How could he be expected to leave his
family? The baby was only three months old, the eldest of the other
three children not yet six. Sending them and Ellen to the Lutheran
mission at Port Clarence was beyond foolhardy. To leave them by
themselves at the Cape was scarcely more prudent. They had never
had a serious problem with the natives; if anything, the Cape Eskimos
tended to be overly protective of Tom, Ellen, and especially the children. On the other hand, too many Cape residents were incorrigible
drinkers, unruly and unpredictable when drunk, and the community
had a history of violence. The Lopps tried not to dwell on the murder
of Harrison Thornton, the missionary who had landed at the Cape
with Tom in 1890 only to be shot dead by Cape thugs three years later.
But still . . . .

If Tom acceded to Jarvis's request—were they orders?—how long could he expect to be away? Could he even get to Point Barrow at all with—or, for that matter, even without—a herd of reindeer? Such a journey was unprecedented. Natives frequently ventured considerable distances by dogsled to hunt or fish. But nobody—not Lopp, not the small group of Eskimo apprentices—had ever driven a herd such a long way. How far was Point Barrow? Maps were sketchy at best. Worse, in the dead of winter there was scarcely any daylight. Nevertheless, Tom Lopp could think of reasons not to say no.

And in the end, Jarvis was very persuasive as he told the extraordinary tale of how he had gotten to this point. Some of the whaling ships on the north coast had managed to slip out, carrying word of the grim prospects faced by those who had not been so fortunate. When news of the icebound whalers was finally telegraphed from San Francisco to Washington, the response was prompt and explicit. In the fall of 1897, the attention of the United States was turned to warmer, more turbulent waters. Cuba was in the midst of revolution, and Washington, fueled by turgid press accounts of gross indignities committed by the Spanish against the freedom fighters of a sugar-rich island so close to America's southern coast, was working up its brief for war. Cuba, however, was not the only theater of expansionist intrigue. Appetite for Hawaiian annexation was growing, as was interest in a canal to shorten the route between the Caribbean and the Pacific. In a recent flurry of sword rattling, the United States had rousted Britain from disputed seal-hunting grounds in the Bering Sea. Consistent with the recent rage for bold nationalist gestures, word went out that no American sparrow, however distant, should be allowed to fall—or freeze.

The *Bear* had barely docked at Seattle on its homeward voyage from the Arctic when it was ordered to reprovision and head out again. By the time it turned north on its voyage of relief, winter had enveloped the Far North in an armor of ice. On December 16, 1897, Jarvis and three others were put ashore at Cape Vancouver, five hundred inhospitable miles south of Cape Prince of Wales. It took Jarvis six weeks to reach the Lopps, traveling most of the way by dogsled, depending on native guides, and sleeping in canvas tents at temperatures sixty degrees below freezing. Along the way, Jarvis had split his team of cuttermen, assigning one officer to establish a supply depot at Point Hope, north of Cape Prince of Wales, while the rest of the expedition struck out along the coast of the Seward Peninsula, where Charlie Antisarlook and Tom Lopp kept their reindeer herds. Antisarlook had 130 deer; Lopp oversaw more than 300.

Lopp did not take long to make up his mind. "After a sleepless night," he revealed in a Congregational newsletter afterward, "Mrs. Lopp and I decided . . . that the deer, herders, and myself would have to go. You can imagine at what cost this decision was made."

Yet no one could imagine what was about to befall not just the Lopps but all of Alaska. In the summer of 1898, while the trapped whalers were awaiting rescue and fending off starvation and scurvy, three Norwegian prospectors struck gold near Cape Nome, a hundred miles southeast of Cape Prince of Wales, not far from where Charlie Antisarlook kept his reindeer herd. Within a year, the white population of northern Alaska would explode from two or three dozen to well over ten thousand. Nothing that the natives had absorbed and applied in their broad span of hardy and not unhappy existence in the North, and nothing that Tom and Ellen Lopp could teach them, could amply prepare them for this abrupt stampede from Outside.

Similarly, the Overland Relief Expedition was overwhelmed by grander events in American history. Two weeks after Jarvis knocked on the Lopps' door, the U.S. battleship *Maine* exploded in Havana harbor. On April 11, the day President McKinley finally summoned the nerve to ask Congress for the power to wage war against Spain, Tom Lopp was far from home on an exposed beach on the Chukchi Sea, crippled by snowblindness. By the time news of the Overland Relief Expedition's remarkable achievement reached the world in September, Theodore Roosevelt had taken San Juan Hill and Admiral Dewey had demolished the Spanish fleet at Manila Bay. Reindeer were hardly front-page news.

Medals for bravery would eventually be awarded to Jarvis and two other Revenue Cutter Service men. Yet Tom Lopp's role in the ordeal—a seven-hundred-mile trek (as long as many of the now legendary cattle drives from Texas to Kansas) accomplished in the dead of winter across ice and frozen tundra, and at temperatures far below zero, in the polar gloom—was no less crucial and every bit as courageous as that of the military men. However, neither he nor the natives who stuck by him throughout the expedition received more than passing acknowledgment for their efforts. More galling, they had to plead with the government to be reimbursed for the reindeer that had been sacrificed to weather, wolves, and the whalers of Point Barrow. The exploits of these men, like the tracks they left in the Arctic snow, were blown into obscurity—only now to be retraced.

# Beyond the Pale

TOM LOPP FAVORED DEEDS over words, heeding St. James's exhortation that "by works was faith made perfect." Perhaps this explains his decision to trade the comparative calm of an Indiana classroom for the hardship of Alaska. His reasons might be clearer if only he had thought to record them, but, true to his character, he allowed his actions to speak for themselves.

Could be it was in his blood. His great-grandfather Jacob Klopp had fled the war-ravaged Rhineland in the 1750s and sought passage to the American colonies, where he dropped the *K* from his surname and took up acreage in North Carolina. His son Jacob followed the frontier westward to Harrison County, Indiana, named for William Henry Harrison, who had wrested Indiana from the Indians at bloody Tippecanoe and became its first territorial governor (and later president). There the Lopps stuck, prospering in the fertile bottomlands of the Ohio River Valley. Two generations later, William Thomas Lopp was born in Valley City on the summer solstice of 1864, in the shadow of the Civil War. Tom was the fourth of ten children, the second son. By necessity or out of choice, he left the farm for Hanover College, a struggling Presbyterian school east of Louisville. He graduated at twenty-four, old for his class. Those who knew him say he appeared taller than his height, which was five-foot-eight. His broad shoulders, dark complexion, and large hazel eyes made him dashingly handsome. "He gives the impression of great strength and endurance," one acquaintance observed. His manner was that of "a mild, patient, yet determined man."

For the next five years he served as principal of various small-town schools in Indiana. He also taught Sunday school in the Presbyterian Church. In the spring of 1890 he read a notice in a church journal, seeking lay missionaries willing to go to Alaska under the auspices of the American Missionary Association. Unattached, in good health, and with experience in education, he believed he was just the man for the job.

The American Missionary Association had its roots in a committee formed in 1839 to support a group of African slaves who had mutinied against the masters of the Spanish ship *Amistad* and pleaded for asylum on the coast of New England. Mostly Congregationalist at first, the AMA became increasingly nondenominational with the establishment of missions in Jamaica, in the Sandwich Islands, and among the Indians of the Great Plains. Always true to its abolitionist roots, it placed thousands of teachers throughout the South during and after the Civil War. AMA teachers helped found several black colleges, including Fisk University in Nashville and Talladega College in Alabama. With its focus turned southward, the AMA might never have added Alaska to its portfolio were it not for the righteous entreaty of the Reverend Sheldon Jackson.

Jackson was a little man (barely five feet tall) who thought big. More than one contemporary compared him to Napoleon, although in place of gold braid he wore the white collar of the Presbyterian clergy. Foremost of his many achievements, according to the most generous of his biographers, is that "he saved the Eskimos from extinction."

True or not, Jackson had a vision of what was best for Alaska's natives and, more important, he sold it to the American people.

After completing seminary at Princeton in 1858, Jackson hoped to be posted to a foreign mission. But he was judged too frail and instead was sent to teach in a Choctaw mission school in Indian Territory, where he quickly found that he had neither the physical nor the moral constitution for whipping recalcitrant students. Jackson's strength, indeed, was not as a hands-on evangelist. Rather, he exhorted and enabled those already converted to carry the Word farther into the field. A "peppery Puritan," he saw himself as a general of Christian soldiers and steered his career accordingly. In the spring of 1869, a month before the completion of the first transcontinental railroad, Jackson was appointed superintendent of all Presbyterian missions in Iowa, Nebraska, the Dakotas, Wyoming, Montana, and Idaho, a parish of more than a half-million square miles. The scale suited him.

To reach his far-flung congregation, he began publishing a newspaper, the *Rocky Mountain Presbyterian*, which became a clarion for his fondest cause: education of natives. Jackson had learned the hard way that he could not beat religion into the "degraded heathen"; nor could he preach it into him—at least not directly, not immediately. When a young frontier missionary complained that he was having difficulty guiding his native charges to the light, Jackson reportedly replied, "They won't come to hear preachers; send . . . a teacher." This was Jackson's method: educate first, then convert. It was also a doctrine endorsed by President Ulysses S. Grant and the Congress. Passed in 1873, the so-called Grant Peace Policy stipulated that Indians be placed on reservations—ostensibly, the law said, to spare them from further aggressions by whites (who wanted their land)—where they would be clothed, fed, and taught "pursuits as are incident to civilization, through the aid of . . . Christian organizations." In the same fashion that Indian homelands had been divided by whites, so then were their reservations. A contract system was developed that dele-

gated to various denominations the task of educating certain tribes—
church schools funded, at least partially, by federal money. (Nowadays
similar arrangements are called, somewhat controversially, "faith-
based initiatives.")

In his first eight years as superintendent in the Great Plains and
Rocky Mountains, Jackson placed dozens of missionaries in reserva-
tion schools. Yet his appetite was hardly sated. In 1877, on a trip to
Portland, Oregon, he impulsively boarded a ship bound for Wrangell,
a slapped-together port on the thickly forested coast of southeastern
Alaska. There he witnessed firsthand the debauchery, disease, and
general woefulness of the Tlingit and Tsimshian Indians, inflicted on
them by rapacious white settlers. The message of misery, he later
wrote, was "a wail as despairing and piteous as was ever wafted from
the jungles of Darkest Africa." Alaska, like Africa, was far beyond the
bounds of Jackson's superintendence, but that would soon change.
His companion on the trip was a devout Presbyterian named Amanda
McFarland, who was determined to sustain a mission at Wrangell.
With Jackson's help she succeeded.

Jackson returned to the States, raised money to keep the Wrangell
mission alive, and thereafter gave his full attention to Alaska. He was,
above all, a brilliant propagandist. He published dozens of tracts and
articles and an engaging travelogue, *Alaska and the Missions of the
North Pacific Coast*. He was an equally effective public speaker, filling
churches and auditoriums throughout the East and Midwest. Aided by
magic lantern slides, native artifacts, and a rudimentary map, he
would expatiate on the plight and promise of Alaska with infectious
conviction. He was not afraid to embellish, estimating that whatever
his listeners knew of this remote corner of the continent was no more
than what he told them. In prim spectacles and close-cropped beard,
he would inflame the women in the audience with shocking tales of
devil worship, cannibalism, infanticide, polygamy, and sexual slavery.
For his male listeners, he chose a different tack, promoting Alaska's

enormous economic potential. The way to ameliorate the former and exploit the latter, he lectured, was to establish mission schools that would mold benighted natives into industrious, peaceable, Christian citizens. With Sheldon Jackson as its chief publicist, Alaska became more than a curiosity, a faraway folly of ice and emptiness; it was now a cause, as urgent as it was worthy.

Jackson got his way. On May 17, 1884, President Chester Arthur signed a bill granting civil government to Alaska. Up to that point, Alaska had been simply a possession; now it was a jurisdiction, governed by rule of law. The Alaska Organic Act, as the legislation would eventually be known, was drafted by Senator Benjamin Harrison of Indiana—grandson of the hero of Tippecanoe, chairman of the Committee on Territories, staunch Presbyterian, and boon ally of Sheldon Jackson. Jackson's fingerprints were all over the final draft, particularly the part that authorized and financed native schools. Under Jackson's guidance, the law was relatively progressive, consciously avoiding, as Jackson noted, "the restrictions and disabilities of our Indian system." Alaskan natives would not be herded onto reservations; they would not be doled annuities; they would not live as public wards. "They ask no favors from the American government," Jackson explained, "but simply to be treated as other citizens, protected by the laws and courts, and . . . furnished with schools for their children."

Jackson's rhetoric was consistent with the latest and somewhat faddish push for Indian rights, a movement led by (mostly eastern) reformers who believed "1st. That the Indians were capable of civilization, and 2d. That it was largely due to the injustice or inefficiency of the government's dealings with him that the Indian had attained civilization so imperfectly." Natives, including Alaskans, must be taught to help themselves. Charles Dawes, the reform-minded U.S. senator from Massachusetts, advocated treating the Indian "not as an insoluble substance that the civilization of this country has been unable, hitherto, to digest, but to take him as an individual, a human being, and treat him as you find him." Thanks to the influence of men like Dawes and Sheldon Jackson, responsibility for Alaska's native schools was assigned to the U.S. Bureau of Education, under the Department of the Interior, not Interior's tarnished Bureau of Indian Affairs. The commissioner of education, John Eaton, was yet another devout Presbyterian, and in 1885 he chose Sheldon Jackson as the first general agent of education in Alaska.

In January 1890, Jackson summoned representatives of various Protestant churches and missionary societies to a meeting at the Methodist Book Rooms in New York, where he revealed his outline for Alaska. To avoid a feeding frenzy, he informed them, the vast field of native souls would be carved up judiciously and, within limits, ecumenically. "[W]e tried to improve on what the churches had done in other lands," he explained some years later. "We did not want Presbyterians and Congregationalists and Methodists and Baptists and Friends . . . working in one corner . . . and leaving thousands of barbarians outside without any chance." And so with Jackson wielding the knife, the pie was sliced into pieces, and later some of those pieces were sliced again. The Yukon River, because of its connection with Anglican Canada, went to the Episcopalians; the Baptists got Kodiak Island and Cook Inlet; the Methodists wound up with the Aleutians; and so on. Presbyterians retained their established presence in southeastern Alaska, and because nobody else wanted Point Barrow, they took this wedge as well. The Congregationalists, under the aegis of the American Missionary Association, were assigned one of the largest portions, from a population standpoint, Cape Prince of Wales. (Exposing a long-standing prejudice against Catholics, Jackson excluded them from the initial apportionment. Nevertheless, Catholic missions took hold on the lower Yukon.)

Dividing and delegating was the easy part. It was one thing for sympathetic brethren to convene in a New York vestry and envision the incremental enlightenment of Alaska. The more difficult task was to find men and women willing to carry the torch and trim the lamps, especially in the most remote outposts of the Far North: Point Barrow, Cape Prince of Wales, and Point Hope, which lay roughly between the two.

The logistics of carrying supplies and providing transportation were staggering. Traders, whalers, and walrus- and seal-hunters had been plying the unpredictable waters beyond the Bering Strait since the 1850s. Yet by 1890, the only year-round white settlements north of Norton Sound were two bare-bones whaling stations at Point Hope and Point Barrow and a stingy mine and trading post at Golovnin Bay. Whaling ships rendezvoused seasonally at Port Clarence, but then retreated in the winter. Post Office Point, where they exchanged mail, was not a fixed address at all but merely the southernmost tip of the polar ice pack between Russia and Alaska. The rest of the coastline, spanning eight degrees of latitude, a distance from Maine to the Carolinas, was, in Sheldon Jackson's view, primordial.

Jackson expected that the three new missions he had in mind for northernmost Alaska would be inordinately dangerous. In the spring of 1890, he posted a brief description of the Cape Prince of Wales position in the *American Missionary*, the monthly newsletter of the AMA. It read more like a warning than an enticement. Jackson made clear that the natives at the Cape were "a turbulent crowd." For this reason, he favored placing not one man, as he had done at other missions, but two. "[I]f difficulties arise, they will be a mutual strength, and if the teacher gets sick, there will be someone to attend him," he counseled. "From the time that the revenue cutter passes south in August and the whalers in September, these men will be shut up with the natives and thrown upon their own resources and God's protection until the following June or July."

And not just any two men would do. "I would advise that the missionaries be large men physically," Jackson wrote, "as size impresses the natives favorably, and there may be times when they will need to remove a turbulent man from their room by physical force." As if these caveats did not give sufficient pause, Jackson closed his solicitation with a final caution: "It is obvious that none need nor will apply who are not Christian heroes who have not in themselves the stuff of which martyrs are made."

Incredibly, there were twenty-four responses; despite Jackson's pointed discouragement, as many women applied as did men. Natural-ly Jackson chose only the latter. For Cape Prince of Wales, he paired Tom Lopp with Harrison Thornton, a thirty-two-year-old Virginian. For Point Hope, he chose John Driggs, thirty-eight, from Delaware; and for Point Barrow, Leander Stevenson, forty-five, from Ohio. Evidently Jackson was satisfied with their qualifications. Stevenson, the eldest, was a Civil War veteran and teacher. Driggs had the distinction of being a doctor. Thornton had taught here and there and stressed his talents as a hunter and outdoorsman. Lopp was the youngest but in some ways the most capable of the lot, given his experience as both teacher and administrator. All four were solid churchmen and keen to serve. Jack-son applauded their zeal, though beneath his own enthusiasm ran the fine print of indemnification. "They enter upon the field with the full realization of its difficulties and even dangers," he wrote to AMA sup-porters, announcing his selections, "and yet, cheerfully trusting them-selves to the hand of God, are ready to go forth with undaunted faith." He instructed the new missionaries to appear at the Occidental Hotel in San Francisco by the first of June. Their ship would embark for Alaska soon thereafter.

On June 6, the four men boarded the four-masted steam schooner *Jeanie*. The age of steam had not immediately obsoleted the age of sail. In the late nineteenth century, many ships were hybrids, with sails, rudder, and keel, but fitted also with coal-fired steam engines. This marriage was particularly well suited for navigation in the Arctic, where sailing saved precious coal, and the increased power and maneuverability provided by steam-driven propellers allowed ships to venture farther, longer, and more safely into latitudes notorious for ice and ill wind.

By midnight the *Jeanie* was through the Golden Gate. After four days of clawing against a stiff northwest wind, it had made only a hundred miles. All the missionaries except Dr. Driggs were sick. The *Jeanie* was a tender of the Pacific Steam Whaling Company, bound initially for Port Clarence, where it was to rendezvous with the Arctic whaling fleet and replenish the coal and provisions that the ships required for their summer hunt north of the Bering Strait. In exchange, the *Jeanie* would take on whatever oil and whalebone the ships had accumulated during the spring cruise along the Siberian coastline. The 1890 season was particularly noteworthy for reasons that had nothing to do with the seasick passengers aboard the *Jeanie*. Two of the whaling ships supplied by the *Jeanie* intended to winter over in the ice at Herschel Island, east of Point Barrow, in order to get a jump on the next summer's whaling—an unprecedented tactic and a measure of the risks that the whalers were now willing to take in order to corner the increasingly elusive bowhead whale.

Finally the wind cooperated, and the *Jeanie* made better progress. In the month-long voyage to Port Clarence, the missionaries had time to get acquainted and contemplate the unknowns awaiting them. Also aboard was Charles Weeks, a veteran whaling captain, who regaled the neophytes with tales of life and death in the Arctic. One story in particular commanded their fullest attention. Today it is known infamously as the Gilley Affair.

Thirteen years earlier, in July 1877, the trading brig *William H. Allen* encountered heavy fog between Cape Prince of Wales and the Diomede Islands, which guard the Bering Strait, dividing Alaska and Siberia. To avoid running aground on the Cape shoals, the ship dropped anchor. Soon an umiak paddled by Cape natives approached and signaled a desire to trade. Some retellings of the story insist that the natives were drunk when they climbed aboard. Others assert that Captain George Gilley traded guns and whiskey for the natives' furs, a patently illegal but common practice throughout Alaska. Whichever version one accepts—whether the natives were already drunk or acquired whiskey aboard ship, carried it to shore, and returned the next day to demand more—the ensuing events were indisputably violent and ghastly. When Gilley refused to trade further and gave orders for the ship to get under way, a fight broke out. The crew of the *William H. Allen* consisted mostly of Kanakas—Hawaiian natives who had become indispensable aboard American whaling ships. "They're a mighty peaceable lot unless they get really mad," Gilley recalled. When a Cape native stabbed one of the crewmen, "Those Kanakas went crazy," and in the ensuing melee, they gave no quarter. "I stood ready," Gilley continued, "and whenever I saw a native raise his knife I shot him." Outnumbered and unable to retreat to their umiaks, the natives made a desperate last stand in the forecastle. Crewmen surrounded the hatchway, and whenever a native showed himself, he was clubbed or shot and his body was thrown overboard. "Toward the last we hauled them out with gaff hooks," Gilley stated with scant remorse. The number of natives killed ranged from thirteen to thirty, depending on the source. The grief and grudge they bore was immeasurable.

Word of the carnage spread quickly along the Alaskan coast, and afterward ships rarely called at Cape Prince of Wales, and those that did would not drop anchor. Only a few natives at a time were permitted aboard, and they were watched with suspicion. Deservedly or not, the Cape now had a reputation as the most treacherous and aggressive village in the western Arctic. Sheldon Jackson, who had never set foot there before 1890, regarded the residents as " barbarous . . . savage . . . beyond the pale of civilization." When he posted the job descriptions for the missions, he did not choose the word "martyr" in jest. Nor did Lopp and Thornton take it lightly: They resolved that they would accept God's will, with eyes wide open. "We determined . . . to disarm the hostility of the natives by a mild and peaceful behavior," Lopp and Thornton declared bravely in a joint letter to the *American Missionary*. Even so, they had no intention of disarming themselves.

The *Jeanie* arrived at Port Clarence on July 3, where the missionaries were pleased to discover the Arctic whaling fleet and the revenue cutter *Bear*, with Sheldon Jackson aboard. As general agent of education for Alaska, Jackson took passage on the *Bear* each summer in order to inspect his ever-lengthening skein of mission schools. The additional goal of this trip was to dedicate three more.

At Port Clarence, Lopp and Thornton got their first glimpse of Bering Strait Eskimos. Each summer, when the sea was open and light abundant, natives loaded their umiaks with skins, ivory, oil, meat, handicrafts, and whatever else they figured might be of value and traveled to one of the great trading fairs—at, say, Kotzebue Sound, to name one of the biggest. On occasion Alaskan natives traveled all the way to the Siberian coast. Their foremost objective was always commerce, an imperative dating back hundreds if not thousands of years. Yet these summer gatherings were also cultural exchanges. Amid the daylight and bounty of a brief season, natives danced, feasted, and pooled their wisdom, dreams, and woes. Eventually, with the increasing presence of whaling and trading ships in the mid-nineteenth century, the role of these trading fairs was usurped, as the umiaks steered for places such as Port Clarence, where Yankee ships could be counted on to disgorge, pots, axes, needles, cloth, flour, sugar, tobacco, and sometimes guns and spirits. And when the natives could not acquire alcohol itself, they could trade for the ingredients to distill their own "hooch," an Alaskan Indian (as opposed to Eskimo) term soon imprinted in the sodden lexicon of drink and drunkenness.

Standing at the rail of the *Jeanie* in the bay of Port Clarence, Lopp and Thornton could make out scores of tents lining the beach, a mile or so distant. Even before the ship reached its anchorage, they watched with a mixture of awe and alarm as umiaks of sun-darkened natives in skin atigis raced to be first alongside. Neither missionary mentioned going ashore or meeting any natives in person, but Thornton remarked that several sailors recognized the brother of one of the natives killed in the Gilley Affair. The old salts told Thornton that they had taunted the fellow, "If we were in your place, we wouldn't allow any damned missionary to settle at Cape Prince of Wales!"

The following morning, the *Bear* steamed toward the Cape and points north. Besides Jackson, its passengers now included Thornton, Driggs, and carpenters from three of the whaling ships who had volunteered to help build the schools. Lopp had agreed to stay behind at Port Clarence for several days to oversee the transfer of his and Thornton's belongings to the whaler *Orca*, which would proceed to the Cape a few days later. At noon on the Fourth of July, the *Bear* dropped anchor several miles from Cape Prince of Wales, and Jackson and Thornton were rowed ashore. Thornton confessed later that he could not help wondering "how it would feel to be knocked on the head and eaten while half alive." Instead the natives gathered on the beach with "excited curiosity." After a brief benediction and a clasp of hands, the two men selected a site for the first public school in Arctic Alaska.

Another supply ship, the *Oscar and Hattie*, had already landed lumber and other material for the schoolhouse. With extra help from the crew of the *Bear*, the carpenters got busy, taking advantage of a night that dimmed but never got dark. By morning they had broken ground and begun laying the sills. When Lopp arrived on the *Orca* on July 10, the walls were up and the rooms framed. The building was compact, sixteen feet by forty. With tongue-and-groove siding, mullioned windows, gabled roof, and a coat of white paint, it resembled many schoolhouses on the American prairie—except that instead of sinking its feet into fertile sod, it clung uneasily to a bed of spongy tundra and impenetrable permafrost. The interior was divided into classroom, bedroom, kitchen, storeroom, and vestibule; Lopp and Thornton would teach in the front, live in the rear. In two more days the work was far enough along that the missionaries were able to sleep indoors. On July 14, ten days after coming ashore, the carpenters returned to the *Bear*. Thornton and Lopp stood at the water's edge and watched as its topsails and smoke became infinitesimal on the northern horizon. With that, they were on their own.

# 2

# The High Place

CAPE PRINCE OF WALES was named by Captain James Cook to honor the heir to the British throne. In 1778 Cook sailed along the Alaskan coast, probing for the Pacific entrance to the Northwest Passage. He did not go ashore at the Cape—he feared running aground—but noted in his log, "We thought we saw some people up on the coast; and probably we were not mistaken."

The people he spied on shore already had a name for the Cape— Kingegan, meaning "high place," for the battered gray mountain that rises fifteen hundred feet above the village. Stark and stalwart, Cape Mountain, as it is now called, is one of the surviving stones in the bracelet of land that once linked Asia and North America. Running northeast from its summit is a jagged ridge, like the dorsal of a stegosaurus, which turns aside the wind and current from one quarter of the compass, albeit the south.

From other directions and in most other respects, the Cape is exposed. The Seward Peninsula, like most of northern Alaska, does not receive an extraordinary amount of snow—only three or four feet a year—but stupendous winds produce frequent ground blizzards and monstrous drifts. Because the Bering Strait is shallow, barely one hundred feet deep in many places, even mild winds churn up the sea, making launching and landing, never mind travel, extremely perilous.

Yet conditions at the Cape, at least by Arctic standards, are not entirely unfavorable. During the winter—which spans nearly nine months of the year—the broad, gradual beach of the Cape is covered with shore ice, from which natives are able to set nets, spear seals, and catch fish. Better still, the combination of shallow coastline, prevailing offshore winds, and the buffer of Cape Mountain wards off the deep-drafted polar pack ice and frequently creates a margin of open water, or lead (pronounced "leed"), that permits hunting by kayak and umiak. Cape Prince of Wales is located at the narrowest point of the bottleneck through which whales must migrate each fall and spring, and the Bering Strait's shallow bottom is superb habitat for walruses, which live on ice floes and grow fat by raking shellfish from the sea floor with their impressive tusks.

A short distance inland, bunkers of dunes give way to a narrow plain of tundra, covered with a mattress of lichen and a surprising diversity of tenacious plants, including berries and edible greens that are integral to the native diet. The tundra eventually surrenders to a slope of coarse talus, tumbling from the scarp above. Away to the north, the mountains withdraw, and the coastal plain broadens to accommodate a large lagoon, frozen most of the year. At the center of the village of Kingegan is a smaller lagoon, fed by a freshwater stream and emptying into the Bering Sea. This source of good water is yet another reason why Cape Prince of Wales became the largest Eskimo settlement in Alaska, if not the world.

At first the village was hard for Lopp and Thornton to comprehend. It bore no resemblance to anything they had ever encountered or read about. It offered no lanes, no plaza, no obvious order. Even the houses were difficult to discern. The native dwellings of Cape Prince of Wales were semi-subterranean burrows hidden from view. To the outsider, they looked like kilns, and to a lesser degree they functioned as such. A typical dwelling was one room, usually no more than twelve or fifteen feet across, dug several feet into the permafrost, domed with rafters made from driftwood or sometimes from the ribs of whales, and then covered with turf. They had no windows save for a small skylight made from stretched walrus intestine. The entrance was via a long, tunnel-like crawlway, a covered trench dug three or four feet lower than the floor of the house. Entering the house from below, through a hole in the floor, created an effective airlock, turning away the Arctic cold. The houses were so snug that body heat and a simple oil lamp with a moss wick were sufficient to keep the residents cozy even when the temperature outside was thirty below zero. Raised benches and sleeping platforms kept them off the frozen floor.

Lopp and Thornton would come to appreciate the efficiency of Eskimo architecture soon enough, but at the beginning the overall effect was ungraceful and off-putting. To measure the cultural gulf between the Cape natives and themselves, the missionaries needed only to compare their own schoolhouse, angular, ostentatious, and exposed, to the blunt earthen mounds that encircled it.

Yet there was nothing very secretive about Cape Prince of Wales. If anything, the opposite was true. Because houses were small, the Eskimos kept many of their possessions outdoors, especially in summer when the ground was free of ice and snow. One of the first Europeans to approach a Bering Strait village in the early 1800s described it as a "forest of stakes"—a cluster of half-buried "yourts" surrounded by a thicket of driftwood scaffolding that displayed the essentials of Eskimo life for all to see. Fish, meat, and hides were stored here, as were kayaks, umiaks, sleds, harnesses, nets, and anything else that was better kept away from the harsh tundra and the jaws of village dogs. Eskimos stealing from other Eskimos was extremely rare; from whites was a different story, as the missionaries would eventually discover.

The reason that few whites had ever stepped ashore at the Cape had less to do with the deviltry of the natives, cruelly embroidered in recitations of the Gilley Affair, and more to do with the lack of reliable anchorage offshore. One of the few white men to actually spend time at Cape Prince of Wales was Henry Trollope, commander of the British ship *Rattlesnake*. While the ship was anchored at Port Clarence in 1854, Trollope led a party overland to the Cape, where he was greeted by natives "holloing, shrieking and tumbling over one another." He was invited into an underground house, where he was warmed and fed while his clothes were dried and repaired. He was struck by the natives' politeness, equally so by their smell. In winter, ice was everywhere, but water, especially warm water, less easy to come by. Natives rarely bathed; nor did they change or clean their clothing. Moreover, they typically went naked from the waist up when indoors, and the oily smoke from their lamps clung to their skin. To remove the residue, they were accustomed to using their own urine, which they stored in a communal chamber pot. Their uncleanliness was "worse than tenement dwellers," according to a later visitor. "Pestiferous," recalled another. "Anyone with a reasonably good sense of smell would know that a native was near whether he could see him or not." During Trollope's stop at the Cape, he happened to drop his handkerchief near a native woman, who retrieved it and began rubbing her skin with it. "I was fain to make her a present of it," he remarked, "although it was my only one."

In spite of the exaggerated warnings passed to them by prankish sailors, Tom Lopp and Harrison Thornton were pleasantly relieved by the civility of the Cape natives. "The natives are peaceable, friendly and intelligent, instead of ferocious, hostile and stupid, as we were led to expect," they wrote to the *American Missionary* shortly after their arrival. And, they added, "The stories about their filth . . . have been very much exaggerated."

If they had an immediate concern, it was that the Eskimos were too curious. "As the natives had never seen an American house before and were not accustomed to being excluded from each other's dwellings, they began hammering away at our doors and windows at a very lively rate," the missionaries commented somewhat drolly. For the first few days, Lopp and Thornton kept their shotguns and pistols loaded and in plain sight, but they quickly realized that the villagers bore no malice; they merely wanted to inspect the outsiders and their exotic trappings. With no common language, looking and touching were a means of understanding. And in such a harsh climate, people did not stand waiting on a neighbor's doorstep. Good sense and etiquette called for entering first and then exchanging greetings.

The missionaries were no less eager to learn about their new neighbors. "They are a fine looking set of people," Lopp and Thornton agreed. The natives of Cape Prince of Wales, like most Inuit inhabitants of the Arctic, from Greenland to Siberia, were stocky, broad-faced, with dark almond eyes and straight, dark hair, which the women wore braided and the men tonsured, not unlike medieval monks. Thornton, the Virginian, thought Eskimos were a cut above African-Americans. They reminded him of "very good-looking mulattoes. . . . Their lips are, perhaps, slightly thicker than those of the average Caucasian; but they do not resemble, even approximately, the blubber-like organs of the genuine negro." The Eskimo skull, he complimented, appeared to have "plenty of room for brains." He and Lopp were also struck, as were most outsiders, by the Eskimos' facial decoration. Most men pierced their lower lips with labrets, ornaments of carved stone or ivory, some as large as glass bottle stoppers; after American trading ships began visiting the coast, some labrets *were* bottle stoppers. Not to be outdone, women tattooed their chins with a series of vertical lines, like seal whiskers painted on a ceremonial mask—elegant and totemic.

If the culture shock was severe in the first days and weeks at the Cape, it only increased in September, when most of the villagers returned from trading trips and summer fishing and hunting camps. The population resumed its normal complement of five hundred, and everyone wanted to meet the newcomers. The Eskimos' only previous exposure to whites had been aboard ships, their only dialogue in the improvised pidgin of trade. How strange that the missionaries had nothing to sell, unless it was words themselves.

Sheldon Jackson's official report on that first season at Cape Prince of Wales noted that because the natives were a "wild people that had never known any restraints, they could not comprehend the purposes of the teachers." In their own first reports, the missionaries referred to the natives as "these savages." The author of this assessment appears to have been Thornton, but Lopp's name was on it, too. The difference was that, over time, Thornton used the term ever more spitefully, and Lopp never chose it when speaking on his own.

From the start, Thornton showed great dedication, but he could be domineering and arrogant. Piety gave him purpose, but his righteousness was untempered by humility or empathy. He was God-fearing but also high-strung, paranoid even. What Thornton's résumé—at least the one submitted to Sheldon Jackson—did not reveal was that he was at worst a serial failure, at best a dilettante who rarely followed through on what he started. His father, a Confederate colonel, had been killed when Harrison was only four. A precocious child, Thornton graduated from Virginia's Hampden-Sidney College at the age of sixteen. Afterward, he took teaching jobs at private schools in Virginia, where, according to a biographical sketch prepared by his nephew, the strapping, six-foot-two Thornton became an unhesitant practitioner of corporal punishment. He left teaching to enter the University of Virginia law school but dropped out due to "severe depression" from which, his nephew relates, "it is by no means certain that he ever fully recovered." He tried an office job in New York, resigning to resume teaching in Virginia and Tennessee. Eventually, like so many malcontents, he moved west, where he dabbled in mining in Colorado. There he drew closer to the Presbyterian Church, which presumably is how he first gained the attention of Sheldon Jackson.

Thornton's photograph presents a study in rectitude and cocksureness: bold chin, flamboyant handlebar moustache, hair parted sharply down the middle. "He was no book-worm," his brother would eulogize. "He loved the outdoor life. . . . With the passion of the scholar he joined the ardor of the sportsman. . . . If he ever swore, I never heard him. . . . His speech and accent [were] correct and cultured." Nevertheless, the brother concluded with a note of tragic resignation, "A nature like his . . . does not escape the scars of life's struggle."

Thornton did his best to keep these scars hidden from Tom Lopp, who was every bit as hale, erudite, and able as the Virginian. Any criticisms Lopp had of Thornton in the early going went unspoken. The two worked shoulder to shoulder getting the schoolhouse in order, and each was bolstered by the other's faith and fortitude. After all, they were two white men among five hundred natives. Common cause and culture vastly outweighed any inchoate differences of conscience and character.

Because Thornton assumed the role of mission correspondent during the first year at the Cape, regrettably we must rely on Lopp's later letters and reports for glimpses of his personal philosophy and methods. "Every teacher is a social worker," he reflected, "who, in addition to performing the routine work of the school room, strives in every possible way to promote the physical, moral and industrial welfare of the natives, adults as well as children. In the schoolrooms the endeavor is made to impart to the children such instruction as will enable them to live comfortably and to deal intelligently with those with whom they come in contact."

In a letter to a young teacher heading for Alaska, he was more succinct, and far less stiff, in his explanation of the best way to enable the natives: "If they learn to love you, you can teach them *anything*." This was the essence of Tom Lopp: somewhat paternalistic, to be sure, but the shepherd in him was well matched by the humble servant.

Harrison Thornton had not come to Cape Prince of Wales looking for love, at least not of the sort Tom Lopp had in mind. It was clear from the start that he regarded himself as the protagonist of a Sunday school saga, a Leatherstocking St. Paul determined to bring, in his words, "light and education into the depths of barbarism and paganism." Here, for instance, is his account of first landing at the Cape:

> The United States revenue cruiser had gone South, and we were completely at the mercy of these savages. . . . We recalled the killing of thirteen natives by the white men on Gill[e]y's ship, and the subsequent ferocity and desire for vengeance said to have been displayed by the rest of the tribe; we reflected that our meager supply of clothes and provisions was richest booty in the eyes of this poverty-stricken people.

Accordingly, Thornton endeavored "to make them understand something of the power of our government and threatened them . . . if they should seriously injure us . . . and [told] them we would not submit tamely to being butchered."

Having made the desired impression with strong words and charged weapons, he next decided to impress the natives with his prowess as an outdoorsman by accompanying them on a seal hunt. "It was really important for the success of my work to inspire the natives with some respect for me as the representative of my race, my nation, and my religion," he explained, "and they would naturally admire intrepidity on the part of a hunter more than any other quality." Instead, Thornton succeeded only in getting lost and would have perished if the natives had not come to his rescue in the nick of time. ("I tried to stir my muscles up to the point of performing their wonted tasks; but, like jaded steeds, they would not respond to the dull spur of my impaired will.") After strength returned and humiliation subsided, he was hesitant to take similar risks again, reasoning that the hunting companions he so wanted to inspire would henceforth devise ways to "get us into trouble for the pleasure and profit of getting us out."

Tom Lopp, on the other hand, was a quick and thoughtful study.

Whenever he was with the natives on their own footing, he happily reversed the role of teacher and student. Ellen Lopp, who would not arrive on the scene for another two years, was an equally quick study, and at times a rather caustic one. After first meeting Thornton, she declared that he "isn't of the variety that takes advice."

. . .

School started with a flurry on August 18. The missionaries had no trouble enticing the Cape natives into the classroom. Almost immediately they had far more students than the sixteen-by-twenty-four-foot space could hold. "Many of them were so desirous of not missing a session," the missionaries reported to the AMA, "that they stood outside the door for hours in the coldest weather and in the worst blizzards." Thornton was slightly unnerved by the constant attention. Even when school was not in session, "twenty or thirty of them were constantly standing about our house peering in at the windows," he complained. "In spite of the old adage: 'A cat may look at a king,' that sort of thing grows wearisome at times."

Once classes began, the gawkers became avid, if clamorous, learners. Excited by the novelty of it all, children and adults would talk, laugh, and leap over benches. Those not able to gain admittance yelled at the windows, beat on the walls, and slid down the roof. The only way for Lopp and Thornton to get them to behave was to threaten to call off school altogether.

Eventually the natives became more courteous, although the number wanting to attend class continued to increase, until more than half of the five hundred residents of the Cape were enrolled. To accommodate them, the missionaries split the day into two sessions: one in the morning for young children and a second in the afternoon for older children; adults could join either group. Thornton suggested that the natives were hungry for English in order to improve their bartering with the whalers and traders. More than that, however, the Eskimos possessed an appetite for learning of all sorts. They had endured as a culture by making use of every resource at hand. And there was no question that they had exceptional powers of concentration and eye for detail. "Although we have a combined experience of some thirteen years in the school-room," the missionaries exclaimed, "we have never had more quick-witted and intelligent students."

At the start, perhaps one out of ten Eskimos knew any English— at most a dozen words. Their teachers had an even weaker grasp of the Eskimo language. They began with a vocabulary of common objects. "Our first lessons were not about 'A fan for Ann,' but about a hair seal," Lopp recalled. Pointing to an object or a picture, the teachers would say the name in English and spell it. They called the exercise "making paper speak," and the villagers caught on with extraordinary alacrity.

The missionaries, meanwhile, labored to learn Inupiaq. There was no written native language (although dictionaries of eastern Canadian Inuit existed), so Lopp and Thornton did their best to cobble a phonetic spelling for each new word; even this was extremely difficult. Predictably, Thornton regarded the Inupiaq language as inferior, primitive. "They speak in a rather slovenly way," he groused, "slurring over their words and running them together." Lopp, a better listener, picked up the nuance of the native tongue more readily and was astounded by the sophistication of its syntax. "Like the Greek, [it] had singular, plural, and dual numbers. Not only that, but we learned that every child of 10 or 12 knew how to use these inflected forms correctly. For example, when speaking of one ship they say, oo-me-ak-puk; of two, oo-me-ak-pak; of more than two, oo-me-ak-pait. It delighted them to see us write these dual and plural forms as they called them off."

Ultimately, Lopp conceded, "We decided to be satisfied with just enough of their language to enable us to teach them English understandingly. But I recall that we were impressed by the thought that a people who could master and speak this unwritten classical language grammatically have possibilities."

Because of the language barrier, the missionaries chose not to wade into religious waters for the time being, beyond offering a brief prayer at the beginning of each school day. In holding off, they were following Sheldon Jackson's doctrine of teach-then-preach. But the way seemed open. As best Thornton could tell, the Cape natives had "no notion of God. . . . Their minds are fallow for the reception of the good seed."

Unfortunately the natives were also vulnerable to germs and viruses. A month after they returned from their summer hegira of hunting and trading, they began to succumb to respiratory infection. Within a few weeks, twenty-six had died. Thornton attributed the extraordinary tragedy to a particularly "cold, wet storm," but countless generations of Eskimos had suffered worse storms without succumbing in such epidemic numbers. Some of the village shamans had a different idea: They blamed the newcomers, if not for their pathogens, then for the curse contained in their teaching. The missionaries had passed out slates so the students could practice their writing. After people began falling ill, the connection seemed obvious. What today might be applauded as a commonsense diagnosis was dismissed by Thornton as pure superstition. For a while, he and Lopp feared that they might be banished from the village and their school dismantled.

But the epidemic subsided, and the missionaries were allowed to remain. Gradually as language skills and trust improved, Thornton and Lopp began to gain a clearer picture of the village. They learned that Kingegan was not one village but two: Agenamete (now spelled Agianamiut), located on the slope below Cape Mountain, and Gaytar-namete (Kiatanamiut), on the flat below. Though the two villages got along, they had not always been so compatible, and old grievances died hard. The schoolhouse, quite by chance, had been built between the two settlements, although a bit closer to the lower. "The principal men of each, if they imagine we are disposed to favor one [village] rather than the other, seem to become greatly exercised," Thornton observed.

Thornton had limited respect for these putative leaders. He preferred to regard the Cape as an "aboriginal republic," where "no man has any legal authority or superiority over another. . . . Custom and public opinion are the only regulating forces."

This assumption was wide of the mark. Kingegan was organized around extended families, each headed by an *umialik*, or chief. In its strictest definition, an umialik was simply the owner and captain of an umiak, a man of superior experience, strength, and hunting ability. Cape Prince of Wales, as Tom Lopp cannily observed, was an "oo-me-ak village, having between 30 and 40 of the largest skin boats in the world." Each individual and family was aligned with a particular umiak, and the authority of the umialiks extended well beyond the strict confines of the boat. "Every lad was ambitious to own and steer his own oomeak when he grew up," Lopp remarked.

Thornton discounted the authority of village umialiks mainly because the most prominent one was a volatile drunkard. Indeed, the presence of alcohol, either acquired from traders or distilled secretly in native houses, had shaken the village's equilibrium—the Gilley Affair being the most grievous but not the most recent disruption.

On September 19, the missionaries were startled by a commotion outside their door. "Immediately," Thornton recounted in the pages of the *American Missionary*, "Elignok, the principal chief, and one of his wives rushed in. . . . Both were in a state of indescribably beastly intoxication, raving and rambling with what seemed to be hostile intent." With the help of several (sober) natives, Elignok and his wife were removed from the schoolhouse, but the tension between the chief and the missionaries did not end there.

On another occasion when a drunken villager became unruly, Thornton lost his temper and shoved the man, sending him sprawling into a cold cellar. "He was furious at the time," Thornton related, "and gave vent to his wrath by howling around the house."

Possession of alcohol or its manufacture by Alaskan natives was strictly illegal, as was the possession of breech-loading rifles. However, Thornton noted bitterly, "The law against trading these people whiskey seems to be virtually a dead letter. The stuff traded them is the very cheapest, vilest and most poisonous made; while under its influence, the natives resemble maniacs or raving wild beasts rather than sane men." On the other hand, Thornton firmly advocated the sale of breech-loading rifles to natives, believing that the threat of a native uprising—the original impetus for the law—was outweighed by the advantage that state-of-the-art weapons would give to native hunters, whose lives depended on the meat they brought in. Like the ban on alcohol, the gun law was ineffectual. That first winter, Thornton counted 152 guns among the 135 adult males in the village; 46 were breech-loading rifles.

Ironically, guns served an end that was highly injurious to natives themselves. Traders had taught Eskimo to distill their own moonshine, using flour, sugar, and, for a condensing tube, the barrel of a rifle. Once established, stills were virtually impossible to eradicate. "Poor old Kingegan!" Tom Lopp would reminisce in a letter to one of his former students. "What wonderful oomeaks and crews and fine hunters it had. Whiskey started it down hill. My oh my! . . . I have seen there when 40 or 50 of them were drunk."

Most of the natives were not drunkards, though, and those who did drink were not always violent. If anything, they tended to become morose. "It was the custom of natives, when drunk, to talk and cry about their dead ones," Lopp explained. "In fact, it was the excuse that many of them gave for imbibing—'When drunk, we're not ashamed to talk and cry about our dead ones.'" At Cape Prince of Wales, many of the dead had perished at the hands of the Gilley crew, including the first-born son of Elignok, remembered as "a mighty hunter." Still, in the missionaries' book there was no excuse for such dissipation, among natives or whites. Lopp and Thornton were both professed temperance men (although in the supply order they drew up for the following winter, they requested a case of claret and a gallon of whiskey, presumably for medicinal purposes).

As winter deepened, the missionaries and natives fell into a calmer coexistence. "We prayed to our God," Thornton recorded, "and trusted him to order all for the best, and to give us the requisite patience, prudence, and fortitude; we soon got used, in a certain sense, to our state of potential siege; we were determined not to let the natives see that we were afraid of them; so we taught school, took our exercise, and went hunting for our fresh meat. . . . By January we felt so confident of our good-will that we did not even take the trouble to shut and bar at night the stout inside shutters."

Their burden was further lightened by the arrival of Sokweena, a twelve-year-old orphan boy, described by Thornton as halfway between "servant and protégé" and by Lopp as "our 'Friday.'" Often clumsy at chores, he was remarkably adept at learning English and proved valuable as an interpreter.

Just as the missionaries' door remained unbarred, so too were those of the villagers. "The people of any establishment always seemed to feel complimented when we paid them a visit," Thornton remarked. Yet despite the hospitality shown the missionaries and for all the white men's curiosity about the domestic life of their hosts, Lopp and Thornton never adjusted entirely to their underground houses. The passageway was tight, the light dim, and the odor overpowering. Eskimos were fanatical about smoking—Russian traders had hooked them on tobacco a hundred years earlier—and their poorly ventilated houses were often thick with smoke, from their pipes as well as from oil lamps. Modesty was another issue. Women, along with men and boys, frequently went shirtless indoors. The missionaries did not, and they never got comfortable with those who did.

Even the villagers' unstinting generosity created awkward moments. "You may find the family eating when you go in; that is, dining on frozen raw fish—which, by the way, is not so unpalatable as one might imagine—and seal meat," Thornton described. "They will heartily invite you to share dinner; but you remember seeing an old single-toothed hag, like the one in the corner, cutting up the meat . . . by holding one end in her mouth, and you therefore decline as grace-fully as you can—alleging, perhaps, that you recently finished your own meal."

Lopp and Thornton found themselves slightly more at ease in the *qargi*, a communal building in which women were usually not permit-ted. Cape Prince of Wales once had as many as four; in 1890 there were two. The qargi was a combination courthouse, church, work-shop, dance hall, and recreation center, two or three times the size of a typical house. Here the elders received outsiders and ruled on fam-ily disputes (despite Thornton's claim that there were no "laws"). In the qargi, men prepared themselves and their gear for the hunt and, upon their return, recounted their exploits, singing, dancing, drum-ming, and paying their respects to the animals that had generously given their lives so that the Eskimo people might live.

Much of the nuance of such occasions went right over the mis-sionaries' heads. In notes scribbled at one qargi ceremony—during which villagers danced in masks and a shaman in a self-induced trance was pierced with a spear—Lopp compared the feverish mummery to a "Methodist revival." He and Thornton took kerosene lamps to anoth-er qargi gathering, but the air was so close that the lamps would not stay lit.

An earlier white visitor to the Bering Strait had described Eskimo religion as no better than "feeble polytheism," and Thornton was inclined to agree. Yet his own judgment that the Cape Eskimos had "no regularly systemized religion to be uprooted" was dead wrong. On the contrary, Eskimos possessed a deeply ingrained creation myth; they believed in an afterlife; and their universe was guided by an elab-orate interplay of spirits, supernatural creatures, charms, taboos, and

superstitions. It was true that the authority of the village shamans—
Lopp and Thornton called these histrionic figures "doctors"—ebbed
and flowed depending on their individual prowess at shaping the
future, curing illness, removing curses, and generally dazzling their
adherents. But it was wishful thinking on Thornton's part to assume
that the overall "power and influence of these spirits seem to be on the
decline." In midwinter, when the Cape natives were having poor luck
netting seals, a local shaman came to the schoolhouse and implored
Lopp not to ring the school bell so loudly. "Many of the older people
came to me saying probably there was some truth in what the doctor
said," Lopp conceded. He saw no harm in assenting to the shaman's
request, and thereafter he rang the bell only two or three strokes at a
time. He did not record whether the hunting improved.

For every native habit that unsettled the missionaries—immodesty,
polygamy, burial of the dead above ground—there were aspects of the
culture that impressed them, such as their kindness toward children,
their infectious sense of humor, and their prevailing honesty, ingenu-
ity, industriousness, perseverance, and courage. Many customs the
missionaries took with a grain of salt; others they took to heart, for
increasingly they found themselves dependent on the Cape Prince of
Wales villagers for survival. Thornton boasted that a "Caucasian work-
ing-man . . . can stand as much as an Eskimo," but he had nearly died
once when he could not keep up with his fellow hunters. In the relatively mild weather of summer and early fall, the missionaries had
gone about in the wool and flannel they had brought in their trunks.
But once the temperature began to fall to zero and below, they recognized the virtue of deer- and sealskin. "At first, with the not unnatural
conceit of civilized men, we tried to make certain improvements,"
Thornton admitted, "but in most respects obtained only laughable fail-
ures. These experiments increased very much our respect for that
thing . . . called 'custom' even though it be among barbarians."

And so the winter passed. Thornton described the Cape as a "lifeless, solemn-looking plain—sublimely awful in its vastness and unbroken silence." The temperature, which was recorded fastidiously, sank to thirty-nine below. At the solstice, the sun rose above the horizon, but only barely and not for long. Day was outweighed by darkness. One storm followed another. "In some of these storms," Thornton noted, "our house, though staunchly built and undoubtedly safe, labors and groans like a ship in a storm at sea. . . . We awoke in the middle of a blizzard . . . and found our deerskin bags and blankets covered with snow that had been blown through a double window, and the vestibule had a three-foot drift in it despite the fact that the door seemed adequately protected." Drifts around the house were fifteen feet deep.

Still, the missionaries found the climate "eminently healthful." The worst that befell them—other than Thornton's close calls on the ice—were mild cases of frostbite and snowblindness. To protect their faces, they both grew beards, earning Lopp, the brunette, the nickname Kavvik (wolverine) and fair Thornton Kayuktuk (red fox). If Thornton's recollections are to be trusted, he suffered from none of the mental and emotional dysfunction that had propelled him, indirectly, to Alaska. ("Notwithstanding the large number of cloudy and rainy days," he wrote, "we experienced no such feeling of depression as one is usually conscious of in lower latitudes as the effect of this kind of weather.") Nor do any of the official reports or extant correspondence mention any strain in Thornton and Lopp's relationship during that first year at the Cape. Their incompatibility would not become evident until later.

In passing, it should be noted that they were not the only white men to spend the winter of 1890–1891 at Cape Prince of Wales. On their journey from San Francisco to Alaska, including the stopover among the whaling fleet at Port Clarence, both Thornton and Lopp had been shocked by the coarse and degraded character of the sailors they encountered. "We are inclined to believe, from what we have seen and heard," Thornton railed, "that in great part the crews of the whaling ships are selected from two classes: greenhorns and drunkards." This impression did not improve with the unanticipated arrival of three deserters at Cape Prince of Wales. One was a "Portuguese half breed from the Cape Verde Islands," who promptly boarded an umiak bound for the Diomede Islands and was never heard from again. The second, according to Thornton, was a "besotted Irishman who had deserted, he said, while drunk." When the fellow was unable to stow away on one of the last ships heading south in the fall, he took up with a Cape woman. "In May a child was born of the illicit union, and the mother smothered it." The third deserter was an Englishman, a "cockney" whom Thornton described as a "whining, effeminate, affected fool—infinitely more disagreeable in his way than the besotted Irishman."

Even so, the missionaries recognized a Christian obligation to feed these white men from their storeroom of supplies throughout the winter. Beyond that, they had little use for the interlopers, except perhaps as object lessons. "We have . . . enlightened the natives as to the true character of these vagabonds," Thornton postured. Moreover, he pledged "to warn the sailors on all whaling ships in these waters that absconders are not wanted at this settlement. If any choose to disregard the admonition, then so much the worse for them. We could not conscientiously see these two men die before our very eyes; but in future deserters will not fare so well." Over the years, this antipathy toward whalers as a breed would continue to harden. Certainly the caliber of whaling crews did not improve.

On May 13, with the days brightening, Thornton and Lopp decided that the time was ripe to begin church services. "Teaching them novel abstract ideas concerning religion or anything else is not so easy nor so satisfactory in immediate results as the teaching of the name of concrete objects they can see and handle," the missionaries acknowledged. Nevertheless, each Sunday they took turns giving "a little talk about God and Christ, and heaven and hell, telling some Bible story with its appropriate lesson, trying to show the natives in words as well as in our lives the beauty of holiness, and to make them see that their hope of a happy and blessed immortality depends upon the love of God and of Christ for them, and upon their own efforts to lead pure and holy lives." They would then lead the natives, as best they could, in prayers and hymns. "We felt very much encouraged by their attention and apparently intelligent reception of the truth."

It did not hurt, either, that the missionaries had demonstrable powers as medicine men. Although helpless to stem the epidemic that had killed and sickened so many villagers, they were effective in treating minor injuries and afflictions, relying on the small stock of emetics, purgatives, powders, salves, plasters, and other nostrums brought from the States. Armed with a pair of forceps, they became wizards at pulling teeth. Not surprisingly, the native shamans resented such blatant usurpation of their role as healers and charmers, but eventually they too became willing and appreciative beneficiaries of modern medicine, such as it was. "We have been remarkably fortunate in our practice, having lost only one patient," the missionaries reported proudly.

At the end of June, with darkness finally banished, the Cape began to thaw. Most of the villagers loaded their umiaks and departed for a summer of hunting and trading. Those who stayed moved from their sodden underground houses to skin tents nearby. Shore ice melted, the ducks and sandpipers returned, and the hills began to turn a mossy green. And as their first year at the Cape neared its end, Thornton and Lopp became restless. So restless, in fact, that they could not wait for the first ship to appear. Leaving Sokweena to mind the schoolhouse, they took passage aboard native umiaks to Port Clarence, where on July 5 they were on hand to greet the *Bear* as it anchored among the fleet of twenty whaling ships and their tenders. Sheldon Jackson was again a passenger. "It was a great relief to see them looking well &

learn they had had a prosperous winter," he remarked after welcoming the two missionaries. Jackson also noted rather curiously, "They were disappointed at finding that no ladies were on board for the mission at Cape Prince of Wales." In all of the surviving correspondence, official and otherwise, this is the only mention, however allusive, of any pledge of mail-order brides.

Thornton and Lopp sailed with the *Bear*, which arrived at Cape Prince of Wales on July 7, almost exactly a year after it had first landed the missionaries. The missionaries were eager to show off their school and students. After the Cape natives helped offload eighteen tons of coal and provisions for the mission, they were invited aboard the revenue cutter. Under the proud gaze of their teachers, the students sang, danced, and demonstrated their progress in reading and arithmetic.

One member of the audience who was not impressed by the recital was Mary Healy, wife of Captain Michael Healy. It was common for whaling captains to bring their wives on long cruises of a year or more. Such conjugal privilege was highly unusual in the Revenue Cutter Service. However, Captain Healy was a man to be reckoned with—and apparently so was his wife. "Mr. Thornton has taught [the Eskimos] to beg in English," she jotted acidly in her diary. "I think his will be slow work if they learn as little in another year as they have in this. I have not much faith in him as a man working for the love of God."

The Healys had not cared for Harrison Thornton from the start. No doubt they found him a sanctimonious prig. Michael Healy had a reputation as a profane, brusk, no-nonsense skipper—a superb sailor but also a tyrannical taskmaster. Yet there was much more to him than met the eye. His father had been a Georgia plantation owner; his mother had been a slave. Michael Healy and his mixed-blood siblings had been shipped north, where they passed successfully as white and lived comfortably on income from the sale of the family chattel in Georgia. Three sisters became nuns; two brothers became priests, one eventually rising to bishop of Portland, Maine, the other to president of Georgetown University. Through raw determination and keen wits, Healy made his way up the ranks of the U.S. Revenue Cutter Service, where the Arctic became his escape and then his fiefdom. His word was law, his gavel an iron fist. By 1891, "Hell-Roaring" Mike Healy, as he was called (though not to his rugged face), had already been court-martialed once—for drunkenness on duty and physical abuse of sailors—but had beaten the rap.

Despite his gruff exterior (and perhaps spurred by his secret burden of shame), Healy took an active interest in native schools and missions. Under his command, the *Bear* became a vessel of aid and protection, as well as authority, to the Eskimos of Alaska. A hard drinker himself, Healy saw firsthand the corrosive effect alcohol had on native lives, and he enforced prohibition with characteristic vigilance, though not with absolute success. "I wish to help where I can," he wrote, "keep[ing] contraband out of the country and help[ing] the distressed. I am not much of a Christian, don't know if I care to be an overzealous one, but I respect everyone's motives and beliefs, though their methods and ways of thinking may be different from mine."

Where his patience ran short was with anyone who put on airs or who smacked of demagoguery. Healy had sized up Thornton the previous July, during the voyage from Port Clarence to Cape Prince of Wales, and had chewed him out for using Healy's cabin to take a Sunday bath without asking permission. The Healys, then, were predisposed to belittle Thornton's accomplishments at the Cape, although they offered no such disparagements of Tom Lopp. Indeed, in the coming years, the Healys became friends and supporters of the Lopps. As one of the few women who understood the hardship of the North, Mary Healy sent clothes and other presents for the Lopp children when the *Bear* went north each spring.

Captain Healy did take seriously Thornton and Lopp's accounts of the pervasive drinking and unruliness at the Cape. He made a big show of lining up his officers and lecturing the natives on the subject of temperance and civility. He selected ten of the villagers as "policemen," presenting them with uniform caps and sacks of flour in exchange for their pledge to keep the community peaceful and sober. To impress upon the villagers the long arm of his command—not to mention the price they might pay for disobeying it—he fired three deafening rounds from one of the cutter's cannons, which sent plumes of water high into the air.

Thornton, too, learned that there was no way to buck the *Bear's* captain. At some point during the ship's stopover, Thornton took Sheldon Jackson aside and announced his intention to return to the States to seek a wife, promising to return the following summer. He had already discussed his decision with Lopp, who had agreed to stay on at the Cape by himself. Jackson had little choice but to accept the plan (although he had yet to determine how the single missionaries had fared at Point Hope and Point Barrow). Captain Healy had his own opinion. Thornton could leave the mission, but not aboard the *Bear.* During any other summer, Healy might have been more cooperative, even toward Thornton, but his sufferance of civilian passengers had been tragically overtaxed in June, when five of the *Bear's* crew had drowned while endeavoring to land a scientific party in heavy surf at Icy Bay, Alaska.

Shortly after the afternoon artillery exhibition, the *Bear* weighed anchor and set sail for East Cape, Siberia, leaving Thornton pacing the beach, doubtless nursing uncharitable thoughts. He was obliged to stew at the Cape for two more months. He finally arranged a ride south aboard a trading ship.

The *Bear* stopped at the Cape again at the end of August just long enough to leave more supplies and check on the mission once more.

Lopp spent the night on board, savoring the company of Jackson, Captain and Mrs. Healy, and the crew, not knowing when he would see another white face. He returned to the village in the morning.

As the *Bear* steamed into the Bering Strait, Sheldon Jackson came on deck for a final glimpse of the mission. The schoolhouse was by now a speck beneath the dark brow of Cape Mountain. Before the continent receded below the horizon, he was heartened to see land's end "encircled with a beautiful rainbow."

# 3

# A Race Worth Saving

THE FIRST FEW DAYS after the *Bear*'s departure, Tom Lopp was occupied sorting the provisions that would sustain him through the coming winter. His groceries included 4 barrels of flour, 640 pounds of potatoes, 60 pounds of beans, 40 pounds of rice, 150 pounds of cabbage, 90 pounds each of bacon and ham, and 120 pounds of lard. For dessert (and digestion), he had a supply of dried apples, peaches, and prunes. Besides the eighteen tons of coal to be stored, a large quantity of lumber was stacked on the beach. It had originally been intended for the Presbyterian mission at Point Barrow, but the ice had been so thick on the north coast that the supply schooner could not make delivery and had dumped the load at Cape Prince of Wales.

With most of the Cape natives gone for the summer, only a few villagers were available to help Lopp shift the wood to safer ground. The task left him "half sick and worn out," he admitted, and at last he was overtaken by a sense of isolation. "Lonesome does not begin to express what I felt," he wrote. "I began to realize what it meant to pass the winter here without the companionship of my late coworker,

Mr. Thornton. I felt more completely than ever before my utter dependence on God's kind providence."

He was not entirely alone, however. In addition to his young helper, Sokweena, he now had the company of Charlie Antisarlook and his wife, Mary. Charlie was a full-blooded Eskimo, born near Cape Nome; Mary had been born at St. Michael to an Eskimo mother and a Russian father. Through their contact with traders, they both spoke a little English, which brought them to Sheldon Jackson's attention earlier that summer as he was making his way north to inspect the new missions at Cape Prince of Wales, Point Hope, and Point Barrow. He hired them to accompany him as interpreters. When the cutter stopped at Cape Prince of Wales on its way south at the end of August, Jackson persuaded Charlie and Mary to go ashore and work for Tom Lopp, instead of returning to their home at Sinuk River, on Norton Sound near Cape Rodney. "They were fair cooks and housekeepers, honest and faithful servants," Lopp reported to the *American Missionary*. Best of all, he had someone to whom he could speak his own language.

With the return of the Cape natives from their summer travels, school began again but with far less hubbub and perturbation. "As I had anticipated, life was more monotonous this year than last," Lopp recorded. "The novelty had passed away." Still, he added, "With teaching, doctoring, hunting, repairing, housekeeping, entertaining, reading and exploring, the time has not dragged."

His health was fine, but less than perfect. He developed a chronic sore throat, which he blamed on "the stench of the over-crowded schoolroom." Whether allergy or infection, the condition would nag him for years.

The natives' ardor for learning was both blessing and burden. "The school had been too prosperous," Lopp remarked. The average daily attendance was 106. Despite the cramped quarters and overwhelming odds, he was pleased to report steady progress: "Many of the children know the alphabet, can spell and pronounce simple English words, read in First Reader, write, sing twenty gospel and patriotic songs; are familiar with several hundred English words and try to keep themselves clean." As rewards for achievement and good behavior, Lopp passed out pencils, papers, pictures, bread, combs, and soap.

Captain Healy's lecture aboard the *Bear* had apparently sunk in, too, for Lopp reported no drunkenness among the natives. He was making headway on the religious front as well. "The pupils are silent in times of prayer and sing with enthusiasm if not with the 'spirit and with the understanding,'" he announced brightly. And unlike Thornton, he sensed that the natives' own spirituality could be a useful bridge to Christianity. "They do not seem to doubt, nor are they moved or astonished at the stories of the Bible, not even the miracle of Christ," he wrote. "They tell and believe legendary 'stories' which they consider equally wonderful. Every child . . . can recite many of these legends relating to 'is-sok' (ages ago), when their doctors were 'un-ut-kooz-ruk' (immortal)."

Even with Lopp's steadfast commitment to the classroom, the natives had difficulty believing that he had been sent to the Cape simply to teach. "The missionary teacher has been a puzzle," he admitted. Because the natives "never do favors or give gifts without expecting others in return," they couldn't understand why "Oo-ma-liks" in the States would give him supplies and pay him to run the mission without demanding that he compensate them in some way. To the natives it seemed only natural that "we were preparing the way for other Americans to settle here," Lopp explained. It was easy for him to chuckle at such a ludicrous assumption, but as events would eventually show, Eskimo logic was not off target.

No matter what, Lopp's gentle touch was refreshing, especially compared with Thornton's starched condescension. Trying to imagine how he must appear in the eyes of the natives, Lopp ventured half jokingly, "Too poor to trade, too stingy to marry, and too effeminate to hunt." Yet there was nothing even vaguely pusillanimous about him.

He was the one who had offered to stay on alone, and his isolation bred neither contempt nor fear. Instinctively he knew when to turn the other cheek and when to stand firm.

The villagers had warned him about Titalk, a boy with a crippled right arm and a reputation for thievery. Lopp and Thornton had caught him stealing bread and suspended him from school. With Thornton away, Lopp allowed Titalk back in the classroom, where he behaved and performed well enough. But then in the spring, Lopp caught Titalk and another boy breaking into the kitchen. When the boys tried to run, Tom fired his revolver, which he kept loaded with bird shot. The warning arrested their flight, and the burglars spent the rest of the night locked in Lopp's bedroom. In the morning they were forced to endure the scolding of the village women as they brought their children to school.

On another occasion, it was the language barrier that kept a bad situation from boiling over. "I still remember the time when A-woot-nuk wanted to make bullets at the school-room stove and I would not let him," Lopp reminisced in a letter to Sokweena many years later. 'He became very mad in the hall and when you heard what he was saying, your face became very pale (no blood). I did not understand what he was saying but I could guess when I saw him reaching for his knife. I think you told me . . . that he was threatening to kill me."

Over time, Lopp's relationship with Sokweena became more than that of teacher and student or boss and houseboy. Out of necessity but also out of a bond verging on brotherhood, Lopp came to defer to Sokweena's judgment in matters regarding native custom and character. "You had a hard time living with white men who did not understand the people of that big village," he confessed to his friend.

Yet understanding came—slowly. Having endured one brutal winter on the Bering Strait, Lopp had deep respect for the resilience and resourcefulness of those who knew no other way of life. Mercifully there was no epidemic during the winter of 1891–1892, and Lopp attributed the overall good health of the village to good hunting. "This has been a fairly prosperous year for our Eskimos," he wrote to the AMA in the spring. "Many white foxes and eleven white [polar] bears have been killed. During the last five days forty-three Oo-ga-rooks [bearded seals] weighing from eight hundred to one thousand pounds have been killed. In a few days they will chase the walrus, the wild buffalo of the Arctic, as he passes northward through the Straits."

But hunting was not always so productive. In December and January, with seals unexpectedly scarce, the villagers resorted to living mostly on tomcod, small fish they caught through holes in the shore ice. Whenever food was in short supply, Lopp noticed that the natives tended to complain of various ailments. "The calls for medicine for boils, scrofulous sores and dysentery were very numerous," he wrote. Mothers came around, asking for bread to feed their babies.

. . .

Of course the cycle of feast and famine was nothing new. Yet outsiders were invariably astounded by how little middle ground existed between the two. "Eskimos [are] probably the hardiest people in the world," wrote twentieth-century Arctic explorer and anthropologist Knud Rasmussen. "Their country is such as to offer but a bare existence under the hardest possible conditions, and yet they think it is the best that could be found. What most impressed [me] was the constant change from one to another extreme; either they are on the verge of starvation, or wallowing in a luxury of abundance which renders them oblivious of hard times past, and heedless of those that await them in the next winter's dark."

For Sheldon Jackson, such blithe fatalism was cause for great concern. He had no faith that the pendulum could swing both ways—from poverty to plenty and back again. Based on his experience among Indians in the American West, he saw only a downward spiral of starvation, disease, and destitution, leading inexorably to extinction.

The evidence, he insisted, was overwhelming, and the cause was shamefully obvious. The greed of white men had obliterated the Eskimos' food supply, and the introduction of alcohol had rendered the natives unable to feed their families. The most graphic case in point, and one frequently related by Jackson to rapt audiences in heated lecture halls across America, was that of the St. Lawrence Islanders.

St. Lawrence Island is a wind-battered scrap of granite and lava anchored stubbornly in the Bering Sea, 120 miles from the Alaskan mainland and less than half that distance from Siberia. Its natives speak a Siberian dialect of Yup'ik, and historically it has had stronger ties to the Asian shore. Nonetheless, St. Lawrence was included in Seward's 1867 purchase, and it has been American property ever since.

Yankee traders, whalers, and fur hunters frequented the island's villages during their Arctic cruises, and too often the currency of exchange was whiskey. In the summer of 1880, the U.S. Revenue Cutter Service vessel *Corwin* (predecessor of the *Bear*) visited the hundred-mile-long island and discovered widespread disaster. At several villages, the *Corwin*'s crew could not find a living soul; instead, they found scores of corpses, many still in their beds. The landing party concluded that the islanders had died of starvation brought on by drunkenness. The story goes that in the summer of 1878 the natives had traded furs and ivory for barrels of liquor. "So long as the rum lasts they do nothing but drink and fight," the *Corwin*'s captain reckoned. Come hunting season, they were too debauched to hunt; over the winter, everybody weakened and starved. The total death toll was estimated in the hundreds, roughly two thirds of the island's population. When Captain Healy visited the devastated villages four years later, decaying bodies were still "lying in and about the falling houses."

More recent historians have surmised that an epidemic such as measles or prolonged bad weather had led to starvation. But Jackson, who learned of the tragedy on his trip north in 1890, had a bigger and much more alarming tale to tell—and sell. Versions of what happened at St. Lawrence were occurring everywhere, he sermonized in an official report to the Department of the Interior. "For time immemorial, [Alaskan natives] have lived upon the whale, the walrus, and the seal of their coasts, the fish and aquatic birds of their rivers, and the caribou or wild reindeer of their vast inland plains." Now those days were gone. "As the great herds of buffalo that once roamed the western prairies have been exterminated for their pelts, so the whales have been sacrificed for the fat that encased their bodies and the bone that hung in their mouths."

Jackson put walruses in the same boat: "Where a few years ago they were so numerous that their bellowings were heard above the roar of the waves and grinding and crashing of the ice fields, this year I cruised for weeks without seeing or hearing one." And so it went for seals and caribou—all depleted by spears, nets, and breech-loading rifles. "Thus," he concluded, "the support of the people is largely gone and the process of slow starvation and extermination has commenced along the whole Arctic coast of Alaska. Villages that once numbered thousands have been reduced to hundreds; of some tribes but two or three families remain. . . . It does not take long to figure out the end."

Another story that became a staple of Jackson's lectures borrowed generously from biblical parable. During a particularly harsh winter, a native father is confronted with a grim choice: "I have a wife and seven children and seven dogs to support, and not a pound of meat or fish to give them," the Eskimo in Jackson's story explains anxiously. "But I have some deerskins and eight fathoms of thong that I can boil up. But these are not sufficient to sustain the family and the dogs too. . . . I do not know where to get more food, as my neighbors are starving too."

Such a dilemma might have taxed the wisdom of Solomon. "If my children perish I will have my dogs left, but if my dogs die how can I [get food]?" the man wonders. "Then my family will starve too, and I will have neither family nor dogs." Jackson usually accompanied apocryphal tales like this with shocking testimony on the prevalence of euthanasia among Eskimos.

At Cape Prince of Wales, however, the situation was not so dire. Disease had taken its toll, to be sure, but the population was not decimated. Lopp and Thornton counted 539 residents in the winter of 1890–1891, and they had noted that food was "generally plentiful."

But as soon as Thornton left the Cape, he began drawing a grimmer picture. In a subsequent report, written after he had reached the States, he testified that "the whalers have so thinned the whales and the walrus that the Eskimos are at times on the verge of starvation; it would not surprise us [Lopp's name was not on the report] that some had actually starved to death." As evidence of the natives' neediness, Thornton noted that they had been "forced to form the habit of eating even the entrails and the blood of their game, and dead fish cast up on the beach." That such comestibles were regarded as savory fare was something that Thornton evidently never considered. Nor did he have any way of knowing that hunting had improved during the second winter, when Lopp was manning the mission by himself. Besides, most outsiders had come to believe that periods of bounty were the exceptions that proved the rule. No surfeit of food could make up for inevitable periods of want.

Thornton, Lopp, and Jackson were in full agreement that the best and perhaps only way to improve the lives of the Eskimos of northern Alaska was to increase the aid of missionary societies and, above all, the U.S government. To do this, they first had to prove (a) that the Eskimo people were on the brink of destruction and (b) that they were worthy of salvation. Jackson had stressed the latter point many times. Admittedly he had called the Cape Prince of Wales natives "insolent and overbearing," but in general he echoed the sentiments of Alaska's second governor, Alfred P. Swineford, who had vouched in 1885: "The native Alaskans, as a rule, are industrious and provident. *These people, it should be understood, are not Indians.* Their appearance, habits, language, complexion, and even their anatomy, mark them as a race wholly different and distinct from the Indian tribes inhabiting other portions of the United States. They are far superior intellectually. . . . They yield readily to civilizing influences, and can, with much less care than has been bestowed upon native tribes elsewhere, be educated up to the standard of good and intelligent citizenship."

To make the other point—that the Eskimos teetered on the brink of extinction—demanded a heavy dose of pessimism. "I myself saw a number of abandoned villages and crumbling houses during the summer," Jackson wrote in June 1890, "and wherever I visited the people I heard the same tale of destitution." To bolster his claim, he sought data and anecdotes from his missionaries. In the summer of 1891, on the first of his two stops at Cape Prince of Wales that year, he had asked Thornton and Lopp to assess the recent harvest of fish and game. The numbers they collected became the basis of a "Report on Food Supply of Arctic Alaska," which is dated July 25, 1891, and carries the byline of both Thornton and Lopp but most likely was written by Thornton after his departure from the Cape. "It is a well-known fact," the report declares, "that the number of whales in these waters has been much diminished by the energetic pursuit of American whalers, and that those which remain have become more wary, and are every year going off further and further from the haunts of men." The report lists only three small whales killed in 1889, none in 1890, one in the spring of 1891. The 1891 walrus season had been similarly disappointing, with only 109 killed.

. . .

That same summer, while Lopp and Thornton had been compiling a census of animals slain, Jackson was making his own reconnaissance. Unlike the missionaries, he focused on a single species: reindeer.

Jackson's first encounter with reindeer had occurred a year earlier, while he was a passenger on the *Bear*. Congress had appropriated

$1,000 in gifts to be delivered to a group of Siberian natives who had aided the lone survivor of an American whaling ship wrecked off the Russian coast. Accompanying Captain Healy on his mission of thanks, Jackson was impressed by the Siberians' wealth of reindeer and their skill at husbandry. He was given a ride in a reindeer sled and afterward witnessed the ritual butchering of four deer purchased by the *Bear* for meat. Throughout the remainder of the summer, he could not shake the image of fifteen hundred reindeer grazing serenely on the Russian shores of the Bering Sea. Returning to Washington, he shared his vision with his superiors at Interior and then with Congress.

Again he stressed the difference between Alaskan natives and the Indian tribes of the United States. "Relief [for Eskimos] can, of course, be afforded by Congress voting an appropriation to feed them, as it has done for North American Indians," he wrote in his year-end report. "But I think that everyone familiar with the feeding process among the Indians will devoutly wish that it would not be necessary to extend that system to the Eskimo of Alaska. It would cost hundreds of thousands of dollars annually, and worse than that, degrade, pauperize, and finally exterminate the people. There is a better, cheaper, more practical, and more humane way, and that is to introduce into northern Alaska the domesticated reindeer of Siberia, and train the Eskimo young men in their management, care, and propagation."

For those who had never seen a reindeer, Jackson described a creature of near-mythic attributes. "I know of no other animal that in so many different ways can minister to the comfort and well-being of man in the far northern regions of the earth," he exclaimed. "It's milk and flesh furnish food. . . . Its skin is made into clothes, bedding, tent covers, reindeer harness, ropes, cords, and fish lines. . . . Its sinews are dried and pounded into a strong and lasting thread; its bones are soaked in seal oil and burned for fuel; its horns are made into various kinds of household implements, into weapons of hunting and war, and in the manufacture of sleds."

The litany of virtues was myriad and endless. "Under favorable circumstances a swift reindeer can traverse 150 miles in a day. . . . As a beast of burden they can draw a load of 300 pounds." A butchered reindeer produced 80 to 100 pounds of meat. Its milk was not plentiful—about a cup per milking—but, as Jackson hastened to emphasize, "this small quantity . . . is so thick and rich that it needs to be diluted with nearly a quart of water to make it drinkable."

Most amazing of all, reindeer survived and thrived on nothing more than the lichen of the tundra—reindeer moss—of which, Jackson pointed out, there were three hundred thousand square miles in central and Arctic Alaska—"an area equal to the New England and Middle States combined, together with Ohio, Indiana, and Illinois . . . [and] practically useless for any other purpose." It was simply a matter of "sound public policy," he argued, "to stock the plains of Alaska with herds of domesticated reindeer and cause these vast, dreary, desolate, frozen, and storm-swept regions to minister to the wealth, happiness, comfort, and well-being of man. What stock-raising has been and is on the vast plains of Texas, Colorado, Wyoming, and Montana, reindeer-raising can be to northern Alaska."

Put in more spiritual terms, *Rangifer tarandus* was "the animal which God's providence seems to have provided for the northern regions." And always Jackson returned to his belief that Eskimos were "a race worth saving." Implicit in this evangelical avowal was that he would be their savior.

Truth be told, however, Jackson could not claim sole authorship of the reindeer idea. In the summer of 1885, the revenue cutter *Corwin*, captained by Michael Healy, had explored Kotzebue Sound and the Kobuk River, north of Seward Peninsula. One of the passengers, Charles Townsend, a naturalist employed by the government, had remarked on the scarcity of caribou, meanwhile observing that the natives favored reindeer-skin clothing acquired from "the Asiatic side of Bering Straits." Assessing this dilemma of supply and demand, Townsend proposed:

> In time, when the general use of fire-arms by the natives of Upper Alaska shall have reduced the numbers of this wary animal, the introduction of the tame variety, which is a substantial support to the people just across the straits, among our own thriftless, alcohol-bewitched Eskimos, would be a philanthropic movement, contributing more toward their amelioration than any system of schools or kindred charities. The native boats could never accomplish the importation, which would, however, present no difficulty to ordinary sea-going vessels. The taming of the American [caribou] is impracticable, for domestication, with this animal at least, is the result of subjection through many generations. Something tending to render a wild people pastoral or agricultural ought to be the first step toward their advancement. In our management of these people . . . we have an opportunity to atone, in a measure, for a century of dishonorable treatment of the Indian.

In this last, Townsend was plainly referring to an inflammatory book by Helen Hunt Jackson (no relation to Sheldon Jackson), *A Century of Dishonor*, a disjointed but widely circulated screed denouncing the U.S. government for its repeated acts of "cruelty and perfidy" toward its native population—the *Uncle Tom's Cabin* of its day. When it came to Alaskan natives, Townsend saw the road to redemption as straightforward—and spanning only fifty or so miles from start to end.

Whether the suggestion to import reindeer originated with Townsend or was prompted by Healy (or someone else entirely) is not clear. Regardless, by 1890 Townsend had faded into the background and Healy was front and center as a fervid advocate—and willing accomplice—of the reindeer scheme. The introduction of reindeer, he testified, was "the

most important question that bears upon the Territory of Alaska." Setting
aside whatever ambivalence he had toward blue-nosed missionaries,
Healy committed the *Bear's* crew, resources, and time to the experiment.

Without Healy's immediate support and encouragement, Sheldon
Jackson might easily have failed. Over the winter of 1890–1891, after first
seeing Siberian reindeer, Jackson had marshaled his full repertoire of
clerical and political savvy to persuade Congress to give him—as Alaska's general agent of education—$15,000 to embark on the reindeer
project. He won an enthusiastic supporter in Henry M. Teller, U.S. Senator from Colorado and former secretary of the Interior, but no amount
of cajolery could win enough votes for the appropriation. Undeterred,
Jackson turned to the public directly, eloquently pitching the plight of
the needy but inherently noble Eskimos in churches and lecture halls
and through newspapers and religious journals across the country.

Reindeer, he discovered, made good copy. "Ten dollars will buy a
reindeer," bruited the *Mail and Express* of New York. "Here is a chance
for those good folk who love Father Christmas. Let them send a full
St. Nicholas team—Dancer and Prancer, Dunder and Blixen, Comet
and Vixen, one and all! Before long the reindeer bells will jingle and
sing through all the desolate land. The Esquimaux shall stop starving,
and work and grow fat." By the time Jackson returned to Alaska in the
summer of 1891, he had collected $2,146 in small donations—enough,
anyway, for a start.

That summer, in addition to its usual duties in Alaska, the *Bear*
cruised the Siberian coast, looking for natives willing to part with their
reindeer. Travel was difficult. The ship was hampered by frequent ice
and fog; charts were unreliable. And on the occasions when crewmen
were able to get ashore, they had extreme difficulty communicating
with the reindeer-herding Chukchi, whose language, Chukotkan, was
distinct from any spoken on the Alaskan side of the strait. Charlie and
Mary Antisarlook were brought along as translators, but they spoke
only Yup'ik and Inupiaq, along with pidgin English and Russian.

Nor did anyone else aboard the *Bear* understand much about Chukchi culture and customs. They had all been ashore the summer before, but most of what Sheldon Jackson knew of these inhabitants of the eastern Siberian capes and uplands he had gleaned from reading the travelogues of Western Union surveyors, who had come to the region in the mid–1860s to map a route for an undersea cable intended to link the two continents. (It was never completed.) One of those travelers, George Kennan (great-uncle of the esteemed twentieth-century diplomat and historian of the same name), had noted that the Chukchi nursed a strong superstition against parting with living reindeer. "You may purchase as many dead deer as you choose, up to five hundred, for about seventy cents apiece; but a live deer they will not give you for love nor money," Kennan advised. "You may offer them what they consider a fortune in tobacco, copper kettles, beads, and scarlet cloth, for a single live reindeer, but they will persistently refuse to sell them; yet, if you will allow them to kill the very same animal, you can have his carcass for one small string of beads. It is useless to argue with them about this absurd superstition. You can get no reason for it or explanation for it, except that 'to sell a live reindeer would be *atkin* [bad].'"

Bad indeed. The Chukchi were a fierce and proud people. They had kept the Russian empire at bay until the late eighteenth century, earning themselves a reputation as "the most untractable, the least civilized, the most rugged and cruel people of all Siberia." For generations they had skirmished with Cossacks, neighboring tribes, and the Eskimos of Alaska, with whom they competed for the bounty and boundaries of the Bering Sea. Eventually the temptations of trade conquered all, and by the mid-nineteenth century the Chukchi had become a vital cog in the new order of commerce that linked Russia to Siberia, Siberia to Alaska, and Alaska to the United States.

For all their purported lack of sophistication, the Chukchi accomplished something few other cultures had done: They turned caribou into reindeer.

No one knows who first thought of taming *Rangifer tarandus*. One of the best guesses is that natives living near the Sayan Mountains, southwest of Lake Baikal on the border of present-day Siberia and Mongolia, began breeding wild reindeer as draft animals, beasts of burden, and docile sources of food and peltry as early as three thousand years ago. The practice spread from there, although reindeer husbandry was evidently not a hugely popular pastime, for today the only ethnic groups who have stuck with it are the Saami (Lapps) of northern Scandinavia and several remote Siberian peoples, including the Chukchi.

The Chukchi, it turned out, were in the right place at the right time. After the caribou herds abandoned the northwest coast of Alaska in the 1880s, the Eskimos became absolutely dependent on the Chukchi for reindeer skins. Sheldon Jackson, on his first trips to northern Alaska, had noticed that the farther he traveled from the Bering Strait—away from the Chukchi homelands in Siberia—the worse the Eskimos dressed. Reindeer skins were expensive and hard to come by. What George Kennan had perceived as "superstition" was more likely deeply ingrained economic protectionism. "The Siberian deermen are a nonprogressive people," Sheldon Jackson had declared after his first encounter with the Chukchi. "They have lived for ages outside of the activities and progress of the world." Perhaps so, but they were not too "uncivilized" to grasp the meaning of monopoly.

Even when Jackson and Healy were able to get ashore and contact Chukchi willing to sell deer, the deer were not at hand. On July 13, the *Bear* anchored in Holy Cross Bay amid treacherous ice and a "cold driving rain storm," Jackson recorded in his diary. "Probably the *Bear* was the first steamer to plough its waters." The following morning, four umiaks approached the ship, and the natives were welcomed aboard. After accepting gifts of the notoriously hard-crusted ship's bread, two of the natives agreed to sell five reindeer each, "but the deer were on the west side of the Bay, which could not be reached until the ice should move, & the ice would not move."

At other anchorages, the Americans were told that the herds had been driven inland for the summer, where the grazing was better. The best they could extract from the Chukchi was a promise to bring herds to the beach the following summer. "Purchasing reindeer in Siberia is very different from going to Texas and buying a herd of cattle," Jackson lamented. "In Texas such a sale could be consummated in a few minutes or hours. But in Siberia it takes both time and patience."

As the summer wore on, Jackson became even more frustrated. He seemed not to display the same warmth and paternalism for the Siberian natives as he did for their Alaskan counterparts. The Chukchi were not his flock; they were not Americans. They looked and lived much like the Eskimos, and they shared many of the same exotic and objectionable habits—tattooed faces, belief in supernatural creatures, weakness for intoxicants. But to Jackson, the Chukchi were one step further down the evolutionary ladder—a "dirty looking set." Chukchi relished the larvae that infested the fur of the reindeer and made gruel of the semidigested contents of the deer's stomach. Most herders carried a small pouch of urine on their belts, a proven perfume for attracting reindeer. Least appealing of all, though, they were rock-ribbed bargainers. Jackson confessed that without the *Bear*'s imposing presence—"moral effect," he called it—"little would have been accomplished in the summer of 1891."

On August 27, with only a few days remaining before the *Bear* needed to turn south for open water, it anchored in the fog off of Indian Point, Siberia. Finally Jackson got his first reindeer. "A large number were offered," Jackson wrote, "but having failed in procuring herders, & having no place ready to receive them, & and not knowing whether we could procure food such as they would eat, we thought it prudent to receive only four." The price was one rifle and two hundred cartridges. (The sale of breech-loading rifles to Alaskan natives was still illegal, but the law did not apply to Siberia.) The deer were wrestled to the ground, and their legs were bound together. They were then hefted into the *Bear*'s boats, rowed to the ship, and hoisted aboard by block and tackle. "They are beautiful creatures and gentle as lambs," Mary Healy wrote in her diary.

Two days later the *Bear* anchored off Cape Prince of Wales. Harrison Thornton and Tom Lopp came aboard. For Thornton, it was a last chance to make a plea for passage home. For Tom Lopp, it was a last chance to see white faces before winter set in. It was also their first opportunity to see reindeer; the four animals were penned on deck and appeared in good shape. In the "Report on Food Supply of Arctic Alaska," dated earlier that summer, he and Thornton had "hailed with delight the proposed scheme for introducing domestic reindeer here," adding that it was "a plan that we often discussed ourselves last winter and had intended to recommend if you [Jackson] had not anticipated us." Now as they examined the four reindeer, stabled so agreeably on the bobbing deck of the revenue cutter, they too were convinced of not only the potential of reindeer in Alaska, but of the feasibility as well. Lopp promised Jackson that he would make scouting trips during the coming months to find suitable grazing land for a larger herd, which the *Bear* hoped to procure the following summer.

After leaving the Cape, the *Bear* turned west again and made one final sweep of the Siberian coast. On September 12, Jackson was lucky enough to buy twelve more deer, making a total of sixteen. The season was quite late at this point, and instead of putting the deer ashore at St. Lawrence Island, as had originally been planned, the *Bear* steamed south toward the Aleutians. The deer showed no signs of seasickness, surviving on a diet of their accustomed moss, sacks of which had been provided by the Chukchi herders. A week later the *Bear* arrived at the Aleutian island of Unalaska, where seven of the reindeer were put ashore; the other nine were set loose at nearby Amaknak Island.

For Sheldon Jackson, the summer had been more than a modest success. He had fallen short of the two hundred reindeer he had originally hoped to acquire. Nevertheless, he had proven the skeptics wrong by accomplishing three important goals: "1. The cultivation of the good will of the Siberians and foundations laid for future purchases; 2, the actual purchase of sixteen reindeer; 3, the proving by actual experience that reindeer can be transported with the same facility as other domestic cattle."

Over the winter, as he again lobbied Congress for funding to expand his project, he had no way of knowing that all sixteen of the reindeer put ashore in the Aleutians had died, of starvation apparently.

. . .

Tom Lopp, alone at Cape Prince of Wales, knew nothing of the reindeers' demise, either. Nor would the news have made him any less sanguine about introducing reindeer to the Seward Peninsula. It was his hope that the first herd would be established somewhere near Cape Prince of Wales. True to his word, he had made a survey of the plains north of the Cape. The first of his two trips was in some ways a trial, for until then Lopp had never ventured very far from the village. In November, he rode a dogsled along the west shore of the twenty-mile-long lagoon northeast of the Cape. In the brief report he submitted to Sheldon Jackson, he called it "Louge Inlet or Lake," although eventually it would bear his own name, Lopp Lagoon. The lagoon is separated from the Bering Strait by a narrow strand of low dunes, and on the east it is fed by a series of shallow creeks. Lopp followed the largest of these creeks (today's Mint River) until it reached the foothills of the mountains. "The mountains . . . were sloping and rolling, not sharp and rocky, and covered with moss," he observed. "Portions of these hills were covered with 3 to 5 inches of snow, but all the exposed portions were free from any snow." In short, ideal grazing land for reindeer.

To have made the journey any earlier would have been vastly more difficult. Before freeze-up, the tundra is an obstacle course of soggy turf, countless bogs, and unavoidable potholes, swarming with mosquitoes. Come winter, though, the soup solidifies, and the bays, lagoons, and ponds become terra firma. The traveler who in July or August must pick his way arduously over, through, and around this untidy topography—hugging serpentine shores, wading frigid inlets, sinking to the thigh in sump holes—can from November to May choose a route that is much more direct and efficient. If he can bear the cold and wind, short days and lengthy blizzards, then winter is the season for making miles.

Lopp's report failed to mention how long this first trip took or whether he made it alone. All the same, he returned encouraged. Two days after Christmas he embarked on a longer journey, again by dogsled, this time accompanied by "a boy," presumably Sokweena. Again he went north, his destination Kegiktok (present-day Shishmaref), a village of eighty maritime hunters, burrowed into the beach seventy-five miles up the coast from Cape Prince of Wales. Each night during the ten-day trip, Lopp and Sokweena were taken in by native families. "Without exception, they were very kind and did every thing in their power to entertain me," he remarked gratefully. His opinion of Eskimo architecture increased commensurately. "After traveling twenty or thirty miles, with the mercury at twenty to twenty-five degrees below zero, I found the underground houses very comfortable."

The children in many of these houses had never seen a white man before. Yet somehow they knew all about the school at the Cape. To Lopp's amazement and delight, some of them had already learned—by word of mouth—to count to ten and to sing "In the Sweet By and By."

Even more heartening was the natives' enthusiastic response when he related the plan to bring reindeer to the region. They complained that the traders from the Cape charged exorbitant prices for Siberian deerskins. "In fact," Lopp reported, "many of the poorer people can not afford a deer-skin artega [atigi] but are compelled to shiver through the winter on one made of squirrel skins." All told, Lopp met more than two hundred Eskimos on the trip; all of them, he said, were "very anxious to have deer introduced."

The habitat looked quite promising, too. In his memo to Sheldon Jackson, he assured that grazing was excellent all along the coast, from Port Clarence in the south to Kotzebue Sound in the north. Moreover, he vouched, "I think these coast people are better situated and adapted for herding than any other Alaskan people." He added only one caveat: "They are all superstitious and are great cowards after dark. Perhaps it will be necessary to have them stand watch [over the reindeer herds] at night in pairs until they become accustomed to the darkness. (One Eskimo never goes any place after dark if he can help it. He sees ghosts; but he is all right with a companion.)"

Lopp arrived back in Cape Prince of Wales brimming with confidence in both the prospects for reindeer and his own ability to journey far from home under trying conditions. If anything, he seemed to thrive on the hardship. "On the whole my trip was an enjoyable one," he wrote in the *American Missionary*, "and when I returned I felt fresh and strong for the five months' work before me."

There was no shaking the loneliness, however. It closed in like the Arctic darkness. Mary and Charlie Antisarlook were homesick as well, not having seen their family in two years. When Mary got word in February that her mother had died, Lopp let them return to their home on Norton Sound.

For the rest of the winter, Lopp immersed himself in learning the native tongue and teaching his own. Yet he was still not proficient enough to sustain a conversation, except with Sokweena perhaps. Unfortunately, Sokweena was only a boy and hardly someone with whom Lopp could share diverse thoughts. Not that he was a complainer. Tom Lopp might describe things as difficult, but he would never say he *minded* that they were difficult. He would painstakingly record the day's temperature—thirty below, for example—but he would never mention that he was suffering from the cold.

Still, he must have been counting the days until spring, when the *Bear* would appear in the roadstead offshore, bearing letters from home and, if all went according to plan, Harrison Thornton and his new bride. A woman—a white woman—at the Cape would be quite a change.

In the meantime, he made another friend. In early spring some natives appeared at the Cape with a dog they had acquired at a distant trading post. Lopp discovered that the dog understood a few commands in English. Thenceforth, until the revenue cutter arrived, he made a habit of visiting the dog every day—two of God's creatures joined by a common language.

# 4

# Just the One for the Place

O N THE SIXTEENTH of June, the villagers took up the cry, "*Tra me! Tra me!*" (A ship! A ship!) From the beach, Tom Lopp could make out the *Bear*, nosing at the edge of the ice, four miles offshore. The revenue cutter had appeared two weeks ahead of schedule, and Lopp realized it would be foolhardy to try to make his way across the rotten spring ice or for the ship to attempt to ram its way nearer. When the cutter withdrew, Lopp decided that he would not wait for it to return. Leaving Sokweena to look after the schoolhouse, he boarded an umiak headed for the summer trading fair at Port Clarence; when the *Bear* arrived there a week later, he was on the beach to greet it.

Besides the *Bear*, seven other ships were anchored in the harbor, including the steam whaler *Newport*, on its first voyage to the Arctic. It was the *Newport* that commanded most of Lopp's attention. Two hours before the whaler had arrived, Lopp had learned that the passenger list included Harrison Thornton, who had indeed found himself a wife, Neda Pratt of Auburn, Maine. Also on board was a second woman, Ellen Kittredge, who had been assigned by the American Missionary Association to share the teaching duties at Cape Prince of

Wales. Whatever Lopp's expectations might have been, he kept them to himself. But from this point forward his laconic exterior would lose its opacity. With Ellen's arrival, not only did Lopp have a reason to open up, but he was also entering the company of a prolific correspondent whose letters and diaries are the basis of so much that is known about her, the man she would soon marry, and the history of Cape Prince of Wales.

As for Ellen's first impression of her future husband, she confided to her sister Frances, "He is very pleasant." Apparently he reminded her of someone from back home in Glyndon, Minnesota. "I would tell you who Mr. Lopp looks somewhat like," she jotted coyly in a postscript, "but then you wouldn't like him, and everybody does, they say." Three days after arriving at Port Clarence, "everybody" included Ellen Louise Kittredge.

She was twenty-four years old, no longer (maybe never) a girl whose head was easily turned. Indeed, she had always set her own course. The oldest of eight children, she was devoted to her family yet fortunate never to have been shackled by the duties of big-sisterhood. Her father, Charles Kittredge, was not one to be hemmed in, either. He had left Dartmouth College to fight in the Civil War. Afterward he married Katharine Forbes, a woman of equally staunch New England lineage, and took up farming in the town of his ancestors, Westborough, Massachusetts, where his first three children were born. By and by he grew restless, as so many did in the years of expansion and upheaval after the war. He worked for a while in the first oilfields of Pennsylvania, then looked about in West Virginia, Illinois, Michigan, and Iowa. Emboldened by the Homestead Act, he finally settled in the untilled Red River valley of western Minnesota, only recently appropriated from the Great Sioux Nation. The nearest town was Glyndon.

Ellen Kittredge—Nellie to her family—was six when she was sent back to Westborough to live with her grandparents, who gave her a rigorous New England education and instilled the moral compass that had guided her Puritan forebears for two centuries. She stayed for six years. Returning home to Minnesota, she enrolled in Carleton College at the age of fifteen. To pay her way, she taught school between sessions. Two years later she enrolled at the State Normal School in St. Cloud and sped through in two years. By 1889, she was principal and head teacher of the school in Glyndon.

It had to be more than money that drew her from her hometown to her next teaching position, for the job promised only $20 a month. The American Missionary Association, true to the wishes of its Congregational founders, was still very active in the South. In the fall of 1891, Ellen Kittredge became a teacher at the AMA-sponsored Gregory Institute in Wilmington, North Carolina. She loved the change of scenery, the adventure of a new place, and, above all, the chance to seek a higher calling. The one thing she did not like was the weather. Raised in the North, she found North Carolina uncomfortably hot and muggy.

In the spring of 1892, Ellen read a notice in a church journal, advertising for a teacher to join a husband and wife bound for Alaska—the Thorntons. On April 3, she raised the question with her parents out of the blue: "[M]ay I go to Alaska to teach?" Her main reason for considering the offer, she said half-jokingly, was, "The climate would be better for me than this because I keep warm so easily. I am warm often when everyone around me is cold."

Of all her many qualifications for the position at Cape Prince of Wales, her abidance of cold was not the least.

Ellen did not wait to receive her family's approval, nor had she truly solicited it. By mid-April, she had accepted the appointment. "I feel so sure I am doing right," she wrote her parents. "I have asked God's direction in every step. As I said when I came here [to North Carolina], I am one of four grown-up daughters. You have more of us at home than most families have anywhere. I am not going into something I can't get out of."

By the end of the month, she was headed to Minnesota to bid

good-bye to her family. On the way, she stopped in Virginia to meet Harrison and Neda Thornton, who were preparing to depart for San Francisco. As best he could, Thornton briefed Ellen on what to expect at Cape Prince of Wales. Surely he mentioned Tom Lopp. Regardless of what he said about the Cape, she had already made up her mind to take the job.

Certainly she gave no hint that she was going to Alaska in search of a husband. "If I were a great many girls I should have been married and away from home for good by this time," she needled her parents affectionately, "and probably would have married someone you were not suited with, for certainly the right young men are scarce, very scarce." Besides, she reminded, "You brought me up for the sole purpose of being of use in the world."

Be that as it may, the news that she would be obliged to live in close quarters with a single man—devout and proper, to be sure—did not dampen her enthusiasm. On the seventeen-day trip north from San Francisco, she had staved off seasickness by remaining on deck even in the roughest seas. The 135-foot *Newport* was a heavily laden whaler, not at all built for comfort. Ellen "won the admiration and respect of everyone on board," recalled one of the other passengers. "I remember full well helping to lash her into her steamer chair on top of the deck-house and then lashing the chair to the rail to prevent it capsizing as the ship rolled."

The Thorntons were neither as beloved nor as seaworthy. As the voyage wore on, they began to find fault with everything. Someone left a hatch open, allowing seawater to flood their cabin, soaking their shoes and precious bundles of books. The tablecloth and dishes were filthy, the canned beef was barely edible, and the ship's officers swore, smoked, and gambled in the presence of the women. "Most seafaring men have a prejudice against all sorts of missionaries," Thornton griped. Sailors were "little educated either mentally or morally" and governed by "natural animal passions and greed." Small wonder that the officers and crew took to playing practical jokes on the righteous Mr. Thornton.

Ellen had quibbles of her own. She lamented that she was not able to curl her hair, and she could not bear the inactivity. "Walks on this deck are like the walks of a caged tiger," she wrote to her father. For the most part, though, she reported that she was "enjoying the trip first rate." To kill time and win favor, she coaxed one of the "dreaded traders" on board to teach her to splice rope. Of all the passengers, she most enjoyed the company of Archibald McLellan, whom Sheldon Jackson had hired to build a new house at Cape Prince of Wales. Besides his carpentry skills, McLellan was also a minister, although Ellen mentioned only that he was "studying theology." A devoted husband and father, McLellan was respectably charmed by Ellen's vivacity and independent spirit. Together they explored the island of Unalaska, climbing one of the steep mountains that surround Dutch Harbor. "When we got to the top the sight was grand, just grand," Ellen exclaimed, despite her soaked dress. "I would climb ten times as high to see it again." When she disagreed with McLellan on some point of theology, he playfully called her a "heathen." He was the one who teased her the most about her imminent encounter with Tom Lopp.

In San Francisco, Ellen had overheard friends of Thornton complimenting him for selecting women who could stand up to the Alaska climate. Ellen's appetite for cold was well-known, and her counterpart, Neda Pratt Thornton, was from Maine and no stranger to winter, either. When Harrison met Neda in New York, she was working as a nurse in a settlement house in lower Manhattan. They were married three months later.

Ellen had taken the remarks on her hardiness as a compliment. But the inference that she was even tacitly a mail-order bride made her bristle—as well as blush. A kindly San Franciscan had told her, "I hope you will be happy up there. I think you have every reason to be." The well-wisher had met Tom Lopp and "like[d] him very much."

Snippet by snippet, Ellen began to form a portrait of the man she would soon be obliged to reckon with. "Speaking of Brother Lopp," she wrote coquettishly to her sister Alice, "was it Fannie [sister Frances] who wanted a description of him? Here are three points for her: He's from Canada, wears number eight slippers and likes cats." (She later corrected the misinformation about Canada; a cat on board the *Newport* was intended as a pet for Lopp; how and why Ellen came to learn Lopp's slipper size can only be conjectured.)

The more time Ellen spent with the Thorntons, however, the more they annoyed her. One day in the Bering Sea, Thornton decided to shoot ducks from the deck of the *Newport*. McLellan tried to coach him on when to fire so that the ducks would fall on deck. It was after Thornton ignored McLellan and the bird fell into the ocean that Ellen first made her spiteful remark, "Mr. Thornton isn't of the variety that takes advice." She also disapproved of the Thorntons' constant display of newlywed affection. One rainy night she was with the Thorntons in the ship's cramped main cabin. When the couple got up to leave, Ellen noticed that they had been sitting on two stools, "though I should have thought when they were there that it was one. She had her head on his shoulder and he managed to have one arm around her and hold to her hands, one of which he kissed at intervals. . . . I confess I am getting tired of it. It is too, too."

As the day approached when she would finally meet Lopp in person, she had already set him apart from the less than winsome Thornton. To her sister Susie she gossiped good-naturedly: "Mamma said once that she thought probably Mr. Thornton was the one to come home and Mr. Lopp the one to stay because Mr. Lopp was the least selfish of the two. Mr. McLellan . . . credits Mr. Thornton with the large share of the bad and Mr. Lopp a large share of the good traits. It amuses me. It is too bad; because if Mr. Lopp is mortal, Mr. McLellan will have to be disappointed when he sees him."

She tried not to set her own hopes too high. "I have said 'Mr. Lopp'

enough now," she wrote with girlish contrition, "and will wind up by
saying I wish I wasn't doing such a silly thing as going [on] this way."

But she had come too far to turn back. On the morning of June 28,
the day after the *Newport* arrived at Port Clarence, Tom came aboard
and met Ellen for the first time. There is no record of their introduction. Tom likely wore deerskin breeches, sealskin boots, and a woolen
shirt and jacket, the only clothes he had brought from the Cape. His
face was deeply tanned, darker even than his eyes. He had shaved his
beard, and his moustache was not so unkempt that it hid his kind
smile.

Ellen's cheeks would have been flushed, from the month-long voyage and from so much else. Her upper lip was firm; her lower much
fuller. Her light brown hair, which she wore pinned, had a natural
wave, with or without the aid of curling iron, and her eyes matched the
sunlit sea, blue and lively. She was shorter than he by several inches.
As always, her dress suited her trim figure and unaffected nature
equally well. She was pretty and poised, far from plain, and nowhere
near pretentious. In the modest fashion of the era, she wore long skirts
and sleeves. Tom Lopp, having spent a year among natives whose faces
were so often framed by a hood of fur, could not help noticing that the
high collar of Ellen's dress encircled her slender throat with a ruffle of
white lace.

So much happened at once that she was unable to write home
until July 3. By then the *Newport* had sailed the sixty miles from Port
Clarence to Cape Prince of Wales and dropped off the missionaries
and their supplies. In her next letter, Ellen remarked on how well
adjusted "Mr. Lopp" had become to the harsh, exotic environment of
the Cape. "I think he is just the one for the place," she observed.

Soon after they had met, Tom had let it be known that if his throat
did not improve, he might return to the States at the end of the summer. Still, things were going well enough, and Ellen did her best to
sooth, if not cure, Tom's ailment. "The maple sugar Mamma put in

[my trunk] was a pleasant surprise," Ellen wrote home gratefully. "Mr. Lopp is helping eat it."

In other letters, Ellen expressed no misgivings about her new circumstances. "This is a pleasant place," she declared. "I can stand . . . to get along without trees because we have the hills and the ocean. We can see East Cape, Siberia, at any time. It looks about fifteen miles away. There are islands [the Diomedes] in between."

They had come ashore from the *Newport* late in the evening, and it was nearly midnight before all the provisions were landed. Ellen tried to be of help but eventually accepted the role of spectator, "as happy as a small boy watching a circus tent put up." She didn't get to bed until three in the morning, two hours after sunrise.

Accommodations were cramped at first. Living quarters built for two bachelors now had to be shared by a married couple, an unmarried man and woman, and Archibald McLellan, who would spend the summer at the Cape building the house that would become the new missionary residence. If nothing else, Tom and Ellen were thoroughly chaperoned. "There have been some Eskimos around the house every minute, night and day, since we landed," Ellen reported. "Imagine what it must be to work under such a fire of eyes. We have made sash curtains for two windows, but I do not like to see them shut out. The first few days it would startle me to look up and see several pairs of eyes gazing at me. But now I don't usually mind it. The women always smile when I look at them. Often they have their babies on their backs."

Most of the villagers were gone for the summer, as usual, and there would be no school until fall. On most days, Lopp and Thornton helped McLellan with the new house. They had chosen a site on the hillside at the far southern end of the upper village, one hundred feet above the beach. Tucked in the lee of Cape Mountain, it was better protected from the wind than was the original schoolhouse. But while the first school was located in the center of things, halfway between the two villages that comprised Cape Prince of Wales, the new house was aloof and looked down on the rest of the community. Nine months out of the year, the path to and from it was extremely slippery.

As soon as the missionaries moved into their new home, the living quarters in the original schoolhouse could be converted into two additional classrooms. Since there had been no room aboard the *Newport* for the lumber to build the new house, McLellan was obliged to use the lumber originally intended for Point Barrow but left at the Cape. After a year lying in the open, much of it was soggy and warped. It would have to suffice.

. . .

While the house was under construction and the new arrivals at the Cape settled in, another project was under way that would change the landscape of northern Alaska. Two other passengers aboard the *Newport* that summer were Miner Bruce and Bruce Gibson, hired by Sheldon Jackson to establish a reindeer station at Port Clarence. The previous winter, Jackson at last had succeeded in persuading Congress to appropriate $6,000—less than half the $15,000 he had originally requested—for the purchase of more Siberian reindeer and for the establishment of a herd on the Alaskan mainland. Jackson had been aboard the *Bear* when it arrived at Port Clarence at the end of June, and he had sailed with the *Newport* when it dropped the Thorntons, Ellen Kittredge, and McLellan at Cape Prince of Wales. He rejoined the *Bear* two days later for its cruise to the reindeer camps on the Siberian coast.

This time the Chukchi were more amenable and better prepared. At the first camp the Americans visited, Jackson succeeded in purchasing forty-one reindeer; at the next camp, another twelve. Additionally, he hired four Chukchi herders to accompany the animals and look after them in Alaska.

Grantley Harbor lies in a protected location within the bay of Port

Clarence. Before leaving for Siberia, Jackson had selected it as the site of the Teller Reindeer Station, in honor of the senator who had made it possible. On the morning of July 4, the *Bear*'s boats began landing the deer. Natives carried the hobbled animals up the beach in litters. Out of the original fifty-three brought ashore, only one was injured. Native dogs killed it almost immediately. While the Chukchi herders kept the herd from disappearing in the moss-covered hills of their new home, Captain Healy ordered that a flagstaff be erected on the spot where the station would soon be built. On July 6, the *Bear* embarked again for Siberia. By the end of the summer, Jackson acquired 118 additional reindeer. He had wished for ten times that number.

But even with such a small herd, Superintendent Bruce and his assistant, Gibson, had their hands full. Neither had any experience with reindeer—Bruce was a Nebraskan, Gibson from California—and at first they were entirely dependent on the Siberians. Fortunately moss was abundant in the hills surrounding the station, so the deer did not wander far. As each new bunch was landed on the beach, "They no sooner found themselves at liberty than they started at a breakneck speed in whichever direction their dazed condition suggested," Bruce observed. But then after running a mile or so, they stopped, took their bearings, and invariably joined the main herd. Bruce and Gibson were pleasantly surprised to discover that the native dogs, for the most part, were not a menace.

In keeping with Jackson's design to train native Alaskans as herders, four Eskimos were hired—two from Cape Prince of Wales and two from the native village at Port Clarence. One of the latter was Charlie Antisarlook. If they stayed with the herd for two years, each was promised ten reindeer of his own. The Chukchi were to be paid more conventionally—$50 a year, plus food and clothing. Five of the eight herders, Alaskan and Siberian, were housed in an eighteen-by-twenty-four-foot driftwood house dug into the side of a hill. The other three lived with Bruce and Gibson in the station headquarters, a frame house built with lumber from the States. Gibson divided the eight into two watches, each tending the herd for twenty-four hours at a stretch. They communicated as best they could through sign language, a few words of shared vocabulary, and the translation of Charlie Antisarlook.

From the start, there was trouble between the Chukchi and the Eskimos. Age-old rivals, neither group liked being pushed around by the other. The Chukchi insisted that they knew everything there was to know about reindeer; the Eskimos used their home-field advantage to treat the Chukchi like dirt. Nor did it help that a number of the natives from the nearby village were unruly whiskey traders. Before long the Eskimos had persuaded the Chukchi that they would soon be murdered, along with the whites at the station and the entire herd. There was no truth to the threat, but such dissembling and disrespect did not bode well for Sheldon Jackson's vision of cross-cultural intercourse. Miner Bruce concluded, not surprisingly, that the Chukchi were "of a nervous temperament."

Yet Bruce was impressed by how quickly the Eskimos picked up the skills needed for reindeer herding. Paying them the highest compliment, he asserted that they "will compare favorably in intelligence with any of the white race." Brains and initiative had their limits, however. Charlie Antisarlook was apparently a bit too ambitious and opinionated, and his wife, Mary, even more so. She knew "just enough English to make mischief," Bruce reported. Unable to muzzle her, he fired Charlie and recommended to Jackson that "no native should be employed by the station who speaks a word of English. If they understand what is said by the white men when speaking to each other they carry gossip to the natives and thus cause dissatisfaction."

· · ·

Sixty miles to the west at Cape Prince of Wales, there was tension of a different sort. The time was nearing when Tom Lopp would have to decide whether to leave Alaska. He had already arranged passage to San Francisco. The reasons for staying, though, grew more obvious every day. It is easy to imagine the respect and admiration Tom and Ellen shared from the start. Each was so determined and capable, thoughtful and self-effacing. Nor was it surprising that they would take such pleasure in each other's company—both of them vigorous and intrepid, educated and sensible, not to mention spiritually compatible. Physical attraction was not to be discounted, either. But what were the odds that they would fall so thoroughly in love?

Neither of them was a breathless romantic, not publicly anyway. But romance flourished nonetheless, fanned perhaps by necessity. An arranged marriage may not be what either had in mind, but under the circumstances and based on the pleasant serendipity of the situation, it was hard for them not to believe that their harmonious convergence and abrupt cohabitation, on whatever terms, was, if not preordained, then at the very least irresistible. Within six weeks they had made up their minds to get married.

If taciturnity was Tom's calling card, then wryness was Ellen's. On August 17, she began a tongue-in-cheek letter of apology to her mother and father: "Mamma said once that she always had felt sorry that she didn't tell her mother as soon as she was engaged, so I was going to write you immediately, but I have waited a week." She made only a halfhearted attempt to mask her elation: "I have thought of the dozens of things I have said about not getting married. Some stand good and some don't. I feel decidedly cheap to think of going back on all I have said. But I am not breaking one of my resolutions, the one not to marry a man who smokes."

Tom's letter to Mr. and Mrs. Kittredge was at once chivalrous and resolute, and, for him, rather effusive: "I have always dreaded the time when I would have to ask fond parents for their daughter, but now I am compelled to write and inform you that I have won the heart of your brave and noble Nellie." Ellen had teased her parents that Tom might prove himself in the Eskimo way, by killing a walrus and presenting the tusks to his in-laws-to-be. Instead, he offered a firm but sincere prayer: "If the announcement of this union, which to us seems to have been brought about by God's kind Providence, is painful to you, I trust that you will let God help you bear it."

Concerned that Tom's bona fides might not speak for themselves, Ellen asked McLellan to vouch for him separately. "I had some thoughts of what he would be before I got there in regard to his ability & usefulness, which I am glad to say [were] fully verified in what I saw of him at his work," McLellan explained to the Kittredges, "and he makes it his work to do anything that needs doing at the mission. He is a college graduate, has plenty of good common sense . . . and as a missionary for northern Alaska I put him a little above any man in the country." McLellan ended with an assurance meant to allay any parental concern that Tom and Ellen were acting on unbridled impulse: "They seem to be well suited to each other, and are not carried away with any emotion, but have been."

Tom and Ellen were married on August 22 by the Reverend McLellan. Ellen worked on her dress until the last minute, finishing just in time for the ceremony. It was made of red flannel and trimmed with mink. Her deerskin jacket and cap were trimmed likewise. In honor of the occasion, Tom wore "American clothes," a switch from his usual native garb. The entire village was invited to the ceremony, performed on a sealskin rug in the schoolhouse; the overflow stood on boxes and watched through the windows. Neda Thornton played the wedding march on the new organ, which had come north on the *Newport*. "The natives were very much impressed," Ellen wrote her sister Frances. "It was made as impressive as possible, for their benefit." Afterward, Tom and Ellen passed out gifts: needles for the women, ammunition for the men, bread for the children. Later the newlyweds, Thorntons, and McLellan sat down to a dinner of scalloped oysters, quince jelly, strawberries, and Edam cheese. For a wedding cake, the Thorntons shared their own, which they had sealed in a tin box and brought from the States as a memento.

By way of a honeymoon, the Lopps took a trip to Port Clarence. Over the summer, McLellan had finished the new mission house at the Cape as best he could, given the constraints of time and material, and now he was heading home. Tom and Ellen decided to accompany him as far as Teller Reindeer Station. Tom was also very eager to inspect the herd.

Ellen had proven that she was game for anything. The closest thing to a manual for missionaries was *Foreign Missions: Their Relations and Claims*, written by Congregational minister and missionary Rufus Anderson in 1869. Based on Anderson's own experiences in Asia and the Sandwich Islands, the most effective missionaries were married men: "With an intelligent, pious, well-educated wife, having good health and a devoted spirit, his value as a missionary is greatly enhanced. She faces danger and endures hardship as well as he. Her courage, faith, and patience among barbarous heathens, fully equal her husband's, and her presence add much to his safety." Whether Tom and Ellen had read this job description is not known, although it seems likely. Either way, Ellen could not have fit Anderson's bill more perfectly. Her pluck was second to none. Shortly after arriving at the Cape, she had enthusiastically accepted an invitation to visit one of the subterranean native houses, crawling through the claustrophobic entrance on her hands and knees. Soon she took up ptarmigan hunting and became an excellent shot. "When I get out in my short dress and one of Mr. Lopp's hats . . . and my Eskimo boots and a gun over my shoulder, I look pretty tough," she boasted.

The short dress was a measure of her ready adjustment to her new environment. The only way to get across the creek that divided Kingegan was to wade, and the summer had been especially rainy. Unlike Tom, she would never adopt native clothing entirely. But, discarding Victorian propriety (and alarming her parents), she shortened the hems on her dresses and took to wearing reindeer-skin trousers underneath her bloomers. Of the Eskimo boots, she soon owned three pairs.

At the reindeer station, the Lopps moved into the dugout recently vacated by the herders. Ellen judged it a "fine place only it is a little too damp"—a cheerful understatement; not even Eskimos chose to live in their sodden underground houses during the summer. Nevertheless, she chirped, "Am having a delightful time here . . . looking at the tame deer . . . hunting grouse [ptarmigan], boating and studying Eskimos." In the only photographs taken of them at the time of the marriage, Tom and Ellen pose smartly in their fur coats. Ellen's hair is curled, Tom's trimmed. In his arms he holds a tame fox. On his wife's face is the beginning of a smile. If there was the slightest discord between them, it was Tom's gentle complaint that Ellen was spending too much time writing letters, which she wished to complete before the ships left for the season. "It isn't very pleasant to write a big bunch of letters when one is enjoying the *Honeymoon*," she acknowledged rapturously.

Not that he was devoting his full attention to her, either. "Just now he is very much interested in reindeer," Ellen wrote her brother Charlie. During the two weeks the Lopps were at the station, Tom spent as much time as possible with the herd. He was impressed by their splendid condition, so sleek and glossy in their summer coats. Their coloring ranged from chocolate to coffee to blond; some had large white spots, while others were almost entirely white. They were not as big as the deer he knew back in Indiana. A full-grown reindeer is barely four feet tall at the shoulder, making the enormous antlers seem oversized. Unlike other horned species, both male and female reindeer grow antlers, though it is mostly the bulls that have shovel-shaped horns protruding over their foreheads, as garish as the plume on a Victorian bonnet. In late summer, the antlers of the Teller herd were enveloped in luxurious velvet.

Their gait reminded Tom of racetrack trotters, heads held high,

legs swinging easily, with scarcely any bounce to the back and with-
ers—efficient for covering long distances or pulling a sled. Reindeer
hooves are broad and cloven, providing superb support on both soft
and frozen ground and functioning splendidly as paddles for swim-
ming and as spades for pawing through snow.

Collectively, reindeer demonstrate an ingenious choreography.
They bunch together as tightly as sheep yet move like a school of
fish—circling and releasing, with those at the center of the herd constantly working to the outer edge, the entire herd turning itself inside
out again and again for communal protection, warmth, and relief from
the torment of flies and mosquitoes. Astoundingly, they never seem to
tangle their antlers. The clicking noise they emit is caused not by their
horns but by the unique flexing of tendons in their supple feet. Often
this sound is accompanied by a mutter of basso grunts, like the belch-
es of satisfied diners.

As diners, too, reindeer are quite exemplary, thriving on the prolific fibrous moss of the tundra—*Cladonia rangiferina*—along with
sedges, willows, and other shrubby vegetation. When full, they will lie
down until weather, predators, or hunger tell them it is time to get
moving again.

At the station, Tom watched the Chukchi walk to within fifty feet
of the herd and lasso the deer with long thongs made of walrus hide.
He was pleased to see that several of the deer had already been broken to harness. Ellen, meanwhile, was surprised to learn that reindeer
provided milk. "When they are out herding," she remarked, "if [the
natives] get hungry or thirsty they catch a deer and take a drink."

Their admiration of reindeer bordered on awe. "When Mrs. Lopp
and I visited your station and viewed the acres of horns, we could
hardly believe our eyes," Tom wrote to Superintendent Bruce afterward. "It seemed as if we had suddenly stepped into the fairy land of
Santa Claus, although, when seen in the distance, the deer resembled
a herd of cattle quietly grazing on a gentle hill slope in the States." By

the time he and Ellen left for the Cape at the beginning of September, Tom was more convinced than ever that reindeer were the answer to saving the Eskimo. Moreover, he was determined to play a more direct role in the future of reindeer in Alaska.

The two-day trip home to the Cape was rainy and rough. Traveling all night, they landed through the heavy surf and were greeted by a group of natives who were busy butchering a whale that had washed up several days earlier. In the Lopps' absence, the Thorntons had moved into the new house, although it still needed a great deal of work. After breakfast and prayers together, the Thorntons had an announcement to make: Rather than sharing the kitchen and living room, they proposed dividing the house into separate quarters. Thornton later defended the decision to the American Missionary Association, explaining that "all who know anything about attempts at combining two families in one domestic establishment will agree that we have been wise and prudent."

The Lopps did not agree. "We objected to secession," Ellen told her family, taking a sideways poke at Thornton's incurable southernness. Nevertheless, "They declared they must go out of the Union." After talking over the matter privately, Ellen and Tom consented, claiming the two front rooms and kitchen, including the new cook stove. Tom and Thornton spent the day installing the old cook stove (from the first schoolhouse) in one of the rear rooms, and that night the couples ate separately. The honeymoon was over.

School resumed at the end of September. The schoolhouse was divided also, the Thorntons teaching in the morning, the Lopps in the afternoon. Later Tom partitioned his room so that Ellen could teach the youngest children separately. In addition to reading, writing, and arithmetic, they offered a steady fare of Bible stories and hymns. The organ was a huge draw, and a duplicating machine called a hectograph made it easier to expand and drill Eskimo-English vocabulary. "Our natives are improving," Thornton declared, "but we find it much slower and more laborious business than we expected to turn a savage Eskimo into a comparatively civilized Christian. Think how long it would take to make the very lowest class of people in your neighborhood clean, truthful, self-reliant, economical, virtuous and God-fearing. Meanwhile, we are sowing the seed with what patience we may."

But Thornton's patience was wearing thin, and the seeds he sowed would not bear appetizing fruit. One of his fundamental problems was that he never truly envisioned a time or circumstance in which native Alaskans would ever become his equal. His mind-set was permanently rooted in his prejudices of race and class. In a letter to the American Missionary Association, Thornton lamented unashamedly: "It looks as if we were going to have more trouble than I anticipated about the 'servant girl question.' The natives, like all uncivilized people, are not accustomed to persistent work or to any routine of duty, so that even an easy position becomes burdensome after a time. Our boy, Sokweena, has taken it into his head that he wants a holiday, so that we have had to take a new girl." Her name was Woodlet. "She has proven quite a jewel, for a savage; but it will take several years perhaps to make a really competent servant of her. Meantime, we console ourselves, when she gives us trouble, with the thought that we are teaching her, and through her the natives, what a civilized Christian household is."

The Lopps also had a girl working for them—an orphan named Kongik. It would be naive to deny that they put themselves above her, but their relationship was nurturing and anything but overbearing. They gave her every advantage possible, and certainly they never abused her or complained about her. Nor did they treat any of the other natives like servants or savages. Occupying the front of the house, they found it easy to receive visitors. Entries from Ellen's diary for September mention variously: "Early in the forenoon three boys were in and looked at pictures and played with small dolls. . . . In the evening a woman came in and looked at pictures. . . . Erahana called before breakfast and drank a cup of coffee and ate some oatmeal." Once school began, Ellen began teaching several of the women how to knit.

The Lopps' neighborliness was repaid in kind. Tom was an honored guest in the qargi. One day in October while the Lopps were out for a walk through the village, Elignok, the chief who had been so hostile two years earlier, stopped them to say that, in their atigis, he had nearly mistaken them for natives. Tom and Ellen took it as a compliment. Others followed. In her diary entry for December 4, Ellen noted for the first time the nickname that the villagers had given to her husband: Tom-gorah— Good Tom. It stuck for the rest of his life.

Ellen, in this instance, held to the custom of her own country. She continued to call her husband "Mr. Lopp" when speaking of him to others and often when speaking to him directly. She laughed at her self-enforced formality, but by her usage and inflection, she made it obvious that his proper name was a term of endearment and devotion—her own way of recognizing Tom's goodness. "It doesn't seem as if anyone could have a better husband than he is," she told her mother.

. . .

With the missionaries' language skills improving and with four of them now making up a Christian community, the time had come to place greater emphasis on evangelism. "We cannot yet record a single unmistakable conversion," Thornton admitted. However, he assured the American Missionary Association, "We believe that God works through human instrumentalities, and that time must be allowed for the heathen to learn what Christianity is before they can accept it."

On November 20, the first Sunday school class was held in the schoolhouse. One hundred natives attended, attracted by the organ playing. Lopp and Thornton began at the beginning—reading the first chapter of Genesis. Depending on the weather, they held Sunday school every week from then on. But even with enthralling music and expanded vocabulary, progress was slow. The miracle of the loaves and the fishes translated easily enough. Loaves became pilot bread, the hard ship's biscuits that were virtually a unit of currency with Alaskan natives. Hell, on the other hand, was a tougher sell. Appreciating the premium Eskimos placed on warmth, Thornton suggested describing hell as a place of extreme cold—with the obvious inference that Eskimos inhabited the land of the damned.

An even bigger problem was that the Thorntons and Lopps could not agree among themselves on what to teach and how—the Thorntons tending to be doctrinaire, the Lopps more flexible. "One thing that troubles me when I think of these people becoming Christians is what to tell them they should or shouldn't do," Ellen wrote to one of her sisters. "They keep their own customs very carefully, [and] there are strict lines between right and wrong that they all agree upon. But we can draw no such line for them, for we don't agree among ourselves. . . . [And] even if we all four agreed, we are not the only ones these people are going to see."

As ever, deeds spoke more volubly than words. They made plans to build a community wash house, which would also serve as a "workshop, reading-room, study, and possibly gymnasium"—a Christian qargi of sorts. Yet for Tom Lopp especially, the gift that would do the most for the Eskimos of the Bering Strait was reindeer.

In mid-October, just before freeze-up, Miner Bruce arrived at the Cape by umiak, out of loneliness presumably but also to see the country. Tom was keen to hear how the reindeer herd was getting along, and he undoubtedly expressed his interest in establishing a herd near Cape Prince of Wales. Learning of Tom's scouting trip of the previous year, Bruce suggested that he take a longer trip, this time exploring as far as Point Hope, three hundred miles to the north, for potential reindeer range. Tom needed little urging. Ellen was no less sanguine; if her husband was going, she was going with him. They discussed leaving right after Christmas, once the country became more passable by sled.

There was only one catch: Ellen was pregnant. Worried that her letters might be opened before they reached home, she was reluctant to share too many details of her condition. By the first of December she was wracked by morning sickness, unable to get out of bed until Tom had brought her a piece of bread to settle her stomach. Nevertheless, she was determined to make the journey to Point Hope. She argued that it would be safer to take a six-hundred-mile sled trip in the dead of winter than to stay at home, where she would be at constant risk of slipping on the steep, ice-covered path that led from the house to the village. Tom assented, but only after she promised to leave behind a letter explaining that she was making the trip on her own free will—in the event, she said, that "we should be carried off on the ice or anything." Such perils were fresh on their minds; several Cape natives had been lost on the ice earlier that month.

On Christmas Eve they made a short trial run up the coast. Tom by now was an able dog driver, and they were home by mid-afternoon in time to stuff the stockings of Sokweena and Kongik. The original plan was to leave for Point Hope a day or two after Christmas, but word had passed down from the natives that Kotzebue Sound was not yet frozen, which would have added several days to the itinerary.

They were not able to get away until January 13. The temperature hovered near zero. "Strange as it may appear," Miner Bruce would comment in his superintendent's report later that year, "among the 500 or more natives at the cape, there was not one who had ever made the journey [from Cape Prince of Wales to Point Hope] in winter, and [the Lopps'] trip was all the more remarkable because it was undertaken in the face of opposition by the natives, who are supposed to know the country and its dangers in winter traveling."

From the brief log they kept, it is evident that they did not make the journey entirely by themselves. On the trip north, there were two sleds, guided by natives about whom little is known except their names, Kerook and Nanok. One of them, possibly Kerook, had been a student at the Point Hope mission a year earlier and was familiar with the landmarks along the coast, at least in summer. The diary makes no mention of Nanok on the return trip, so perhaps Tom drove the second sled on the homeward leg. The only passenger was Ellen, who at the outset was about three months pregnant—she wasn't exactly sure. The others ran behind the heavily laden sleds.

Traveling by dogsled is exhausting and fraught with hazards. Dogs are forever tangling their harnesses, testing the authority of the driver, and fighting among themselves. Sleds tip over easily and require constant repair. For pregnant Ellen the trip was doubly arduous. For the first three days, she rode bundled in deerskins, vomiting up everything she put in her stomach. When they stayed in native houses, the stifling air nauseated her even more. Tom's diary entry for January 18, the sixth day of the trip, reads tersely: "Start at 8. Cold wind. Hard trip on shore ice most of time. Mrs. Lopp's sled fell over—no harm." That night they slept in a native house packed with fifteen others. The ceiling dripped, and there was not enough room to stand, barely enough to lie down. Remarkably, the next day Ellen felt better. The journal recorded: "Nice day. . . . Mrs. Lopp ran part of time."

On the twentieth, they lay over for a day in a native house, and Ellen was feeling well enough to take over the duties of diarist: "Started at 6:30. New dog disappeared just after he had been harnessed. Probably the son of the man who sold it . . . let it loose. Traveled nine hours and reached To-o-tet a little after dark. K[e]rook froze his face a little. Mr. Lopp got his very cold. . . . The house we are in has an addition on one corner. Seems to belong to one branch of the family. Kitchen just high for me to stand straight in. . . . They killed a walrus here a few days ago. They can't chop wood after dark here, because it would injure the seal hunting. Lamps smaller here than any place but the last. Can't get through the passage without getting down and crawling. Little water. Slept well."

The next morning they breakfasted on tea and walrus liver. "Very good," Ellen noted cheerily, failing to mention whether the meat had been served cooked or raw.

They hugged the coast, often running along the shore ice. Their preference was to stay with natives, and often they stayed for more than one night—resting the dogs, buying new ones, and replenishing the supply of fish and meat. At each stop they would pass out pictures depicting the life of Christ, followed by a brief sermon and prayer. Tom also took the opportunity to spread the gospel of reindeer. "The farther north we went the more poorly clad we found the people," he wrote to Miner Bruce. "Most of their [atigis] were made of squirrel or rabbit skins." When he explained to the natives that reindeer were being introduced to the Alaskan coast, "some looked as though they thought it too good to be true. . . . They would often say, 'Hurry up,' 'Bring the deer next year,' 'Plenty moss,' etc."

The biggest obstacle of the trip was Kotzebue Sound, a forty-mile-wide scoop in the bulging brow of northern Alaska. Under the right conditions, the crossing from Cape Espenberg to Cape Krusenstern, the two nearest points, could be made in one long push. Tom and Ellen had been told that the ice was locked in for the season, and they made no objection when local shamans "doctored up" the weather for them as they neared land's end. But when they arrived at the low spit of Cape Espenberg on January 25, they were greeted by a broad expanse of open water. The wind had shifted to the south, separating the pack ice from the shore ice. The detour along the shore added three days to their journey.

The diary entries for the next ten days are a staccato of hard knocks borne stoically.

January 29: "One of our best dogs dead. . . . Deep snow. . . . No tea for breakfast. Thirsty. . . . Wind blew sled over me [Tom] and dogs. Afraid to go out far on shore ice. . . . Worn out. Blizzard."

January 31: "Windy. . . . Turn sled over twice. Mrs. Lopp OK. Lost mit[ten]. 3 grouse. Camped about 3 in ice drift. . . . Slept well."

February 3: "Wind stronger. . . . Wet socks. Lost boot. . . . Rough sliding. Perpendicular cliffs. Mrs. Lopp turned over twice. . . . Freshly fallen rocks—danger—whirlwind. Mrs. Lopp walks—lifting. Dogs confused. . . . Bad blizzard. Not sure about location . . . ."

On February 4, they arrived at Point Hope, an outpost even colder and more wind-swept than the one they had left twenty-three days earlier. Eskimos had an apt name for this bar of sand, gravel, and ice poking fifteen tenuous miles into the Chukchi Sea: Tigara (forefinger). Archaeologists estimate that maritime hunters were living here, 125 miles above the Arctic Circle, a thousand years before Captain Frederick Beechy renamed the bleak promontory for a seafaring friend in 1826. In the late nineteenth century, Point Hope, with a robust population of nearly three hundred Eskimos, was often the first stop for whalers and traders after leaving Port Clarence, and their impact was in some ways worse than the most brutal barrage of bad weather. From whites, natives readily acquired great proficiency in distilling whiskey. Venereal disease became commonplace.

Unlike Tom Lopp and Harrison Thornton to the south, Dr. John Driggs was not the first white man to winter over at Point Hope. A shore-whaling station had been established in 1887, manned by a handful of hardy, hard-bitten Americans, and at least one sailor had jumped ship and settled in Tigara with a native wife.

Alaska had not been Driggs's first choice. Born in Cuba to American parents, he spoke Spanish and sensibly had asked the Episcopal Church to send him to Mexico or South America. Instead, he had sailed with Lopp and Thornton on the *Jeanie* and landed at Point Hope on July 11, 1890. Most of his winter's supply of coal and many of his belongings were lost in the surf; the lumber for his twenty-by-forty-foot schoolhouse did not arrive until the end of August. Fueled by evangelical zeal and blessed with a stout constitution, Driggs made a go of the mission. The first winter, he rigged a harness out of rope and dragged driftwood from the beach to burn. The nearest freshwater, other than melted snow, was six miles away. He had to keep his inkwell on the stove to prevent it from freezing. In the spring, he had to drill holes in the floorboards to drain a winter's worth of condensation that had accumulated on the ceiling and then thawed in torrents. Sizing up his new life, he wrote to a church friend, "A man in civilization and the same man up here are two different individuals." This was hardly a revelation from someone whose previous job had been as physician for an opera company.

With snow drifted around the Point Hope schoolhouse, Tom had difficulty finding it in the failing afternoon light. Leaving Ellen in the sled, he pushed open the door and found Driggs sweeping the empty classroom. "I was greatly surprised to see a stranger walking in," Driggs recalled. "Through the furs which protected his face I could see that he was a white man. I was yet more puzzled when he informed me that his wife was outside. I went out to see her and there was the first white woman who had ever paid Point Hope a visit."

They stayed with Driggs two weeks. They were gladdened to discover that he had made considerable progress. He was, if anything, more fluent than Tom in the Inupiaq language. He had fewer students—fifty or so—but he taught them alone, rewarding attendance and achievement with small cakes made of flour and molasses. After only two years, the best students were already beginning to read the Bible, and many honored the Sabbath. And as a doctor, Driggs had brought great comfort to the community. "Little by little we are gaining their hearts," he assured his Episcopal sponsors.

Tom and Ellen lent a hand in the classroom and with Sunday school. The natives found Ellen's bread a big improvement over Driggs's bachelor biscuits. One of the first things they noticed was that

Tigara was quite deserted, with many of the houses empty—the opposite of Cape Prince of Wales, whose natives left in the summer but returned to fill the village in winter. The Lopps learned that whaling had worsened at Point Hope in recent years, and many natives had moved north to Point Barrow to work for the American whalers who wintered there.

There were still American whalers at Point Hope, however. In addition to the men who occupied the two whaling stations six miles east of Tigara, the whaling schooner *Nicoline* was wintering over in Marry-at Inlet, the lagoon formed by the finger of the point. When the Lopps paid a visit, the ship was frozen in the ice and banked with snow for insulation. Captain Benjamin Tilton received them kindly, the highlight of an otherwise tedious winter. The Lopps found him cordial but were dismayed to learn that the crew had been robbing the scaffolding of native graves for firewood and fornicating with native women.

Bad weather kept them from leaving until February 20. The return trip was no easier than the run north. Sleds broke; dogs died or disappeared; Tom's sore throat acted up; Ellen was sick to her stomach. In addition to the wind and bitter cold, the sun now rose by ten and set at four, and the reflection off the snow and ice stung their eyes. On March 1 they reached Kotzebue Sound. Kerook tried to talk them out of crossing. Tom was determined to try.

They left the north shore at 3:30 P.M., just at dusk. Within an hour they encountered floating blocks of ice. "Had some trouble getting sleds over cracks of water two or three feet wide," Tom wrote in the diary. "Lead dog was jerked back into the stream. Trouble to get all them out." They made camp at 5:30; mercifully the wind subsided. They were off the following morning by 4:45. "Very bad traveling, floe after floe with little ledges to lift the sled over. . . . Nothing to guide us most of the time but snow drifts." Just before nightfall, they spied land but were forced to spend a second night on the ice. "Wood scarce. Use up one of our boxes. Clear and cold. Throat bothers me all day. . . .

Dogs fighting." Finally, at noon on the third day, they made landfall.

Comparatively speaking, the next ten days were uneventful, aside from the usual aggravation of storms, blinding sun, fractious dogs, and unwieldy sleds. On March 10, Ellen turned twenty-five. Now nearly five months pregnant, she walked gamely behind the sled for hours. A day out from Cape Prince of Wales, the snow blew so hard they lost their way. "Dogs worn out and blinded—dive their heads into snow," Tom noted. "Sled stuck in drifts. Mrs. Lopp off. Dogs refuse to go past [Pinguk River]. We stop. Shawl and lunch bags blow away. Thaw—wet—stay overnight. Eat seal heart, beans and rice. . . . Start out with light."

When they arrived at the Cape the next day, the Thorntons seemed stunned to see them. They had feared that the Lopps had been lost on the ice while crossing Kotzebue Sound. Cape natives had reported seeing ghosts in the schoolhouse. Also on hand to greet them were Miner Bruce and one of the few other white residents of northern Alaska, John Dexter, who owned a trading post on the eastern end of Norton Sound.

That night, after the Lopps had told of their winter adventure, the conversation turned to reindeer. Lopp reported that the reindeer range looked promising. In a letter that he wrote to Bruce later on, Tom calculated how the trip might have gone if they had done it with reindeer instead of dogs: "We traveled from here to Point Hope, more than 300 miles, in twenty-three days, sixteen days of actual traveling. The other seven days we were laid up on account of bad weather or to rest our dogs. With deer I think we could have reached Point Hope in half the time, especially had herds of deer been available at two or three settlements along the route, so that we could have changed our team occasionally. At times we were compelled to haul dog food 100 miles, while with deer they could have picked their food, as there is an abundance of moss all the way."

Further stressing his advocacy of reindeer, he added: "It may be of interest to note that while on this mid-winter journey we were clothed in deerskins, carried a deerskin tent (seven winter skins sewed together) and sleeping bag of the same, and escaped without a frostbite, although there were days when the thermometer registered 33 below zero, and we camped out when it was as low as 22 below."

The Lopps had been away exactly two months. All things considered, they were no worse for wear. Miner Bruce even complimented them on how well they looked. The same could not be said for Harrison Thornton. Ellen and Tom were shocked by the change that had come over him. He seemed distracted, agitated, and angry. Almost before the Lopps had unbuttoned their coats and eaten a hot meal, he presented a litany of crimes, threats, and slights that had been perpetrated by the villagers while the Lopps were away. After one of the natives stole some matches, Thornton had closed school for a week. He alleged that another villager had tried to stab him. When Bruce had sent a letter announcing that he was coming to the Cape, the Thorntons had warned him not to come; they didn't have time for visitors.

It was now evident to all that Thornton was losing his grip.

# 5

# Not So Much to Be Pitied

To hear Thornton tell it, he and Neda had spent the past two months under virtual siege.

Even the house had turned against them. Winds cascaded over the brim of Cape Mountain and funneled down the chimney, choking the kitchen with smoke and ash. The siding had shrunk and warped in the Arctic air, and drafts whistled through cracks so wide "we could thrust a knife between the boards," Thornton grumbled. Not long after the Lopps had departed for Point Hope, the Thorntons had moved the cook stove to the sitting room and closed off the other rooms of the house.

What once had been regarded as minor nuisances now became gross intrusions. "They demand unreasonable things of us," Thornton complained of the Cape natives, "[and they] are sometimes offended if we do not comply, as, for instance, to furnish the whole community with matches, nails, boards, etc., when their lack of such things is generally due to their lack of industry and forethought; or to interrupt us at our meals or in our sleep (if we would allow it) to trade with them."

The Lopps were not swayed by Thornton's carping. The previous fall, Thornton had claimed that his old nemesis, Elignok, had tried to shoot him while he was walking with Neda on the beach. Tom was skeptical, but Thornton insisted that he had heard the rifle shot hit the water. Later, when Thornton claimed that another of the village umialiks, Erahana, had tried to stab him, Tom conducted his own investigation, concluding in his diary: "Small knife. Didn't want to stab T."

Ellen had her own take on Thornton's behavior: "He doesn't mean things [to] appear different from what they are, but he forgets very easily and fills in the places he forgets from his imagination."

There was no placating Thornton. He grew increasingly obsessed with the notion that the natives were bent on murdering him. Indeed, murder had never been far from his mind since the day he had first sailed for Alaska in 1890. Two years later, when he was returning to the Cape accompanied by his wife and Ellen, he was shaken by a rumor, passed from ship to ship, that Sheldon Jackson had been slain by natives. The story turned out to be false, but Thornton remained on edge. More recently, a Cape Prince of Wales native had shot a neighbor to death during a drunken quarrel. "We did not fear the people when they were sober, but feared from the whiskey," explained the formerly quiescent and stoical Neda Thornton, "for when they were drunk they shot at us, and Mr. Thornton felt the peril."

After the alleged attempt to stab him, Thornton announced that he would shoot any native who came to his door at night without identifying himself. He carried a gun with him everywhere. "It has since occurred to me," Lopp wrote to Neda Thornton many years later, "that some of his apprehensiveness might be attributed to advice Dr. Jackson gave him about being prepared to defend our lives with our rifles. He repeatedly referred to the Jackson advice. . . . Doctor meant well but it was not the advice [that] Harry needed."

At the least excuse—the incident of the stolen matches, for instance—Thornton would refuse to teach, and as he grew more and more defensive, he came to regard the Lopps' lenience and equanimity as a betrayal. In early April, he castigated them for "feeding natives at our table, giving them the same kind of food we ate," a plainly peeved Ellen wrote in her journal. Thornton urged the Lopps to treat the natives "less as social equals" and to stop "visiting them, etc. and inviting men and wives to come together." Thornton announced that he was going to write to the American Missionary Association, requesting that both couples be recalled and the mission closed. Tom and Ellen thought Thornton was being extreme. "Mr. T is the one who is afraid now, not we," Ellen confided to her mother.

The Lopps were not so blithe as to disregard the potential volatility of certain villagers, but experience had taught them that steadier members of the community usually stepped forward to keep the troublemakers in check. The Lopps felt confident enough, anyway, that Tom had no qualms about taking a trip to the Teller Reindeer Station. Ellen was by now too pregnant to travel.

Tom was away five days. The six-hour, sixty-mile dash by dogsled was scarcely worth mentioning, compared with the thrill of seeing the reindeer herd. The day after Tom arrived at the station, Miner Bruce took him on an inspection of the herd, each man riding a sled pulled by reindeer. Tom described his first reindeer ride as "a pleasure which I shall always remember with pride." Later on he gushed his enthusiasm in a letter to Bruce that was obviously intended for a wider audience: "[W]hen I visited you in April, and rode out to the herd behind two fleet-footed deer, saw the fawns gamboling over the snow, and the big herd feeding in almost the same place where we had sent them in August, witnessed four deer drawing four sleds loaded with driftwood, which would have required twenty dogs, I realized more fully than ever before how completely and admirably the domesticated deer are adapted to the wants of the inhabitants of these frozen waste lands."

While at Port Clarence, Tom discussed with Bruce the idea of starting a second herd north of Cape Prince of Wales. He knew firsthand that the country was suitable and that the natives were amenable, but the final decision would have to wait until Sheldon Jackson arrived in June, two months hence.

Meanwhile, the drama at the Cape was building. Shortly after Tom arrived home, Titalk, the troublemaker with the crippled arm, burglarized the schoolhouse again, breaking several windows and stealing some chalk and pencils. Two days later, he broke two more windows.

Deliberations over how to respond to Titalk's chronic mischief were interrupted by the arrival of three umiaks towing a bowhead whale. For the next several days the entire village was engaged in landing and butchering the catch, which Tom estimated was fifty to sixty feet long—fifty to sixty tons in weight. He and Ellen made several trips to the site, a two-mile walk across the ice. "The natives had dug a trench in the snow and ice on the edge of the water, at right angles. . . . The whale was partly dragged into this, tail first," Ellen described, "and when we got there the tail had been cut off and Kokit[uk] was wearing a piece. . . . Five men in waterproof suits [sewn from walrus intestines] were on the whale halfway between his head and tail and were cutting him up. . . . The skin was slate color from an inch to two inches thick, pieces of blubber of different shades of pink with the dark skin, cut off like pieces of side pork, looked pretty floating in the water. Some of the boys were running around eating small pieces of blubber and skin . . . that looked like candy made of layers of chocolate and pink candy. . . . We tasted some and it was good." Tom and Ellen were impressed by the efficiency and cooperation of the natives and by their thoroughness: "Nothing but blood wasted. Every scrap saved."

The Lopps' diary notes that the whale had been "speared first, then shot with Kokit[uk]'s gun." Presumably this meant that it had been struck first with a harpoon, a lance with a barbed iron (in earlier times it was ivory) point, followed by an exploding "bomb lance." Federal law still forbade the sale of breech-loading rifles to Alaskan natives, but this regulation did not prevent whites from providing natives with whaling guns, which came in several designs. All of them carried an explosive charge, which detonated after the lance penetrated deep into the flesh of the whale. A bomb lance was fired by a shoulder gun configured somewhat like a shotgun; a darting gun looked and functioned more like a harpoon, with the exploding charge mounted at the tip. Eager to help the natives help themselves, Lopp and Thornton had acquired two of these weapons, which they loaned to the natives and stored in the schoolhouse when not in use. Whaling had been lean lately, and it was in the interest of all for hunters to gain every advantage. Loaning the guns was also a good way to build trust, although Thornton was not so sure.

The hunting had been slightly better that spring than in recent years. Two weeks after the first whale was killed, another was taken. Other successes were reported in the first edition of the *Eskimo Bulletin*, a blurry but sprightly one-page newsletter printed on the mission's hectograph and eventually distributed to family and supporters in the States. Besides noting the inventory of whales, seals, and polar bears killed during the winter, the *Bulletin* posted the Lopps' wedding announcement, news from the reindeer station, and a one-line notice of the trip to Point Hope. The meatiest article appeared at Thornton's insistence under the headline, "Whisky in the Arctic":

> The liquor question in the Arctic is a question of self-preservation to white residents and the Eskimo race. The missionary teachers have been shot at and their lives threatened by drunken men this year. When sober, the natives are friendly. When drunk they want to avenge their relatives killed in the 'Gill[e]y affair.' One bottle of liquor might be the death of us all.

Several days before publication of the *Bulletin*, Thornton announced that he was giving up teaching, at least until the fall. He was disgusted with the natives' tardiness and their general lack of obedience. He again accused the Lopps of being too tolerant of late arrivals. Principle, he said, took precedent over popularity. Tom replied that "too much liberality or not enough were things that would correct themselves." In the meantime, school must continue no matter what, he urged. Begrudgingly Thornton agreed to continue with Sunday school, but nothing more.

Each day, fifty or more students attended the Lopps' classes, and on Sundays nearly twice that many came to Sunday school. Since Easter the missionaries had been teaching the New Testament with "good results." Momentum faltered, however, on Sunday, May 28, when Ellen felt too ill to help out with Sunday school, her first absence since arriving at the Cape. She blamed indigestion, which had nagged her since the start of her pregnancy; she was not expecting her baby until July. Unable to sleep, she sat up most of the night, sewing baby clothes. Still feeling poorly at 3:00 A.M., she consulted a medical manual, altered her diagnosis to "false pains," and went to bed. An hour later, "This small girl was in the clothes basket on a chair in front of the stove," she wrote to her mother. "She weighed five pounds though she was far from fat. From all counts she must have been a seven-months baby. . . . She wasn't strong enough to suck much, so we fed her with spoon or rag. . . . I suppose she looks very homely to everyone else, but we think she is quite good looking."

Ellen and Tom took their time naming the child. The natives called her Elidlenok, after the point of land on which the house was built. Finally, after two months, Tom and Ellen settled on Lucy—Lucy Alaska Lopp.

The baby gained weight slowly. She was so small and weak that Ellen was hesitant to bathe her, and she had difficulty waking her to eat. Isolated and inexperienced, Ellen was grateful for the help of Neda Thornton, who had worked in a dispensary in New York. The natives, too, were full of advice. When Lucy's umbilical cord was slow to fall off, one of the village women was sure it was because the mission house was located too near a cemetery.

· · ·

By June, everyone was anxious for the *Bear* to arrive. Tom was keen to present his plan for a second reindeer herd. He was likewise determined to distance himself and his family from the feckless Thornton.

Even on occasions when Thornton tried to get along with the natives, he seemed jinxed. Earlier in the month, he had accompanied a party of walrus hunters, but on the way home he had insisted on taking a shortcut across a stretch of ice, against the advice of his companions. When the ice began drifting away from shore, "He jumped in and tried to swim, with his boots and heavy fur clothing on," Ellen wrote. "He found he couldn't get close to land so he held on to a small piece of ice and called and the canoe heard him and came back for him. . . . [The natives] said to Mr. Lopp that if he had been drowned, Captain Healy would have killed them all."

Thornton thanked his rescuers with a gift of flour, but his regard for the village as a whole did not improve. He wanted desperately for Captain Healy to line the natives up and deliver a stern lecture on manners and the price of misbehavior. He especially wanted Healy to remove Titalk and his other adversary, Elignok, from the Cape.

The way things turned out, Thornton was left more exposed than ever, and Lopp got everything he wished for. On June 27, the *Bear* anchored off Cape Prince of Wales with Sheldon Jackson aboard. Natives paddled Lopp and Thornton to the ship, where, according to Jackson, they separately "poured out their troubles & grievances." Thornton had also put his concerns in writing.

Describing the break-ins and the alleged attempts on his life, Thornton appealed to Healy "for protection for my wife and myself as a law-abiding citizen of the U.S. and as teacher in a U.S. school—engaged in trying to civilize U.S. subjects and therefore at least a quasi U.S. official." Thornton felt that if Healy failed to deport Titalk and Elignok, "We shall be left the alternative of facing probable death—or of abandoning the mission." As Thornton warmed to his subject, his pen raced across the page in manic strokes: "These people are utterly without law. The chiefs profess to deplore Titalk's burglary, but no one has the authority to inflict upon him the slightest punishment. If we punished him, it would be at the risk of having to shoot his father or be shot by him."

He then issued a backhanded denunciation of Tom Lopp: "Mr. Lopp does not join with me in advocating such severe measures because he says he thinks it will have a bad effect on the mission; how far his judgment is unconsciously influenced by the fact that he thinks of leaving . . . this summer and that most of the overt acts have been against me . . . I cannot say."

His own character, he insisted, was unimpeachable: "I am sure I have done nothing to provoke an attempt at murdering my wife and me. But as [Lopp] may be absent and I am to stand the consequences, it would seem that my voice should have more weight in the matter. However, there is no dispute about the facts, and you can judge for yourself."

When it was Lopp's turn to tell Jackson and Healy about the occurrences of the past year, he pulled no punches. He suggested that most of the ill will toward Thornton had been brought on by the missionary himself. Specifically, Lopp alleged that Thornton had doctored school reports to indicate that he had taught more students on more days than he actually had. Worse, Lopp testified that Thornton, despite his stance against the liquor trade and native drunkenness, was a drinker himself.

Thornton's suspicion that the Lopps would be leaving the Cape was not ungrounded, however. During his meeting with Jackson aboard the *Bear*, Lopp issued his ultimatum: He wanted his own reindeer herd, and he wanted no more of Thornton. Otherwise he and his family would leave. Jackson had to think fast. Worried that he might lose one of the most able men in Alaska, he told Lopp that if he would serve a year at the Teller Reindeer Station, he could then establish a herd nearer to Cape Prince of Wales. Within a week, Jackson was able to offer much more.

. . .

Miner Bruce's term of employment was due to expire on June 30. It is impossible to know whether or not Jackson went looking for reasons to terminate the appointment; either way, he had little difficulty finding one. Arriving in Port Clarence with Tom Lopp, Jackson learned that the reindeer herd had wintered well and increased in number. But in most other respects, Superintendent Bruce and Assistant Superintendent Gibson had conducted themselves shamefully. The station house was in deplorable condition. Sewage and stagnant water had been allowed to seep into the provisions. The foundation of the house was sagging where Bruce and Gibson had removed timbers to make storage space for sleds. Inside, heaps of fish and meat had been left to rot.

Such negligence was insignificant compared with the other sins of the two reindeer men. On July 3, Captain Healy alerted Jackson that Bruce had been trading breech-loading rifles to the natives. To be fair, by 1893 the matter should not have raised eyebrows. Most whites, beginning with Sheldon Jackson and his missionary teachers, favored native ownership of guns. The U.S. Revenue Cutter Service, which continued to police rigorously against the sale of liquor, devoted little energy to chasing gunrunners. Under the circumstances, Healy's charge that Bruce had sold as few as three or four rifles to natives seems trivial and token—a legalistic way to solve a more egregious transgression.

What Bruce was really guilty of, it seems, was entrepreneurism, a virus that infected many newcomers to Alaska. The reindeer herd had done so well that Bruce had decided to go into the reindeer business himself. Not long before the arrival of the *Bear*, he had contracted with a trading ship to purchase deer from the Chukchi for his own private herd. The deer would be paid for with either guns or whiskey, or so Healy suspected. Jackson was outraged. The U.S. government had experienced enough difficulty locating and buying reindeer in Siberia; the last thing Jackson needed was a competitor.

As for retaining Bruce's assistant, that was out of the question, too.

Over the winter, Gibson had taken up with a native woman—a not uncommon practice among traders, whalers, and other whites who wintered in the Arctic. Tom Lopp, who had observed the relationship firsthand at the reindeer station in April, called the affair a "scandal." Thornton demanded that Gibson be prosecuted for adultery.

The upshot of Jackson and Healy's investigations was that Bruce's and Gibson's contracts were allowed to expire, and on July 4 Tom Lopp was offered the superintendent's job at an annual salary of $1,200. Ellen was invited to teach school to the natives who lived nearby for $300, an offer she was not inclined to refuse. The total equaled what they had made together at the Cape. As successor to Bruce Gibson, Jackson hired the *Bear*'s quartermaster, John Grubin, at a salary of $500.

Tom and Ellen spent the next two weeks preparing for the move. On July 10, the *Bear* collected them, baby Lucy, and the house girl, Kongik, and steamed to the reindeer station. After Tom had gone ashore and looked over their new home, he jotted in his diary, "Horrible looking place for wife & young babe." The house was in such wretched shape that Ellen and the baby remained on board ship for three days until Tom, with the help of Grubin and three crewmen from the *Bear*, could make it habitable. In addition to the filth left behind by Bruce and Gibson, he found the house occupied by a mate from one of the trading ships, who was dying of an undetermined illness. Lopp gingerly transferred the man to the dugout and assigned one of the herders to nurse him. The dugout collapsed after a week, nearly burying the patient. Two days later he was dead.

Lopp and his helpers spent the next month re-flooring, insulating, partitioning, and painting; they added a lean-to along the length of the house as a storeroom and dormitory for the herders, who would not have to suffer another season in the pestilential dugout.

To his great disappointment, he found the herders in not much better shape than the house. Three of the disgruntled Chukchi had returned to Siberia; their replacements were hardly more convivial. One of the experienced Alaskan herders had gone to the States with a group of Eskimos whom Miner Bruce intended to exhibit at the World's Columbian Exhibition in Chicago. "The three remaining herders were dissatisfied," Lopp reported to Jackson. "They have all been sick with the 'grip' or a bad cold, and unfit to work or herd since I have been here, so that I have had to depend on the two Siberians and 'green' herders. . . . All the natives seem thoroughly disgusted with the 'herding school,'" he continued, "and claim that they had few comforts last year to make them forget what they suffered standing out in blizzards and living crowded together in that low dug-out."

Unlike Miner Bruce, Lopp never lost sight of the reindeer station's purpose, which, first and foremost, was to establish a herd but also to empower natives as herders. "I think while natives are learning to herd they should be clothed and fed and paid a small salary, from $1 to $4 a month, according to age, efficiency, etc.," he lobbied Sheldon Jackson, "and at the end of one year, in some cases two, [we should] loan four or five of [the] best herders 20 or 30 deers each. Let them put them together and keep them on a new range of pasture 10 or 20 miles from here, the superintendent of this station giving them general direction as to the management. At the end of two or three years their [number] will have increased so much that they can pay back the Government what they have borrowed, and will have become so thoroughly acquainted with the best methods of breeding, managing, . . . etc., that they can be trusted to assume the whole management of their herd."

By treating natives with respect—taking care of them, rewarding them for good work, and setting self-sufficiency as a goal—Lopp hoped to develop a model that could be replicated throughout Alaska. He would fight for these principles for the rest of his life, at times making great strides, at others suffering demoralizing setbacks.

In the short term, he built his program with the tools—and personnel—he knew best. That summer he enlisted several natives from Cape Prince of Wales as apprentices, including Sokweena, Ootenna, and Keok—all of them in their teens, smart, ambitious, and devoted to Tom-gorah. Tautuk, from nearby Cape York, was another welcome arrival, and at the end of August, Lopp reinstated his old friends Charlie and Mary Antisarlook, who had been fired by Miner Bruce. Mary had adopted a baby from an impoverished mother who otherwise would have let it die, an exigency still common throughout the Arctic. "[Mary] is truly a Christian soul, and a good example for others to follow," vouched Mary Healy, who was accompanying her husband on the *Bear* that summer. Lopp wanted to make an example of Charlie, too, by selecting him as the first native to be entrusted with his own reindeer. "I think it is important to do something like this next year," he proposed to Jackson. Putting Charlie in charge of a herd "would do much toward educating the people up to the advantages of becoming deermen."

Concerning the herd itself, Lopp regretted being too busy that summer to devote much time to its management. Fortunately the deer seemed to be getting along well enough on their own. Only two dozen had died, and that spring seventy-nine fawns had been born. During July and August, the *Bear* delivered 127 more from Siberia, boosting the herd total to more than three hundred.

As the new herders learned their way around the animals, so did Tom Lopp. Once when the night watch was shorthanded, he joined the two natives on duty. "The deer are less trouble to herd than I expected," he noted afterward. "During the night most of them lie down. Occasionally a few of those not asleep straggle away and have to be driven in. Jack our black Shepherd dog did very nicely. At first they got scared and stampeded and ran about 3 or 4 hundred yards. I think the dangers of a stampede have been greatly overestimated, these fat deer are too unaccustomed to running and consequently to[o] short winded to run in this mossy, marshy pasture land. . . . Day break we drove the herd northward. I took the left wing and several times sen[t] Jack back to bring some stragglers."

By late summer, life at the station became less frenzied. The *Bear's* carpenter, who had remained to help with renovations, found time to build a twenty-foot scow. When not being rowed up and down the bays of Grantley Harbor and Port Clarence in search of driftwood, it provided a pleasant diversion for Tom, Ellen, and the baby. Ellen, as always, was quick to adapt to her new circumstances. Cooking for Grubin and the three crewmen from the *Bear* was more than she was used to, and the mosquitoes were much worse than at the Cape. But the house, once refurbished, was "very comfortable," she assured her family, and the setting better than she had anticipated. "I thought I was losing a great deal in the view . . . but I find the view here better than at the Cape—more variety and more changing. There is as long a view of the sea in one direction and in the other directions distant hills, something I could see none of at the Cape."

. . .

Sixty miles to the northwest, Harrison and Neda Thornton were not faring so favorably. Captain Healy had rejected Thornton's request to have Elignok and Titalk removed from the Cape. "I have made inquiries . . . and find it extremely doubtful if Mr. Thornton was shot at at all, and believe it comes more from his imaginings," Healy wrote to his commanding officer. Healy had disliked Thornton from the start and now liked him even less. "Mr. Thornton does not seem of that temperament to govern the natives rightly," he continued. "From all I can learn of the case I do not see that I am called upon to take any action and I do not apprehend any trouble to Mr. Thornton from the natives if he treats them in the way he should." Healy conveyed no more sympathy to Thornton than he had shown toward Miner Bruce and Bruce Gibson at the reindeer station. "In all these cases"— at Port Clarence and Cape Prince of Wales—"I am supposed instantly to hang or otherwise punish the natives if even an accusation is made against them. Some of the whites seem to think that the laws are made only for the repression of the natives but too often upon investigation the breaking of the laws is [done by] the white men themselves."

In a separate letter written to Thornton personally, Healy told the missionary that the government would take no "aggressive action" at the Cape. "But if you wish it and will assemble the natives," Healy offered, "I will speak to them, though I doubt the advisability of threatening a whole community in this manner."

Thornton was past the point of appeasement, and no amount of fawning could mask his rising panic. "I am most anxious to have your friendship and protection and have never intentionally done anything to offend you," he responded to Healy. "Your not taking any action in Elignok's case will leave a woman (Mrs. Thornton) at the mercy of these savages and in great danger—not to speak of myself."

The *Bear* left the Cape without the Thorntons and devoted its attentions to purchasing Siberian reindeer, boarding American ships in search of liquor, and calling on the missions and stations at Point Hope and Point Barrow. It did not return to the Cape until August 24, and by then Thornton was beyond rescue.

Titalk and two other boys, Kongok and Idloowaseuk, had broken into the schoolhouse several more times. Titalk had also stolen a revolver from the grave of a young chief, an even more serious offense in the eyes of the Eskimos. Drinking at the Cape had been heavy that summer, and the Thorntons agreed that if it got any worse, they would leave when the *Bear* returned. "It was only after frequent prayer for guidance that Mr. Thornton reached this decision," Neda Thornton recalled. "He was so anxious to do what was right; even at the blessing at the table he would pray for guidance."

On Saturday, August 19, two barrels of whiskey—"more than at any one time before," Neda declared—arrived by umiak from Siberia. The

Thorntons locked their door and turned in early. The next day they would begin preparations to depart the Cape.

The night was moonless and spitting rain. Sometime after midnight, the Thorntons were awakened by a knock at the door. Their initial thought was that one of the villagers was sick and needed medicine. Thornton arose, assuring Neda that he would be only a minute or two. "Everything was quiet, and oh! the first thing I heard was this awful report," Neda told the *American Missionary*.

Earlier in the evening Titalk, Kongok, and Idloowaseuk had stolen a whale gun and muzzle-loading rifle from the schoolhouse. American newspapers later described the three boys as "rum-crazed Esquimaux," but the Cape villagers insisted that that they were sober and that the motive was simple robbery. Remembering Thornton's stern vow to shoot first and ask questions later, the thieves did not wait to be admitted to the mission house. As soon as Thornton unlatched the outer door, one of the boys fired the whale gun. The bomb lance, capable of killing a fifty-ton whale, slammed through the stout timbers of the door, making a hole "the size of a door-knob," Neda estimated. Her husband was standing directly in the line of fire not six feet away, and the brass projectile plowed a comparable hole in his midriff, passing through his body and slamming into the paneling over the hallway door. At nearly the same instant, another of the boys fired the rifle. The bullet hit Thornton in the hip, an indecisive wound under the circumstances. As boldly as they had attacked, the boys could not bring themselves to enter the house. They dropped their guns and fled down the hill.

Amazingly, Thornton did not die instantly. Somehow he managed to shut both the outer door and the hallway door and stagger to the sitting room, where he and Neda had been living since they had moved the stove. "How he ever did it, I do not know," his wife wondered. "He said in quite a strong voice, 'I am shot.'" Lighting a lamp, she found him slumped on the floor, already unconscious. "I got the brandy right away and put it to his lips; he did not move; I do not think he suffered."

Neda sat with her husband's body until daylight. "I did not know what to do," she confessed. "I just stayed in the room and walked to and fro. . . . Then I looked through the hole in the door and saw the whaling gun; and lying down beside it, the [other] gun. I could not tell whether any one was there." Finally she gathered her courage, opened a window, and shouted until she got the attention of a neighbor, Kitmesuk, who lived below the mission house. When Kitmesuk and his wife arrived at the house, they discovered the two guns lying beside the door and flung them down the hill. They then helped Neda lift Thornton's body onto the couch. Leaving his wife to comfort Neda, Kitmesuk departed for the village to spread the news. "He went out and said there was going to be some shooting," Neda recalled. How this was communicated is uncertain, for Neda knew very few words of Inupiaq, and Kitmesuk's English was not much better.

Native justice was swift. The identities and guilt of the perpetrators were never in doubt. Titalk was the ringleader, but the other two had done the shooting. Kongok and Idloowaseuk did not attempt to hide. They were escorted from the village down to the beach, where, without compunction or hesitation, one of the umialiks, a man who presumably knew both boys well, shot them. Their bodies were then dragged up the hill, stripped naked, and left for the dogs. Titalk, in the meantime, had taken to the hills.

Nothing that the villagers could do or say would allay Neda Thornton's fear that she too was about to be murdered. Yet by afternoon her prayers for mercy were answered, or so it seemed. One of the natives rushed in to announce that the *Bear* had been sighted offshore. Now it was the villagers' turn to be frightened. "[At the Cape] the people don't [have] faith in God," Ellen Lopp had once observed. Instead they placed their faith in Captain Healy's "power to kill the people and blow the town up with guns." Despite their dread of severe reprisal, the villagers allowed Neda Thornton to fly a flag of distress from the mission house. To her great dismay—and surely to the private relief of many natives—the *Bear* did not notice the signal and continued southward.

Assuming that the revenue cutter had departed the Bering Strait for the year, Neda Thornton reckoned that her only hope for survival lay in the reindeer station at Port Clarence, sixty miles away. For once, chance was in her favor. Kitmesuk informed her that an umiak—skippered by Sealhok, one of the Lopps' most loyal friends—was leaving the next day for Port Clarence to trade seal and walrus oil for salmon. Sympathetic villagers found her a place among the boat's nineteen passengers, most of them women and children.

As the boat rounded the Cape, it was pummeled by a fierce southeast wind, and Sealhok wisely put into shore to keep from being swept out to sea. For two nights and a day, Neda huddled under the overturned umiak, quaking with grief and uncertainty while the natives sang songs and beat on walrus-skin drums. Possessing little Eskimo vocabulary and having paid only passing attention to native customs, she assumed that the "ceremonials," as she called the singing and drumming, were her death knell, when in fact her fellow travelers were beseeching the spirits to improve the weather so that they might reach their destination sooner.

While waiting for the wind to change, Sealhok sent one of the villagers on foot back over the mountain to tell Kitmesuk of the delay. Commandeering another boat, Kitmesuk made his way around the point to where Neda and the others were beached. By then the weather had improved somewhat, and Kitmesuk transferred Neda to his boat and made all possible haste toward Port Clarence, sailing or paddling when possible, at other times pulling the boat along the shore by a rope of braided sinew. Finally, just past midnight on August 25, five days after Thornton's murder, Kitmesuk and Neda arrived at the reindeer station. When Tom Lopp opened the door, Neda blurted, "Harry was shot," and then fell into his arms.

When she was able to speak again, she told Tom and Ellen the harrowing story of Thornton's murder and her escape. And at some point she revealed an intimate detail that helped to explain why she and Thornton had become so alarmed during the summer: She was five months pregnant.

Captain Healy knew nothing of Neda's condition—or of Thornton's, for that matter—when, two days later, the *Bear* dropped anchor off Cape Prince of Wales with twenty-five Siberian reindeer on board. He was keeping his promise to take the Thorntons south, if that was still their wish. "We were surprised to find no one came off to meet us, and the village seemed deserted of Indians," Mary Healy remembered. More curious than alarmed, Captain Healy sent a party ashore the next morning to see about the Thorntons. The cuttermen, led by Lieutenant David Jarvis, were not greeted by the usual throng of natives. Eventually, though, several villagers came forward and sheepishly related the details of Thornton's murder and his widow's flight to Port Clarence. They handed Jarvis two letters left by Neda and accompanied him to the mission house, where Thornton's bloody body still lay on the sitting-room couch. They also made sure that Jarvis understood that two of the murderers had already been killed and that the third would soon be caught and executed.

Learning of the retribution already exacted by the natives on their own people and wishing to hear the full story directly from Neda Thornton, Healy withheld judgment. He ordered a coffin built, and crewmen buried Thornton on the hillside not far from the drafty house where he had lived and died.

The *Bear* was away by early afternoon; when it anchored off the reindeer station at six o'clock, Tom Lopp brought Neda Thornton aboard. The reindeer were landed as quickly as possible, and early the following morning the *Bear* departed again for the Cape. Escorted by Lopp, Neda went ashore to pack up her belongings and visit her husband's grave. The *Bear*'s carpenter had made a cross bearing

Thornton's name, and children from the village made an offering of flowers they had picked from the surrounding hills. "Of course [the cross] would not last very long," Neda reflected, "but it was some kind of good wood, well oiled, . . . [and] it will remind them of what we told them about Jesus, and of the sacrifice of Mr. Thornton's life while seeking their good."

Afterward, Healy asked the villagers to come aboard the *Bear* for a talk. Fearing a repetition of the Gilley massacre, they declined. As an alternative, Lopp persuaded Healy to go ashore, where the villagers assembled on the beach and, with Lopp interpreting, gave their version of the events of the previous week. Lopp, it must be said, was as much advocate as translator. He knew the natives as well as any white man, just as he knew of Thornton's shortcomings and prejudices. There was no point in revenge, he urged. Not only had the villagers imposed their own justice; their behavior throughout the affair was proof of their lack of complicity.

Summarizing his argument in a letter to Healy several days later, Lopp averred: "The fact that the people, when they heard of the murder, drove the two young men out of their house, shot them and refused to give their bodies the customary burial, but instead stripped them naked and left their bodies for the dogs to eat; and that they say they will kill Titalk when they find him; and the kindness and sympathy which they showed toward Mrs. Thornton, all proves beyond a doubt, I think, the people had nothing to do with the murder, are very sorry it happened and will be glad to have an opportunity to prove to the whites that they have no hostile feelings towards them."

In the end, Healy seemed satisfied with Lopp's evaluation and saw no need for further punishment. Before letting the matter drop, however, he impressed upon the villagers just how close they had come to much harsher punishment. "Had the [natives] not avenged Mr. Thornton's death," Mary Healy assured, "[the captain] would not have left a single one of them alive."

As for the capture and punishment of Titalk, Healy again heeded Lopp's suggestion to leave the matter to the discretion of the villagers. Shortly after the *Bear* departed from the Cape, Titalk crept back to the village to face the consequences. An uncle led him to Thornton's grave, where he let the boy choose how he wanted to be put to death—shot, stabbed, or strangled. "He chose to be shot," Ellen wrote to her parents, "so he and his executioner sat down and waited for a revolver to be brought. When it came, he was told to hold his head down. He did and was shot."

The *Bear* with Neda Thornton aboard left Port Clarence on September 4. At Unalaska, she transferred to the revenue cutter *Corwin*, which docked at San Francisco four weeks later. The news of Thornton's murder provoked predictable outrage in the States. A typical account cast the missionary as a martyr slain while "protecting the parents of his pupils from the evil influences of chance traders, whose principal stock for barter was liquor." But at least one newspaper dismissed Thornton as an insensitive southerner "inclined to be a little imperious in his dealing with the natives."

Thornton's legacy was indeed mixed, thanks in no small part to a book he had been writing about his experiences at Cape Prince of Wales; the rough draft was among the papers Neda took from the Cape. Edited by Neda and her son (born December 1893) and published thirty-eight years after Thornton's death, *Among the Eskimos of Wales, Alaska* offers equal measures enlightenment and indictment. In the book's final paragraphs, Thornton attempts one last time to parade his hauteur as humility:

> We have not felt justified . . . in wearying the reader with a detailed account of the petty annoyances of daily occurrence to which we were necessarily subjected at first: of the oft-recurring conflict with stupidity; . . . of the many unreasonable demands that the natives made upon us; of their natural, but annoying,

curiosity; of our patience-trying troubles with the drunken or the ignorant; of the nervous tension produced by dealing with natures that had never before been accustomed to discipline, and did not appreciate our legitimate rights as householders and as teachers; of the almost hourly risk of becoming involved in a personal (and perhaps deadly) conflict; of the consequent feeble appetite and unrefreshing sleep; . . . of the longing that would sometimes come over us to be once more in a country with laws and policemen; of the tedious days and nights, when blizzards prevented us from going out; . . . of these and many other items the reader would soon tire, were we to relate them at length.

These many travails, Thornton begs thinly, are insignificant. Due to the "many novel manifestations of Divine Creative Power" that watched over him and Neda in Alaska, "we are not so much to be pitied after all."

He had a point: Harrison Thornton was beyond pity, a sentiment shared by many who were familiar with his full story. One of those was the wife of Archibald McLellan, the reverend carpenter who had built the mission house and married the Lopps. Writing to Ellen Lopp's parents in October 1893, she confided, "To a few who knew how matters stood, Mr. Thornton's murder was not a surprise."

. . .

Ellen Lopp had been a busy correspondent herself that fall. She had fallen into the habit of writing letters in installments, never finishing them until just before the last boat headed south. She filled them with cheerful descriptions of native curiosities, the weather, and exotic menus—all meant to assure her family that life in Alaska was indeed extreme but quite agreeable. In one such letter, begun on August 2, Ellen sang the gustatory praises of whale blubber—*maktak*. "I am afraid I can't get you whale blubber this year," she apologized to her brother Charlie, who, of all her siblings, was the most enthralled by Ellen's tales. "If I don't you can make a fair imitation. Take a piece of fat pork that has been baked with beans and pour some castor oil over it." A month later, before closing the letter, she added a hasty postscript: "The Bear will soon go and with it our last chance to send mail. You will hear of Mr. Thornton's death and it may scare you, but it need not. We are not as safe as we would be living in Glyndon, but as safe as in the past. There has been no change."

This final sentence of the letter, which she assumed would be the last of the season, may not have achieved the desired effect of quelling the anxieties of her family, but, if nothing else, it convinced them of her undiminished confidence and courage. "I should be perfectly willing to go back," she scribbled. She did *not* mean back to the peace and comfort of Minnesota. Back meant back to Cape Prince of Wales, where the school and mission house had sat empty since Thornton's murder.

For the time being, though, Port Clarence was home. The upcoming winter would be Tom Lopp's first as superintendent of the reindeer herd, and he was determined to bring the animals through in the best possible shape.

Three Chukchi herders remained, and the more time Lopp spent around them the more he desired to be shut of them. Ever since the notion of importing Siberian reindeer had first been formulated, he had regarded the Chukchi as stand-ins at best. But until he could live without them, he made a point of gleaning as much of their knowledge as possible, as quickly as possible. By observing the Siberians, Lopp and his dozen or so Eskimo herders began to get the hang of lassoing, harnessing, and sledding. Likewise, they acquired a better sense of when to close-herd the reindeer, like a flock of sheep, and when to let them drift more loosely, like cattle. Before long the Alaskan natives had adopted the Chukchi practice of carrying a container of urine to attract the deer.

Lopp, while pleased with the Eskimos' progress, eventually took issue with the not-so-fine points of Chukchi husbandry. For centuries, Siberians had harnessed their deer with a simple leather strap around the neck, connecting to a trace that ran between the animal's legs. Lopp observed that during long drives or when hauling heavy loads, the straps chafed the deer, sometimes disabling them. Over the winter, he worked on devising a more humane and effective harness. Nor did he care much for the Chukchi habit of wrestling a deer to the ground and sucking milk directly from its teats. (When Lopp tried to milk a deer by hand, he extracted barely a spoonful—much to his own chagrin and the disappointment of Ellen, who yearned for fresh milk.) But what turned Lopp against the Chukchi once and for all was the deliberate insubordination and cruelty of the head herder, Anker. Defying Lopp's strict orders against killing reindeer, Anker repeatedly slaughtered them for food, when he and his fellow Chukchi were supposed to be guarding them. Worse still, when an exhausted deer refused to get to its feet, Anker kicked the animal to death.

Even when everyone, Chukchi and Eskimo, was doing their jobs well, the herd was not always easy to manage or even to locate. Daylight was scarce and blizzards frequent. A series of storms between Christmas and New Year were the worst they had experienced that year, Lopp recorded in his journal. The night watch would lose the herd, and in the morning the next watch would spend the brief hours of daylight looking for it. In early January, when the bad weather had abated somewhat, Lopp ordered a new camp established ten miles to the north, where the moss was more plentiful. On the first clear day, the deer were driven across the ice of Grantley Harbor, and for the next three months the herders lived in tents near the new grazing ground. The strategy worked well enough; during the winter, only twenty deer died, and despite temperatures of thirty below zero, 145 of the 186 fawns born in April and May survived, a very satisfactory increase. By the end of Lopp's first year at the Teller station, the herd had grown to nearly five hundred.

His family had borne up admirably, too. "The baby is fat and well, laughed out loud for the first time a month ago," Ellen was pleased to observe in late November. She had weaned Lucy in favor of a traditional Eskimo feeding method: a length of cured seal intestine knotted like a sausage and punctured at one end, which she filled with a gruel of oatmeal and condensed milk. She also began carrying Lucy on her back in the folds of her deerskin atigi, Eskimo style. And to make life a bit easier, she had hired Woodlet, who had previously worked for the Thorntons, to help Kongik around the house.

Entrusting the baby to the Eskimo baby-sitters, Ellen began teaching school on the first of January. Attendance fell short of the enthusiastic crowd that had packed the classrooms at the Cape; at most, she had thirty students. By March, with the herders away at the deer camp and the village children off seal hunting with their parents, she reluctantly stopped teaching altogether.

But two months later she had her hands full again. "You will be surprised to hear we have another baby, a boy this time, born May 2," she wrote her mother. "He wasn't as thin as [Lucy] though he wasn't fat." She was reluctant to accept the help of a native midwife. "I got along well when the baby came, had an easier time than with Lucy," she related brightly. "I let the woman I had planned to have with me go fishing about nine because I wasn't sure enough she would be needed, and he was born at one. The woman I did have . . . was troubled because I . . . didn't let her help me by pressing with her hands as the Eskimos do." They named the child Dwight Thomas Lopp.

Ellen was not one to complain, but the new baby made her increasingly homesick for Minnesota. She longed to introduce her husband and children to her family. Perhaps in another year or so they could go home. Short of that, she set her sights on Cape Prince of Wales. The Cape was safer, she reminded her parents, especially after Captain Healy had read the riot act to the natives. And even though the house at the reindeer station was roomier and better provisioned, she much preferred the house at the Cape. "The only thing about this place more comfortable than the Cape," she stated, "is that the ceiling is two feet lower so the room can be heated more easily and snow banks all sides of the house, helping to keep it warm."

The likelihood of the Lopps returning to the Cape was actually quite good. Sheldon Jackson had told Tom that after a year at the reindeer station, he would be allowed to return to the Cape with his own herd. The death of Thornton and the unanticipated vacancy of the Cape mission gave urgency to Jackson's pledge.

Over the winter, Jackson had taken steps to find replacements for both the Lopps and the Chukchi herders. A few years earlier, he had read Paul Du Chaillu's travelogue *Land of the Midnight Sun*, which offered an admiring portrait of the Lapp reindeer herders of northern Scandinavia. Echoing Du Chaillu, Jackson pronounced that "the Lapps of northern Europe, because of their superior intelligence (nearly all of them being able to read and write and some of them being acquainted with several languages), are much superior to . . . the barbarous deer men of northeastern Siberia." He also might have added that the Lapps were God-fearing Christians.

In the fall of 1893, shortly after returning from Alaska, Jackson placed an advertisement in Scandinavian newspapers around the United States, seeking "a Laplander . . . who has been brought up to the care of reindeer, and who would like to go to Alaska to take charge of reindeer." He received more than two hundred responses, and eventually he was steered toward William Kjellmann (pronounced "*zhell*-man"), a Norwegian immigrant living in Madison, Wisconsin. Kjellmann was a native of Finnmark, Norway's northernmost province. He had grown up around reindeer and knew many reindeer herders.

Jackson hired Kjellmann to replace Tom Lopp as superintendent of the Teller Reindeer Station, and in February he dispatched him to Norway to look for a half dozen herders willing to trade their lives in

Lapland for the heathen tundra of northern Alaska. "The fact that there is not a single colony of Lapps in the United States or elsewhere shows their intense love of home and great unwillingness to leave it," Jackson remarked. Kjellmann persevered anyway and, fighting his way through an abominable Arctic winter, succeeded in recruiting six Lapp families and a bachelor, sixteen in all. By May they had passed through Ellis Island; by the end of June they were in San Francisco, waiting for a boat to Alaska. Accompanying Kjellmann and the Lapps were Kjellmann's wife, son, father, and brother-in-law. Once again, Congress had declined to pay their salaries or their travel expenses, and Jackson had to coax the money from private pockets.

The Lapps had signed three-year contracts. They would receive salaries of $320, plus food, clothing, and a place to live. Additionally, they would be permitted to kill as many reindeer as they needed for food and clothing. There was one final stipulation: The Lapps wanted to be able to attend church in their new home, and so Jackson hired Toleef Brevig, a Norwegian-speaking Lutheran pastor also from Wisconsin. Brevig, along with his wife and infant son, were with the Lapps aboard the brig *W.H. Meyer* when it arrived at Port Clarence on July 29, 1894. To balance his budget, Jackson had given the pastor the official assignment of schoolteacher and assistant superintendent of the reindeer station.

Tom Lopp knew of Jackson's intention to hire Lapp herders, and by June he had received word that Kjellmann and the Lapps were on their way. However, he had not been informed in advance of the Lapps' precise terms of employment. Had he known that they would be granted privileges denied the Eskimos, he might not have awaited the arrival of the new herders quite so amiably. To Lopp's frustration, the terms of the Eskimos' apprenticeship were still quite vague; two of the only constants were that they could not kill deer and that they would be paid only in deer, the number depending on how many years they stayed.

Lopp had bid good riddance to the Chukchi earlier in the winter, and now he was anxious to turn over responsibility for the station to Kjellmann and his recruits. The Eskimos, too, were quick to size up the new herders as they disembarked at the Teller Reindeer Station. Over the years, as more and more ships passed through the Bering Sea, the Alaskan natives had been exposed to an astonishing array of humanity, from swarthy Russian traders to rawboned Yankee seadogs; from golden-skinned Hawaiians to shiny-buttoned Revenue Cutter Service officers. The Lapps, though, in their colorful smocks, curled-toed boots, and floppy, four-cornered hats, were not entirely unfamiliar to the Eskimos. Why, of course! The curious newcomers bore an uncanny resemblance to the faces on the playing cards that the whites clutched and shuffled so enthusiastically.

# [ 6 ]

# Good Faith

THE ARRIVAL OF THE *W.H. Meyer* at the end of July signaled a population explosion of sorts for Arctic Alaska. Besides Toleef Brevig, William Kjellmann and his family, plus the sixteen Lapps, the passenger list included three more missionaries. Vene Gambell and his wife, Nellie, had left small-town Iowa to open a new Presbyterian mission and school on desolate St. Lawrence Island in the western Bering Sea. The Episcopal Church had endeavored to start a mission there in 1891 but could find no one willing to inhabit "the schoolhouse farthest west." The Gambells would be the first white residents of the island. Also on board the *Myers* was the Reverend Elijah Edson, en route to relieve John Driggs, who had become understandably "worn"—some would say "unbalanced"—by four years of isolation at Point Hope. Counting the missions at Barrow, Cape Prince of Wales, Port Clarence, and the Swedish Evangelical missions at Unalakleet and Golovnin Bay in eastern Norton Sound, Sheldon Jackson in five short years had managed to light a chain of Christian beacons along the entire coast of northern Alaska. Granted, the mission at Cape Prince of Wales had been vacant since the murder of Harrison Thornton, but that would soon be corrected.

Tom Lopp was unquestionably one of the brightest and most ambitious of Jackson's soldiers. While other missionaries had merely endured in the North, Lopp seemed actually to have thriven. Indeed, what Lopp needed from Jackson was not personal encouragement so much as official approval to carry on with his reindeer plan. It was an easy sell, for not only did Tom Lopp exude total confidence, but by his achievements and character he also set a splendid example for all other missionaries. One other thing: Lopp had never failed to make Jackson look good.

Jackson had arrived at Port Clarence aboard the *Bear* on July 24, five days before the *Myers*. In three weeks of picking its way along the icebound Siberian coastline, the *Bear* had purchased only thirty-eight reindeer, and Captain Healy was impatient to get on with his summer's patrol. He had been a proponent of the reindeer idea from the beginning, and he was under orders to assist Jackson in acquiring and transporting deer as well as supporting the missions. Yet the flinty skipper had grown tired of being used as "a tool for other's uses"— referring to Jackson in particular. Privately Healy complained that Jackson had become extraneous to the actual acquisition of reindeer, an annoying tourist who took up valuable space aboard the *Bear*. Nevertheless, Healy continued to do Jackson's bidding.

On July 26, while still at Port Clarence, Healy loaned Jackson the *Bear*'s steam launch, the *Bear Cub*. After picking up Tom Lopp at the reindeer station, the two men spent the day on the water. They motored across Grantley Harbor, following the Tuksuk Channel inland toward Imuruk Basin, a vast lagoon dotted with summer fishing camps. One of the advantages that Port Clarence had over Cape Prince of Wales was its abundance of salmon, which migrated up the nearby Kuzitrin and Kaviruk rivers. Along the beach were scores of racks laden with fish, exuberant swatches of crimson flesh offered to the sun like beads on an East Indian tapestry.

Lopp and Jackson spent the day enjoying the blessings of light and warmth. Along the way, they had plenty of time to exchange views on the future of reindeer and the natives who herded them. Jackson was more expansive than ever. He wanted to begin stocking the Aleutian Islands with reindeer. He wanted to establish a purchasing station on the Siberian mainland to obviate the hit-or-miss game of procurement that had hamstrung the growth of the Alaskan herd for the past four years. He also shared with Lopp his outline for an Arctic version of the fabled and defunct Pony Express. Jackson's "reindeer express" would carry the mail via a network of reindeer trails linking Point Barrow in the north to the coastal missions along the Bering Sea, and from the upper Yukon all the way to Haines in the south, where mail could then be put aboard ships and carried Outside at any time of the year.

The commercial necessity of such a network was manifest, Jackson declared. Since 1890, whaling ships had been wintering at Herschel Island, near the mouth of the Mackenzie River, four hundred miles east of Point Barrow, to avoid having to make the dangerous four-thousand-mile trip to and from San Francisco each year. In 1894, a record fifteen ships were headed for this remote winter harbor, two hundred miles above the Arctic Circle. "Millions of dollars of capital are invested in these vessels and their outfits," Jackson explained. "If their owners in San Francisco, Cal., and New Bedford, Mass., could hear from them during the winter, it might make a difference of thousands of dollars in the supplies sent the following spring."

Miners, too, were a growing presence in the Alaskan wilderness. Since the 1870s, hunger for gold had been propelling prospectors across the Canadian border into the upper Yukon, and in 1882 the first steamboat had navigated the tricky bars and timber-choked flood of the Yukon all the way to the junction of the Tanana River, a thousand miles inland. By 1894, two hundred gold seekers were living in the interior, and with the United States in the midst of economic depression—the so-called Panic of 1893—even more fortune hunters were on their way to the gold camps of Alaska. "But a large

number of miners can not be maintained in that barren country,"
Sheldon Jackson warned. River steamers could not ascend tributaries such as the Tanana, "and it is upon the tributaries that the rich
mines, so far as are known, are situated. The river steamers land
their supplies at trading posts at the mouths of these tributaries, and
then the difficult question presents itself of getting the supplies to
the mines. They can partly be taken on dog sleds, and partly on the
backs of Indians. There are not dogs enough to take in an ample supply. Hence," Jackson concluded, "the miners are clamorous that reindeer should be secured in large numbers so that they can have some
for transportation purposes."

In fact, there was no groundswell of evidence to suggest that miners were desperate for reindeer, and Jackson's imagination may have
exceeded his anticipation by a wide margin. The reindeer express was
a case of wishful thinking; even granting the urgency of such a network, the logistics were prohibitive. The mail or freight schemes could
only work through the contractual support of the postmaster general
and with substantial private investment by those who believed that the
miners were as needy as Jackson purported. Neither was immediately
forthcoming.

Leaving aside the question of feasibility, the notion of reindeer as
a medium for commerce and communication represented a dramatic
shift in Jackson's original motive for bringing reindeer to Alaska,
which, it must be recalled, had been "inspired by a desire to provide a
new and permanent food supply for the half-famishing Eskimo." Now,
however, his tune had changed. In a memorandum subsequently
delivered to the Department of the Interior, he listed his priorities in
the following order:

First. *The opening up of the vast and inaccessible regions of northern
and central Alaska to white settlers . . . .* Since [1890] the discovery
of large and valuable gold deposits upon the streams of arctic and

subarctic Alaska has made the introduction of reindeer *a necessity for the white man* as well as the Eskimo. . . . [Italics added]

Second. *The opening of a vast commercial industry.* Lapland, with 400,000 reindeer, supplies the grocery stores of northern Europe with smoked reindeer hams, 10¢ per pound; smoked tongues at 10¢; dried hides at $1.25 to $1.75 each; and 23,000 carcasses to the butcher shop, in addition to what is consumed by the Lapps themselves. . . . Fresh reindeer meat is considered a great delicacy. . . . The tanned skins . . . have a ready sale for military pantaloons, gloves, bookbinding, covering of chairs and sofas, bed pillows, etc. . . . On the same basis Alaska, with its capacity for 9,200,000 head of reindeer can supply the markets of America with 500,000 carcasses of venison annually, together with tons of delicious hams and tongues, and the finest of leather. Surely the creation of an industry worth from $83,000,000 to $100,000,000, where none now exists, is worth the attention of the American people.

Almost as an afterthought, Jackson expressed his concern for the "perpetuation, multiplication, and civilization" of Alaskan natives. "The Eskimo are a hardy and docile race," he explained, although he now seemed to be looking at them through the eyes of a prospective employer surveying the labor pool. "Their children learn readily in the schools, and there is no reason why they should not be made an important factor in the development of the land. The density of population in any section being largely dependent upon the quantity of food supply, the increase of food supply will naturally increase the number of hardy Eskimo."

Whether Jackson revealed his entire agenda—and in this order— to Lopp during their day together in July 1894 is not clear. Given Lopp's feelings toward native self-sufficiency and self-improvement, it seems unlikely that Jackson would have made the case for white advancement quite so bluntly. Or perhaps he did. Lopp was a pragmatist, too, and he would have grasped the opportunity in Jackson's upended priorities.

The steam launch returned to the *Bear* in time for dinner, and that night Jackson and Lopp went ashore to the reindeer station, where they continued talking until nearly midnight. By breakfast the following morning, Lopp had what he wanted: Sheldon Jackson drew up a letter giving the American Missionary Association at Cape Prince of Wales one hundred reindeer. At the same time, he agreed to loan Charlie Antisarlook and four other natives one hundred deer, on the conditions that after five years they return that same number to the government (keeping the increase for themselves); that they not kill any female deer; and that a family of Lapps assist Antisarlook in caring for the herd.

At first Antisarlook doubted that Jackson would follow through on his promise, and for good reason. Antisarlook had been promised deer before but had been fired by Miner Bruce without receiving any. Even Jackson acknowledged that "the Eskimo have been so little accustomed to assistance from the whites that they have been somewhat skeptical concerning their being permitted to ultimately own the deer." The loan to Antisarlook was an act of "good faith," Jackson announced, explaining that he had chosen him as the test case because natives such as Antisarlook, "who most completely come under mission influence, civilization, and education are the coming men of affairs among their own people, and therefore are the best men to lead in a new movement."

Cutting through the rhetoric, Jackson trusted Antisarlook because he trusted Lopp. It was Lopp who trusted Antisarlook. And by vouching for his friend, he had inaugurated the next phase of reindeer herding in Alaska. Jackson's pipe dream of a reindeer express was, by Lopp's reckoning, now a separate matter that would succeed or fail on its own merits. More significantly, the natives of the Bering Sea had been offered, if not absolute independence, then at least a pathway toward it.

· · ·

The *Bear* did not stay at Port Clarence long enough for Jackson to greet Kjellmann and the Lapps on the twenty-ninth. The Lopps chose to remain another two weeks, helping the new superintendent and herders to get settled and greeting the new missionaries. "Someone with fresh enthusiasm ought to be sent to a mission often," Ellen admitted after meeting the newcomers. "Ours gets blunted considerably, coming up against a language in which we can't express ourselves."

Finally on August 14, the Lopps, accompanied by John Grubin, left for Cape Prince of Wales aboard the reindeer station's scow. That same day, the five herders whom Tom had hired from the Cape— Keok, Sokweena, Ootenna, Kivyearzruk, and Netaxite—and one of the remaining Siberians began driving the reindeer overland. Each of the Alaskan natives had been given two deer apiece as reward for his year of apprenticeship, and as they were gathering the hundred deer for the mission, an additional eight animals broke away from the main herd and joined the group bound for the Cape, making a total of 118. Back at the reindeer station, Charlie Antisarlook was not due to take charge of his herd until the first of the year.

The Lopps arrived at the Cape the following morning. Four-month-old Dwight rode most of the way on Ellen's back, protected from the wind and spray in the hood of her atigi. Only about sixty natives were on hand to greet them, and the village's near-desertion could not be explained entirely by the usual summer dispersal for trading and fishing. Rumors had continued to circulate that ships would arrive any day to destroy the village. Another rumor had Thornton's brothers coming to exact revenge.

Before leaving the Teller Reindeer Station, the Lopps had received a letter from Neda Thornton taking Captain Healy to task for his lax policing of the liquor trade and for belittling the danger posed by the Cape natives. "Doubtless you will be given the protection we were denied," Neda had forecast rather bitterly. Figuring that her family would learn of Neda's public deprecations and become upset, Ellen had hastened to rebut Neda on all counts. Healy had not been to blame for Thornton's murder, she insisted, and they had no misgivings about returning to the Cape—unless it was the loss of Ellen's garden. She had started onions, radishes, and lettuce at the reindeer station in June with great optimism, the only garden she would attempt in all her years in Alaska.

They found the mission house and school covered in mold but otherwise intact. They were thrilled to discover that the organ still worked. Tom lit the stoves to drive out the dampness, and the family spent the first night tenting on the beach. Nothing had been touched in the mission house since Thornton's burial nearly a year earlier. Ellen reported to her family that there were three holes in the outer door: one from the whale gun, one from the rifle, and a third apparently from a revolver—the only evidence, contrary to other accounts, that Thornton had fired a shot from his own gun before being killed. Tom and Grubin replaced the door with one from the schoolhouse. After three washings, the bloodstain on the sitting-room floor was still visible. If Ellen or Tom were at all hesitant about living in a house where a murder had been committed, neither said so in their diaries or letters. Curiously, they installed an "electric" doorbell, apparently powered by a battery. The natives took great glee in ringing it, which diminished its usefulness and shortened its life.

While Ellen concentrated on putting the house in order, Tom situated the reindeer, neither too close to the village nor too far from it. With most of the Cape natives away for the summer, their dogs roamed at will, unfed. When the herders first brought the deer over the mountain and onto the tundra north of the village, the pack launched a ravenous assault. The boys fought them off with sticks and whips, but not before two deer had been dragged down and killed.

After several days of scouting, Tom settled on a spot with abundant fresh water seven miles to the north, and that fall he and the natives built a log house out of driftwood, which they heated with a stove brought from Port Clarence. For a time, he and Ellen tried keeping a reindeer cow and her calf in a pen near the mission house. She was gentle enough that with one person holding her antlers, she would stand still to be milked. "It is worthwhile experimenting," Ellen wrote, "for if we can have milk every day, there won't be any food we will miss very much up here."

In the end, milking, like gardening, proved too difficult—the yield did not justify the work—and it was eventually abandoned. Ever resourceful and increasingly open-minded, the Lopps were drawn more and more to native food. "We are eating seal meat often now," Ellen remarked. "We didn't used to think we liked it." The children, Lucy and Dwight, adapted even more readily to Eskimo food and customs. Constantly in the company of the Eskimo house girls, they heard at least as much Inupiaq as English. "Lucy talks a good deal more Eskimo than English," Ellen confessed unashamedly and a bit proudly. Nor did it occur to Ellen and Tom to segregate their children from the rest of the village. On Dwight's first birthday, forty-one native boys and girls were invited to a party at the mission house. "They all sat on the floor and left very little room to walk," Ellen wrote to her family. "We made three kettles of paste, added a little molasses and served it hot."

If anything, Ellen worried that her children were becoming spoiled, a notion that hardly seems possible, given the Spartan rigors of the Cape. Yet as a rule Eskimo children were spoiled—showered with attention, never scolded, granted whatever they wished whenever possible. Kongik and Woodlet treated Lucy and Dwight much the same, singing to them, slipping them treats of seal blubber, and carrying them about in their atigis. More doting nannies would be hard to imagine.

Of the two Lopp children, Dwight was the more robust by far. "He is smarter than Lucy," his mother allowed, "not that she is stupid at all, but she has been backward always." Born prematurely, Lucy had grown slowly, whereas her brother had filled out with every mouthful of gruel or maktak. Within a year, he was the same size as Lucy and wearing the same clothes.

For the most part, the children's health was quite good. In December a vicious cough, which Ellen identified as whooping cough, swept through the village, killing several native babies. Lucy and Dwight both caught it, throwing a scare into their parents, but they were fully recovered by January.

Confinement was a big concern throughout the winter months. Tom was always on the move, dashing back and forth to the school or the herders' camp, but Ellen, who had felt like a "caged tiger" aboard ship, tolerated being hemmed in at home even less. Like the Thorntons, the Lopps found it more efficient to close off all the rooms in the house but two. To cope with claustrophobia, Ellen took to pacing back and forth in a long passageway dug in the deep drift alongside the house. But then one side of the tunnel caved in and she had to give up. Once the weather brightened, which was none too soon and none too often, she or one of the house girls would place Lucy and Dwight on the roof of the coal shed to soak up the sun and fresh air. By early May, Ellen knew that she was pregnant again.

It never occurred to her to forego teaching school. The path to the village was precipitous and slippery; one errant step could prompt a disastrous toboggan ride to the beach. Still, Ellen made her way to the schoolhouse each morning to continue where she and Tom had left off more than a year earlier. To their gratification, one of the most steadfast pupils was Elignok, the umialik whom Thornton had regarded as so incorrigible.

The adults in general were as ready to learn as the children. "I am giving them physiological lectures from a mannequin chart," Ellen wrote to one of her sisters. "They don't like to believe that the brain does the thinking. Their idea is that the 'insides' . . . is the organ of the intellect. A few days ago they brought a Diomede Island native to school and asked me to prove to him that the earth was round. But he is still a doubter. Our natives here all seem to believe it."

Persuading the Cape villagers that the brain was the seat of intellect or that the earth was spherical were remarkable accomplishments indeed, but the Lopps set their goals higher still. At the first Sunday service, conducted on August 19, the anniversary of Thornton's murder, Tom explained to the assembled villagers that "God had sent us back to Cape Prince of Wales to take up the work on the same day in which they by the wickedness of three of their people had caused it to be suspended." The message was not lost on the natives. "We have prospect for a very successful year's work," Ellen wrote home in early October, once Sunday school had begun. "We trust that before you again hear from us, several of these people will have been led to Christ."

Her optimism had no doubt been fueled by the marriage of Kongik to Netaxite, the oldest of the herders. At the end of September, the Reverend Toleef Brevig and his wife and infant son arrived by umiak from Port Clarence to conduct the first Christian wedding of Eskimos in northern Alaska. Kongik, who was rather plump, wore a modest Mother Hubbard dress, presumably sewn by Ellen, with a red sash. Netaxite wore a suit borrowed from Tom. Brevig noted that the groom had on a starched shirt and collar, "but he wore the shirt backside front and the collar upside down."

The entire village turned out for the ceremony. With Tom acting as interpreter—and with one of the natives, perhaps Sokweena, translating Tom's "broken Eskimo" into more fluent Inupiaq—Brevig made sure to stress the tenets of the sacrament: honor and obey . . . in sickness and health . . . for richer or poorer . . . till death do them part . . . so help them, God. The service was interrupted briefly by a suitor who tried to win Kongik's attentions by presenting her with a pair of deer-skin pants—a more traditional expression of affection and betrothal. She declined the gift and whispered that he be sent away.

For all its idiosyncrasy, the wedding was an important milestone in the Lopps' long campaign to Christianize the Eskimos. Much as Charlie Antisarlook had been chosen as an example for other reindeer herders to follow, the Lopps were anxious to convert one or two natives who could then proselytize to their fellow Eskimos in their own language. Short of this, they hoped that they could at least train two full-time "helpers" to whom they could assign greater responsibilities as teachers and translators. If funds could be raised, they proposed sending one or two Cape villagers back to the States for a fuller immersion in American civilization.

The downside of this approach was well understood. In his influential book, *Foreign Missions*, Rufus Anderson quotes a minister who had served among the Choctaw Indians for forty years: "Those who acquired the most knowledge of the English language seemed the farthest from embracing the gospel. . . . They regarded themselves as elevated above their parents, and the mass of their people, and became vain in their imaginations, and their foolish hearts were darkened." In short, Anderson warns, "civilized" natives become "foreign in their manners, foreign in their habits, [and] foreign in their sympathies."

The Lopps also recognized the unintended consequences of this sort of initiative. "More bad than good could result from such an experiment unless watchful and patient care were exercised toward the pupils," Ellen conceded. She also mentioned that Sheldon Jackson was "firmly opposed to anything of the kind." Nevertheless, she and Tom were willing to take a chance, leaning on Rufus Anderson's counsel that "the child will never stand and walk firmly, if always in leading-strings."

Quietly they set their sights on a day when natives would be in complete charge of their own Christian souls, not to mention their own reindeer. "A foreign missionary should not be the pastor of a native church," Rufus Anderson had directed. "His business is to plant churches in well-chosen parts of the field, committing them as soon as possible to the care of native pastors." The Lopps had a long way to go before Cape Prince of Wales would achieve such a desirable goal. Yet anything they believed in was worth striving for.

Throughout the fall and early winter, Ellen and Tom tried harder than ever at Sunday school. Their diary notes the theme of each week's service:

> September 9: "Rest in Jesus."
>
> September 16: "Forgiveness."
>
> October 21: "And if I be lifted up . . . ."

The turning point came at the end of February with the arrival of David Johnson, the Swedish Evangelical missionary at Unalakleet, accompanied by two native translators, Stephen and Lincoln, whose acceptance of Christian names suggest that they had been baptized.

The format was that of a revival. Regular school was suspended, and the missionaries took turns preaching and leading the natives in hymns and prayers from morning until late at night. The Lopps' diary again gives only the sketchiest glimpse of the evangelical marathon:

> March 1: "I [Tom] used the interpreters to give them a general outline of the Bible & the object. Mr. Johnson preached at night on the Prodigal Son."
>
> March 3: "The Commandments"
>
> March 5: "The Crucifixion"

March 6: "Resurrection"

March 7: "The Second Coming"

On the final day of Johnson's visit, Ellen wrote to her parents that many of the natives had said that "they believe the Bible and what they have heard preached. . . . They have never before heard the gospel preached in correct Eskimo language and, I suppose, have learned more in this week than they have learned before, in all." The best news was that forty of the Cape natives expressed a desire to become Christians.

Throughout the spring, Tom and Ellen worked diligently to sustain the momentum. Every Sunday afternoon, they conducted a prayer meeting at the mission house for the two dozen or so natives who had "made their peace with God" during the revival. On one Sunday at the end of March, Tom and Sokweena held a prayer meeting at the small settlement of Mitletok (today's Mitletukeruk), twenty miles up the coast. The natives "listened to catch every word," Tom rejoiced in his journal. "This was the second Sunday they have kept and some of them have tried to pray. . . . They want us to come up again." Tom assured them that "in a few years some of the pupils at the Cape school would be sufficiently advanced to teach them."

Keeping the Sabbath was a major accomplishment, regardless of whether the natives dedicated the day to worship. Days of the week were a white man's metric, and the Lopps regarded it as a great triumph when Kokituk, one of the most prodigious whale hunters in the village, elected to keep his crew ashore on a Sunday that also happened to be the first good whaling day of the season. "So we feel that he is earnest about being a Christian," Ellen exalted.

In April, right after Easter, Tom sent a sled to Port Clarence to collect Toleef Brevig, his wife, and eighteen-month-old son. "Mr. Brevig is not an active man and had to ride almost all the way," Ellen chuckled to her sister Susie. Still, she and Tom were grateful to have an ordained minister who could preach to their nascent congregation. The Lopps had achieved a great deal since returning to the Cape the previous August. Their perseverance was fueled to a great extent by the expectation that sometime in the coming summer they would be leaving the mission for a much-needed hiatus in the States. And they hoped—expected—that their replacement would be a clergyman. "God's spirit has surely been working in the hearts of this people," Tom wrote to the American Missionary Association, "and we trust many of them will be ready for baptism when the long-looked-for minister comes to relieve us."

By June Tom was so eager for the mail to arrive that once again he went down to Port Clarence to meet the ships. On the tenth he was stunned to learn that, due to lack of funds, the American Missionary Association could not afford to send a missionary, much less a minister, to replace him and Ellen. Technically the Cape would cease to be a "contract" school, a joint effort of church and state. Instead, the U.S. Bureau of Education had agreed to take over responsibility but with no commitment to fulfill any religious obligations. Tom and Ellen were nearly heartbroken by the thought of the Cape falling into the hands of anyone besides committed Christians. "We have counted so much on the work of the minister and his wife we thought would be sent this summer that we were very badly disappointed to hear that the American Missionary Association had given up the mission for this year," a plainly irritated Ellen informed her parents on July 3. "Alaska missionaries are not much like the ideal missionaries I used to believe in before I went behind the scenes, but a government teacher is worse. I had much rather the buildings would be vacant than have . . . government teachers."

Then suddenly the outlook improved. The new teacher appointed to the Cape turned out to be a minister after all—the Reverend Thomas Hanna, an Englishman by way of California. Nowhere in any of the government reports or in the correspondence and diaries of Ellen and Tom Lopp is there any mention of his denomination. Given the alternative, it hardly mattered.

But just as the horizon seemed to brighten, it clouded over again. On July 17, the *W.H. Meyer*, carrying the Hannas, their belongings, and most of the year's supplies for the missions of northern Alaska, lost its anchors in a gale at Port Clarence and wrecked on the beach directly in front of the reindeer station. The keel was ripped from its hull as waves broke over the decks. Remarkably no one drowned, but the provisions for Cape Prince of Wales were not recovered. The Hannas, shaken but unharmed, were finally delivered to the Cape on July 28. "We like the Hannas," Ellen wrote home.

The Lopps did their best to make the Hannas comfortable. There was no time to teach them the language or even the lay of the land. Mostly they hoped that the newcomers could learn from the gaffes of their predecessors. "Mr. Lopp and Mr. Thornton did some funny things the first years," Ellen laughed in hindsight. "For instance, [they] had their clothes made of such heavy deerskins that they couldn't wear them, and salted ever so many ducks for winter use. . . . And more important, [they] made some mistakes in dealing with the natives because they didn't understand their ways."

The nearer the day came for Tom and Ellen to leave the Cape, the more they realized how thoroughly they had adjusted to their Alaskan surroundings—and how unprepared they were for the Outside. Tom had not been in the States in five years; Ellen had been away three. While their missionary zeal had not slackened during their term at the Cape, they had become enmeshed in the rhythm of native life. Tom had spent a good part of June aboard an umiak, hunting walruses amidst the hazardous ice floes of the Bering Strait, at times venturing as far as the Diomede Islands, halfway to Siberia. His main reason for participation was to help lay in oil and meat for the herders; yet he was obviously thrilled to be part of such a magnificent pursuit.

Tom's umiak, which was crewed mostly by the reindeer herders, managed to kill only six walruses, but the other twenty or so boats from the village took more than two hundred, each weighing as much as an ox. For weeks the entire village was absorbed with rendering the meat and extracting the oil. Tom and Ellen offered prayers of thanks for the bounty that the season had provided, but their benedictions hardly superseded the rituals of the natives as each umiak was welcomed home and its catch divided and preserved.

Had Sheldon Jackson arrived amid the bloody, all-consuming slaughter and witnessed the Lopps' immersion in the gory harvest, he might have wondered who was converting whom. Half facetiously, Tom and Ellen had begun to wonder the same thing themselves. "This is something I never thought of in regard to missionaries," Ellen wrote home. "In a foreign country, to *Christianize* heathen people, they are inclined to become somewhat heathenized themselves."

It had been a good year for the Cape reindeer herd, too. The winter had been harsher than usual, but the spring had been milder. Having been given only young bulls from the Teller herd, several of which had died, Tom had expected a modest calf crop at best. Instead he was pleasantly surprised when seventy-five were born in April and May. Losses over the winter had been minimal, and as he prepared to leave the Cape, Tom was happy to report that the Cape herd now numbered 174, including more than half a dozen that could pull sleds.

Meanwhile, the news from Port Clarence was not nearly so sunny. The native herders did not like the new pecking order of Lapps bossing Eskimos, and they resented the special privileges afforded the interlopers—most especially that Lapps could kill reindeer for their own use and Eskimos could not. Nor did it help that Captain Healy had sided against the Lapps. "At best the Arctic Natives have a hard struggle for existence," Healy lectured in a letter to the commissioner of education, Sheldon Jackson's boss, "and it does not seem exactly just to them that a low class of foreign laborers should be brought over and settled in their midst, at rates of pay equal to four or five times that paid our own Natives for the same work."

Such xenophobic rhetoric was typical of an era in which Main Street Americans felt inundated by waves of immigrants. Healy's African-American parentage (however secret) doubtless added fuel to his resentment. Not that he regarded Eskimos as much better than "beggars," but he failed to see the merits of entrusting their uplift to outsiders of questionable stock. "We would make Americans of our Alaskan natives, cultivate a spirit of patriotism in them and teach them to live, but with Laplanders for their models how can this be done?" he vituperated. "The very language they hear is that of the servile foreigner. God's word is preached to them in some Scandinavian tongue. It's very well to make Christians of these people, but let us make Americans of them first." Others have suggested that Healy was simply eager to come across as whiter than most whites.

Tom Lopp expressed no such bigotry toward Lapps in general, but he did not hide his favoritism toward Eskimo herders, whose distaste for the new batch of reindeer men was growing by the week. "The natives bring bad reports about the new Superintendent and Lapps at Port Clarence," he wrote to Ellen's family.

Bad blood aside, the Lapps were living up to their advanced billing as capable herders. They were better—gentler, more attentive—at handling the animals than the Chukchi had been, and their skills with harness, sleds, and taming of deer were superb. They had a good eye for range as well; they quickly realized that the fragile tundra surrounding the reindeer station was depleted after four years of grazing, and they urged that the herds be moved to an area with more plentiful moss. The Lapps were the first to suggest that bigger herds of a thousand or more reindeer were better than several small herds; they grew faster and were more easily managed. However, Sheldon Jackson did not heed their suggestion, and the herd of five hundred was splintered to make herds for Cape Prince of Wales and Charlie Antisarlook.

Both Lopp and Antisarlook were gratified by how well their herds had wintered. Kjellmann, on the other hand, was dispirited, as the Lopps discovered when they arrived at the reindeer station aboard the *Bear* on August 27. Kjellmann's wife was in poor health, and he was getting fed up with the lack of respect and appreciation shown to him and his herders by both the Eskimos and the U.S. government. The wreck of the *Meyer* was the last straw. When Kjellmann asked Captain Healy if his father could claim salvage rights to the cargo, Healy refused on grounds that the senior Kjellmann was not an American citizen. Pressed by Kjellmann to cite a specific statute, Healy reportedly replied, "If it isn't the Law, I make it a Law because *I am the Law.*" With that, Kjellmann turned in his resignation and booked passage to the States. For want of a better appointment, the job of superintendent devolved to Kjellmann's brother-in-law.

The unhappy severance of Kjellmann clouded the future of the reindeer station, and the American Missionary Association's withdrawal of support for the Cape mission cast doubt on whether the Lopps would be able to return to Alaska. Ellen and Tom might have been more disturbed by the recent downturn of events if they had not been so consumed by the chore and excitement of going home.

. . .

The trip was a trial in itself. They were two weeks getting to Unalaska. The entire family was seasick, except for sturdy Dwight, who played merrily among the baggage on the cabin floor. At St. Michael the *Bear* picked up sixteen miners who had gone bust on the upper Yukon and fled on the last steamboat to depart the interior before winter closed in. Arriving at the coast, the miners threw themselves on the mercy of Captain Healy, whose timely appearance likely spared them from utter destitution, if not starvation. Even as the Lopps were making their own exit, they were provided a glimpse of Alaska's future: It was only a matter of time before more men like these would be pushing north toward the Seward Peninsula and Cape Prince of Wales. The second edition of the homespun *Eskimo Bulletin*, published in June, had reported a promising strike near Golovnin Bay. "Gold! Gold! Gold! A New Eldorado for Yukon Miners," the headline ballyhooed in a playful parody of the big-city papers.

The *Bear's* next stop was at St. Lawrence, where the Gambells were bracing for their second winter at the Presbyterian mission. Ellen and Tom were sympathetic, up to a point. The Gambells were solemn and dedicated, but also stiff and superior, not unlike the Thorntons. They were initially repulsed by the natives' "greasy, flat faces, pug noses and broad mouths." The Gambells slept with doors bolted and eventually strung barbed wire around the mission house to keep the "semi-savage" gawkers at bay.

Arriving at Unalaska on September 11, the Lopps transferred to the *Dora*, a mail steamer bound for Sitka, the territorial capital. The new boat made numerous stops as it worked its way southeast. "It was very pleasant to come into civilization very gradually . . . [and to] see cattle and trees, stores and churches once more," Ellen wrote to her family. After so much time in the tundra, even the rudest trading post seemed like a metropolis. "The first store I was in was at Kodiak, and I stood and stared so much that folks probably thought that I had never seen a store before," Ellen laughed at herself.

Her sisters had tried to prepare her for the dramatic change in fashions —"the reign of big sleeves," they teased. This only made her more self-conscious when she, Tom, and the children landed, out of style and unkempt, in San Francisco, seven weeks after leaving Cape Prince of Wales. By mid-October they were at last in Glyndon, Minnesota, where they were showered with love and forgiven their feral ways.

The visit was more than a reunion, for none of Ellen's family had met Tom or the children before. Lucy and Dwight were passed from sister to sister, but it was Tom who stole the show. Ellen's father and brothers were fixated by his tales of reindeer herding, walrus hunting, and the atavistic ways of the natives. None of Ellen's letters had prepared the family for just how dashing he looked, thick muscled and deeply tanned from months in the open. In a family photograph taken shortly after their arrival at Glyndon, Tom stood out among his tamer, paler in-laws like a knight among yeoman. Ellen, who was eight months pregnant, distinguished herself from her three unmarried sisters by wearing the most voluminous sleeves.

Sarah Louise Lopp was born at Glyndon on December 20, 1895, the third Lopp child in thirty months. After several enjoyable weeks at Glyndon, it was time for Ellen and the children to meet Tom's family. However, Tom did not stay long in Valley City, Indiana. If he and Ellen were going to continue their mission at Cape Prince of Wales, they had to persuade the American Missionary Association to restore funding or raise the money themselves somehow. In the meantime, Tom also had to support his family, since his salary had ended before he left Alaska.

He began by giving lectures in nearby towns, sometimes earning as little as three or four dollars a presentation. America's interest in "the Esquimaux" specifically, and "primitive" cultures in general, had expanded significantly in recent years due in no small part to the astonishing anthropological "villages" at the World's Columbian Exhibition in 1893, where fair-goers by the tens of thousands traipsed wide-eyed past living dioramas of "dusky Bedouins," bare-breasted Fijians, "little people" from Java, and even "lowly" Irish women tending the turf fire of a "quaint little cottage." Miner Bruce had not arrived in the States in time to arrange for the Port Clarence Eskimos to appear in Chicago, as he had hoped. That exhibit had already been filled by several families of Inuit from Labrador, who passed the sweltering summer paddling their kayaks among the gondolas in the fair's man-made lagoon. Bruce had better luck the following winter, when, with the help of Sheldon Jackson, his deerskin-clad entourage was invited to perform "In the Sweet By and By" for Mrs. Grover Cleveland in the Blue Room of the White House.

Tom Lopp had no such accompaniment for his talks on Alaska. Nor would it have occurred to him to shock or titillate his audiences. On the contrary, his goal was to emphasize that Eskimos, despite their harsh habitat and profane practices, were God's children and not nearly so savage as one might imagine. In December, Lopp was invited to present his case directly to the American Missionary Association at its annual gathering in Detroit. The speaker who preceded him was a "Christianized Indian." When Lopp's turn came, he won a warm round of laughter by introducing himself as a "heathenized American." The thrust of his message was that the hardest work had already been done, and it should not be wasted. "Our school at Cape Prince of Wales has always been a success," he declared. "We have had a Sunday service every Sunday . . . and we have found that the Eskimos are quite capable of understanding the plan of salvation, and that many of them gladly accept it." For the sake of these native souls—not to mention the memory of the martyred Harrison Thornton—the mission must continue.

Through winter and early spring, Tom continued to campaign for reinstatement by the AMA. At the end of March, Ellen joined him in Westborough, Massachusetts, where together they won support from the Congregational church where Ellen's relatives were long-standing members. A Congregational church in Southport, Connecticut, also made a donation. Visit by visit, speech by speech, letter by letter, they raised the money—more than $1,000—and by April, the AMA relented, renewing its support of the mission.

Suddenly they had less than a month to gather up their things, say good-bye to family and friends, and make their way to San Francisco. The spring had been lovely in Indiana. "The petals are falling off the peach blossoms but they are still pretty and the pear trees are in their glory," Ellen wrote to her family. But as the season expanded, she was reminded of why she had left the States in 1892. "It has been ninety-four in the shade here," she complained on April 19. "I 'most melted."

By the end of May, they were in San Francisco, procuring more supplies and waiting for their ship. By June 6, they were aboard the schooner *Ida Schnauer*, headed north. Their freight included high chairs, a sewing machine, wallpaper, a new organ, and a marble obelisk for Harrison Thornton's grave, on which was carved, "A good soldier of Jesus Christ."

During their eight months in the States, Ellen and Tom seemed never to have considered forsaking the Cape mission in favor of safer, warmer, and surely no less constructive lives within reassuring reach of their families. Yet in their case, the recommitment to Alaska was not a matter of resisting temptation or honoring an oath of sacrifice, for the ties that bound them to each other and made them whole were inexorably woven into the landscape, climate, and community where they had met and made their start. They might miss Minnesota and Indiana, but they felt physically and spiritually drawn to the battered coast of the Bering Sea. "These Eskimos are a fine race of people," Tom had told the AMA, "and while we are down here in civilization our hearts are in Alaska."

For better or worse, they were heading home.

# Camels of the Far North

BESIDES THE FIVE MEMBERS of the Lopp family, there were only two other passengers aboard the *Ida Schnauer.* One was William Kjellmann, whom Sheldon Jackson had rehired as superintendent of the Teller Reindeer Station. The other was Dr. Albert Kittilsen, who would serve as Kjellmann's assistant and the station's physician.

Over the winter, while Ellen and Tom had been soliciting aid for the Cape Prince of Wales mission, Jackson had been no less vigorous in promoting the role of reindeer in Alaska's future. He had enticed Kjellmann to return north with the promise that the reindeer program was on the verge of exhilarating expansion—expansion that would include bringing more Lapp herders to Alaska, importing more deer, and distributing more herds throughout the territory. Shortly after Kjellmann and Dr. Kittilsen had left San Francisco aboard the *Schnauer,* Jackson also headed north to make the rounds of the Alaskan missions.

Tom Lopp had kept up with Jackson while both were in the States. He had visited him in Washington, D.C., and Jackson had joined Lopp in New York for an important meeting with the American Missionary Association. The newspapers also had followed Jackson's uphill campaign. Some viewed him as an Arctic Samaritan; others regarded reindeer as just another flavor of pork. Jackson had lobbied Congress to increase its annual appropriation for reindeer to $45,000—six times the amount allotted the previous year. "Are the Natives Really in Any Danger of Starvation?" a skeptical *Washington Post* had inquired in February. An Alaskan trader who happened to be visiting the capital told the *New York Times*: "The story of starving natives is all bosh. The fellows who are running this reindeer job know what they are about even if you people down here are fools enough to believe them, but I want to say that, as far as the natives of that region are concerned, the importation of Siberian reindeer is absolutely of no earthly use or need to their lives."

To refute the doubters, Jackson produced a sheaf of letters written by missionaries in the field (though none by Tom Lopp), attesting to the dire need for reindeer in the native villages. A letter by a Yukon River trader vouched for the tremendous boon reindeer would provide to the gold mining camps. Meanwhile, congressional cynics ribbed Jackson for "adjusting" his justifications to fit his audience: First he had declared that reindeer were needed to relieve starving Eskimos. Next reindeer became "industry" for those same natives. And finally they metamorphosed into an essential means of transportation for white settlers. In the end, Congress was unmoved, voting Jackson the same appropriation as the year before. More provoked than chastened, Jackson returned to Alaska doubly determined to prove both the necessity and the soundness of the reindeer program.

Meanwhile, the *Ida Schnauer* took forty-five days to reach Port Clarence, by which time the Lopps had traded seasickness for a yearning to don sealskin boots and walk once again on Arctic tundra. Two more weeks would pass before they were able to get ashore. With high winds churning up the shallow bay, the captain would not risk landing Ellen and the children through the heavy surf. Native umiaks were more daring, and shortly after the *Schnauer* anchored off of the reindeer station, familiar faces clambered aboard with greetings and goods to trade. "We have found [them] friendly and glad to see us," Ellen noted happily. She and Tom were pleased to discover that their grasp of Inupiaq, which had never been thorough, had survived a year of disuse.

The news from the reindeer station was mixed. In March, the Brevigs' son had died of fever; a month later, Mrs. Brevig gave birth to a healthy daughter. By all reports, the native herders at Teller had gotten along well enough with the Lapps, but the herd itself had been infested with hoof rot, killing at least two dozen and hobbling many more. In January, 130 deer had been driven to Golovnin Bay—fifty each as a loan to Episcopal and Swedish Evangelical missions, the other thirty divided among four native apprentices.

The Lopps were delighted to learn that the Cape Prince of Wales herd had done well in their absence, increasing from 169 to 250. "It must be said that our herders have been faithful in detail during all seasons of the year," Thomas Hanna had stated in his annual report.

But when the Lopps inquired about the Hannas, the natives from Cape Prince of Wales were reluctant to divulge all that they knew. Slowly, though, bits of gossip began to emerge. In her first letter home from Port Clarence, Ellen mentioned, "We are so disappointed about Mr. Hanna. I won't say any more about that now, except that I think he will go down." Several days later, she added no less enigmatically, "Things at the Cape have not been going as we hoped. We may have to be alone there again . . . though there is such a thing as being worse off than alone." The dark cloud hovering over the mission made Ellen and Tom only that much more eager to arrive.

By the time the family was able to land at Cape Prince of Wales on August 24, summer was nearly over. The homecoming might have been more touching if it were not for the nagging issue of the Hannas. The hardships of a year in the Arctic had not brought out the best in the reverend, though no aspersions were ever cast on his wife (a woman so inconspicuous that her first name is not mentioned in any of the correspondence or government reports of the period). While they were at Port Clarence, the Lopps had learned that the *Bear* had tried "to take [Hanna] away early in July because his life wasn't safe." Heavy ice had thwarted the cutter's intervention, and the Hannas remained, beleaguered but unmolested.

The memory of Harrison Thornton lingered palpably, yet Hanna, who had helped the Lopps place the marble monument on Thornton's grave, apparently had not spent a great deal of time reflecting on Thornton's missteps. "The natives do not like or respect [Hanna] as they ought," Ellen explained, "partly because they believe some very bad things about him which may or may not be true." Over the first days and weeks at the Cape, Ellen and Tom tried discreetly to gather the natives' grievances against Hanna. They learned that during a dispute over trade goods, Hanna supposedly had pointed a shotgun at one of the natives. The worst accusation, however, was that Hanna had made inappropriate advances toward several native girls. Ellen and Tom had no reason to disbelieve the natives; nor were they anxious to confront Hanna.

For the time being, they elected to give Hanna the benefit of the doubt. "You must make allowances for what I say," Ellen equivocated to her mother. "We Arctic people are too much inclined to criticize each other. In comparison with later people, some of Mr. Thornton's good points come to the front quite conspicuously." Upon fuller reflection, she reversed her earlier prediction: "I expect the Hannas will stay. . . . I do so much want another family here with us."

Ellen and Tom had been planning all along to build a new house, and not just because they had expected that the Hannas would continue to occupy the house on the hill. The old house was difficult to keep warm, and with three children to look after, the treacherous footing by the front door was even more worrisome. Most of all, though, the Lopps desired to be in the center of the village, not at its fringe, hovering above it.

Until Tom could finish the new building, the family lived in the schoolhouse, partitioning off a bedroom and kitchen with boxes of provisions. Three-year-old Lucy and two-year-old Dwight were at first scared to be surrounded by so many natives, despite having been born into their company. Soon, however, their temperament improved under the attentions of two new house girls, the cousins Nowadluk, whom Ellen named Nora and Alice in order to tell them apart. By winter, the two elder children were again talking "considerable Eskimo." Baby Sarah, meanwhile, was cutting her first tooth and learning to crawl. "I think she is smarter and sweeter than the others were at her age," Ellen bragged.

Several of the villagers pitched in to help Tom with the house. They brought driftwood logs from as far as ten miles away, which Tom split painstakingly with a pit saw. He sited the house beside the shallow stream that divided the village, back from the beach and a short walk to the schoolhouse—"a fine place all around for the children," Ellen noted, with "water handy in winter and summer." Within a month, the house was inhabitable, if not quite done. It was smaller than either the school or mission houses—twenty-four feet by twenty—and much cozier. "What it lacks in architectural beauty is made up in comfort," Tom remarked. The front door opened onto a narrow hall; on either side was a storeroom and a small waiting room for natives when they came to visit and trade. At the center of the house was a combined living room and kitchen, which connected to two bedrooms and a storage room. The house was heated by a stove in the kitchen and another in one of the bedrooms. Ellen had bought wallpaper for the sitting room. She had wanted to put linoleum on the floor but could afford only oilcloth.

As an afterthought, Tom added a temporary sod lean-to on the front of the house, which he used as a woodshed and carpentry shop. Lacking proper glass, he installed sheets of ice as skylights—"ice windows," he called them. Also that fall he built a separate log house for the reindeer herders not far away. Throughout the weeks of hurried construction, Hanna proved to be a big help, which made it even harder for Ellen and Tom to think badly of him. "The more Tom tried to run down stories, the more [the natives] tell, but none with any proof," Ellen wrote. "We are not worrying about it and are feeling quite good over getting our house made."

School began at the end of October. To enliven Sunday school, they had acquired an ingenious moving-picture invention called a zoetrope. Simple Bible stories were depicted on a sequence of panels mounted on the inside of a lighted cylinder. As the cylinder was spun, the pictures appeared to move—enthralling the natives, most of whom had never even seen a photograph before the missionaries arrived. The Lopps also brought with them a new printing press, which made preparation of lessons much easier. A typical primer bore a simple drawing of reindeer, under which was printed:

> We-mok has ten deer.
> *We-mok ko-le-nik kon-a-rok tuk.*
> Have you seen his deer?
> *Ki-ming-e-ve-ge oo-ma kong-ne-a?*

With the Hannas to share the teaching duties, Tom was able to devote more time to the deer herd. His five herders had done a good job in his absence. Over the previous winter, the Cape herd had lost only seven deer, none of them to the horrible foot rot that plagued the Teller herd. Tom's principal regret was that the government did not provide enough supplies so that the herders could get by without taking time off to hunt. They were still forbidden to eat reindeer meat. Nevertheless, they remained loyal to Tom-gorah, and he reciprocated with praise and high expectations. "We hope that in a year or two, when they can live independent of mission support, that the influence which they will exert as Christian deermen will do much toward leading the natives along the coast 'out of darkness into light,'" Tom wrote. "What a pleasure when visiting in camp to see them bow their heads and offer thanks to God."

Such piety was not the case with all of the Cape natives. Drinking had become more widespread while the Lopps had been away. "They are having a terrible time here with the liquor," Ellen recorded in November. "They make it themselves and there are some drunk almost all the time. We hear them shouting sometimes when we first go out in the morning. Often natives can't sleep because other natives, drunk, shout and come into their houses so much." One day while Tom was off with the herders, a drunken native appeared at Ellen's door. "He rapped and I opened the outside door and he started right in without an invitation," she recounted. "I . . . jumped back into the sitting room [and] locked the door. . . . He said he wanted medicine for a cut finger. I offered to tie it up through [the window of the waiting room], thinking he would go then. But that wouldn't do. . . . He howled and threw himself against the door and broke the lock." Finally neighbors heard the commotion and came to her aid. "When I unlock and open the outside door now, I open only a crack and keep my toe braced against the bottom of the door."

Several weeks later the missionaries were awakened in the middle of the night with the news that Kokituk, the village's most able hunter, had been killed. As reported in the hand-printed *Eskimo Bulletin*, Kokituk had been drinking with a man named Setartuk. A disagreement arose, and Kokituk, "armed with a revolver and crazed with rum, went to the north end of the village, where he found S. and opened fire upon him. After he had emptied the chambers of his revolver, he and S. were in the act of using their knives, when a young man, attracted by the noise, came up and took a knife away from each of them and started [Kokituk] towards his home. But it seems that S. had a knife secreted under his [atigi] and pursued the unarmed [Kokituk]. S. was soon joined by his brother, Ereheruk, who was armed with a rifle. They stabbed and shot K. several times before they succeeded in killing him."

By way of eulogy, Tom noted, "Kokituk was a shrewd, intelligent, and ambitious young man about twenty-eight years old. He had always been a successful trader and hunter, having killed one whale, and more white bears than any other native here. . . . Whisky was his worst enemy and he knew it."

As winter lengthened, Tom feared a repeat of the famine that had struck St. Lawrence Island in 1888. "Distilling and drunkenness . . . often prevented many [native hunters] from making the most of a favorable wind," he noted ruefully. Ellen observed in one of her letters: "Food is quite scarce. I know a great many people don't get two square meals a day. I wish we had food to pay them for work. There are many women who would be thankful to sew all day for their dinner and ten cents worth of food for their children. There are quite a number of women who are nursing two children, the older three or four years old."

If there was a positive aspect to the shortages, it was the lack of flour. Without it, natives could not distill whiskey, and by early spring much of the drunkenness had subsided, at least temporarily. What little flour Ellen could spare, she made into bread before giving it to the villagers. Thankfully spring brought a bounty of walruses, and the cycle of native life began all over again. With the change of season, Tom and Ellen hoped that once again they could turn the village's attention to God. They had not made much headway over the winter, Ellen lamented. "The liquor they have made has hurt our work a great deal."

· · ·

The shore ice was gone by June, much earlier than usual, and the *Bear* arrived, bringing the first letters from Outside. For Tom Lopp, it was also a chance to catch up on the latest developments in the reindeer program.

Before leaving Alaska the previous fall, Sheldon Jackson had discussed with William Kjellmann a plan by which they could dispel any lingering doubts about the efficacy of reindeer. "Having shown by actual experience that they could be bought, transported, and successfully propagated," Jackson wrote, "it remained to give a practical demonstration of their ability to traverse any part of the country under the most unfavorable circumstances." At the end of December, with temperatures well below zero, Kjellmann and two Lapp herders had left the Teller station with nine sleds and seventeen head of reindeer "to demonstrate the capacity of the hardy and swift animal for winter travel in Alaska."

Over the next four months, they made a round-trip journey of two thousand miles, traveling alongside and then across frozen Norton Sound, overland to the Yukon River, then south as far as the Moravian mission at Bethel on the Kuskokwim River. On the best days, they covered nearly one hundred miles; on the worst, they were lucky to hold their ground and remain alive. In late January, a blizzard overturned the sleds and knocked the Lapps and deer off their feet. "Small stones and flakes of ice crashed and hurled by in clouds," Kjellmann wrote in his log. "Tried to pitch tent, but had to give up. . . . Had a fearful night." On February 5, the temperature fell to seventy-three below. "Our deer broke loose in the middle of the night and kept . . . running around the tent, in order to keep warm," Kjellmann reported. Approaching the Yukon, the snow was too deep for the deer to graze. They sledded through deep drifts for four days without rest or food for the deer. Five animals dropped dead in harness.

The return trip was less eventful—except for one frightening interlude in which one of the sleds fell through a crack in the ice while crossing Norton Sound. Writing to his superiors in Washington, Sheldon Jackson described Kjellmann's odyssey as "the longest ever recorded in any land as made by the same reindeer." Its success, he testified, should persuade "missionaries, miners, traders, and others residing in northern and central Alaska that domestic reindeer can do for them what they have been doing for centuries in Lapland. That when introduced in sufficient numbers they will supplant dogs, both for traveling and freighting, furnish a rapid means of communications between widely separated communities, and render possible the full and profitable development of the rich mineral interests."

Jackson had another reason for dispatching Kjellmann on his rigorous winter jaunt. A year earlier, before Kjellmann had agreed to return as superintendent of the reindeer station, he and Jackson had discussed establishing a permanent Lapp colony somewhere in Alaska. A series of disputes between Norway and its neighbors had drastically restricted the movements of the semi-nomadic Lapps and their herds. "I have seen that it is only a matter of time when the Lapps will be compelled to migrate on account of the increase in population and decrease in pasturage for reindeer," Kjellmann, a Norwegian émigré himself, had predicted. "If simple calculation is to be taken into account, America must become the future home of the Laplanders."

Jackson was sympathetic. Unlike Tom Lopp, he believed that Lapps were indispensable to the growth and legitimacy of reindeer herding throughout Alaska. The biggest sticking point was location. After a year at Port Clarence, Kjellmann had concluded that the station was not a place where Lapps would choose to raise their own deer, despite its nearness to the Siberian reindeer herds. "If the Lapps are kept at those stations [in and around Port Clarence] . . . and sent home directly," Kjellmann warned, "I am convinced of the fact that all prospects for the formation of Laplander colonies in Alaska will be in vain." He and Jackson agreed that it would be wise to scout for someplace more suitable before the Lapps' three-year contracts expired that summer.

In the end, nine of the sixteen Lapps who had come over in 1894 decided to repatriate to Norway. One was Per Rist, whom Tom Lopp described as "the wealthiest and most influential" of the group. Rist had traveled with Kjellmann to Bethel and back and was impressed by the country between Norton Sound and the Yukon River. Impressed enough, at any rate, that he consented to return to Norway, accompanied by Kjellmann, to recruit other Lapps willing to establish a new reindeer-herding colony.

The site that Rist and Kjellmann had selected was at the mouth of the Unalakleet River, 350 miles east of Port Clarence. "The new station," Jackson explained in his annual report, would be "central for distribution of the herds either northward to Kotzebue Sound, Point Hope, and Point Barrow; southward to the Roman Catholic and Moravian stations on the Lower Yukon, Kuskokwim, and Nushagak rivers, or eastward to the Episcopal stations and mining settlements on the Upper Yukon Valley. Located in the neighborhood of the leading mission stations among the native populations, it will be able to draw and educate as herders and teamsters a larger number of the native young men." It went without saying that Kjellmann and Rist selected the site to draw a larger number of Lapps.

These developments did not catch Tom Lopp entirely by surprise. But as things worked out, he did not get a chance to meet with Jackson in person until the end of the summer; even if he had desired to voice his ambivalence toward Jackson's scheme to import more Lapps to a new station, by then it was too late.

. . .

On June 25, Jackson arrived at St. Michael, sixty miles from the Yukon's gaping delta, where he awaited the *Portus B. Weare*, one of the first boats to emerge from the interior that year. At first glance, there was nothing impressive about the flat-bottomed river steamer; nor did the eighty or so seedy men crowding its decks command immediate envy. Yet their arrival at St. Michael on June 28, 1897, was momentous. Stacked and stashed on board in all manner of crate and satchel were

nearly three tons of gold, most of it in the form of dust but some reportedly in chunks the size of "shelled corn." Virtually all of the gold had
been panned in streams that flowed into the Klondike River, which
entered the Yukon seventeen hundred miles upstream, in Canadian territory. The previous summer, on a boggy, mosquito-ridden creek aptly
christened Bonanza, three dumb-lucky prospectors—Tagish Charley,
Skookum Jim, and George Washington Carmack—had extracted a
nugget from the muck that triggered one of the most explosive gold
rushes in history.

Now more than ever, gold was the bedrock of the nation. In the
election of 1896, the plutocratic William McKinley had run against
William Jennings Bryan with a pledge of allegiance to the gold standard. Bryan, the flamboyant populist, had campaigned in favor of
bimetallism—currency based on both gold and silver, a dilution that
was said to favor the little guy. Bryan lost, and despite his epic forecast
that McKinley would inevitably "crucify mankind on a cross of gold,"
average Americans now grasped, begrudgingly perhaps but with
heightened surety, that they were better off possessing gold—the actual metal—than not. Tens of thousands who previously could not find
Alaska on the map would soon regard it as the end of the rainbow.

At the time of the Klondike gold strike in 1896, several thousand
prospectors, trappers, and traders were already living in the remote
interior of the Yukon country. When they caught wind of the fantastic
find on Bonanza Creek, many of them had dropped everything and
stampeded to the Klondike by any means possible. The rest of the
world did not hear of the discovery until after the ice broke up the following June.

Sheldon Jackson was one of the first outsiders to learn of the
Klondike bonanza. Booking himself on the Weare's very next trip
upstream was, without question, highly fortuitous but not entirely
coincidental. At the request of the secretary of agriculture—a request
that Jackson may have prompted himself—he had agreed to devote

most of the summer to evaluating the "special conditions which will meet the introduction of reindeer freighting" to the interior of Alaska. He could not have picked a better moment to make his case.

Two weeks after leaving St. Michael, the *Weare* reached Circle City, more than a thousand miles upstream. Gold mining in the upper Yukon had been robust for at least a decade. Soon after its boom began in 1894, Circle City boasted an opera house, two theaters, eight dance halls, and twenty-eight saloons. Named originally for its nearness to the Arctic Circle, it began to promote itself as "the Paris of Alaska." By the time Jackson arrived on July 19, he estimated that the population, which a year earlier had exceeded one thousand, had plummeted to fewer than one hundred; everyone had decamped for the Klondike.

At Circle City, Jackson was joined by William Kjellmann, who had come upriver on an earlier boat, allowing him time to size up the suitability of the surrounding country for reindeer grazing. A week later, he and Jackson arrived together at Dawson City, the raw heart of the Klondike, still not much more than a farrago of soiled tents and hastily stacked cabins. "Nearly the entire population seemed to be at the landing," Jackson noted, "either to greet friends or from curiosity to witness the landing of newcomers. . . . The town is situated in an undrained swamp, and much sickness prevails. . . . Although it was Sunday, the sawmills were running day and night." Already the population had reached three thousand, more than a few of them millionaires.

Jackson and Kjellmann remained in Dawson City only thirty-six hours, long enough to make some basic calculations. What struck them most of all, other than the profane pulse of the town, was the prohibitive cost of feeding it, due to its remoteness; to make matters worse, the Yukon is navigable only four or five months of the year. Jackson noted that in Dawson City a barrel of flour sold for as much as $100; to haul a ton of freight from Dawson City to the Klondike mines, a distance of fifteen miles, could cost $500 per ton. And the problem was about to get exponentially worse. As Jackson and Kjellmann steamed downriver aboard the *Portus B. Weare*, they met several boats headed upstream, "crowded with gold seekers and adventurers . . . also [with] many special correspondents of newspapers." The real gold rush was just beginning.

Jackson had seen the future, and, with characteristic boldness, he grasped what needed to be done. "The only solution of reasonable land transportation and rapid communication and travel between mining centers hundreds of miles apart in subarctic Alaska is the introduction and utilizing of domestic reindeer," he asserted in his report to Washington. To drive home his point, he added, "The reindeer is to the far north what the camel is to desert regions." After Kjellmann's successful winter experiment and his own observations on the upper Yukon, he was confident that he could now bend even the most recalcitrant congressman to his will. "The possibilities are so great," he opined, "that in the days to come it will be a matter of surprise that the utilization of the deer was not vigorously pushed at the start."

Jackson's vision caught fire well before he returned to the States. As soon as word of the Klondike strike reached the Outside, the nation was thoroughly infected with "Klondicitis," as the the press dubbed the epidemic. Within days—within hours—after the first Klondike miners strode down the gangplanks onto the Seattle docks in mid-July, lugging their fortunes in nuggets and dust, thousands of wildly optimistic, grossly unprepared argonauts had mortgaged the farm, closed up shop, packed their kits, and booked passage north. To reach the Yukon and then the Klondike goldfields, they had to make a choice. The easier, but slower, route was by ship to St. Michael, transferring there to river steamer, as Jackson and Kjellmann had traveled earlier in the summer. The other way was shorter but more brutal, leaving ship at Dyea or Skagway in southeast Alaska and proceeding by foot, usually with one's gear in a backpack, over one of two nearly vertical, thoroughly merciless passes, Chilkoot or White, that separated the coast from the upper reaches of the Yukon, upstream from the Klondike.

By the end of August, nearly four thousand gold seekers had reached Dawson City. Many of them had arrived broke and worn out, expecting to be succored by instant riches. Instead they discovered that they had arrived too late in the season to begin prospecting; their only choice was to wait eight months until spring. How they would get by in the interim was a topic of colossal concern. Charles Constantine, the North West Mounted Police's man in Dawson City, had already sent a dispatch to Ottawa, advising that "the outlook for grub is not assuring for the number of people here."

Come September, with the creeks beginning to freeze and nighttime temperatures falling toward zero, anxiety escalated to near panic. Constantine tacked up a notice, urging exodus before the Klondike and Yukon became fully icebound. "For those who have not laid in a winter's supply to remain longer is to court death . . . or at least the certainty of sickness from scurvy and other troubles," he warned. "Starvation now stares everyone in the face."

Help was on the way, in fact, but the Yukon was not cooperating. By the end of summer its torrent had subsided, and there were stretches that were now too shallow for bulky steamboats to pass. Two hundred miles below Circle City, the river enters a broad plain, known as the Yukon Flats, where the current braids into a labyrinth of shallow channels. At Fort Yukon, in the midst of the flats, 100 miles below Circle City and another 250 miles below Dawson City, five steamboats had become stranded in the low water of autumn. The cargo was offloaded into the Army's warehouses.

Two boats, however, did make it through the Yukon Flats that September. One was the *Portus B. Weare*, on its next run upriver for the year; the other was the *Bella*. By halving their cargoes and cutting loose the barges they ordinarily towed behind, they succeeded in reaching Circle City at the end of September—whereupon they were plundered by armed miners. The Wild West was alive and kicking in the Far North. More than fifty tons of provisions intended for Dawson City never reached their destination.

Sheldon Jackson was halfway to California when this brigandage occurred, but he had seen enough. On his way home, he had noticed stacks of provisions piled along the shore at St. Michael; there was no way they would make it to the interior by winter. He arrived in San Francisco on October 13 and did not reach Washington, D.C., until November 1. Already West Coast newspapers were warning that the "hideous spectre" of starvation was stalking the "ice-beleaguered miners," who toiled "under the fitful gleam of the aurora along the rim of the Arctic Circle."

Government officials had long ago turned a jaded eye on Jackson's bulletins on "starving" natives, and if his had been the only voice raising the alarm in 1897, he might not have won much sympathy. But that same summer, the U.S. Army had ordered Captain Patrick Henry Ray to Alaska to observe the sudden influx of prospectors in the distant borderland of the upper Yukon. Ray's initial dispatches to Washington measured the rashness of the stampeding miners against the inability of shipping companies to deliver supplies to the interior, where they were sorely needed. These advisories were soon seconded by Revenue Cutter Service reports of a "perfect mob" of frustrated prospectors building at St. Michael. This time the higher-ups in Washington did not drag their feet. On September 18, two weeks before Sheldon Jackson had arrived in the capital, the Interior Department ordered William Kjellmann to "assemble at once all of the available reindeer trained for harness, teamsters, and sleds, and report at St. Michael, to U.S. Army [Lieutenant] Colonel [George M.] Randall to transport supplies to Dawson City if necessary. Obtain all deer trained to harness that can be spared from Cape Prince of Wales, Golov[n]in Bay, and Cape Nome [Antisarlook's herd], together with apprentices trained as teamsters and willing to go."

For Jackson, years of letters and lectures and lobbying had finally paid off. Sending reindeer to the rescue would not have been considered if he had not advocated their usefulness so relentlessly. His prayer had been answered. Now the challenge was for the reindeer and their herders to live up to Jackson's lofty billing.

What no one—neither Jackson nor the government—could have anticipated was that by the time Interior ordered a herd to be assembled at St. Michael, William Kjellmann was already en route to Norway, along with Per Rist and the other Lapps who had chosen to return home. Responsibility for the Teller herd—its transference to the new station at Unalakleet and then to St. Michael—fell to Dr. Albert Kittilsen, Kjellmann's assistant.

. . .

At Cape Prince of Wales, the Lopps had heard bits and pieces of the plan to establish a new reindeer station at Unalakleet, but they did not glimpse the full picture until the *Bear* arrived late in September. They had never favored increasing the role of Lapps in the reindeer program, yet they were not eager to see the Teller station abandoned altogether. "We had been anxious for some weeks to know . . . whether we were to be without neighbors or not," Ellen wrote in one of the final letters sent from the Cape that year. It was with considerable relief that she learned from Sheldon Jackson that Dr. Kittilsen would remain until at least December. She had managed without doctors in the past, but she was comforted by the thought that one was not too far away. Her next baby was due in October.

Ellen and Tom had already lost their closest white neighbors, the Hannas, in August. Although the Hannas had proven to be "very pleasant and kind," the Lopps were not sorry to see them go. In the end, the testimony against Hanna had been overwhelming. When Sheldon Jackson had first told Hanna that his appointment would not be renewed—and that the contract for government teacher would be given to Tom

Lopp alone—he avoided confronting Hanna with the real reason for his dismissal. Instead, Jackson had informed Hanna that he was letting him go for his own safety. But the Lopps knew the true reason.

In March 1896, while Mrs. Hanna was away visiting the Teller station. Hanna apparently had lured Woodlet, who had worked for both the Thorntons and the Lopps, into the mission house, locked the door, and made sexual advances. Somehow Woodlet managed to spurn him and fled in tears. On another occasion, Hanna plied two native girls with drink, hoping to soften their resistance. Whether he achieved his prurient goals this time is not clear, but afterward villagers began referring to one of the girls teasingly as Hanna's "wife." Shamed and stigmatized, she subsequently became the companion of the captain of a whaling ship bound for Herschel Island.

When Tom Lopp presented Hanna with these allegations in July, the reverend denied them. After Tom brought Hanna before his accusers, the reverend insisted that he had given the girls liquor for medicinal purposes. Refusing to admit to any wrongdoing, Hanna at first vowed to stay on at the Cape, with or without a government salary or support from the American Missionary Association. Tom, however, would not waver. "Mr. H. and Mr. L. talked and talked," Ellen confided to her family, and finally Tom prevailed. "If [Hanna] had persisted in remaining here another year," Ellen remarked, "there would have had to have been a . . . scandal investigation"—which was the last thing any of them wanted. "Now that I have written all this I feel as if I might be doing great harm by spreading it," she confessed in closing. "I will meditate until the ship comes [to collect the mail] and decide whether or not to send it. If I knew it wouldn't get out of the family I would feel better. Couldn't I swear you all to secrecy? Just saying that he left . . . will satisfy. Not mentioning him unless it is necessary. And if more must be said, say there was nothing proved against him. But that the natives' opinion of him hindered his usefulness. He didn't like it very well here anyway."

The Lopps, on the other hand, liked the Cape a great deal. Save for the confrontation with the Hannas and disturbing bouts of drunkenness among the natives, the family passed a pleasant summer. By July, the tundra and mountainside were blooming with a dozen types of wildflower. "We have a little stream in front, and the sandy beach on one side, and a bank of earth covered with moss and grass on the other two sides of our house," Tom wrote to a Congregational journal, adding, "Our children seem to enjoy life up here."

Lucy, Dwight, and Sarah were by now fully acclimated to their surroundings on the Bering Strait, able to chatter away in Inupiaq with a fluency that was the envy of their parents. They had also acquired a native's tolerance of cold. Not even spanking would keep Dwight from wading and playing in the frigid water. One of Ellen's favorite diversions was to write letters imitating the voice of one of her children. On August 29, she had twenty-month-old Sarah describe a typical day at the beach: "I go outdoors all the time when the sun shines, and sometimes it rains and we put on our ke-urt-uks [waterproof coats] and stay out. I lie down in the sand and make houses and put up sticks, and Lucy and I wash shells, and Dwight has a little canoe and sails it in the water."

Like the season itself, such tranquillity did not last long. Up until that fall, the gold rush in the upper Yukon had affected the Lopps only slightly. Over the summer, Cape natives returning from Siberia had reported a dramatic hike in the price of reindeer skins—an indication of increased demand by the miners. And there was some hope, due to the increased activity on the Yukon, that a regular winter mail route might soon be established between St. Michael and the Outside. Other than that, the gold stampede was so much distant thunder. But then on October 5, Albert Kittilsen arrived at the Cape by umiak, carrying orders from Washington to purchase reindeer for the relief of the miners in the Yukon.

Tom Lopp was taken aback. Three years had passed since the herd had been established at Cape Prince of Wales, and still native herders were forbidden to slaughter reindeer, even though many in the village were chronically short of food. Lopp had held his tongue earlier in the year when he had learned of the decision to drive the Teller herd to Unalakleet to benefit an enlarged colony of Lapp herders. But this was another matter entirely. Here came Kittilsen, requesting deer to freight provisions to the greedy miners of the Klondike.

For the moment, at least, Lopp had the upper hand. Kittilsen could not demand; he could only request. The Cape herd belonged not to the government but to the American Missionary Association—and to the natives who had husbanded it so diligently. When Kittilsen offered $15 a head, the highest price authorized by the government, Lopp turned him down, and Kittilsen had to return to Port Clarence empty-handed.

The events of the coming winter would ultimately obscure Lopp's act of stubbornness, but his initial decision to stand up to Kittilsen— and by extension, the U.S. government—was nonetheless a measure of how far he had diverged from the philosophy of his superiors. In the years to come, his advocacy of native ownership and industry would become increasingly more strident and controversial. Eventually his outspokenness would cost him his job.

In October 1897, however, he had little time to dwell on matters so far in the future. On the thirteenth, a week after Dr. Kittilsen had departed, Ellen gave birth to Katharine Kittredge Lopp, named for her grandmother. "She weighs a little more than seven pounds," Ellen reported merrily. "Lucy found the scales in the bedroom and asked if Papa had 'scaled the baby.' She offered to make a dress for it and said she would carry it in her [atigi] on her back the way she had been carrying her puppy that day."

In typical fashion, Ellen made light of the ordeal of childbirth. In the same letter in which she noted the latest addition to the family, she seemed more concerned with the paucity of food among the natives.

In passing, her letter also mentioned that one of the miners who had traveled through Port Clarence had tried to tempt Tom into filing a claim on a gold mine. Ellen reported that Tom had declined on the grounds that he was too busy with school and getting ready for winter. "So he won't go even if he wanted to." Tom's disposition toward gold miners and gold mining required no further elaboration.

Ellen wrote one more letter that fall, which she knew was unlikely to be delivered until the following year. "I am writing with the baby in my lap and the three others close," she jotted on November 18. "The people are getting drunk a good deal, but I haven't seen any drink. . . . We didn't get an addition to our house. I am sorry, as I wanted a room where the Natives who wanted to keep Sunday could spend Sunday afternoon singing, reading and looking at pictures, and where we could let them wash their clothes and take baths."

She made one last observation: "No ships came in this fall. The lights of one were seen one night, and another light was seen from the Diomedes. A third ship anchored at East Cape [Siberia]. That is all we have known of, so perhaps some were frozen in or wrecked up north."

Another two months would pass before she learned just how correct she had been.

· · ·

While the Lopps watched for ships in the Bering Strait, Albert Kittilsen was still faced with the formidable task of rounding up "all of the available reindeer" and driving them to St. Michael. On October 25, Kittilsen set out for Cape Rodney, near the mouth of the Sinuk River, where Charlie Antisarlook kept his herd. Antisarlook had proven to be a capable enough reindeer man, with only intermittent assistance from Lapp herders. During the winter of 1895–1896, he had lost a dozen deer in a snow slide, but he had come through with nearly two hundred animals. The following winter he had kept his herd close to the coast, where reindeer moss was less abundant. Like the rest of the

Eskimo herders, Antisarlook was forbidden to kill reindeer for food, and so he and his herders were obliged to catch fish to stay alive, making it hard to keep track of the deer. Still, his herd had survived and grown, and when Kittilsen arrived at Cape Rodney, he was able to claim 120 deer—three years ahead of the deadline specified in the original agreement between Antisarlook and the government—which he then drove back to Port Clarence to merge with the main herd.

Two weeks after returning to the Teller station, Kittilsen was off again, this time to Cape Prince of Wales, where he at last struck an agreement with Tom Lopp, who allowed fifty-two sled deer to be taken from the mission herd with the understanding that Kittilsen would secure fair payment from the government. To show his earnestness—and perhaps his misgivings—Lopp sent along Keok, one of his native apprentices, to look out for the interests of the Cape herd and herders.

. . .

After another month of preparation, Kittilsen was finally ready to start. The plan was to drive the assembled herd, which now totaled more than five hundred deer, as far as Unalakleet, where the new station was to be built, and from there deliver the required sled deer to the Army at St. Michael, farther down the coast of Norton Sound. Seventeen Lapp and Eskimo herders, including their wives and children, left Teller station on December 16. The caravan consisted of forty sleds.

The trip went smoothly at first, and by Christmas they had completed nearly half of the 350-mile trek. But then in early January the herd bogged down in deep snow east of Golovnin Bay. To push farther would have exhausted the deer, which had trouble pawing through the drifts to the moss below. Prudently Kittilsen turned the herd back toward Golovnin Bay, where the grazing was better. Assigning two men to accompany the reindeer, Kittilsen and the rest of the herders pitched camp at the foot of the Kwiktalik Mountains and waited for conditions to improve.

On the evening of January 10, the camp was aroused by the arrival of three dogsleds, led through the drifts by two deerskin-clad men on snowshoes. Once the dogs quit barking and the strangers' hoods were thrown back, Kittilsen recognized Lieutenant David Jarvis and Dr. Samuel Call of the Revenue Cutter Service. He had last seen them aboard the *Bear* when it had stopped at Port Clarence in September, on its way south for the winter.

The surprise of encountering two seafaring men in the snowbound tundra of eastern Norton Sound in the dead of January was extraordinary enough. But Kittilsen's astonishment only increased when Jarvis explained that he was now the commanding officer of the Overland Relief Expedition, bound for Point Barrow to rescue two hundred or so whalers trapped in the ice with not enough supplies to last the winter.

Clutching mugs of steaming coffee, Jarvis and Call described their overland journey, beginning a month earlier five hundred miles to the south at Cape Vancouver, where they had left the *Bear*. The most startling revelation came when Jarvis dug into his pack and handed Kittilsen orders from Lieutenant Colonel Randall at St. Michael, directing the reindeer superintendent to turn over whatever deer Jarvis might need to get him as far north as Cape Prince of Wales, where the relief expedition then expected to press Tom Lopp and his herd into service for the final push to Point Barrow.

Kittilsen was doubtful at first. "I asked if [Jarvis] had any instructions for me from Washington," he recalled. "He thought so, but was unable to find any." In the end Kittilsen agreed to offer his own services as well as his deer. Without the former, the latter would do Jarvis and Call little good. "After considering the matter I told them that it was useless to give them deer," Kittilsen explained, "because they would be unable to do anything with them, but that we would take them to Port Clarence."

Two days later, Kittilsen, Jarvis, and Call, accompanied by one of the Lapps and the Eskimo herder Keok, set off for Port Clarence on reindeer sleds, leaving the rest to mind the herd. Handling harnessed reindeer, as Kittilsen warned, was an art not easily mastered. In the coming days, it was the rescuers who needed rescuing more than once. Although Jarvis and Call had already traveled many miles, Point Barrow still seemed frightfully far away. The imperiled whalers would have to wait their turn.

## [ 8 ]

# Floe Monsters

WHILE IT IS TRUE that the Overland Relief Expedition might never have been dared if Sheldon Jackson had not pushed for the importation of reindeer and trumpeted their usefulness, the fact that the expedition was necessary at all can be pinned on one distinct and, but for the circumstances, benign expression of Gilded Age vanity: the corset—more specifically, corset stays, so essential in defining the female form in an era of Gibson girls and six-course suppers. Most often they were made of baleen, the frond-like bones that hang by the hundreds in the cavernous mouths of bowhead whales, which employ them in sieving the extraordinary bounty of nutritious crustacea that thicken the shallow waters of the Chukchi and Beaufort seas.

Baleen, like Ahab's ivory prosthesis, was the leg propping up an American whaling industry that had flourished so grandly in the eighteenth and nineteenth centuries but now was beginning to falter. Since the drilling of the first petroleum well in Pennsylvania in 1859, the price of whale oil had dropped steadily; a barrel of oil in 1897 was worth one quarter of what it had commanded at the end of the Civil War. And as demand for whale oil had fallen, so had supply. During the heyday of whaling, from the 1830s to the 1860s, American ships had slain more than a quarter million whales, decimating the global fishery. To stand any chance of turning a profit, whalers were obliged to voyage even farther and stay at sea longer. Such was the downward spiral of ecology and economy that drew the fleet through the icy jaws of the Bering Strait into the redoubt of the western Arctic.

The first (non-native) vessel to chase whales north of the strait was the *Superior*, captained by Thomas Roys, in the summer of 1848. The whales he encountered were different from any he had hunted before, blue-black in color with a distinctive curve to the upper jaw, like the bend of an archer's bow. Roys guessed correctly that these were Greenland whales, a species already hunted in the northern Atlantic. He was delighted by the richness of their oil and baleen. The largest of these bowheads, as *Balaena mysticetus* would soon be known, were more than fifty feet long and weighed as much as fifty tons. The two-foot-thick rind of blubber rendered from a single bowhead boiled down to 120 barrels of oil. And while Herman Melville had been impressed by the mouth of the right whale—with its "scimetar-shaped slats" of whalebone, fringed with "loose hairy fibers . . . like the top-knot on some old Potowattamie sachem's head"—the author of *Moby-Dick* had never peered inside anything so marvelous as the maw of a bowhead, which holds more bone than any other species. Many of its six hundred or so wands of baleen are twelve feet long; a good-sized adult yields more than three thousand pounds of whalebone.

In a month-long hunt, the crew of the *Superior* killed eleven whales, filling its hold with sixteen hundred barrels of oil and fifteen tons of baleen. Roys arrived triumphantly in Hawaii, tantalizing his audience with reports of pleasant weather in the Arctic and an ocean remarkably free of ice.

His description of an open polar sea struck a familiar chord. More than a few of Roys's contemporaries in nautical and scientific circles had speculated that the North Pole was not frozen but in fact quite

"Mediterranean," once a vessel got past the impasse of ice that ringed the upper latitudes of the earth. (A similar theory applied to the South Pole.) It was postulated that this open polar sea could be reached via "thermometric gateways"—warm currents that in the Pacific flowed north through the Bering Strait and in the Atlantic past Greenland. (More than a few who should have known better still clung to the notion of a hollow pole, wherein was secreted the Garden of Eden. The aurora borealis was explained as the glow of forest fires burning at the center of the earth. And so on.)

Roys did not claim to have found the Northwest Passage, much less the hollow pole, but he was delighted to report that the whales in the northern reaches of the Bering Sea were not only plentiful but also "quite tame." Furthermore, he pointed out that at such extreme latitudes, ships could hunt around the clock. The following summer, fifty whalers followed in the *Superior*'s wake; a year after that the fleet was nearly three times larger.

In a few short years, however, productivity declined dramatically. By 1853, with 160 ships cruising the Bering Sea, the average yield was less than six hundred barrels. By 1856, whalers had killed seven thousand bowheads, roughly a third of the estimated population, and the survivors had become more cagey, keeping close to the pack ice, where, as Melville had written, "in a charmed circle of everlasting December, [they] bid defiance to all pursuit of men." Once again, the ante was raised: To catch more whales, captains had to push still farther north.

Slowly, through trial and error and also by listening to native hunters, Yankee whalers began to gain a better understanding of the migratory patterns of the bowhead. Pods of bowhead spend each winter in the relatively open water of the Siberian coast. In spring, as the polar ice pack begins to break up, they make their way northeastward through the Bering Strait. By early summer the ice pack recedes—but only slightly and never reliably—creating ephemeral corridors of open water, known as leads, along the northern shore of Alaska. Hugging the coastline, the bowhead thread a labyrinth of broken ice to spend the summer in the Beaufort Sea, east of Point Barrow. Come fall, they reverse their course, lingering in the Chukchi Sea above Siberia until the ice pack drives them south again.

To follow the bowhead, the whalers of the Arctic fleet had to run the same gauntlet, first rendezvousing at Port Clarence, then feeling their way north as early as conditions would allow, hunting madly for as long as they dared, and sprinting home before winter slammed the lid. All told, the season was frustratingly short. Ships from New England took eight months just getting to the whaling grounds of the northern Pacific; by the 1880s most of the Arctic whalers sensibly had begun homeporting in San Francisco. But even then whalers could figure on spending no more than three months in the Bering Sea and points north, and those that did were brave, foolish, desperate, or lucky—often all of these at once. "With the opening of navigation in high latitudes . . . came increased perils," Alexander Starbuck noted in his benchmark *History of the American Whale Fishery.* "Not sufficient were the dangers from their gigantic prey, or furious gales, or the losing sight of the ships; to these must be added the risk of being ground between two mighty icebergs, in being caught in some field of ice and being forced ashore, of having the stout timbers of their vessel pierced by the glittering spear of some stray berg as it was driven by the force of polar currents. . . . Yet the temptation to incur many risks for the sake of rapidly filling the ship is too great to be withstood."

Two things emboldened the Arctic whalers at the close of the nineteenth century. One was the technological advantage of steam power. Traditionally whaling ships were never in a hurry. They were built to remain at sea for years, and in hunting whales, capacity, not quickness, was of the essence. In the Arctic, though, the rules changed. Ships needed to be able to maneuver among the ice floes and, in many instances, through them. Along shallow coastlines, in the fierce storms and unkind currents of the Arctic, with ice liable to envelop, bludgeon, and crush anything in its path at any time, sails could not be counted on. Steam power, on the other hand, gave ships a fighting chance. Most, but not all, of the ships that frequented the Arctic in the 1880s and 1890s—whalers, traders, revenue cutters—employed a combination of sail and steam, unfurling the former to conserve coal but pouring on the latter when necessity demanded. Then again, steam also stoked the hubris that thrust ships into predicaments that no means of propulsion could undo.

The other factor that kept whalers coming back to the Arctic was the price of baleen. Between the Civil War and 1890, the price of whalebone more than tripled. Until the invention of spring steel in the early 1900s, manufacturers could find no suitable substitute for supple, lightweight baleen. It was used for buggy whips, umbrellas, fishing rods, but most of all for corsets. Just as the vogue for beaver hats in the early nineteenth century had incited trappers to explore the wilderness of the American West, the appetite for slimness created its own grail.

Ellen Lopp's anxieties notwithstanding, the focus of femininity was not limited to the proper billow of sleeves. The waist was what mattered most, and the way to accentuate it was by means of a whalebone corset, regardless of the hardship. "It was usual for ladies who received in the evenings to wear . . . a close-fitting armour of whale-boned silk," Edith Wharton noted in her mordant novel of the era, *The Age of Innocence*. A more apt designation for the period might have been the Age of Whalebone.

Eventually the demand for whalebone became so great and the price of whale oil so dismal that many ships ceased the laborious and exceedingly messy chore of "trying out" whale blubber into oil, and they began harvesting baleen exclusively. (When the polar explorer Roald Amundsen learned that bowheads were killed solely to make corset stays, he fumed, "I would vote for a fashion reform.") Whalebone was much easier to clean and store, which had great appeal to the growing number of Arctic whalers who either hunted from semi-permanent shore stations or wintered their ships in the ice in order to eliminate long, annual journeys to and from the Arctic. By the late 1880s, shore-whaling stations had been established at Point Hope and Point Barrow. (The Lopps had been to the Point Hope stations in 1893 when they visited John Driggs at the Episcopal mission.)

Shore whaling ensured that whalers were on hand when the bowhead migrated along the coastal leads during the spring and fall. A shore station was also cheaper to operate than a whaling ship. For manpower, the stations hired natives, the best shore whalers in the world, who worked for next to nothing. By 1890, twenty white whalers and traders were living at Point Barrow, employing fifty umiak crews of Eskimos. Although there were many years when the pack ice left Point Barrow very late or closed in far too early, John W. Kelly, proprietor of the Pacific Steam Whaling Company's station, and Charles Brower, of the Cape Smythe Whaling Company, were invariably in position to maximize their chances, and they prospered accordingly.

The first steam whalers to winter over in the Beaufort Sea were the *Grampus* and the *Mary D. Hume* in 1890–1891. (In fairness, two small sailing ships, the *Spy* and *Nicoline*, had survived the previous winter at Point Barrow.) In more than eight hundred miles of coastline between Marryat Inlet at Point Hope and the mouth of Canada's Mackenzie River, there are any number of lagoons, bights, spits, and shoals that provide a nominal buffer from the onslaught of the polar ice pack. But none is a sure bet; sooner or later all are overrun by massive hummocks of ice, some forty feet high, their titanic force capable of reducing the stoutest ship to splinters. The one reliable exception is Pauline Cove on tiny Herschel Island, four hundred miles east of Point Barrow, just east of the Canadian boundary. Herschel Island also has the good grace to sit directly in the path of the bowhead migration. Here the *Grampus* and *Mary D. Hume* installed roofs over their decks, banked their sides with snow as insulation, and passed the winter by burning driftwood, trading for caribou meat with the natives, and enduring blizzards, snowblindness, frostbite, melancholia, and forty-four consecutive days without a glimpse of the sun. The ice finally turned them loose on July 10, and over the next two months they killed twenty-seven whales. Their daring experiment had paid off royally.

Yet there was a huge difference between intentionally tucking oneself into winter harbor and being "nipped," or trapped, in the open ocean. Ships that traveled in polar latitudes were usually strengthened with double-thick bottoms. But no amount of reinforcement could repulse Arctic ice when it chose to take a ship in its clutches. Perhaps the most vivid account of being captured by ice while at sea is provided by Elisha Kent Kane, who in 1850 was aboard the *Advance*, one of a long parade of ships to go looking for Sir John Franklin, the famously doomed Northwest Passage explorer. There was nothing at all monolithic about pack ice, Kane observed, and rarely was it at rest. He described gargantuan "floe-monsters" that collided with the combined force of "tempest, explosion, and earthquake," heaving "[t]ables of white marble" into the air "as if by invisible machinery." Equally arresting to Kane were the "voices of the ice." By turns, he was tormented by the humming of bees, the whining of puppies, the grating of nutmeg, or more ominously, the racket of "musket fire in an empty town."

When the *Advance* was finally nipped, Kane envisioned the grip of a cold-blooded serpent:

> The water-lane of yesterday is covered by four-inch ice; the floes at its margin more than three feet thick. These have been closing for some time by a sliding, grinding movement, one upon the other; but every now and then coming together more directly, the thinner ice clattering between them, and marking their new outline with hummock ridges. They have been fairly in contact for the last hour; we feel their pressure extending to us through the elas-

Tom Lopp

Ellen Lopp

The Lopp family, Seattle, 1902. Standing, from left: Lucy, Dwight, Katherine. Seated, from left: Ellen, Weyana, Irene, Tom, Sarah

Harrison Thornton

Neda Thornton

The mission house, Cape Prince of Wales, built 1892; site of Thornton murder, 1893; village and mission school in distance

The Lopps' second house, built 1896, with natives in foreground

Villagers with umiak, Cape Prince of Wales, 1895

Sheldon Jackson (right) with
Lapp reindeer herders

Captain Michael Healy aboard
the *Bear*

The U.S. revenue cutter *Bear* with dogsleds in foreground

Mary and Charlie Antisarlook with adopted children

The Five Quints at 1915 reunion, 17 years after the Overland Relief Expedition. From left: Kivyearzruk, Keok, Tautuk, Sokweena, Ootenna

Reindeer being loaded aboard
the *Bear*

From left: Ellsworth Bertholf,
Samuel Call, and David Jarvis

Reindeer with revenue cutter *Bear* off shore

Whaling ships icebound at Point Barrow, 1898

Freeing ships from ice, Point Barrow, 1898

Tom Gordon, Fred Hopson,
and Charlie Brower, Point
Barrow, 1898

Edward Avery McIlhenny, 1897

Stranded whalers and bunkhouse, Point Barrow, 1898

tic floe in which we are cradled. There is a quivering, vibratory hum about the timbers of the brig, and every now and then a harsh rubbing creak along her sides, like waxed cork on a mahogany table. The hummocks are driven to within four feet of our [deck], and stand there looming fourteen feet high through the darkness. It has been an horrible commotion so far, with one wild, booming, agonized note, made up of a thousand discords; and now comes the deep stillness after it, the mysterious ice-pulse, as if the energies were gathering for another strife.

Kane's ship survived the grip of the pack ice, but hundreds of others did not. Rarely did a year pass without a ship being lost somewhere in the Arctic. The worst by far was 1871. Forty whaling ships sailed through the Bering Strait that summer in search of bowhead. The pack ice was especially late in receding, and the fleet did not reach the whaling grounds paralleling Alaska's northern coast until the first week of August, and then only barely. Within three weeks, an unkind shift in the wind hurled the pack ice down upon them. The nearest harbor was hundreds of miles distant (Pauline Cove was unknown and beyond reach), and by September 12, twenty-seven ships were locked in the ice and being driven inexorably toward shore. Five had already been crushed. In the end, the largest disaster in Arctic whaling history was also the largest rescue, for while thirty-two ships were abandoned, not a single crewman was lost. More than twelve hundred souls, including three women and five children, were taken aboard the ships that had narrowly avoided being nipped, and all made it to safety.

Never again would so many whalers test the Arctic in a single season. But still they came. Five years later, a fleet of twenty ships headed north. Two were lost even before reaching the whaling grounds. In mid-August, a northeast wind pushed the ice pack southward, forcing fourteen of the remaining eighteen ships to seek refuge in the tenuous lee of Point Barrow, a slim finger of sand and gravel that seems mostly just to taunt the furies of the North Pole. One by one, as each ship made a run to open water, it was seized by the ice; ten never broke free. Unlike the wholesale rescue of 1871, this time fifty or so crewmen remained on board the icebound ships, electing to winter over as best they could in order to claim salvage rights. When the first whalers arrived at Point Barrow the following summer, they found only one ship, the *Clara Bell*, intact, and only two of the fifty crewmen had survived. That same season, two more ships sank at Point Barrow.

. . .

Given the vicissitudes of Arctic whaling, it is no wonder that ships that pursued the bowhead did not employ the cream of America's workforce. Even in the glory years of sail, as Richard Henry Dana observed firsthand, life and labor aboard ship were "the worst part of a dog's life." Men went whaling because they were drunkards, scofflaws, runaways, degenerates, paupers, or, in the case of the Hawaiians, Cape Verde islanders, and Negroes, because they had no better prospects. Melville's Ishmael, it should be remembered, embarked on the *Pequod* not as a lark but to flee the "damp, drizzly November" that gripped his soul.

By the latter half of the nineteenth century, there were too many good reasons *not* to go whaling. The gold and silver strikes of the American West provided sure romance, if not always tangible treasure. The Homestead Act offered every man a swatch of the American Dream, and the industrial boom that accelerated after the Civil War drew millions to the cities and their factories, where conditions were far from ideal but leagues better than the wretched particulars of Arctic whaling.

Whaling anywhere was rough. Crews worked not for salaries, but for a percentage of the catch, called a lay, which was always portioned in the most niggardly of fractions—1/179$^{th}$, for instance. If the ship did not fill its hold with bone and oil, or it came home "clean," without anything at all, which was often the case, a crewman might not make a cent. Worse, necessities acquired from the ship's stores—wool socks, a suit of foul-weather gear—were charged against a crewman's lay, a form of gouging that guaranteed that many whaling men arrived home in San Francisco at the end of an eight-month voyage in debt, leaving them little choice but to sign up for yet another voyage.

During their time at sea, whalers lived in a cramped, rank-smelling forecastle, where they slept on a straw mattress, known unaffectionately as a "donkey's breakfast," and nourished themselves on wormy hardtack and salted meat, dourly called "horse." This for the honor and reward of chasing whales through the icy polar sea in open whaleboats too easily broached by ice, which they endeavored desperately to avoid, or whales, which they recklessly sought to harpoon. Butchering a fifty-ton whale—flaying and boiling the blubber and cleaning the baleen—was a more vile job than any to be found in sweatshop or packing plant—except that in place of sweat, crews of whaling ships were alternately soaked to the skin in thirty-degree salt water or begrimed by the ripe oil and smoke of the bowhead whose massive corpse they slaved to mince and render. Often they slept in the same clothes for weeks on end.

Discipline aboard whaling ships was notoriously despotic and brutal. Not surprisingly, the rate of desertion among whaling crews was high. After months of confinement on a whaling ship, the pristine beaches of Hawaii or the fleshpots of the East Indies presented far too great a temptation. Yet it was one thing to jump ship in a tropical clime, where beachcombers could live off the land, betake of the carnal pleasures, and, when the time came, find passage on any number of ships, most of which were sufficiently shorthanded not to ask questions. What was more astonishing was that men deserted even in the Arctic—the most scathing commentary of all on the cruel conditions aboard Arctic ships and the misery of those who manned them.

To leave a whaling ship in the Arctic was less an act of courage than of foolhardiness. Natives were famously hospitable toward lost and hungry travelers, but a winter in an Eskimo dwelling, living on raw seal and ripe blubber, when and if available, was a far cry from palm huts, grass-skirted natives, and sweet coconut milk. Tom Lopp and Harrison Thornton found nothing to admire in the three deserters who appeared at Cape Prince of Wales during their first summer at the mission. To Thornton especially, they were worse than worthless, and he made it known that future deserters who turned up at the Cape would not be received with Christian charity. No such charity was extended to two whalers who stupidly deserted the *Mary D. Hume* and *Grampus* during their first winter at Herschel Island. Their aim was to make their way overland by dogsled to the goldfields of the Yukon. A day later they were tracked to a native house, where two of the four were too frozen to travel farther. Escorted back to the ships at Pauline Cove, they were lashed and put in irons; one suffered the additional punishment of having frostbitten toes amputated with a butcher knife. You could run in the Arctic, but you could not run far.

Tom Lopp and Harrison Thornton were not the only missionaries with a low opinion of whalers. While missionaries frequently extended their ministry to the souls of sailors, most of the time whalers and missionaries worked at cross-purposes. "There is about as much affinity between them as between oil and water," Toleef Brevig, the Lutheran minister at Port Clarence, declared. The whalers were to blame for supplying alcohol to natives and for teaching them how to distill their own. Native women who exchanged sexual favors for flour, fabric, or sewing needles were infected with venereal disease in the bargain. Gilbert Borden, superintendent of the government station at Point Barrow, vouched that by 1889 half of the natives at Point Barrow were infected.

No missionary was more critical of whalers than Leander Stevenson, who had come north in 1890 on the same ship as Lopp, Thornton, and John Driggs. Stevenson, with his dark eyes and Old Testament beard, was not one to turn the other cheek. He possessed

"the right combination of sincerity and horse sense," one of his admir-
ers observed, and he expected nothing less than hard work and good
deeds from his fellow man. After his first year at Point Barrow, Stevenson composed a series of blistering philippics against certain whalers
and traders at Point Barrow who were corrupting the local Eskimos:
"They . . . introduced rum, started them by this baleful influence to
degrade themselves, and, when their supplies of trade were exhausted[,] gave them the idea by direct instruction to trade the virtues of
their women to gain more rum to satisfy the cravings of the false
appetite now created; and after all these deeds of infamy and shame[,]
they have the impudence to call these people a set of devils. If they be
devils, who made them such?"

To Stevenson, the shameless hypocrisy of the whites was almost
more galling than their actions. "Some of these same persons who per-
petrate such outrages, as soon as they return to civilization and their
families, frequent with long and doleful countenance the church, the
prayer-meeting, the Sunday-School . . . anxious to jump up and testi-
fy how much they have suffered among the heathen . . . and gain the
sympathy and applause of men. A good question, and one directly to
the point, would be to ask [them], 'How long have you had venereal
disease, and how many have you inoculated with it . . . ?'" The worst
offenders, Stevenson emphasized, were not the crew members of the
whaling and trading ships, as base as they might be, but rather the
ships' officers. "The typical whaling Captain," he fumed, "is a tripartite
composed of hog, villain, and supreme selfishness."

In this last, he was referring especially to Gilbert Borden. In the
summer of 1888, five more ships had been lost near Point Barrow. The
following January, after years of constant pressure by owners, mer-
chants, and the families of whalers, Congress finally appropriated
$15,000 to establish a refuge station there. Erected in August 1889, the
station was thirty by forty-eight feet, with fifty bunks and a well-
stocked storeroom; an adjoining shed could hold twenty tons of coal.

Borden was chosen as superintendent because of his previous experience as a whaling captain in Hudson Bay and his pull with influential Republicans. He turned out to be a self-righteous reprobate who got along with neither whites nor Eskimos. "We must remember the Esquimaux are a peculiar people," he wrote to his hometown paper, "harmless more like beasts of prey, living entirely on other beasts." To attempt to educate or Christianize such a primitive race was a waste of time and resources, he insisted—a direct slap at Stevenson, who had dedicated his life to achieving just that. When the revenue cutter *Bear* delivered Stevenson to Point Barrow in 1890, Captain Healy had given him the title of assistant superintendent of the refuge station, a formality that allowed Stevenson to live and teach school at the station until the time when a proper school and mission house could be built. (Heavy ice prevented delivery of lumber the following year; the load was dropped at Cape Prince of Wales and became the mission house in which Thornton was murdered. A separate school/mission house was finally completed at Point Barrow in 1895.) Stevenson and Borden were at each other's throats almost immediately.

Stevenson was a fierce nemesis, but in the end Borden's undoing was his own. In the fall of 1890, shortly after Stevenson's arrival, Borden hatched a scheme with the captain of the schooner *Silver Wave* whereby they would declare the ship a loss—a determination that, according to admiralty law, allowed them to purchase it and its contents as salvage for a nominal fee. In fact, the *Silver Wave* had not been wrecked at all; it had merely run aground, and apparently not ruinously so, in the Sea Horse Islands, sixty miles southwest of Point Barrow. Regrettably for Borden, there were too many witnesses and too few accomplices to the *Silver Wave* fraud, and when the *Bear* was finally able to reach Point Barrow in 1892—heavy ice had prevented the cutter's appearance in 1891—a livid Captain Healy wasted no time in firing Borden, whom he called "an old scoundrel," and naming Stevenson interim superintendent of the station.

The refuge station carried on for another four years, briefly under Stevenson and then under another superintendent, Edward Akin. Doubtless its existence brought peace of mind to the dozens of ships that whaled and traded each summer in the Beaufort Sea and wintered at Herschel Island, but from the time the station opened in 1889 until the winter of 1896, only once did it actually serve its purpose of providing refuge to stranded whalers, and then just for a few days. By 1896, the U.S. Revenue Cutter Service had concluded that the station was a waste of resources and recommended that it be closed, an opinion seconded by Josiah Knowles, manager of the Pacific Steam Whaling Company of San Francisco, whose ships dominated the Arctic whaling fleet. Ironically, Knowles was one of the station's original proponents. "I never could see the real benefit that it would be to any of the whaling fleet to have a station there, as ships are seldom lost in that vicinity," he now pronounced. "There has never been a wreck there [Point Barrow] to my knowledge when the station would have been of any use . . . and should a wreck occur in that locality there are other [shore-whaling and trading] stations that would provide for the crews."

Knowles's business instincts were sharper than his memory. In the spring of 1896, the government declared the refuge station closed (news of the decision would not reach Point Barrow until midsummer), and the facility was put up for auction. The Pacific Steam Whaling Company outbid Charles Brower's partners, shrewdly purchasing the station and its assets for $4,000—a steal, although not quite in the same sense as Gilbert Borden's shady acquisition of the *Silver Wave*.

. . .

Josiah Knowles died not long after purchasing the refuge station, and the Pacific Steam Whaling Company decided to close its shore-whaling operation at Point Barrow. The following summer, Leander Stevenson, who had visited his wife and children only once in seven years, departed on the *Bear* for a long-anticipated sabbatical in Ohio. Steven-

son's position as missionary and teacher was filled by a recent graduate of the New York Homeopathic Medical College, twenty-three-
year-old Dr. H. Richmond Marsh, and his bride of nine months, Mary.
Arriving a day ahead of the Marshes were three more Arctic newcomers: twenty-five-year-old Edward Avery McIlhenny and his two assistants, Norman Buxton and Will Snyder. Ned McIlhenny was an avid
sportsman and amateur naturalist who had grown up on a plantation
in New Iberia, Louisiana, where his family was engaged in the manufacture of a popular and piquant condiment called Tabasco sauce. A
college dropout, McIlhenny carried a letter from the University of
Pennsylvania, agreeing to purchase any zoological or ethnological
specimens he happened to collect in the Arctic. Toward this end, he
had leased the vacant refuge station for one year.

Topping this cast of characters was Charles Brower, who was
already a near-legendary figure in the Arctic. Brower had gone to sea
as a young boy and had seen most of the world by 1884, when, at the
age of twenty-one, he was put ashore at Corwin Bluff, a god-forsaken
stretch of the northern Alaska coast, east of Cape Lisburne. He and
three other men had been hired by the Pacific Steam Whaling Company to spend the winter trading and developing a seam of coal that
their employer hoped would simplify the task of refueling steam
whalers in the Arctic. The coal venture was a disappointment, but
Brower took to the Arctic as if it was his long-lost home. In 1886, the
Pacific Steam Whaling Company sent him to Point Barrow to man its
nascent shore-whaling operation.

Brower was tough and tempered from years of hard labor and harsher elements; above all, he was a keen student of native ways, especially
their approach to whaling. Whites possessed technological advantages
such as whale bombs and binoculars, but natives *knew* the bowhead.
Rather than dismiss Eskimo rituals and superstitions— always launching an umiak bow first or pouring fresh water on the snout of a dead
whale, for instance—Brower took them at face value and hired the

natives to hunt for him. Merging his own know-how with the ingrained methods of the Eskimos, Brower made a success of shore whaling at Point Barrow. By 1893, he had formed the Cape Smythe Whaling Company, with backing from a San Francisco furrier, H. Liebes & Company. He built his headquarters a half-mile from the Pacific Steam Whaling Company, beyond the Presbyterian mission, the refuge station, and Ukpiagvik, as the native village that burgeoned around the white settlement was called. For the next fifty years, Charlie Brower was the man to see in Point Barrow—"the Northernmost American." He was respected and trusted by whites and natives alike, and when trouble arose, he was the one they looked to for guidance and salvation. Never would his leadership and resources be in such great demand as in the summer of 1897 and the winter that followed.

. . .

In early July, Brower and several native employees loaded an umiak and set out for Icy Cape, hunting polar bears along the way. Brower was thirty-four and at the peak of his prowess. His thick moustache and burly physique suggested a bull walrus, but one with markedly greater agility. The previous year, his San Francisco partners had proposed establishing another shore-whaling station at Icy Cape, 160 miles to the southwest, and Brower was eager to learn what they had decided over the winter. Besides, he confessed, Point Barrow was in the midst of a "tobacco famine."

Arriving at Icy Cape at the end of July, the first ship they sighted was the *Navarch*, a three-masted, 140-foot-long steam whaler built in Maine. "I went aboard at once to get the latest news from her skipper," Brower would recall, "and for the first time met the man whose extraordinary behavior was to go down through the years as an ugly blot on my memories of the sea."

The skipper, Joseph Whiteside, was a veteran of the Arctic; on this trip he had brought along his wife. Whiteside informed Brower that plans for the whaling station at Icy Cape had been scrapped. When he invited Brower to ride back to Point Barrow aboard the ship, Brower declined at first but then agreed to send his umiak crew home on its own. It was a decision he would soon regret. Later that day, the whaler *Karluk* appeared, anchoring near the *Navarch*. Normally the two whalers would have engaged in a "gam"—a time-honored tradition in which the officers and sometimes the crews of ships at sea socialize back and forth. But the wives of the two captains "had some kind of grudge against each other," Brower revealed, so Captain Whiteside weighed anchor and moved the *Navarch* farther offshore, to the north of Blossom Shoals—"a very unwise thing to do," Brower noted.

The following morning, the *Navarch* was completely surrounded by drifting ice. "There was not even room to turn around in," Brower recalled in his memoir. "Each minute the ice seemed to pack harder around us. Then we drifted northwest until the [other whaling] ships were out of sight. . . . As we drifted the ice just [kept] pushing the *Navarch* further and further in the pack, until we could not see the edge." Over the next several days, wind and current carried the ship northward deeper into the pack ice, while "the ice crushed around the ship, listing her to first one side then the other." On the evening of August 3, Captain Whiteside issued the order to abandon ship. The goal was to haul the *Navarch*'s three whaling boats to the edge of the pack and from there try for the Alaskan coast, by now more than twenty-five miles away. When Brower offered his advice on what provisions to take and how to prepare the boats, Whiteside ignored him.

They hauled throughout the first night until the men were exhausted and the boats so battered by the ice that they were useless. "Then the Capt broke down crying like a kid," Brower reported. The only sensible option was to return to the ship, the masts of which were still in sight. "For a while every one stayed together, the men that were all right helping those that were all in." Leaving his wife in the care of a crewman, Captain Whiteside struggled along on his own, fortified by frequent nips from a bottle. In scrambling over a jumbled, twenty-foot-high pressure ridge, many of the crew became separated. Somehow all made it back to the ship eventually. The first to arrive startled two polar bears feasting on the carcasses of the hogs that had been shot and left behind when the ship had been evacuated. Captain Whiteside was asleep in his cabin when his wife was at last helped aboard.

A week later, estimating that the ice had carried the ship opposite Point Barrow, they abandoned it again. Brower had overseen the building of a small boat, stout, watertight, and light enough to be carried by two men. To protect it from the abrasive ice, he lashed polar-bear skins to the bottom. Whiteside asked Brower to forge ahead, "thinking [that] with my ice experience I could pick out a better road." The captain with a small contingent would bring up the rear, hauling the boat, much of the food, and the compass.

By the end of the day, Brower's vanguard had traveled near enough to the edge of the pack to recognize two ships in the distance, the *Bear* and the whaler *William Baylies*, presumably anchored in open water not more than six miles away. "I waited where the ice was safe for the men to come up," Brower related. "As they straggled in I kept asking where the old man and the boat was. None had seen him since leaving the ship. The last man was John Egan, the second Mate. He told me he had been with the boat, that after coming two miles from the *Navarch* the Capt ordered them to return to the ship taking the boat Food Compass and ammunition. . . . We were in a fix, trying every way we could think to make the ships see us to no use. In an hour it shut in foggy[;] then we did not know which way to turn, the ice was drifting fast to the north, the nearer we came abreast of the point [Barrow] the faster we traveled, the piece we were on separated from the pack and we were marooned. Every one was hungry, no one had anything to eat . . . [and] not more than two besides myself had taken spare boots with them." There were thirty-two in Brower's group; Mrs. Whiteside had stayed with her husband.

Any other white man besides Charlie Brower might have lost heart. But his years in the ice saved him. He knew that in the summer the pack ice north of Point Barrow typically splits in two, one part drifting westward, the other east-northeast. Not only could he decipher the ice, but he could also read the sky. In the Arctic (and Antarctic as well), a phenomenon known as "water sky" makes it possible to detect open water, often from a great distance, by the dark reflection it casts on the clouds above. On the morning after losing contact with White-side, Brower could see by the sky "that we were soon coming to the loose ice where the pack separated." Gathering the men, they made their way onto the heavy ice that would take them east. Brower tried to boost morale by explaining that if they worked their way to the southern edge of the eastward-drifting ice, they would likely be picked up by a passing ship. The *Navarch's* steward was not convinced; he wandered away from his shipmates and shot himself.

The next day two more men perished. "They just gave up," Brower stated. "It was just that they could travel no longer, so we left them." A day later the chief engineer lost his mind, then collapsed and died. The rest of the group trudged south, sharing a few pieces of hard bread and drinking from pools of freshwater that collected on the ice. "[S]leep was out of the question, there was no place except the wet cold ice to sit or lay on." Brower carried a rifle, but "there seemed nothing alive on the ice." Finally he shot a bird, a black jaeger, but it offered little more than skin and bones.

By continually studying the water sky, Brower realized that, as doggedly as they were traveling south, the ice pack was drifting toward the northeast at a faster rate. He saw no advantage in sharing this knowledge with the men, who were now no better than zombies. "On the fourth and fifth day we lost six more men," Brower related somber-ly. "Not being able to keep up some would cry out not to be left behind. This was heart rending, I never deserted a man in my life before, there was nothing we could do. . . . One of the Portuguese we left was a young man, strong and able when we left the ship. He played out by not wanting to leave his good clothes behind. When we left he had on three suits of clothing all new, these when they got wet were a weight to carry. He finally had to discard some of them. . . [but not before he was all in]. A day later we left him."

The suffering worsened. Egan, the second mate, went snowblind. The ship's blacksmith walked until the soles of his boots were worn through and the bottoms of his feet were raw. "When we had to leave him all he said was good bye boys I hope you get out, the gamest man I ever knew."

They had not eaten for days, other than to chew on their sealskin boots and deerskin pants and jackets. "For a while I thought I could not stand it," Brower admitted, "then the feeling . . . passed [and] day by day we just tightened our belts and kept going."

Finally, eight days after leaving the *Navarch* for the second time, they reached the southern edge of the pack ice. Beyond them lay open water and pieces of drifting ice as far as they could see. Here Brower made his most daring decision of all. "I talked them into trying my way, saying to them, if the wind changes all this loose ice will come back to the solid pack [and] we will be so far from the edge no one would ever see us even if we lived that long, and if we had to die, we could do it just as easy on the small ice as [on] the larger pack. I picked a fairly large cake to drift on. It was 60 feet long and nearly as wide."

Two of the men chose cakes of their own. "Before I could prevent them, one colored fellow from Martinique got on a small cake and shoved away from the pack, the piece was so small he had not gone far when it rolled over, and that was the last of him. The second engineer Scanl[a]n walked a short distance . . . to get up on a high piece of ice, trying to look off in the distance, the piece he was on was adrift, [and] when he started back, he tried to jump to the solid ice, he did not reach that far, I suppose he was so weak from hunger he could not keep afloat. . . . He sank and never came up again."

For the next four days they drifted. Brower's calculation had been correct. The wind and current took them steadily southeastward. "The further we got from the pack the faster we seemed to drift, passing all the other pieces, big and small." On the first night Brower shot a seal only to watch it sink before the men could retrieve it. The next morning, as the ice opened up even more, they were suddenly surrounded by hundreds of whales migrating toward the west. Killing one, much less catching it, was out of the question. That same day they spotted a steamer in the distance—the *Karluk*, they would later learn—but it was too far off to notice the shirt that they lashed to a pole and waved frantically.

The next day Brower shot two more seals; both sank. That evening the schooner *Rosario* passed within three miles of them. "Again we set our flag, it was no use they just kept sailing away from us. . . . This was too much for one of the men . . . Enos by name . . . went insane. If he had not been so weak we would have had some trouble with him. For a few hours he was raving trying to do all kinds of things, hardly able to stand, he finally settled in a stupor and never moved again."

On the morning of the fourth day on the ice cake, Brower spotted land, which he recognized as Cape Halkett, a bluff located one hundred miles to the southeast of Point Barrow. As they drifted to within two miles of shore, Brower looked in vain for the camps of natives whom he knew traveled the coast each summer. "Now there was no one around."

Salvation came at last. In the afternoon, the *Thrasher*, a steam bark owned by the Pacific Steam Whaling Company, passed through the narrow lead between Cape Halkett and the pack ice. A Siberian native at the masthead signaled to the watch below that he had spotted a group of walruses on the ice—an unusual occurrence, since walruses seldom appear east of Point Barrow. Through binoculars, the officer on deck quickly determined that the specks were something other than walruses. "Then the ship headed our way," Brower recollected, "and soon was alongside taking what remained of the crowd aboard." Of the thirty-two men who had accompanied Brower, sixteen were still alive. Several men later had frostbitten feet amputated, and one died on the way back to the States. "The others," Brower remarked, "just disappeared as sailors do anywhere."

As for Captain Whiteside and his wife, fortune had been perversely kind. After rudely leaving Brower and his group to plod ahead on their own, the captain and his contingent had returned to the *Navarch*. The next day they had set off again; eight men elected to remain on the ship. It took them only one day to reach open water, which they crossed easily in the small boat that Brower had helped to build. They were camped with plenty of food east of Point Barrow, where the *Bear* spotted their tents three days later. When Lieutenant Jarvis, who led the rescue party, asked the captain what had become of the rest of the *Navarch*'s men, Whiteside said that the others had been gone from the ship for four days and were presumably dead. And when Jarvis asked Whiteside why he had returned to the *Navarch* without notifying the rest of the crew of his decision, the captain reportedly turned away without uttering a word.

Whiteside left Alaska without ever having to account for his actions. Meanwhile, Charlie Brower's trials were far from over. Earlier in the summer, he and his native wife, Toctoo (also spelled Taktuk), had arranged for Leander Stevenson to take their two older daughters back to Ohio, where they could receive a better education. During the weeks that Brower was missing and presumed dead, Stevenson had been undecided whether to take the girls. Mercifully, he was spared further hand-wringing by Brower's stunning return, two days before Stevenson and the girls were to depart on the supply ship *Bonanza*. Yet for Brower it was a bittersweet homecoming, having to bid his daughters good-bye so soon after being reunited with them. Sadder still, his third daughter, the youngest, had taken ill during his absence. She died on the same day her two sisters left Point Barrow. "It was a

sorrowful home for some time," the normally stalwart Brower confessed, unhinged at last by a summer of horrendous suffering and
needless loss of life.

. . .

By now it was the end of August and the whaling season was coming
to an end. Twenty or so whaling ships had been in the Arctic that summer, a half-dozen of them intending to winter over at Herschel Island
or even farther east at Langton Bay in Canada. The whales had been
elusive and the ice unfavorable that year, as the *Navarch* had been the
first to discover. By the first week of September, several of the ships—
the steam barks *Orca*, *Belvedere*, *Jesse H. Freeman*, *Alexander*, and the
sailing schooner *Rosario*—were anchored off of Point Barrow, waiting
for the pack ice to ease so they could continue homeward. They
received no such reprieve. "The pack came last night and now the ice
is hard on the beach," Ned McIlhenny noted on the seventh.

The whaling captains understood that few ships had ever remained
so far north so late and made it out before winter. Already the small
patch of open water where the ships were anchored had begun to solid-
ify—first thickening into a scum the texture of aspic, known as grease
ice; then clotting into an undulating terrazzo of shield-shaped slabs,
called pancake ice; and finally setting up as a continuous frozen sheet,
like troweled plaster. "Much young ice," the *Orca*'s logbook recorded on
the eleventh. "Ice making fast," echoed the *Belvedere* that same day.

As dangerous as this development was, it was nothing compared
with what would happen if the ships could not break free. Pack ice
from offshore, built up over years, has a nasty habit of buckling the
weaker shorebound ice—and anything in its grasp—with incalculable
ferocity. As had been grimly proven in 1871 and 1876, the prospects for
any ship anchored here were stark indeed. "The ice is still hard on
shore," McIlhenny recorded on the thirteenth, "and it begins to look
doubtful if they will get out."

Of the five ships, the *Alexander* had positioned itself the farthest west, protected for the moment behind a ridge of ice that had broken off from the pack sometime earlier and grounded close to shore. Its captain, Benjamin Tilton, recognized that even if he were able to get free, other ships would not be so lucky. Already the Pacific Steam Whaling Company's supply ship *Jeanie* was overdue on its return from Herschel Island. Fearing the worst, Tilton ordered all the provisions he could spare to be landed at Brower's whaling station, and on September 14 he began to fight his way out of the ice. For eighteen hours the *Alexander* rammed the ice repeatedly at full steam. "Back and forth we went," chief engineer Michael McKinnon described, "and every succeeding crash seemed to us down in the engine-room as though it would be our last. It did not seem possible that wood and iron could stand the strain much longer." Finally, miraculously, the *Alexander* broke free, only to be confronted by miles of quickly forming ice. "I can tell you when we reached Sea Horse Island and saw open water before us we were a happy set of men," McKinnon confessed.

All the while, the *Orca, Belvedere, Freeman,* and *Rosario* hesitated. "I suppose they think the ice will go off from the shore, and they can get out without bucking," Norman Buxton, one of McIlhenny's assistants, speculated in his diary.

Jim Allen, an engineer aboard the *Freeman,* had his own opinion of why the four ships dawdled. "About September 10," he recalled (actually, it was the end of August), "we reached Point Barrow, where we found the steamers *Orca* and *Belvedere.* Every evening Captain Porter [of the *Freeman*], along with Captain Sherman of the *Orca,* would go aboard the *Belvedere* for a drinking party with the *Belvedere's* skipper, Captain Millard. This went on for several days. . . . The captains didn't pay much attention to the ice, or anything else during those parties. So when the ice was first seen and reported to them they didn't regard the situation as serious. They reckoned that when a nor'easter came it would drive the ice out again. A few days later came the northeast wind, and oh boy, she blew, believe me! But the ice never moved."

Nor did the four blithe and jolly captains.

The *Alexander* was the last of the Point Barrow ships to make it home from the top of Alaska that year. Having barely managed his own narrow escape, Captain Tilton steamed toward San Francisco to deliver the troubling news. Besides the *Orca, Freeman, Belvedere,* and *Rosario,* four other ships—the *Jeanie, Fearless, Newport,* and *Wanderer*—were still missing somewhere between Point Barrow and Herschel Island. Perhaps some or all of them might find their way to safety, but in the Arctic one had to be prepared for the worst. Even if the overdue ships, or just their crews, could somehow get as far as Point Barrow, there was no assurance that they would have enough food to last until relief ships could reach them the following summer—nine, perhaps ten, months hence. The closing of the refuge station a year earlier had made their chances even slimmer. And for those who contemplated a darker scenario, they needed look no further than the recent calamity of the *Navarch.*

# [ 9 ]

# Godspeed

ONCE NEWS OF THE icebound ships finally reached the States, it traveled fast, thanks in no small part to the alarums of the San Francisco *Call.* In the 1890s, the *Call* was in the midst of a feverish circulation war against two formidable rivals, the *Chronicle* and especially the *Examiner,* the latter owned by the brash multimillionaire William Randolph Hearst. Each day, the *Call* and *Examiner* endeavored anew to trump each other with provocative headlines and stories, the most bombastic pertaining to the Yukon gold strike or the incivilities of Spain toward Cuba and the Stars and Stripes. The *Call,* whose kettle was quite black, referred to the *Examiner* as "the Yellow Journal."

The *Call* seized on the plight of the Alaskan whalers as its own personal franchise. On October 30, while the *Examiner* ran an uncharacteristically tame one-column notice, "Whalers in Peril on the Crushing Ice," the *Call* draped a somber banner across its front page: "Crews of Whaling Vessels Ice-Bound in the Arctic Have No Hope of Rescue." Subsequent headlines in the *Call* were no less lugubrious: "Suffering and Death Will Be the Portion of Imprisoned Whalers". . . "With the

Setting of the Arctic Sun the Hopes of the Ice-Bound Whalers Grow Darker."

Since the *Call* had no way of knowing the actual plight of the whaling ships, it canvassed veterans of the Arctic for likely scenarios of tragedy and survival. "The Arctic is one of the shiftiest things in the world and it would not surprise me to hear that all the vessels had got out," ventured one ship captain, "nor again would I be surprised to hear that all of them that expected to get out had been crushed."

To many, the shuttering of the relief station at Point Barrow now seemed a crime. Then, too, there was no shortage of opinions on the feasibility of rescue. "An expedition should be dispatched by the Government without an hour's delay," exhorted Lieutenant George M. Stoney of the Navy, who had led several Arctic expeditions himself. He naturally urged that the heroic mission be assigned to his branch of the military, not the Revenue Cutter Service. "The distance is so great that the chances of rescuing them are decidedly against success, but the attempt should be made at once," Lieutenant Stoney intoned bravely.

Another whaling captain, unnamed by the *Call*, laid out a scheme that, plus or minus a few particulars, was essentially the first draft of the plan that would become the Overland Relief Expedition. "What I would suggest is this," the skipper proposed. "Let the Government instruct Colonel Randall [at St. Michael] to do the same for the whalers that he has to do if necessary for the miners in Dawson City. Then the revenue cutter Bear should be fitted out and Captain Healy placed in command of her. I'll gamble on it that he will take the cutter as far as Nunivak Island [350 miles south of St. Michael]. From there the relief party could reach the deer station on the north side of Norton Sound with the aid of dog teams. At Norton Sound, Charlie [Antisarlook], the Indian keeper, has about 200 deer, and they could be used to take the party to Cape Prince of Wales, where there is another herd of 350 or 400 deer. From that place to Point Hope would be the hardest part of the journey, but when Mr. Lopp made it for pleasure [in 1893] surely the rescue party could make it when human life is at stake."

The clamor of the *Call* turned the plight of the whalers into a cause célèbre. "Let the *Call* agitate the matter," declared whaling captain Lew Wallace, "and the Government will act speedily." And how the *Call* agitated! On November 6, the newspaper's proprietor, John D. Spreckels, sent a telegram to President William McKinley, sketching a plan for a relief expedition and pleading with the president to take swift action. "There are over 300 men with the whaling fleet in the Arctic Ocean now in imminent danger of starvation," Spreckels warned. "Their pitiable condition has aroused profound interest among our citizens, and must awaken sympathy all over the country." His telegram was hand-delivered by the *Call's* correspondent in Washington, who also gained an audience with secretary of the Navy John D. Long.

The following day, at the *Call's* urging, the San Francisco Chamber of Commerce and members of California's congressional delegation sent letters to McKinley and Long, exhorting the cabinet to make "every possible effort" on behalf of the icebound "American sailors." By beating the drum of patriotism, the *Call* and its adherents captured the broadest possible audience. "If we can afford to send relief to the starving natives of India and aid the struggling Cubans in their fight for liberty," a member of San Francisco's Merchant Exchange scolded, "we can surely afford to dispatch an expedition to the relief of 300 of our own people." To cover its bets, the *Call* let the White House know that it would "guarantee that the provisions [for the expedition] be furnished if the Government decides that it cannot use . . . public funds for the purpose."

The plight of the icebound ships struck a nerve in Washington, where the McKinley administration, still in its first year, was just beginning to find its voice. The U.S. battleship *Maine* would not explode in Havana harbor—killing 260 American sailors—for another four months, but already America's hotspurs, led by Theodore Roosevelt, assistant secretary of the Navy, and William Randolph Hearst, who owned the *New York Journal* as well as the *Examiner*, were urging the White House and Congress to flex their muscles in Cuba and around the globe generally. McKinley, who had won election without ever leaving his front porch in Canton, Ohio, was becoming sensitive to charges of indecision and passivity. Compared with any number of uncertainties facing the nation and the world—insurrections in Cuba and the Philippines, a boundary dispute in Venezuela, war in South Africa, the annexation of Hawaii—the matter of aiding stranded whalers was easy enough to address, if not to solve.

On November 8, a day after receiving the barrage of telegrams from the West Coast, President McKinley met with War secretary Russell A. Alger, Treasury secretary Lyman J. Gage, Navy secretary Long, and Captain-Commandant Charles F. Shoemaker of the Revenue Cutter Service to determine the best way to bring relief to the whalers. As chance would have it, Sheldon Jackson was also in Washington, busy promoting his scheme to dispatch reindeer in relief of the "starving" Yukon miners. Judging from a remark that Jackson made to the *Call*, the crisis of the whalers and the proposal to use reindeer for their relief had taken the canny reverend by surprise. His first instinct had been to shepherd the Yukon expedition exclusively, which meant withholding favor from the new expedition to Point Barrow. "Dr. Jackson does not think it possible for any vessel to reach the imprisoned whalers and others in distress before the spring," the *Call* reported, "and therefore does not like the idea of sending deer on the whalers' relief expedition." In the end, though, Jackson knew better than to belittle reindeer in any fashion, and he suppressed his worry that there might not be ample deer to accomplish both goals. On the morning of the cabinet meeting, he met with Secretary Alger and sang the praises of the "camels of the north," retelling the story of William Kjellmann and Per Rist's successful two-thousand-mile trip the previous winter.

Jackson was not invited to the meeting at the White House, but his counsel both beforehand and afterward was welcome and persuasive. For the moment at least, he was one of the few men available to the cabinet who had actually been to Alaska. He had visited Point Barrow numerous times; he knew many of the whaling captains and traders there; and he could describe in reliable detail the likely conditions confronting them. Once again Sheldon Jackson was in the right place at the right time, as were the reindeer.

Over the next few days, speculation swirled around whether the Navy or the Revenue Cutter Service would be called upon to command the expedition. Twenty crewmen and officers from San Francisco's whaling fleet sent an open letter to the *Call*, beseeching the paper to use its influence "to have Captain Healy placed in charge of the expedition, not only on account of his ability as an officer and seaman, but also for the great influence he has over the natives." Those most familiar with the Arctic endorsed Healy as "the one man above all others who should be given command of the relief ship."

Healy, who was living in San Francisco, had been one of the first men the *Call* had interviewed when the story of the trapped whalers had broken, and Hell-Roaring Mike had been unequivocally sanguine about the possibility of a rescue expedition: "A suitable vessel—one that is capable of battling with the ice [clearly he was thinking of his old ship, the *Bear*]—would have to be obtained and start at once. . . . There is no reason that I can see why such a ship cannot reach the north shore of Norton Sound or even Cape Prince of Wales, where the first reindeer station is located. There the stores could be landed and the land expedition prepare for its part of the work."

Healy then mapped out the overland part of the journey. "The distance from Cape Prince of Wales to Point Barrow . . . ought to be made in from thirty to fifty days, according to the weather conditions," he stated authoritatively. Responding to Lieutenant Stoney's supposition that the whalers would attempt to make their way southward,

Healy scoffed: "It would be imprudent for them to start down the coast with their limited stock of food for they could not get any relief from the natives. The natives would be willing to help them with all in their power, but it requires a strong stomach to retain what those people consider delicacies." Much better, Healy advised, for the whalers to sit tight and wait for supplies to come to them. "Such a journey as the relief expedition . . . I do not regard as particularly hazardous," he declared, "provided it takes with it all the available reindeer."

When pressed on the question of whether he would be willing to lead such an expedition, Healy replied, "Yes, if I were asked." But in truth he doubted that he would be, for his past had finally caught up with him.

During his dozen years patrolling the Arctic, Captain Healy had saved hundreds of lives. In 1885, while skipper of the *Corwin*, predecessor to the *Bear*, he had steamed fearlessly into the very edge of the surf to save the whaler *Mabel*, which had dragged its anchor in a gale off Point Franklin, not far from where the *Orca*, *Freeman*, *Belvedere*, and *Rosario* found themselves trapped twelve years later. He knew the *Belvedere* particularly well, having rescued it once already in 1888. Yet for all the whalers indebted to Healy, others resented his domineering ways. "I wish to say . . . that while in the north when I act officially I do it without fear or favor to anyone," he wrote in 1893. "The consequence is that while I have the confidence in the fullest of all honest people interested in the north, I have made no small number of evil wishers who would like an opening to say something. I never return home without the chance of a suit in court or a scorching from the newspapers."

In 1895, he had received both. At the end of its summer patrol to Alaska, the *Bear* had stopped at Unalaska to rendezvous with four other revenue cutters, all of them homeward bound. (The Lopps had been passengers onboard the *Bear* that summer, en route from Cape Prince of Wales to Unalaska, where they transferred to a commercial vessel for the remainder of their journey to the States.) Captain Healy's drinking was one of the worst kept secrets in the Arctic, but finally his imbibitions had become too blatant to ignore. While a guest aboard a British warship anchored at Unalaska, he became drunk and obstreperous, embarrassing his fellow officers and shocking his host. Two days later a still wobbly Healy committed the faux pas of falling off the pier into Dutch Harbor in front of aghast officers and enlisted men. When Healy docked in San Francisco the following month, he was brought up on a charge of drunkenness, to which was added a litany of long-festering misdeeds, including "tyrannous and abusive conduct to inferiors," endangerment of his ship, and conduct unbecoming an officer and a gentleman. The newspapers had a heyday, and when the affair was over, Healy had been found guilty on all charges, removed from command for four years, and dropped to the bottom of the list of Revenue Cutter Service officers.

But even with Healy hors de combat, the Revenue Cutter Service could still boast unparalleled experience in Alaska's icy waters—not to mention the best ship for the mission at hand, the *Bear*. The matter was decided on November 15, when Treasury secretary Gage, whose department oversaw the Revenue Cutter Service, issued a detailed letter of instruction to the skipper of the *Bear*, Healy's successor, Captain Francis Tuttle: "The best information obtainable gives the assurance of truth to reports that a fleet of eight whaling vessels are icebound in the Arctic Ocean, somewhere in the vicinity of Point Barrow, and that the 265 persons who were, at last accounts, on board these vessels are in all probability in dire distress. These conditions call for prompt and energetic action, looking to the relief of the imprisoned whalemen. It therefore has been determined to send an expedition to the rescue."

Recognizing that the "advanced season" would prevent any ship from getting as far as the Bering Strait, Gage directed Tuttle to "establish communication by means of an overland expedition . . . not only for the purpose of succoring the people, but to cheer them with the information that their relief and ultimate rescue will be effected as soon as the condition in Bering Strait will permit your command to advance." Gage was very specific on how the overland expedition ought to proceed. The *Bear* was to press as far north as possible. When it could go no farther, Tuttle was to put ashore three officers, who would then begin the overland phase of the rescue. "There are several plans deemed feasible, all leading to the same end," Gage noted, but each recognized the same exigency: "The first and great need of the whalemen will probably be food. It is believed that the only practicable method of getting it to them is to drive it on the hoof."

Regardless of where the *Bear*'s men landed, they were to make haste to the Seward Peninsula, where they were to "communicate as quickly as possible with W. T. Lopp at Cape Prince of Wales [and] with a native named A[n]tisarlook (generally known as Charlie), at Point Rodney. . . . The purpose is to collect from the herds at Rodney and Cape Prince of Wales the entire available herds of reindeer, all to be driven to Point Barrow."

Gage offered no suggestions on how the Revenue Cutter Service men should go about soliciting the cooperation of Lopp and Antisarlook; nor did he imply that either of them had a choice. "Mr. Lopp is to take charge of this herd and make all necessary arrangements for herders," Gage stated firmly. "Mr. Lopp must be fully impressed with the importance of the work in hand, and with the necessity of bending every energy to its speedy accomplishment." Finally, the secretary urged the cuttermen to assure Lopp and the natives he employed that they would be "amply rewarded for their labor."

That was it: Officers of the U.S. Revenue Cutter Service would appear unexpectedly at Tom Lopp's door in the dead of winter. Not only would they commandeer all of Lopp's reindeer—which belonged not to the U.S. government but to the American Missionary Association—and those of Charlie Antisarlook; in addition to this extraordinary demand, the officers would expect Lopp to leave his wife and

children, not to mention his mission, to drive the herd many hundreds
of miles overland to Point Barrow. Nowhere in Secretary Gage's letter
of instructions did he bother to spell out what to do if Lopp or Antisarlook declined such an incredible offer.

"Mindful of the arduous and perilous expedition which you are
about to enter, I bid you, your officers and men, Godspeed upon your
errand of mercy," Gage offered in closing.

. . .

The *Bear* had spent most of September and the beginning of October policing the tumult of gold miners and supplies at St. Michael,
now nicknamed Fort Get There. The revenue cutter had waited until
Army troops arrived on October 8 to reinforce the military post, and
then it continued on its homeward patrol, stopping at Unalaska in
the Aleutians and at the Pribilof Islands. At Dutch Harbor, Lieutenant Jarvis, the ship's executive officer, had transferred to a faster
vessel and hurried to the States to be with his wife and newborn child
in New Bedford. The *Bear* did not arrive in Seattle until November 7.
Tuttle and his men looked forward to a tranquil winter in port. It was
not to be.

While still at Dutch Harbor, Tuttle had heard from several whaling
captains that other whaling ships might be trapped in the ice up north.
Even so, he was unprepared for the high pitch of public concern that
greeted him when the *Bear* docked in Seattle—a hysteria he did not
share. From what he had gleaned from the captains at Unalaska, he
doubted that the whalers were in grave danger of starvation. "While it
probably will be necessary to abandon the vessels, I do not apprehend
the crews will meet with anything worse than privations and hardships," he stated calmly. His opinion had little sway, however; the critical cabinet meeting to address the plight of the whalers took place in
Washington one day after Tuttle's arrival in Seattle, too soon and too
far away for him to have any influence.

But that did not stop Tuttle from sharing his views with the *Seattle Post-Intelligencer*. "When . . . it was learned that the heads of departments in Washington were seriously considering [an overland relief expedition]," the paper reported, "Capt. Tuttle, of the Bear, was open in his expression of disapproval, declaring that he could do nothing, and that even if he could he believed the whalers amply able to take care of themselves without relief. He substantiated his reasoning with facts he had learned during the cruise of 1897 in regard to the supplies of provisions known to be in the vicinity of the imprisoned whalers. Since the issuance of the order on which the Bear will return to Alaskan waters Capt. Tuttle has maintained an attitude discreetly neutral. It is as though he said: 'Well, if I must go, I must, and I will not dampen the ardor of my men by doubts as to the expediency of the going. But I think—well, no matter what I think—I am going, and that ends it.'"

Francis Tuttle was in all ways a capable cutter captain. He had enlisted in the Navy at nineteen, serving in the Civil War, and had spent the rest of his life at sea, including ten seasons cruising in the North Pacific and Bering Sea. At fifty-four, he stood trim and erect, his generous moustaches draped across his weathered face like the bow wave on a close-hauled schooner. The *Call* spoke of his "indomitable courage," determination, modesty, and rapport with subordinates. Yet despite Tuttle's impressive press and profile, he did not cut as flamboyant a figure as his predecessor. In his two years as skipper of the *Bear*, he had not been called upon to rescue any ships, seize contraband, or transport reindeer from Siberia. Shutting down the Point Barrow refuge station and monitoring the mining stampede at St. Michael had called for firmness and finesse, but neither chore had pushed Tuttle to the limit.

The expedition to rescue the icebound whalers was unprecedented, even for a Michael Healy, and Tuttle's reservations about the endeavor were justified. "It would be hard to imagine a proposition on which it is more difficult to plan ahead," the *Post-Intelligencer* opined. "Capt. Tuttle, who is responsible for the success or failure of the attempt, is forced to say in reply to all queries, 'I don't know what I am going to do. . . . Everything will depend on where we are stopped by ice, and that is something not to be calculated upon.'"

While the papers pondered how far the *Bear* might get before bumping up against the polar ice pack, debate persisted over the underlying urgency of the expedition. Those least informed were the most certain that starvation was inevitable and imminent. "There are provisions enough at Point Barrow, including what is likely to be secured by hunting, to last twenty five people for one year," the *New York Evangelist* fretted, "and it is probable that as many as three hundred men from the whalers will attempt to reach Port Barrow." Wiser heads were cooler, tending to share Captain Tuttle's imperturbability. O. J. Humphrey, a representative of the Pacific Steam Whaling Company, which owned five of the eight imperiled ships, was downright blasé. "The vessels will unquestionably be crushed," he predicted, "[but] the relief expedition will find a lively lot of sailor corpses when they arrive at Point Barrow. Ten to one the whalers will meet them with the joking inquiry, 'Well, what under the Arctic aurora borealis are you fellows doing here?' But they will take advantage of the opportunity to borrow smoking and chewing tobacco and add a few unexpected entrees to the menu. You need not worry about those men starving for the larders of all the steamers are well filled."

Humphrey then added, "I do not believe the expedition will do any good, yet I believe in its going for if one whaler's life was lost and nothing had been done it would be a very black eye for the government."

In the days that followed, the *Call* kept the public apprised of every detail of the expedition's preparations, saving plenty of ink for self-congratulation. "Outfitted by 'The Call,' A Rescue Ship Will Sail into the Frozen Ocean," bruited a typical headline. Ultimately, however, the newspaper was not required to honor its pledge to provision the entire expedition. Its financial contribution amounted to $7,000 worth of socks, underwear, gloves, tobacco, books, sheet music, and other sundries for the stranded whalers. The *Call* cattily pointed out that the *Examiner* had contributed only a few hundred dollars. The funds of the *Call*'s "saffron contemporary" had gone to purchasing flimsy sheepskin coats, which, the *Call* declared, were better suited for "the sheepherder on the upper slope of the sunny Sierra."

. . .

The *Bear* finally departed Seattle on November 27, three weeks after returning from its previous patrol and only two weeks after Secretary Gage had issued his letter of instruction. The earliest that the cutter could expect to return to the States was the following September; if all went as planned, the *Bear* would spend the winter at Dutch Harbor, which was generally ice-free. The ship could count on replenishing its coal there and consequently had dedicated most of its onboard bunkers to provisions for the whalers. The decks were likewise crowded with barrels of salted meat. A place was found for everything—except the eggs; cases and cases of them had to be dumped over the side.

The secretary had given Tuttle "full authority and the largest possible latitude" in executing his mission, stressing, however, that the captain "leave no avenue of possible success untried." Regarding the men to be put ashore for the overland portion of the expedition, Gage advised: "This party should be prepared while you are en route and be ready . . . to take advantage of the first opportunity afforded for its landing. . . . You will make your own selection from the personnel of your command, volunteers preferred."

The first two choices were easy. First Lieutenant David Jarvis and Dr. Samuel Call were seasoned Arctic hands and quick to volunteer. Jarvis had hurried back from the East Coast just in time.

Jarvis's appearance belied his toughness. He was short, jug-eared, and surprisingly smooth-faced for his forty-five years. One fellow officer described him as "boyish of build and almost shy in manner." Jarvis had served much of the previous decade aboard the *Bear*, acting as Michael Healy's adept and, when the situation necessitated, emphatic right arm. Beyond Jarvis's considerable talents as a seaman, he also acquitted himself ably on shore. He knew reindeer as well as any man in the Revenue Cutter Service, having accompanied Sheldon Jackson on his trips to Siberian villages, and he had spent time among the herd at the Teller station. Moreover, he was well acquainted with Alaskan natives. Over the years, he had learned to speak their language passably well.

Dr. Samuel Call was thirty-nine in 1897. Raised in California, he had spent most of his adult years in Alaska, first as company physician for the Alaskan Commercial Company and then as a contract surgeon aboard Revenue Cutter Service vessels. In his extensive travels throughout the Arctic, he had been called upon to treat every sort of ailment and injury, from epidemics of influenza to amputations of frostbitten limbs. Clearly he enjoyed the adventure of his job as much as the medical duties. Like Jarvis, he was often in the parties that went ashore on reindeer forays, and Call's extensive photographs of Arctic natives, both Siberian and Alaskan, are regarded as some of the most valuable records of the era. Above all, Call was game, and his medical expertise would be valuable during the expedition and especially once he reached Point Barrow.

The third choice for the expedition was not so obvious. Round-faced and balding, Second Lieutenant Ellsworth Bertholf looked more like a Salvation Army officer than a man tempered for winter travel. His previous billet, before joining the *Bear* in November, had been as executive officer aboard the *Salmon P. Chase*, a ship that trained Revenue Cutter Service cadets in the Atlantic. In his ten years at sea, Bertholf had sailed through the Strait of Gibraltar but never the Bering Strait. Until arriving in Seattle in November, he had not even laid eyes on the Pacific Ocean, much less the formidable coastline of

Alaska. Yet whatever the thirty-one-year-old lieutenant lacked in experience, he overcame with a hearty self-confidence.

The *Bear* arrived at Dutch Harbor ten days after leaving Seattle. Here Jarvis purchased seven sled dogs and assigned Frederick Koltchoff to manage them. Very little is known about Koltchoff; the *Call* described him enigmatically as "an explorer of experience." Evidently he had spent several years in Alaska and knew his way around dogs and natives. Jarvis did not expect Koltchoff to stay with the expedition all the way to Point Barrow. Rather, his job would be limited to assisting the other members of the expedition, who were not experienced dog handlers, in getting to St. Michael or perhaps Unalakleet, where they hoped to meet up with the reindeer herd, recently relocated from Port Clarence.

The weather had deteriorated as the *Bear* neared the Aleutians, and conditions worsened once the cutter left the shelter of Dutch Harbor on December 11. In his letter to Tuttle, Secretary Gage had suggested optimistically that the *Bear* attempt to get as far as St. Michael, on the eastern shore of Norton Sound. Steering northeast, the ship encountered ice shortly after crossing latitude 63 degrees north, to the east of St. Lawrence Island. The *Bear* had been built in Scotland for hunting seals in the fierce North Atlantic. Its oak planking was six inches thick and reinforced with Australian ironwood. Its bow was strengthened with steel plating, and its propeller could be readily raised to prevent it from being crushed by ice. Altogether, it was as stout as any ship in the Arctic. Even so, Captain Tuttle was not willing to test the limits of its strength, given the stakes.

As the *Bear* steered to the southeast, what began as a "thin scum of ice" became "fields of broken ice mixed with slush ice." Continuing at half speed under reefed sails, Tuttle skirted the edge, hoping for an opening. "But the farther we worked south the thicker the mush ice became," he explained. "Knowing that as soon as the wind died out the sea would go down and the mush ice would form into a solid mass which it would be impossible for us to get through, I went full speed to SSW." Still west of Norton Sound, yet within one hundred miles of Cape Rodney, Tuttle reluctantly chose discretion over reckless valor. On the morning of December 14, he turned his stern to the clotting field of ice and beat toward Cape Vancouver, "the next nearest and perhaps available place" to endeavor a landing, two hundred nautical miles to the south. This rebuff, while not entirely unanticipated, added more than five hundred miles to the overland journey that Jarvis and his men were about to begin.

Cape Vancouver marks the western tip of Nelson Island, midway between the broad deltas of the Yukon River to the north and the Kuskokwim River to the south. (And it is not far from Nunivak Island, where one of the whaling skippers in San Francisco had predicted the voyage would wind up.) On the morning of the sixteenth, the *Bear* dropped anchor off the native village of Tanunak, and Jarvis rowed ashore to see about landing his men, dogs, sleds, and supplies. As he neared the boulder-strewn beach, he was met by several native kayaks, one of which was paddled by a half-breed Russian trader, Alexis Kalenin, who immediately offered to help transport the expedition's gear to the village. The *Bear* lingered offshore long enough to make sure that the expedition landed safely, but with great chunks of ice beginning to run from the northwest, Tuttle got under way and steamed again toward Unalaska.

The appearance of Kalenin was indeed fortuitous, for not only did he facilitate a difficult landing, but he also offered to guide Jarvis and his men across the daunting Yukon delta to St. Michael, a trip that he estimated would take twelve days. Due to recent demand by stampeding miners, dogs were hard to come by in Alaska; at Unalaska the most Jarvis had been able to buy was seven. Kalenin, however, owned plenty, and he agreed to let the expedition have as many as it needed, for a price of course. Jarvis had acquired two sleds in Seattle, which he now determined were more cumbersome than those made by the natives. He purchased three from Kalenin, discarded one of his own, and in the morning darkness of December 18, the expedition left Tanunak on four sleds pulled by forty-one dogs.

They had winnowed the gear to thirteen hundred pounds, still quite a load. A tent of lightweight cotton had been stitched aboard ship. Their clothing was made mostly of wool and dog skin. A sheet-iron stove burned wood; a smaller stove burned oil, fifty pounds of which was packed on the sleds. Sleeping bags, made of goatskin with covers of canvas and rubber, weighed two hundred pounds; food, not including frozen fish for the dogs, weighed another three hundred. They wisely cooked the beans and meat before leaving the ship to minimize meal preparation along the trail. And although they cut down on their personal gear as much as they dared, they still found room for seventy-five pounds of mail to be delivered to St. Michael and Point Barrow.

With Kalenin leading the way on snowshoes and each sled driven by a native, Jarvis, Bertholf, Call, and Koltchoff followed behind on foot. Right off, they had to climb a steep mountain "in the midst of a furious storm of wind and snow," Jarvis recorded. After "much tugging and pushing," they reached the summit, unharnessed the dogs, and tobogganed exuberantly down the far side, two men to a sled. Arriving at the village of Ookagamiut (today's Ukak) at the end of the first day, they were invited to spend the night in the qargi, the communal house. Jarvis judged it "too crowded and filthy," and they opted for their tent and a supper of tea, hard bread, and warmed-over pork and beans.

The following morning they crossed the ice to the mainland and continued northeastward through a confusion of frozen streams and lakes. "We did not make good time," Jarvis lamented, "as the crust on the snow was thin, and the dogs and sleds were continually breaking through." By the time they made camp, several of the young dogs were all in, and Kalenin informed Jarvis that it would take two days to find replacements.

The delay was more than Jarvis could tolerate. That night he announced that he and Call, along with two of the native guides, would press ahead with the two best teams. Kalenin would come along with Bertholf and Koltchoff as soon as he had procured more dogs.

The overland expedition was barely three days old, and Jarvis had already divided his men. A more tentative officer might have kept the group together for the safety of each individual, as well as to increase the likelihood that, through teamwork, at least one of them would complete the mission. None of them was so experienced on the trail that he could get by without assistance from others along the way. Jarvis and Call knew each other well, and perhaps they figured that the untested Bertholf and the now extraneous Koltchoff would slow them down in the long run. But why discard them here, so soon? For whatever reason—vaulting ambition, hidebound duty, or heartfelt humanitarianism—Jarvis threw caution to the wind. "There was . . . the chance of the weather turning bad, rendering travel impossible," he reasoned in the official report he filed a year later, "and now that the weather was favorable, I decided to get ahead as far as we could while the good spell lasted."

The next morning the men divided their outfit in the dark. Jarvis and Call took the sheet-iron stove, the tent, half the food, two of the sleds, and the best dogs. With two native guides, they set off across a flat terrain of frozen bogs and pothole lakes, angling north by northeast. Darkness descended by four in the afternoon, and they made camp on the bank of the Azun River. The temperature had been dropping continuously, and when they awoke the following morning, the thermometer registered four degrees below zero. "As the wind had freshened from the northward," Jarvis wrote, "it made the weather quite sharp."

For the next four days, the sleds were unable to maintain a straight course. The trail chosen by the natives coiled along creek beds, across random lakes, and over rumpled tundra. The solstice made travel even more challenging. With the sun now absent nineteen hours of every day, their time on the trail was limited, and each morning seemed colder than the last. On the twenty-second, the temperature was fifteen below zero. "We had hardly accustomed ourselves to such cold," Jarvis confessed, "and our clothing was not well suited for it, so we had to be moving quite lively during the day to keep warm." For lack of better wood, they burned willows in their stove.

On Christmas Eve, they arrived on the brushy shore of the Yukon and crossed on the ice near the abandoned Russian trading post of Andreafsky. At last they were in country that, if not entirely familiar to them, was better mapped and more regularly traveled by white men. Eight miles or so farther on, they came to the trading post of the Alaska Commercial Company, where several traders and their families were burrowed in for the winter. In other years, a steamboat or two would have wintered at the post, but in the stampede to the Klondike the previous summer, many of the boats had been caught by low water at inconvenient points along the river and then frozen in. There were no boats at the trading post when Jarvis and Call appeared at the door, but a number of "steamer folks" had made their way from camps along the river to spend Christmas. Playing Santa Claus, Jarvis produced letters for many of them from his bulky mail sack.

Also like Santa, he and Call were gone by Christmas morning. "Our mission would admit of no unnecessary delay," Jarvis remarked nobly. After restocking their provisions from the stores at the post, they started down the river with the sleds and the same pair of native guides from Tanunak (whose names Jarvis never thought to record). Despite the bravest intentions, they did not get far. As they rounded a bend in the river at midday, a northeast gale struck them head on. "[T]he dogs were unable to face it," Jarvis regretted, "and we were compelled to camp and wait for better weather."

The wind eventually subsided, and over the next five days, as they traveled downriver, Jarvis and Call encountered several groups of miners wintering in poorly built cabins. On the twenty-seventh, they spent the night aboard the steamer *Alice*, stranded like so many others until the spring.

By now the dogs were nearly played out. Jarvis had demanded speed and long hours from them, remorselessly so. On stretches of the Yukon where the ice was smooth, he put the sleds to a gallop. But it was impossible to anticipate the spots where the ice had frozen in two layers, leaving a gap of a foot or more between the thin upper ice and the firmer ice below. "Often when the dogs were speeding along over the smooth surface," Jarvis recalled, "the sled would strike one of these places and suddenly, with no warning, the whole outfit, dogs, sleds, and men, would go through and bring up on the solid ice below. Then we would have to go ahead and break through the [upper] shell so the dogs could follow until the firm ice was reached again." As they approached the *Alice*, the dogs' paws left a trail of blood.

The Eskimo guides were hardly in better shape; both of them were suffering from bad colds that had settled in their chests. Leaving the natives in the care of the steamboat's purser, Jarvis hired new guides and coaxed some fresh dogs from the Alaska Commercial Company, the ship's owner. The following morning, he and Call were away again, racing along the Yukon delta toward the Bering Sea. "We must have made fifty miles this day, for the ice was good and smooth, and our fresh native runners spurred the tired dogs up to a first rate."

They struck the sea at Pastol Bay, on the southern shore of Norton Sound. They turned north along the shore ice, picking their way around the fractured headland of Point Romanof. Overcome by a fierce snowstorm, they were less discerning in their choice of sleeping accommodations. "It was long after dark before we came to the village [of Pikmiktalik]," Jarvis wrote, "where we were glad to accept the offered shelter of the [native] huts."

On the afternoon of December 30, they sledded into St. Michael, where the commanding officer of the Army post, Lieutenant Colonel George Randall, offered "every assistance in his power." In two weeks, they had covered nearly four hundred miles. "At first such work seems killing," Jarvis commented on his trial by dogsled, "but you get used to it like anything else and take it as a matter of course."

Jarvis and Call allowed themselves one day at St. Michael. Although Bertholf and Koltchoff were likely only a day or two behind, Jarvis decided not to wait for them. He was in a hurry, as ever, and besides, he had other plans for Bertholf.

The first leg of the journey from Cape Vancouver to St. Michael had been arduous enough, and the next leg, to Cape Prince of Wales, promised to be no less daunting. Yet Jarvis knew that both of these treks would seem trifling compared to the final challenge of driving a herd of reindeer from Cape Prince of Wales to Point Barrow. While he was counting on Tom Lopp and Charlie Antisarlook to supply the deer, he dared not assume that they could muster the provisions to sustain themselves and the herders who accompanied them. Accordingly, he left orders at St. Michael for Bertholf to proceed immediately to Unalakleet. Jarvis figured to arrive at Unalakleet ahead of Bertholf; there he would arrange with the agent of the Alaska Commercial Company to supply Bertholf with one thousand pounds of provisions and the dogsleds to transport them. Bertholf's job was to deliver these sleds and supplies to Cape Blossom on Kotzebue Sound via a trail across the throat of the Seward Peninsula, an overland journey of some three hundred miles—roughly half the distance Jarvis and Call were about to cover by following the coast to Cape Prince of Wales and then north to Kotzebue Sound. If all went smoothly, Jarvis, Call, Lopp, and the herders would rendezvous with Bertholf at the Quaker mission that had been established near Cape Blossom the previous summer. By Jarvis's estimate, Bertholf's supplies would be sufficient to get the expedition as far as its next point of replenishment, the mission and whaling stations at Point Hope.

As for Koltchoff, Jarvis left orders for him to report to Lieutenant Colonel Randall for duty. His service to the Overland Relief Expedition was over.

Before leaving St. Michael, Jarvis and Call discarded their heavy woolen and dog-skin clothing and outfitted themselves with the clothes used by Arctic natives for generations. On their feet they wore deerskin—caribou or reindeer—boots soled with the tough hide of bearded seal. Their pants, atigis, and mittens were also of deerskin. The atigis were double-layered, the inside layer worn with the hair next to the skin, the top layer with the hair on the outside. Atigi hoods were fringed with wolf hair, which did not collect frost. On top of everything they wore a shirt of canvas drilling to ward off driving snow.

Deerskin is extraordinarily warm without being heavy. Like many mammals, reindeer have two layers of hair. The outer layer is hollow, and the air in each follicle provides flotation and a perfect baffle of insulation that both disperses and captures body heat. Warmth can be as dangerous as cold in the Arctic, for sweat can kill a man just as surely as a fall through the ice. This is the other marvelous quality of deerskin clothing: Wearing it in layers allows for even greater air circulation and freedom of movement. The same goes for deerskin sleeping bags. Jarvis and Call's new deerskin bedding was half the weight of their goatskin and canvas sleeping bags and much more comfortable.

Replacing the worn-out dogs was not so easy. "Only the urgency of our mission induced the agent of the Alaska Commercial Company to let us have the station team as far as Unalalkik [Unalakleet]," Jarvis wrote. After that they would impose on another agent at Unalakleet to loan them enough dogs to carry them to the point where they finally would meet up with the reindeer herd.

They left St. Michael on January 1, expecting to cover the sixty miles to Unalakleet in two days. But east winds had driven the ice away from the shore, obliging them to take to the tundra. The wind had blown the ground almost bare, "making progress one continual, hard, grinding, pull," Jarvis reported. The next day was no better. "We shoved and pushed over bowlders and almost bare, grassy mounds, and up and down steep gullies and cliffs, and when darkness overtook us, 15 miles was all we had accomplished."

On the third day out from St. Michael, they had a fortunate encounter. They had returned to the shore ice and were picking their way around a low headland when they saw a native woman on snowshoes approaching from the north. As she came closer, Jarvis recognized her as someone he had met at Point Hope on one of the *Bear's* annual visits. When Jarvis inquired what she was doing by herself so far from home, she explained that she had forgotten her pipe at Unalakleet that morning and had returned to get it. She was now hurrying to catch up with her husband, Tickey, and a white man who had come from Point Barrow and, with their help, was trying to reach St. Michael.

The two men, it turned out, had passed over the bluff within a few hundred yards of Jarvis and Call, and if the woman—whose name is recorded in some accounts as Cunuanar, in others Kauyoana—had not gone back for her pipe, they would have missed one another. The white man, Jarvis and Call soon learned, was George Fred Tilton, third mate of the *Belvedere*. He had left Point Barrow on October 17 and had been traveling on foot and dogsled ever since, intent on carrying the news of the stranded whalers to the Outside.

"On the morning of [January 3] we started early and had gone perhaps five miles when I missed Tickey's wife," Tilton recalled in a memoir, published seventy years later. "He told me that she had left her pipe at the mission and had gone back after it. I was just a bit peeved at this, but . . . I considered that she could go about three times as fast as we could, so I kept on. . . . When we reached the summit of the [bluff] I looked back to see if the woman was coming, and I saw two men running toward me, waving their hats."

# [ 10 ]

# Sorry-Looking Bunch

AFTER LISTENING TO George Fred Tilton and reading the mail he carried on his sled, Jarvis and Call had little difficulty visualizing the situation at Point Barrow— starting from the time the last whalers got out in early September until Tilton had volunteered to make his journey one month later.

The dire predictions made by the whaling ships fortunate enough to leave Point Barrow had, for the most part, come true. On September 17, the *Orca, Belvedere, Jessie H. Freeman,* and *Rosario* were anchored to the southwest of the point, hemmed in by a long ridge of pack ice that had grounded itself just offshore. With the shore ice beginning to close around the ships, the skippers mounted a final effort to escape entrapment. "It was a splendid sight to see the 'Orka' back off and come against this great mass of ice at full speed, often going half her length out of water on it, and mashing it down as if it were so much paper," Ned McIlhenny wrote in the journal he kept throughout his year at Point Barrow.

McIlhenny had overestimated the ship's strength, however. While the *Orca's* ironwood bottom and 280-horsepower steam engine could break through five inches of young ice, the vessel was no match for the much denser pack ice. Explosives were the only way. The blasting was accomplished by attaching charges to long poles, which were shoved under the lip of the ice and detonated. By September 19, the *Orca*, *Freeman*, and *Belvedere* had succeeded in gouging through six miles of ice to the open water beyond. But in breaking free, the *Orca* had snapped the fittings to its rudder. The rudder of the *Belvedere* was also in bad shape, and the ships lost another day addressing the damage. The sailing schooner *Rosario*, meanwhile, had not even tried to keep up and continued to hug the shore, praying that a shift in the ice would allow it to sneak northeast around the point, where it stood a better chance of surviving the winter.

While the ships were making hasty repairs, a native arrived with messages from the *Fearless* and *Newport* that they were icebound just off Pitt Point, ninety miles to the east of Point Barrow; the *Jeanie* was trapped twenty miles farther east of them. As for the missing *Wanderer*, the presumption was that it had scrambled back to Herschel Island, where it would spend the winter with the well-provisioned *Mary D. Hume*. The 860-ton *Jeanie* was well-stocked, too. It was a supply ship, after all, and earlier that summer it had taken on board the surplus from the abandoned refuge station at Point Barrow.

Of the four eastern ships, the *Fearless* and *Newport* were facing the most uncertain plight. If there was any good news to be reported, it was that they were in no immediate danger of being crushed. When the two ships had been nipped, they were within one hundred yards of each other, encased in the shore ice and close enough to land that the pack ice was not likely to get at them anytime soon. But like the *Wanderer*, both the *Fearless* and the *Newport* had figured on only enough provisions to get home. Their captains estimated that they had food to last two months, no more.

As an eerie postscript to an already chilling bulletin, Captain James McKenna of the *Fearless* and Captain George Leavitt of the *Newport* reported that the *Navarch* had been spotted drifting in the pack ice, twelve miles to the north of them.

By comparison, the captains of the *Orca*, *Freeman*, and *Belvedere* considered themselves lucky. Having broken free of the pack ice, they at least had a fighting chance of making it home that winter. Mindful of the needs of those who would not get out, they offloaded all the coal, clothing, and food they could spare before steaming southwestward on the twenty-first, the *Belvedere* in the lead, nudging through a continuous sheet of young ice. By evening the three ships had reached Peard Bay, a shallow scoop in the coastline fifty miles from Point Barrow.

Before leaving Point Barrow, Captain Albert Sherman of the *Orca* had made a rather morbid wager with Ned McIlhenny. "He asked me what I thought of the wind," McIlhenny noted in his journal. "I . . . bet him a hat that it would be North West before tomorrow. He took the bet and said if it moved North West, the ice would be on the Sea Horse Islands before the ship[s] could get around them."

Regrettably McIlhenny won the bet. The Sea Horse Islands are scarcely islands at all—really no more than spits of sand and gravel strewn inhospitably across the mouth of Peard Bay. When, as McIlhenny had predicted, the wind shifted to the northwest, it drove the pack ice toward land, buckling the weaker shore ice. On the twenty-second, the *Belvedere* had muscled its way ten miles west of the islands and was nearly free. But the *Orca*, following close behind, was nipped between two great wedges of ice. The force crushed the sternpost, propeller, and steering gear with such force that the wheel was thrust through the pilot house. Assessing the damage, Captain Sherman ordered his forty-nine crewmen to abandon ship.

The *Belvedere* had no choice but to turn back. "We on the *Belvedere* knew that we were near clear water, as we could see the dark cloud that always shows where it lays," George Fred Tilton explained. "But there were the *Orca*'s crew on the ice and we just had to swing

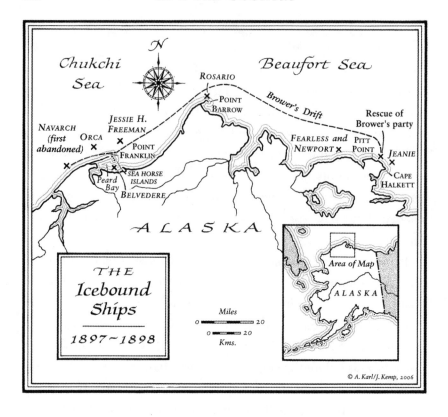

Chukchi Sea

Beaufort Sea

ROSARIO

POINT BARROW

Brower's Drift

Rescue of Brower's party

NAVARCH (first abandoned)

JESSIE H. FREEMAN

ORCA

POINT FRANKLIN

FEARLESS and NEWPORT

PITT POINT

JEANIE

SEA HORSE ISLANDS

Peard Bay

BELVEDERE

CAPE HALKETT

ALASKA

THE *Icebound Ships*

1897~1898

Miles

Kms.

Area of Map

ALASKA

© A. Karl/J. Kemp, 2006

around and work our way back for a mile to a place where we could pick 'em all up." Not all, actually. About half of the *Orca's* men were taken aboard the *Freeman*.

The day went downhill from there. Captain Martin Van Buren Millard of the *Belvedere* now gave up any ambition of reaching open water and turned toward the northeast, seeking refuge from the pack ice behind the Sea Horse Islands. The *Freeman* followed, but two hours later it too was crushed irreparably. Like the *Orca*, it did not sink, but lingered—not so much afloat as clutched in the talons of the ice, undevoured. Forty-nine crewmen from the *Freeman*, plus the men it had rescued from the *Orca*, scrambled across the ice and were taken aboard the *Belvedere*, which at last succeeded in gaining the shallow water of Peard Bay. The number of men on the *Belvedere* was now 147.

"[F]or a time we were comparatively safe, but we also knew that the ice might pile up like a mountain and smash [us] . . . for the ice was drifting in all the time," Tilton recounted. The three captains agreed that the most prudent action would be to remove most of the provisions from the *Belvedere* and set up camp on one of the islands, as desolate as they might be. While some of the men unloaded the ship, others were sent back to the *Orca* and the *Freeman* to salvage its provisions and strip it of bulkheads, spars, and rigging for building shelters. Natives who observed the wreck and abandonment of the two ships had a similar idea, and on September 24, while picking through the cabins of the *Freeman*, one of them knocked over an oil lamp, setting the ship on fire. "All the yards were lit up," recalled James Allen, one of the ship's engineers. "We could hear the cracking of the bombs that were to have been used for killing the whales. It sounded like a New Year celebration in Chinatown." In a few hours, the 140-foot bark burned to the waterline.

The *Orca* survived another three days. By then the salvage crews had taken all they could from its flooded hold. Tilton was the last to go aboard. "I hadn't been on the ship three hours when I felt her give a funny motion," he reported. "There was half a case of canned meat on the deck and I picked it up, threw it as far on to the ice as I could, and jumped after it. Well sir, the ice slacked up and the ship careened at the same time, sliding slowly under the ice. Down, down she went, out of sight, and that was the last of the *Orca*."

On the same day, three mates arrived on foot at Cape Barrow, bringing the news of the two lost ships and the imprisonment of the *Belvedere*. Charles Brower, now recovered from his own harrowing ordeal on the ice, promptly took charge. The following morning, he dispatched his associate Fred Hopson to Peard Bay to alert the captains that help was on the way and that the whalers would be welcome and cared for at Point Barrow. A few hours later, a caravan of sleds driven by natives departed from the whaling station to begin bringing in the men.

"A sorry-looking bunch they were," observed James Allen of his fellow whalers. "Most of these men were past middle age, and a couple were past 65. They had been cooped up in ships for a long time . . . and the [trek was] quite a contest for them." Most of the men had to walk. The snow was two feet deep in places, the temperature well below freezing. In the evening they camped in makeshift tents and ate hard bread with tea. Men moaned all night from the pains in their legs. The worst-off were allowed turns riding on the sleds. When one overweight engineer got too demanding, his shipmates interceded. "When it was not his turn to ride," James Allen stated, "we would make a rope fast around his waist and attach it to the stern of the sled. We would half drag him along."

The first group of sixty-five men arrived at Point Barrow on October 5, three days after leaving Peard Bay. "They finally reached the [whaling station]," McIlhenny wrote, "and none too soon, for many of them could hardly put one foot before the other, they were so stiff. Several of them were stretched on the sleds unable to walk and at least 20 of them were frozen about the face and hands." When he had a chance to take a closer look at the men with whom he was now obliged to spend the winter, McIlhenny, the southern scion, was none too pleased. "I have never seen a worse looking lot of men than these," he grumbled in his journal. "They are the skum of humanity from a dozen nations."

Even before the whalers had stumbled into camp, McIlhenny had come to accept that his prospects for a bracing winter of shooting and specimen gathering were "knocked in the head." His one previous trip to the Arctic had been in 1894 on a generously funded expedition to explore the coastline of Greenland. The trip was aborted when his ship struck a rock, ripping a hole in its bottom. Inconvenienced perhaps but not significantly endangered, McIlhenny and his colleagues were rescued by a fishing schooner and returned safely to Newfoundland. The thrill of that summer had only whetted McIlhenny's appetite for similarly romantic diversion. Yet the events now unfolding at Point

Barrow were of a different order entirely—dark, dangerous, and considerably less collegial.

To his credit, McIlhenny had pitched in without hesitation. Several days after receiving word that the *Newport* and *Fearless* were icebound east of Point Barrow, McIlhenny and Brower's other associate, Tom Gordon, set off by dogsled to inform the ships that there were plenty of supplies at Point Barrow to see them through the winter. They completed the seventy-five-mile trip in sixteen hours. After a day's rest, McIlhenny left Gordon—who had stayed in order to make contact with both the *Navarch* and *Jeanie*—and returned to Point Barrow, guided by natives, again completing the run in a single day.

Back at the whaling station, Charlie Brower had already begun preparing for the arrival of the whalers. With help from the natives, he set to work fixing up the Pacific Steam Whaling Company's old station. In the year since it had last been occupied, much of its lumber, including a great deal of the floor and ceiling, had been scavenged for other uses. Because he did not have enough lumber to restore the building fully, Brower chose to shorten it from sixty-five feet to fifty, using the scraps to renovate the rest. Two stoves were installed, and the walls were lined with forty-eight bunks in tiers of three. McIlhenny estimated that the station could accommodate 144 men, assuming they took turns sleeping in eight-hour shifts.

From the standpoint of the men who would have to share these bunks, this arithmetic was offensive in the extreme. By contrast, McIlhenny, his two assistants, and a cook were the only occupants of the former refuge station, which had been built to hold a hundred men. His name was on the lease, but given the emergency of the moment, his decision to allow only sixteen officers to share his quarters did not sit well with the considerably more cramped rank and file, even less so as the winter wore on.

Fortunately for everyone, the number of men who made their way to Point Barrow was not as great as had been initially anticipated. The

Overland Relief Expedition expected to find nearly three hundred whalers stranded at Point Barrow. The actual number was closer to 150. (No two sources agree, some estimating as low as 130, others as high as 180.) For one thing, the *Wanderer* had succeeded in returning to Herschel Island. Also subtracted from the total were thirty officers and crewmen of the *Belvedere,* including Captain Millard, who elect-ed to remain with the ship, making do on the limited provisions and sheltered from the pack ice behind the slim bulwark of the Sea Horse Islands.

Likewise, nearly all of the officers and crewmen of the *Jeanie, New-port,* and *Fearless* had chosen to sit tight. They banked snow along the sides of the ships for insulation and built roofs over the decks. If need be, they could get to shore without much difficulty and then to Point Barrow. They would not be comfortable, but at least the routine was familiar. The *Newport* had spent the previous five winters at Herschel Island; the *Fearless* and *Wanderer* the past three.

Their decision to remain onboard was influenced by the law of the sea that assured that if the men left ship, they would lose all that they had earned. Officers and crews were paid not for the weeks, months, and years they spent at sea, but only in proportion to the whalebone and oil they delivered to the wharves of San Francisco. Once aban-doned, their ships would most likely be destroyed in the spring break-up. And at any time, an abandoned ship and its cargo were fair game to salvagers. Consequently Captain Edwin Coffin of the *Rosario* had taken a calculated risk. Unable to keep up with his steam-powered brethren when they had departed Point Barrow or even to gain the dubious refuge of the lagoon behind Point Barrow, Coffin had brought the *Rosario* as close to the beach as he dared, where it now lay encased in the shore ice, still intact and still under his watchful eye.

As stubborn as the crews of the *Newport* and *Fearless* were about remaining onboard, they still had to eat. The initial estimate was that they had enough food to last two months. Beyond the provisions already onboard, Charlie Brower had promised to supply the ships from the stores at Point Barrow. But seventy-five miles was a long way to drive heavily laden sleds throughout an Arctic winter. Not long after McIlhenny returned from the ships, the indefatigable Brower decided to make his own trip to confer with the captains. He was also curious about the *Navarch*. From a mate who had completed the twelve-mile trip to the doomed whaler, Brower was astonished to learn that eight crewmen were still onboard. Their aim, however harebrained, was to stay with the ship and claim salvage rights when and if it ever worked free of the ice.

Brower had his own notion. He summoned natives from shore and had them open a crude path across the ice to the *Navarch*. To its skeleton crew he announced that the stores in the hold would be transferred to the *Newport* and *Fearless*. When one of the *Navarch's* men protested, Brower put him in irons. Over the next several days, two dozen sleds, making six trips each, hauled several tons of food to the *Newport* and *Fearless*. Because these stores were still not enough to sustain both crews for the entire winter, Captains McKenna and Leavitt elected to send a few of their men to Point Barrow.

Of the *Navarch's* remaining crew, several were taken aboard the *Newport* and *Fearless*; the others, including the man in irons, were escorted to the whaling station. The day after Brower had removed the last load, the wind changed direction, and the *Navarch* was again spirited away into the great polar ice pack, presumably toward oblivion.

Brower was still not done. After leaving the *Newport* and *Fearless*, he sledded another thirty miles east to the *Jeanie*, which was icebound off of Cape Halkett. Captain P. H. Mason assured him that the ship was in good shape and in no immediate danger of being crushed. The only foreseeable shortage was of meat—a problem that was rectified by trading with the Eskimos for caribou, which grazed all along the coast. Thus there was no need to bring any of the *Jeanie's* men ashore or to maintain a supply line from Point Barrow.

By the time Brower got back to Point Barrow, the situation had stabilized somewhat. About eighty men had moved into the old whaling station, now called "the bunkhouse." The officers had been divided between the refuge station and the Cape Smythe Whaling Company building occupied by Brower and his assistants, Hobson and Gordon. Captain Porter of the *Freeman* and Captain Sherman of the *Orca* shared their own small cottage. Dr. Marsh and his wife continued to live by themselves. Since neither of the stoves in the bunkhouse was adequate for cooking meals of any quantity, most of the cooking and baking for the crewmen was done in the refuge station by McIlhenny's Japanese cook, known as Frank, and the steward from the *Freeman*, John Gibson. For the time being, each man was rationed one pound of meat and one pound of flour a day, along with a small amount of tea, coffee, and sugar. Meals were served twice a day: breakfast at nine, dinner at five.

. . .

Lieutenant Jarvis and Dr. Call listened raptly as Tilton unreeled his narrative of shipwreck, rescue, and refuge in the Far North. Later in the afternoon they made camp on the shore of Norton Sound in order to debrief the trail-worn whaler more fully and go through the sack of letters he had carried from Point Barrow. They regretted the loss of the *Orca* and *Freeman* but were cheered to learn that no men had perished, at least not by the time of Tilton's departure on October 12.

They paid particularly close attention when Tilton reported on the food supply at Point Barrow. The considerable provisions in Brower's storehouse were supplemented by the food from the *Belvedere* and the two wrecked whalers. Ned McIlhenny had brought supplies to last him and his assistants two years, just as a precaution. In addition, McIlhenny, a wing shooter extraordinaire, had shot several thousand ducks, including 430 in a single day. (He was so proud of the slaughter that he recorded it in an affidavit, signed by witnesses.)

As best Jarvis and Call could tell, the whalers had enough food to last until July, a month short of when the *Bear* was expected to arrive. The supply was "not large but will be sufficient," Jarvis wrote in a letter that Tilton eventually mailed to the secretary of the Treasury. Tilton, however, was not so optimistic—perhaps because his gloomy outlook made his own accomplishments appear more heroic but also because he knew better than his auditors just how tight things really were at Point Barrow. "Our entire stock from all sources would allow two meals a day . . . until July 1," Tilton calculated, "but the meals would have to be mighty scant ones. This meant that half of the men would probably get weak and die, and even if most of them did hold out until July there was no guarantee of relief. I tell you, the winter prospects looked pretty doggone blue."

Without question, Tilton was a good storyteller, and the events that had occurred at Point Barrow were only a fraction of his extraordinary chronicle. For twelve weeks he had traveled by dogsled, following the coast to Point Hope and Kotzebue Sound. A strapping Vineyarder with years of experience whaling in the Arctic, "Big Foot" Tilton, as his shipmates had nicknamed him, had persevered through blizzards so fierce that he had roped himself to his guides to keep from losing his way. On the portage across the Seward Peninsula—the same route Bertholf would soon travel in reverse—he had to kill two of his dogs to feed the others.

When Jarvis and Call told him of their intention to drive a herd of reindeer from Cape Prince of Wales to Point Barrow, Tilton wished them luck but figured their chances of success at one in a hundred. Still, reindeer were a better bet than dogs, he allowed. Later that night, Jarvis wrote to Secretary Gage, "Mr. Tilton has been over the road from the north and agreed with me thoroughly in the utter impossibility of carrying anything there by [dog] sledges and that the only possible way was to drive the reindeer."

That Tilton had been dispatched on his perilous mission in the first place was the clearest indication that things at Point Barrow were less than satisfactory. Before he had left, the whalers had already begun grumbling about the short rations and claustrophobic quarters. Yet even if Tilton had come down the trail bearing tidings of abundant victuals and intramural harmony, it hardly seems likely that Jarvis and Call would have altered their plans. Their orders described no circumstances under which they should call off the expedition. Whether or not the reindeer arrived at Point Barrow, and whether or not they were needed in the first place, the Overland Relief Expedition was still expected "to take charge in the name of the Government and organize the community for mutual support and good order." Besides, Jarvis and Call had come too far to quit or turn back. Like Tilton, they saw themselves as knights-errant, embarked on a quest that, once begun, must not pause until it had reached its gallant conclusion. "The information Tilton brought hardly altered the situation," Jarvis declared almost defensively.

The following morning, Tilton and his native guides resumed their southbound journey. While they were crossing the Yukon and Kuskokwim deltas, the temperature fell to fifty below. Reaching Shelikof Strait, at the base of the Aleutians, in mid-March, he commandeered a leaky dory and rowed thirty miles to Kodiak Island. From there he caught a steamer to the States, arriving in Portland on April 8, after six months of continuous travel. Only then did the outside world learn what had happened at Point Barrow the previous fall.

Jarvis and Call pressed on as well. They paused in Unalakleet the next day to acquire fresh dogs and arrange for the provisions that Bertholf would haul to Kotzebue Sound. For the next three days, the trail was well marked and easily traveled, until they reached the mouth of the Koyuk River. Here the terrain turned mountainous and wooded, and the snow got steadily deeper. "The runners would sink to the body of the sled, and dogs go nearly out of sight in their struggles to drag along," Jarvis mentioned grimly. "It took four men to tramp down a trail in order to make any progress at all, and at night . . . our dogs were so exhausted they simply laid down and refused to go any farther."

On the evening of January 10, as they plunged through more drifts, flanked on one side by frozen Norton Bay and on the other by the slopes of the Kwiktalik Mountains, they came upon a scene that brought smiles to their chapped faces. Spread out before them at the foot of the mountain were the government reindeer and the camp of Dr. Albert Kittilsen and the Lapp and Eskimo herders.

. . .

Kittilsen had been on the trail nearly a month when Jarvis and Call appeared at his camp on Norton Bay. In another week he would have delivered the government herd of five hundred reindeer to Unalakleet, an unprecedented trek of 350 miles. But now, so close to the end, he was obliged to reverse his direction. The orders from Lieutenant Colonel Randall had stipulated that he provide Jarvis and Call with deer and sleds to get them to their next destination: the reindeer herd of Charlie Antisarlook and the mission at Cape Prince of Wales. But merely turning over the deer and sleds would not be enough. Kittilsen knew that Jarvis and Call could not make the trip on their own. Reluctantly he called his Lapp and Eskimo herders together and explained that they would have to continue on without him.

On the afternoon of January 11, Kittilsen led the Overland Relief Expedition back over the trail he had just traveled. They kept to the coast, rounding Cape Darby, and on the following day arrived at the trading post and mission at Golovnin Bay, near which the main reindeer herd was still being held. Here Jarvis dismissed his dog teams and native guides, sending them back to Unalakleet and St. Michael. For the next week, the two Revenue Cutter Service men would travel by reindeer sled.

Jarvis and Call had been around plenty of reindeer. They had been ashore at Chukchi villages to buy deer for the Alaskan herd. From the bridge of the *Bear*, they had watched over pens of reindeer during the brief but nerve-racking voyage across the Bering Strait. And each summer when the *Bear* stopped at Port Clarence and Cape Prince of Wales, they had monitored the growth of the herds with vicarious pride. Yet despite their frequent contact with these remarkably resilient creatures, neither Jarvis nor Call had ever handled a reindeer sled. They were about to receive a crash course.

They remained at Golovnin Bay for one day, long enough to have their deerskin clothes mended and acquire provisions for the next two legs of the trip. First they would follow the coast west to Cape Rodney, at the mouth of the Sinuk River, where Antisarlook kept his herd; from there they would head northwest to Cape Prince of Wales. Along with Kittilsen, Jarvis, and Call, the party included one of the Lapp herders, Mikkel Nakkila, and Keok, the Cape Prince of Wales herder whom Tom Lopp had sent to gain experience on the drive to Unalakleet.

On the trip from Cape Vancouver to Golovnin Bay, Jarvis and Call had relied on native guides to take charge of the sleds. From here on, they would have to handle their own. With a dogsled, the driver usually walks or runs alongside, ready to push when necessary. With reindeer, it is almost impossible for the driver to keep up on foot; he is either a passenger or he is soon left behind. "I was very anxious to try the change and note the difference, wishing for anything that would hurry us along," Jarvis wrote enthusiastically. He learned quickly that reindeer are abrupt starters. "All hands must be ready at the same time when starting a deer train," Jarvis advised, "for, just as soon as the animals see the head team start, they are all off with a jump, and for a short time keep up a high rate of speed. If one is not quick in jumping and holding on to his sled, he is likely either to lose his [sled] or be dragged along in the snow."

Jarvis and Call did well enough the first day, as the sleds crossed Golovnin Bay and then flanked the foot of Iknutak Mountain to the shore of Norton Sound. "We tried to keep on the ice where the traveling was easier, but the crushes along the shore grew so rough that we were compelled to take to the hills," Jarvis explained. Coming down the final hill to the coast, his deer spooked, pitching him off the sled. Hanging onto the rein attached to the halter, he was dragged violently through the snow until the sled crashed into a fish rack. "When I saw that fish rack loom up, I though my time had come," Jarvis calculated, "but my bones seemed stronger than the rack."

Later that same day, with the wind now blowing a gale, Jarvis lost the trail in the afternoon darkness and ran into a driftwood stump buried in the snow. This time the harness snapped, and his reindeer galloped into the gloom, leaving Jarvis alone with his sled. He dug out his sleeping bag and prepared to wait for daylight. But after an hour, Kittilsen and Nakkila appeared, leading his deer. "They had a good laugh at my expense," Jarvis admitted, "but I think all hands were very glad it was nothing more serious than a laugh."

For the next six days, they struggled through a near-constant blizzard. The temperature fell to thirty below, and the wind blew so hard they could barely stand up. "It was all the deer could do to keep going ahead, and it required all our efforts to keep them from turning tail and going out to sea," Jarvis commented.

On the afternoon of January 15, the expedition came upon two men toiling in the opposite direction, also on reindeer sleds. One was Nels Hultberg, a Swedish Evangelical missionary from Golovnin Bay; the other was H. L. Blake, a mining engineer. The encounter prompted barely a mention in Jarvis's journal; nevertheless, Hultberg and Blake were making history in their own right. Two weeks earlier they had set off from Golovnin Bay to prospect for gold. Guided by a native with the storybook name of Too Rig Luck, they had been delighted by the color they found in a frozen creek near Cape Nome. Jarvis, who met them on their way home, noted only that the two prospectors had paid for their outing "with frozen cheeks and noses." Whatever the discomfort, it would soon be assuaged by extraordinary rewards. The following July, Hultberg and Blake, along with several partners, would return to form the first mining district at Cape Nome, and by the end of the summer— well before Jarvis, Call, and their companions had concluded their expedition to Point Barrow—the next great Alaskan gold rush was under way.

Oblivious of these momentous developments, Jarvis and his companions carried on with the task at hand. When they finally struggled into a native settlement on the west side of Cape Nome, they were greeted by a pack of native dogs. "Only after a hard fight were we able to drive them off," Jarvis commented.

On January 19, a week after leaving Golovnin Bay, they at last reached the house of Charlie Antisarlook. In December, the *Bear* had steamed to within one hundred miles of this spot before being turned away by the ice. It had taken the Overland Relief Expedition five weeks and five hundred additional miles to make up the difference.

Antisarlook was not at home when they arrived. His wife, Mary, told them that he was out hunting seals. While they waited for Antisarlook to return, Mary chatted away in English, Inupiaq, also in Russian, which Call understood. But as hard as she tried, she could not persuade the men to reveal the true purpose of their visit. "Told her we were looking for whisky-making Indians," Call fibbed. Jarvis remained quiet, pulling on his pipe. "I had looked forward to this day so long that now it had come I almost shrank from the task it brought," he confessed. Toward evening, Antisarlook appeared, dragging a seal, which he divided among his family and neighbors. The best parts, the heart and liver, were served to the guests.

Jarvis did not reveal his true reason for coming so far in the dead of winter until after the meal. "Jarvis knew well the disposition and character of those he had to deal with," Call explained. "He had for years met the Antisarlooks in the country, had never deceived or lied

to them, had always been kind and never failed to bring to them anything which he had promised. So he first began by appealing to their
sympathy and related minutely the condition of the unfortunate people of Point Barrow."

Three months earlier, when Antisarlook had surrendered half of his
reindeer herd to Dr. Kittilsen, he had been given no say in the matter.
This time he had a choice. "I explained to him . . . that I had not come
with power or force to take his property from him," Jarvis wrote, "and
that he must let me have them of his own free will."

At first Antisarlook and Mary resisted. Call remembered Mary saying, "Tell Mr. Jarvis we are sorry for the people of Point Barrow, and
we want to help them, but we hate to see our deer go, because we are
poor and the people in our village are poor, and in the winter when we
can not get seals we kill a deer, and this helps us through the hard
times. If we let the deer go what will we do?"

As proficient as Antisarlook and Mary were at hunting, fishing, and
herding, they were even more adept at bargaining. In the end, they
agreed to let Jarvis take their deer, but only after he wrote letters
authorizing them to draw a winter's worth of supplies from the trading
post at Golovnin Bay and the reindeer station at Port Clarence. More
significantly, Jarvis also promised that next summer the Treasury
Department would replace the deer he was taking from Antisarlook's
herd with an equal number of animals—plus "the estimated increase
in the herd for the coming spring, about 80 fawns."

The deal was not quite done, however. Besides Antisarlook's 213
reindeer, another five deer belonged to the other natives who helped
with the herd. Jarvis was obliged to buy them outright at $15 a head.

Jarvis was enormously relieved to secure Antisarlook's herd and
assistance, yet he allowed himself no pause. Once again he decided to
split the expedition. Entrusting Call and Keok to drive Antisarlook's
reindeer to Cape Prince of Wales, Jarvis departed for Port Clarence
the next day, guided by Kittilsen and the Lapp herder Nakkila. Despite

a temperature of forty below, they made a brisk run along the shore. When Jarvis arrived at Port Clarence, his face was "bloody with sores from the cold," recalled Toleef Brevig, the missionary who was also the acting superintendent of the reindeer station. The long trip and relentless pace had likewise taken a toll on the sled deer, and they were in need of extended rest.

This was also the end of the road for Kittilsen and Nikkala. (They would return to the government herd at Unalakleet the following month.) In their place, Jarvis hired a dogsled and driver for the sixty-mile push to Cape Prince of Wales. A blizzard delayed departure for a day, giving Jarvis time to have his clothes repaired and to acquire more deerskin boots, socks, shirts, and atigis. "Nothing would keep one warm in the weather we were having but deerskins," he noted, "and we were fortunate to be able to obtain what we needed, for the miners had pretty well cleaned out the supply in all other parts of the country."

At this point, there is a curious gap in Jarvis's official report. He does not mention that Charlie Antisarlook was in the party traveling from Sinuk River to Port Clarence, but Antisarlook in fact made the trip. Perhaps he had first put things in order at home and come along later. Regardless, he appeared in Port Clarence in time to accompany Jarvis on the next leg of his journey.

The two-day trip from Port Clarence to Cape Prince of Wales was "the most trying and fearful" of the entire expedition, Jarvis judged. The morning Jarvis and Antisarlook left the reindeer station with the native guide, the temperature was minus thirty, and the blizzard still raged. After a few miles, their guide found an excuse to return to Port Clarence, leaving Jarvis and Antisarlook to drive the sled on their own. Antisarlook, who had been over this route many times, walked ahead, picking a path through the ice heaved against the shore. "I was left to manage the heavy sled, which was continually capsizing in the rough ice," Jarvis recalled.

By eight that night, Jarvis was exhausted and suggested to Antisarlook that they make camp. Antisarlook counseled otherwise, insisting that it was far too cold to camp without firewood and that the ice "was in danger of breaking off from the shore at any minute." Stumbling along in the dark, Jarvis slipped through a crack, soaking one of his legs to the knee. "Though almost ready to drop where I was, I had to keep on, for to stop meant to freeze," he acknowledged. "Pushing and lifting our sled, and urging the dogs, we dragged along until midnight, when we came to a house high up on the shore. . . . It was a small hut, about 10 by 12, and five feet high, and 15 people were already sleeping there. It was most filthy and the worst house I have seen in all my Alaska experience; but I was too tired then to care for that, too tired even to eat; and though I had had nothing but a couple of crackers since morning, I was quite satisfied to take off my wet clothing, crawl into my bag, and sleep."

The blizzard had not abated by morning, but Jarvis and Antisarlook could not bear to stay put in the cramped, foul hut. They hitched their dogs and pushed on another ten miles to a small village—Pelazuk probably—where they cooked a hot meal and hired another sled to lighten the heavy load. Even then they made poor progress. As they approached the Bering Strait, southeast of Cape Prince of Wales, the mountains grew steeper and the slabs of broken ice along the shore more riotous. "Darkness set in long before we had come to the worst of it, and a faint moon gave too little light for such a road," Jarvis wrote. "It was a continuous jumble of dogs, sleds, men, and ice—particularly ice—and it would be hard to tell which suffered most, men or dogs. Once, helping the sled over a particularly bad place, I was thrown eight or nine feet down a slide, landing on the back of my head with the sled on top of me. Though the mercury was -30°, I was wet through with perspiration from the violence of the work. Our sleds were racked and broken, our dogs played out, and we ourselves scarcely able to move."

In this sorry state they finally arrived at the door of Ellen and Tom Lopp on the evening of January 24.

## [ 11 ]

# Errand of Mercy

THE LOPP FAMILY WAS eating supper at the kitchen table when Jarvis knocked. "I met him at the door and thought he was a Native until he held out his hand and spoke English as no Native speaks it," Ellen wrote to her family. (She made no mention of Charlie Antisarlook; perhaps he was tending to the dogs or was in another house in the village.) "I told him I didn't know who he was."

Nor did Jarvis disclose his identity right away. Instead, he let them guess. "I could see only a very little of his face, and that [was] back in his hood," Ellen puzzled. "He was too tall to be Mr. B[revig]. . . . I went into the kitchen and told Tom, who had been so busy with the children that he hadn't heard [Jarvis enter]. He asked if he was Dr. Dexter [the trader from Golovnin Bay]. He said, 'Dr. Dexter can't walk like this.'" They next asked if he was Dr. Driggs from Point Hope, if he was Robert Samms, the new Quaker missionary at Kotzebue Sound. "He seemed to be enjoying our suspense," Ellen elaborated. "His parka was too small and Tom had to help him out of it. He took him by the top of his hood and pulled. The children were . . . at the table and I knew I ought to go to them, but curiosity held me to the spot for there was no one person . . . more likely to appear than any of a few hundred others." At last they got a good look at the visitor's wind-burned face. "It was Mr. Jarvis."

Recognition unleashed a flood of questions. Where had he come from? Why was he here? Jarvis finally abandoned his coyness. As he thawed before the stove, he spilled the entire story of the Overland Relief Expedition and his long journey from Cape Vancouver to Cape Prince of Wales. Once the warmth had returned to his bones, he dug out the official instructions written by Treasury secretary Gage: "The purpose [of the Overland Relief Expedition] is to collect from . . . [the Sinuk River] and Cape Prince of Wales the entire available herds of reindeer, all to be driven to Point Barrow. . . . Mr. Lopp is to take charge of this herd and make all necessary arrangements. . . . Mr. Lopp must be fully impressed with the importance of the work at hand, and with the necessity of bending every energy to its speedy accomplishment."

The wishes of the government were quite clear. But the choice was still Tom's, the same as with Antisarlook. Jarvis could "impress" and flatter, but he could not dictate. He carried no orders from Tom's superintendent, Sheldon Jackson, or from the Department of the Interior, which oversaw the schools of Alaska. The only leverage Jarvis had, beyond his own power of persuasion, was a letter from the American Missionary Association, the owner of the Cape reindeer herd, permitting Tom "to dispose of the herd on requisition of the Government."

Tom and Ellen lay awake all night, mulling over the meteor that had just crashed into their midst. They felt no great affection for whalers, but they trusted Jarvis's assertion that relief was imperative and time of the essence. Tom especially understood that such an expedition, if successful, would be received as a resounding validation of the reindeer program. Unlike the recent drive from Port Clarence to Unalakleet—or the proposed reindeer rescue of the Yukon miners—there would be no Lapps involved in this endeavor. Tom and his native herders would be in charge of the deer, and their efforts would determine the outcome. He probably did not articulate his thoughts so grandly to Ellen—or to Jarvis—but undoubtedly they were at the front of his mind.

The more Tom studied the trip, the more convinced he became that he and his herders could make it. Jarvis estimated the distance from the Cape to Point Barrow at seven hundred miles. No one had ever driven an entire herd of reindeer that far. Yet Tom had been over the trail as far as Point Hope. In 1893, he and Ellen had crossed over the ice of Kotzebue Sound—while Ellen was pregnant. Indeed, the logistics, hardships, and unforeseeable mishaps of the trip were not what worried him. It was not the going so much as the leaving behind. The expedition might take three, four, perhaps as many as six months. Tom had never left Ellen and the children by themselves for that long. He understood only too well how lonely winter could be—never mind the danger.

Ellen had no such reservations, at least none that she divulged to her husband as they whispered back and forth throughout the night. She would be fine without him, she assured. She had the children to keep her company. Nora and Alice would continue to help around the house. Netaxite and his wife Kongik were close by, as was Sokweena's wife, Elubwok. She would continue teaching, and they would all pray for Tom and the herders while they were gone.

By morning it was decided: Tom would lead the drive to Point Barrow. "You can imagine at what cost this decision was made—separation of family . . . loss of deer, and breaking our plans for this year and next," he reflected in an article published the following year. "But it was an 'errand of mercy,' and we were glad to have an opportunity to show these people that our government cared . . . and would go to great expense to save a few in distress."

A mission of mercy perhaps, but not one of charity. Before agreeing to join the Overland Relief Expedition, Tom requested a written pledge from Jarvis to replace the deer taken from the Cape, plus the increase of fawns. Of the 301 reindeer in the Cape herd, 292 belonged to the American Missionary Association. The other nine were owned by native herders, and Jarvis had to purchase them, just as he had done at Sinuk River. And like Antisarklook, the Cape herders were hired at a dollar a day. Tom's pay would be $150 a month.

Ellen, who voiced no qualms over Tom's decision to leave home on such a long, perilous journey, was not so cheerful about seeing the reindeer depart. Nor did she have full faith that the government would live up to its promise. "It is hard to give up our deer," she confided in a letter home. "I don't know when we can get more. . . . We expected at least 140 fawns in the spring. Mr. Jarvis allowed for them in the contract, but that is only paper."

. . .

Jarvis and Lopp spent the next four days preparing for the odyssey ahead. All told, they figured on eighteen sleds to haul their food and camp gear. They would kill reindeer for meat, rounding out their diet with bread, flour, butter, lard, dried fruit, sugar, tea, coffee, and cocoa. "We carried little or no canned goods," Lopp noted. "We did, however, carry Eagle [condensed] milk, and maple syrup." They packed two sheet-metal stoves and two tents. Their sleeping bags, as well as their clothing, were made of deerskin.

Gathering enough reindeer to pull so many sleds was a more difficult proposition. Only a small number of the deer in the Cape herd had been broken to harness. A few of these had names, including one that had been reverently dubbed Moses and another cheekily called Healy. When it looked as if Lopp might come up short, he sent one of his herders to Port Clarence to collect two more. Antisarlook had also gone back down the trail to help bring up his herd from the Sinuk River.

Because the number of sleds exceeded the number of seasoned

drivers, Lopp adopted a technique he had learned from the Lapps at Port Clarence. He would link the sleds together in trains—two trains of five sleds, one train of four. The lead sled in each train would be driven by an experienced herder; each of the "trailer" sleds would be pulled by its own deer but tethered by a rope to the sled in front. Four other sleds, the lightest ones, would be driven separately. Fast and maneuverable, they would follow closely behind the herd to keep it moving, like drovers on a cattle drive. Three herding dogs would help discourage laggards and quitters.

The herd was grazing twenty miles north of the Cape at the Mint River, on the moss-rich hills that Lopp had selected on his scouting trip seven years earlier. When he and Jarvis arrived at the herders' camp on January 30, Call, Antisarlook, Keok, and the Sinuk River herd still had not arrived. Finally, on February 2, the deer were spotted to the south, urged along by the sleds of Antisarlook and Keok, who, by their efficient maneuverings, succeeded not so much in steering the animals in the direction they ought to go but in subtracting the directions that they ought not. As the newcomers drew nearer to the larger herd, Lopp and Jarvis could make out the vapor from a hundred muzzles. Another quarter mile and they could hear the familiar grunting of the leaders. Then the two herds were one, each welcoming the security of the other. Soon the deer were arrayed across the wind-swept hillside, cropping unhurriedly at tussocks of gray moss. The total head count was 438.

The next morning the Overland Relief Expedition was ready to begin. "The harnessing and hitching . . . seemed to take an endless amount of time, and got on poor Jarvis' nerves," Lopp remarked. "He became very impatient and nervous. . . . We did not really get started until about noon." Jarvis's frustration was nothing new, but now he had even greater reason to be restive. A month earlier, George Fred Tilton had told him that the whalers had enough food to last until July. Suddenly an even more pressing deadline had presented itself. If the herd did not arrive at Point Barrow by April, it might not make it at all, Lopp warned him. Most of the cows were pregnant; once they began having their calves, it would be impossible and senseless to push them farther. Five months had shrunk to three.

The going was slow at first. "We could not get them into a trot," Lopp regretted. "In fact, it was difficult for us to keep them in a brisk walk." Seeming to sense the long ordeal ahead, the deer kept stopping to paw the snow and feed on the moss beneath. They made only seven miles the first day. "Though it was not much in distance," Jarvis said with mixed emotion, "[at least] we had moved from our base, and it seemed that we had made a good start at doing something."

In the morning, it took hours to prepare breakfast and pack the sleds. They did not get away until 9:30. The day was sunny and warm—twenty degrees above zero—but again the reindeer could not be persuaded to move with any conviction. The route that Lopp had chosen kept to the hillsides, where the moss was more abundant and blown clear by the wind. In many places it grew in thick clumps, known as niggerheads, which were appetizing but very difficult to travel through. A cow that kept straggling was finally allowed to fall behind, the first of the deer to be lost. They made fifteen miles that day, which improved Jarvis's spirits only slightly.

What nettled him even more than the slow pace was his passive place in the scheme. Lacking experience as a sled driver, he was obliged to ride as a passenger in one of the trains. His only previous attempt at reindeer sledding, from Golovnin Bay to Port Clarence, had been punctuated by a series of spills and near disasters. Call's talents as a deer handler were not much better. He had managed his own sled on the drive from the Sinuk River, but when he tried to drive one of the Cape sleds, he failed miserably. "He furnished much amusement for the boys," Lopp chuckled. "His deer made many circles, some large and some small, turned his sled over a number of times, and gave the Doctor more exercise than he had had for some time."

By the third day, Jarvis could stand no more. In the evening they made camp beside the Nuluk River, sheltered from the north wind by a thicket of alders and willows. The temperature had dropped to ten below. The next day would likely bring more of the same. Pulling Lopp aside, Jarvis suggested—for the third time since landing in Alaska—that the expedition split up. His original letter of instruction had called for him to remain with the herd as far as Kotzebue Sound. Now he announced that he and Call would forge ahead to the Quaker mission located there, alerting the villages along the way that the herd was coming. "The natives beyond Cape Prince of Wales had never seen domestic deer," he explained, "and they could easily mistake them for caribou and go gunning for them." Moreover, he conceded, "We were not essential to the progress of the herd, Mr. Lopp and his herders having all the knowledge and experience necessary for the work in hand, and we . . . were just so much more to be hauled."

The next morning an Eskimo named Perningik appeared at the herders' camp. Lopp had met Perningik several years earlier, and he introduced his friend to Jarvis as "a splendid hunter and trapper and a good trail man." If Jarvis was keen to hurry ahead, he could not find a better guide.

The only one displeased with the plan was Call, who, despite his poor showing as a deer man, nonetheless preferred riding in a reindeer sled to running mile after mile behind a dogsled. But when he tried to make his case for staying with the deer herd, Jarvis turned a deaf ear and ordered the doctor to pack his things.

Lopp and one of the herders took Jarvis and Call by reindeer sled as far as the coastal village of Sinrazet. "It was a mean little trip," Lopp noted. "The wind increased and there was much snow blowing." Leaving the cuttermen in Perningik's hands, Lopp made it back to the herd the following day. Responsibility for the reindeer herd was now his entirely. To be sure, the circumstances were not of his design, but once the challenge had presented itself, he had not sought deliverance. Instead he put himself in God's hands. Then, too, he had utter faith in the ability of the seven natives he had handpicked for this improbable, if not impossible, journey.

. . .

Charlie Antisarlook was by far the oldest of the group. Lopp guessed him to be about thirty-four in 1898, which was Lopp's age, too. As helpful as Antisarlook had been to Jarvis, first in agreeing to let go of his deer and then in guiding Jarvis to Cape Prince of Wales, there was something about Antisarlook—his lack of subservience, his obvious prowess as hunter and guide—that made Jarvis uneasy. Lopp was convinced that if he had not insisted on taking Antisarlook on the overland expedition, Jarvis would have sent him home. Lopp and Antisarlook, on the other hand, had forged an unshakable bond over the years. "If you will pardon the immodesty," Lopp remarked later on, "I doubt if there was another man that Charl[ie] . . . would have gone with on that doubtful drive."

The same was true for the other six herders. Had Lopp refused to lead the drive or been otherwise unavailable, it is hard to imagine Jarvis persuading them to take the herd seven hundred miles to Point Barrow. With Lopp, however, they would go almost anywhere, and the feeling was mutual. They were all between the ages of eighteen and twenty-one. Five of them, whom Lopp would later label "the Quints," had been with him since the first reindeer were brought to the Cape. Sokweena had befriended Lopp even earlier and had guided him on his first sled trip to Shishmaref.

As far as Lopp was concerned, there was much more to being an apprentice reindeer herder than simply learning how to look after reindeer. Four of the Quints knew how to read and write, and they were accustomed to praying and keeping the Sabbath. These four had also accepted Christian names: Thomas Sokweena, James Keok, George Ootenna, Stanley Kivyearzruk. The fifth Quint, Tautuk, had joined the group a year after the others; he was a "bright, active lad," Lopp assured, "but had no schooling." The last of the herders, Ituk, was a nineteen-year-old orphan who had been an apprentice for only a year or so.

Lopp's fondness for all of them was unqualified. Years later as he reminisced on the Overland Relief Expedition, he drafted a short memorandum, "Eskimo Boys on Drive of 1898," lest these seven estimable herders be overlooked by histories that tended to favor the deeds of white men. Of Stanley Kivyearzruk, for example, he wrote: "[He] was a strong st[oc]ky boy . . . of much determination and will power." George Ootenna was "industrious, honest," a talented artist and mechanic as well as a very capable herder.

Lopp's regard for James Keok exceeded all others: "[He had] a rather slender build, well proportioned body, . . . a very pleasing expression, very bright eyes and always wore a smile that meant something because it was part of him. . . . He was a polite boy but never a yes, yes one. He was uncomplaining and always willing to do more than his share, and never shirked a difficult task as a deerman. . . . He was neat and cleanly. Although modest, he was not bashful. He was a boy of unusual good judgment & was thrifty without being stingy. If he was ever jealous I failed to observe it or learn of it, consequently I never heard of his having an enemy. He was the most likeable human being . . . that I have ever known."

Whereas Jarvis rarely bothered to record the names of the natives with whom he traveled, Tom Lopp stood ready to nominate his "boys" for the highest honors. Beyond mere boys, he often called them "gentlemen." And even more important than their individual virtues, for the sake of the Overland Relief Expedition, was the camaraderie of the Quints. "To my knowledge," Lopp attested, "not one of the five ever made an unkind, critical, or jealous remark about any of the other four. They were five jolly jokers, but hard and willing workers."

. . .

On February 8, the Overland Relief Expedition, now numbering eight, set off again, driving the reindeer herd into the teeth of a north wind, the thermometer holding at thirty-five below zero. "There were no willows or alder where we camped [that night]," Lopp wrote. "We found that we now had a surplus sled since relieved of the baggage of Jarvis and Call, so burned it for fuel."

For a variety of reasons—personal chemistry, gentler geography, and not least of all the adapatability of the deer—the drive at last began to gel. On the ninth, they crossed the foothills west of Ear Mountain and angled toward Shishmaref Inlet, where the trail was more level. "We had made up our minds it would be better for us to follow the coast than go overland across the tundra," Lopp recorded in his diary. "On the latter we could make only twelve or fifteen miles a day. Our three hours across the inlet demonstrated to us that on a lagoon we could drive the herd at the rate of twenty or twenty-five miles per day. Our boys were all glad to be on the sea coast again." As a measure of their high spirits, "Charlie sang for the first time."

They camped three miles from present-day Shishmaref, far enough away to keep the native dogs from attacking the herd. The route from there to Kotzebue Sound, sixty miles to the northeast, was straight and unimpeded. To allow for more time on the trail, they began sending one or two sleds ahead each morning to ready the next night's camp. On the afternoon of the twelfth, Antisarlook and Ituk, who had been assigned to the cooking detail, chose to set up their stove in a house occupied by several natives. For once Lopp was a less than appreciative guest. "The air was so close and the smell so strong that I had little appetite," he confessed. "I decided not to attempt to sleep in it, so we pitched our tent outside."

One of the natives with whom they shared the camp that night, a man named Kiktoo-oisuk, had just come from Cape Espenberg on the southern shore of Kotzebue Sound, twenty miles or so up the trail. Kiktoo-oisuk's news was discouraging. Two days earlier, he had attempted to cross the sound from Cape Espenberg to Cape Krusenstern—the same route Lopp had traveled in 1893 and over which he now hoped to take the herd. But Kiktoo-oisuk had been turned back. A stiff offshore wind had separated the pack ice from the shore ice, creating a formidable lead of open water. Kiktoo-oisuk also mentioned that Jarvis and Call were at Cape Espenberg, purportedly short of food, waiting for Lopp and the herders to arrive.

Very soon, perhaps the next day, Lopp and the herders would have to make a difficult choice, one that would surely affect the outcome of the expedition and the fate of all involved. If the ice across the sound was passable, they could drive the herd to Cape Krusenstern, a distance of forty miles, in one long push of twelve or fourteen hours, or at the very most, in two days. But if the ice turned out to be impassable, they would have to keep to the coast, which would add seven or eight precious days to the trek.

For his own peace of mind, Lopp decided to scout ahead. While the herders continued to push the deer northeastward, he hired a native named Mukiuktuk to take him by dogsled to the village of To-otet, on the coast of the Chukchi Sea, where he anticipated Jarvis and Call would be waiting. Ten miles south of Cape Espenberg, Lopp and Mukiuktuk met up with several natives traveling down from Point Hope. One of them carried a letter from Jarvis saying that he and Call had left To-otet a day earlier and headed across the ice of Kotzebue Sound. Lopp took their departure as a hopeful sign that the ice had improved. He was more eager than ever to see for himself.

But the nearer they got to the cape, the slower they traveled. Every few miles, Mukiuktuk would pause, claiming he was out of breath or that the dogs needed rest, when in fact he was deliberately playing on Lopp's impatience. Each time the sled lagged, Lopp would promise a bonus to Mukiuktuk if he would put on speed. "Since I was paying him with an I.O.U. [for cotton fabric], I gave him two more raises in his pay and we made splendid time and reached the village of To-otet on the point of the cape an hour before dark," Lopp recalled happily. "The people gave a hearty welcome. In January 1893, Mrs. Lopp and I had stopped there on our way to Point Hope, and had been detained there some three or four days waiting for a northwesterly wind to drive the ice in and bridge over the sound."

The next morning Lopp and a boy from the village went out to study the ice. The wind was not from the northwest, as he would have liked, but blowing strongly from the southwest. Standing on the shore, he gazed across the sound toward the ragged ramparts of the Igichuk Hills. On a day so clear and crisp (twenty-eight below), he had trouble believing they were forty miles away.

Lopp and the boy walked a ways onto the ice. It looked "safe but too rough," he assessed. "In places it was piled in great heaps." The pack ice had barged ashore, crumpling the weaker shore ice into a grotesque garden of rubble and shards. "I was sure that we could never get deer sleds through these ice jams without breaking them." Climbing to the top of one of the hummocks, he could see nothing but more of the same in the distance. "I returned to the village very much discouraged."

At To-otet he found that the herd had caught up and was grazing two miles away. Later that day several of the herders made their own trip onto the ice, choosing to explore not due north toward Cape Krusenstern, which was the nearest point to Cape Espenberg, but northeastward, toward Cape Blossom on the Baldwin Peninsula, where they hoped the ice might be friendlier. They hiked much farther than Lopp had dared, and, while the going was no less rough, they returned to report that crossing in this direction was possible.

It was a measure of Lopp's leadership and of his respect for the herders that he put the matter up for discussion. If Jarvis had still been with the expedition, the conversation would not have been so democratic. And if Lopp had not spoken Inupiaq, he would have been less comfortable allowing everyone a say. "The question was . . . shall we risk taking the short cut [across the ice] or follow the coast," Lopp remembered. "The cows were showing the effects of the trip. In two months they would commence dropping their fawns. We realized that they were too heavy to keep up the speed at which we had been driving them during the past four days. Therefore, we reasoned that the five or six days which we could save by crossing the ice were absolutely needed."

When at last the question was put to a vote, they were all in favor of the shortcut.

Once a plan had been agreed upon, there was no sense in waiting. While some of the herders began preparing the sleds for the crossing, others gathered firewood and foraged for reindeer moss to be packed on the sleds; there would be no other food for the deer during the crossing. To lighten the loads on the reindeer sleds, Lopp hired two dog teams from the village; one of them was Mukiuktuk's.

That night as they prepared their last supper on land, spirits ran high. "The boys were very much pleased with the prospect of the undertaking," Lopp observed. "They were all experienced ice men, having had much experience in traveling over the Bering Strait ice when seal hunting and bear hunting." To boost morale further, Lopp promised bonuses to everyone if the herd reached Point Barrow on "schedule time"—meaning April, before the calves came.

When they arose the morning of February 15, the temperature was thirty-four degrees below zero. The sky remained clear. The wind was once again in their favor, from the north. They reached the shore an hour after sunrise: fourteen deer sleds, two dogsleds, and more than four hundred reindeer. Before driving the deer onto the ice, they allowed the herd one last chance to graze. And then they committed themselves to Kotzebue Sound.

For a short while, they were accompanied by an old man from the village and his grandson. "This was their first experience with reindeer," Lopp remarked cheerily. "When the going was good they jumped on the reindeer sleds and had their first ride behind what to them were domesticated caribou. Our boys swelled with pride when these natives complimented them on their ability to handle those *toc-too* (caribou). While traveling with us they constantly marveled at the advantage of reindeer over dogs."

But then, as they reached the point where the shore ice collided with the less stationary pack ice, the road got more challenging, and the old man and his grandson climbed off the sleds, bid good-bye to the reindeer men, and turned toward the relative comfort of home. For Lopp and his herders, the mountains on the far side of Kotzebue Sound still beckoned, but they hardly seemed closer. Not that anyone noticed, but they had just crossed the Arctic Circle.

# [ 12 ]

# Labyrinth

THE FIRST TEST CAME where the pack ice met the shore ice. The former was at the mercy of current and winds; the latter was bound tightly to the coastline. Two days earlier, the pack ice had drifted seaward, creating a lead of open water six feet wide. But now as Lopp and his herders drove the deer north across Kotzebue Sound, they were relieved to discover that the gap had frozen over, although only barely. There were patches where the ice was still so young that it seemed to undulate with every roll of the water underneath. The deer could sense its newness and hesitated. Finally after some coaxing, they eased across on their saucer-shaped hooves.

There were other places, however, which the herd simply could not be induced to cross. Some of the hummocks of fractured ice were ten feet tall. Even if the reindeer could pick their way through these warrens of rubble, the heavily laden sleds could not. Eskimo sleds were ingeniously flexible, crafted of supple wood and bound together by leather thongs, but they could not withstand the constant bending and twisting inflicted by the biggest ice upheavals. The only recourse was to seek a way around them.

Painstakingly, reindeer and sleds clambered through the labyrinth, like crabs upon a reef. "Our course during the day meandered in so many directions that it was difficult to estimate how many miles we covered toward our goal," Lopp lamented. Under such conditions, his compass was of no help. By afternoon, as the light began to fail, the mountains to the north seemed nearer, but Lopp knew that he had no chance of reaching the far shore that night. At the very best, he hoped to reach the midway point. Then, if the deer took a notion to seek terra firma, most likely they would go forward toward Cape Krusenstern and not retreat in the direction from which they had come that morning.

They kept moving well past dark and resigned themselves to traveling all night. But by eleven they came upon a particularly formidable bulwark of ice. "It was impossible to continue our journey without tearing our reindeer sleds to pieces," Lopp explained. Tying the sled deer to blocks of ice, they made a rudimentary camp. They had brought along enough driftwood to build a fire, and they had enough moss to feed the sled deer. The rest of the herd would have to wait until they reached land.

Nor could they do anything about the herd's obvious thirst. During the frozen months of the year, reindeer rarely drink water for the simple reason that none is available. Instead, they eat snow, which they scoop up in their mouths as they trot across the tundra. This is what they had done while crossing Kotzebue Sound. But the snow that had accumulated on the ice was saturated with salt, which further dehydrated the deer.

That night Lopp assigned no watch, still figuring that if the herd drifted at all, it would continue north. "We were very well pleased with our day's work," he recalled, "and went to bed feeling that a few hours drive the following day would land us on the north side of Kotzebue."

He guessed wrong. On the morning of February 16, they roused themselves at 3:00 A.M., cooked breakfast, repacked the sleds, and set off in search of the herd. "As nearly as we could discover in the darkness, from the tracks, the herd had started toward the north shore. Therefore, we did not worry," Lopp wrote. "We scattered out 100 to 300 yards apart but we were unable to follow [the tracks] because of the roughness of the ice. When the day finally broke, we soon discovered that the deer instead of going north had turned southward."

All the hard-won progress of the previous day had vanished. To make matters worse, the sled deer were already near exhaustion, and the herd—wherever it had gone—could scarcely be in better shape. To drive them back over yesterday's ice would be doubly difficult. Lopp knew that he had taken a huge risk by attempting the shortcut across Kotzebue Sound. Now the entire Overland Relief Expedition depended on whether the herd could be found and turned around in time.

Lopp sent the four best herders, Tautuk, Keok, Ootenna, and Kivyearzruk, after the reindeer. The rest of the party—Lopp, Sokweena, Ituk, Antisarlook, and the two dogsled drivers—continued slowly northward toward Cape Krusenstern. "We were confident that the boys would soon overtake the herd," Lopp explained. "Therefore, all through the day, we were constantly looking southward for a black streak under a cloud of steam coming in our direction. Every high ice jam we passed we would climb to the top of it to look for the lost herd and herders."

Tautuk, Keok, Ootenna, and Kivyearzruk had expected to find the deer in a few miles and be back with the others in an hour or two. But by noon they had not returned. At midday, Lopp's group took a long rest and fed the last of the moss to the sled deer. Still the other herders did not appear. "We began to worry," Lopp confessed. "They had taken no food with them." Before going on, he had the herders unharness the heaviest and most unwieldy sled—made not by an Eskimo but by a blacksmith at Port Clarence—and stood it on end in the middle of a long stretch of smooth ice, where it would be impossible to miss. They also left a pail of food and a few sticks of firewood.

Reluctantly they resumed their march north. "As darkness was approaching," Lopp wrote, "our position became more and more appalling. . . . Here we were in the middle of Kotzebue Sound . . . with thirteen hungry sled deer and no moss to feed them, and the herd and four of our herders lost as far as we knew. We were constantly condemning our poor judgment." They pitched camp and cooked supper in silence. "We were all glum. There was not the usual joking and hilarity. We sat around our grub box to eat our supper with long faces."

Just as they were starting the meal, they heard the unmistakable sound of deer approaching—the jostling of the leaders, the crunch of hooves on ice. "We rushed out to greet them and there was great rejoicing," Lopp recorded.

Between mouthfuls of food, the herders told the story of their long day. They had tracked the herd south, running along the back trail as fast as they could. Even so, they did not overtake the herd until just before it left the ice on the south shore of Kotzebue Sound, a distance of twenty, perhaps thirty, miles. Rather than allow the reindeer to reach land, where they would lose more time as the animals grazed on moss, the four herders managed to circle the herd and turn it north again. Throughout the rest of the day, they kept the animals at a steady trot, "covering in one day what it had taken us two days to travel," Lopp marveled. Along the way, they came upon Lopp's favorite sled deer, Moses, who had become exhausted earlier in the day and been turned loose either to perish or to catch up on its own. They again left him behind. By superhuman effort, Keok, Ootenna, Tautuk, and Kivyearzruk had snatched, if not victory, then at least a second chance at victory from the jaws of disaster.

Still, there was no rest for the weary. Not wanting to risk a repeat of the day before, they decided to drive the herd through the night until they reached the north shore of the sound. But by now most of the sled deer were too hungry and worn out to negotiate the jumbled icescape. The only solution was to unharness the weakest deer and let them trail along with the herd, as they had done with Moses. Because the native dogs had proven to be better scramblers, the herders packed their sleeping bags, tent, and a bit of food on the dogsleds and left the rest of their gear behind with six sleds, hoping that natives could retrieve it later. With the remaining sleds pulling much lighter loads, they set off into the darkness.

"Our poor, overworked sled deer could scarcely keep up with the herd," Lopp wrote in his log. His shorthand bespoke his own fatigue: "In places we found it very rough. We break the [dog]sled, but repair it, drive ahead of the deer with the sled in order to pick the trail. Soon find a level stretch of ice, but there was a very rough gorge about 50 yards wide between this level area and the herd. Deer cross it very slowly. Leave a male fawn behind."

This was the nastiest night by far. The temperature dropped to forty below. Navigating the uneven ice was demanding enough; staying awake was harder still. They took turns lying across the dogsled, closing their eyes for a minute or two before the cold forced them to their feet again. At some point while riding on the sled, Lopp froze his heels, a potentially disabling injury if not cared for properly. Yet he trudged on, saying nothing. His greater concern was the herd. "It was pitiful, indeed, to watch the deer drag their legs along," he observed. "They had evidently [eaten] more of the salty snow than was good for them."

The night was not entirely bereft of blessings, however. The air was mercifully still, and as they staggered along, they were comforted by a brilliant display of the aurora borealis—a shimmering curtain of purples, reds, and yellows draped lavishly across the frigid dome of darkness.

When dawn approached at last, they could make out the shape of the mountains a few miles ahead. Staring across the ice, they also discerned a "long black streak," which they took to be the shoreline. "When we finally approached it," Lopp wrote forlornly, "I found that instead of land, it was a lead of water from six to forty inches wide. It was the lead separating the float or drift ice from the shore or grounded ice, and [we] reasoned that the land was not more than five or six miles distant."

But unless they could get the herd across the lead, five miles might as well have been fifty. The front-most deer pushed up to the edge and balked. Instinctively the herd began to mill, circling on itself, those on the inside pushing to the outside, the outside absorbed within the swirling mass. For once, there was no safety in numbers. "As the herd bunched up along the narrow crack," Lopp wrote, "their combined weight broke the thin ice and about half of the herd struggled around in the cold icy water."

There was absolutely nothing the herders could do but watch. They dared not get close for fear that they too would fall through the ice. Lassoing the antlers of one or two deer was pointless. Amazingly, the reindeer did not panic. For all their vaunted "domestication," they were still caribou at the core, a species well accustomed to immersion in Arctic waters. For countless millennia, their forebears had forded ice-choked rivers during their annual migration. To escape wolves and mosquitoes, they readily plunged into chilly lakes and lagoons. And in the pre-dawn gloom of February 18, 1898, having fallen unexpectedly through the ice of Kotzebue Sound, the reindeer did what any caribou would do: They swam about until they found a spot where the ice was thick enough to support their weight, heaved their front hooves onto the lip, and pulled themselves out.

As much admiration as Tom Lopp had for the resilience of reindeer at the start of the expedition, it now swelled to the magnitude of utter reverence. "After the herd came out of the water," he wrote, "they shook themselves thoroughly, making a noise like distant thunder." And that was the extent of their shivering. None of the deer had eaten a mouthful of food in forty-eight hours. They were thoroughly dehydrated. The air temperature was seventy degrees below the freezing point. Yet, Lopp noted, "They seemed none the worse for the wetting."

· · ·

The most harrowing part of the crossing was now behind them. With

Lopp and Keok leading the way, the herders drove the deer toward land. "It seemed as if we would never reach the shore," he sighed. At a point fifteen miles east of Cape Krusenstern, near the tiny village of Aniyak, they finally made landfall. The deer immediately fanned out across the coastal plain and began pawing for the small amounts of moss that grew underneath. Exhaustion ensured that they would not wander far.

From the villagers who came out to greet the herd, Lopp learned that he had missed Jarvis and Call by only a day. The cuttermen had crossed Kotzebue Sound in fourteen hours with the help of native guides, and before leaving Cape Espenberg, Jarvis had left a note for Lopp, advising him not to take the herd over the ice. But Lopp had never received Jarvis's letter. On the night that the herd fell through the ice, Jarvis and Call were camped less than ten miles away, comforted no doubt by the thought that the deer had taken the long, and safer, way around the sound.

Believing that the herd was at least a week behind, Jarvis and Call chose not to wait around. (For Jarvis, there was never a point in waiting.) The original orders from the Treasury secretary had stipulated that after the herd had reached Kotzebue Sound, "one officer and the necessary drivers should then push on along the coast to Point Hope, leaving the other officers to follow along with the herd." But by the time Lopp and his herders arrived at Aniyak, both Jarvis and Call were racing north.

Lopp had stopped at Aniyak on his trip with Ellen in 1893, and, as Eskimo houses go, the ones in this village were comparatively roomy. He and his herders were invited to stay in what Lopp jocularly called a "hotel." Three alcoves radiated from a large central room. The entire house was heated by a central stove and lit by a skylight made of seal intestines. Out of the cold and off their feet at last, the herders ate a much-needed meal of frozen and dried fish and then gave themselves up to sleep.

Lopp, though, could not relax. After napping for barely an hour, he donned his deerskins and walked a mile to the house of Pumeuktuk, the native with whom he and Ellen had stayed five years earlier. Through his old friend, he arranged for a messenger to take a letter to Jarvis at Point Hope, reporting the herd's successful crossing of the sound. Pumeuktuk also sent three dogsleds to retrieve the gear and sleds that had been left on the ice. "They did not get back until after dark," Lopp wrote. "They were told to kill any of the seven [sled] deer . . . if they found they were unable to walk to shore." One of the deer the natives put down was Moses, who, sadly, had lacked the stamina of his biblical namesake.

That night, when Lopp returned to the house where he and the herders were staying, he was struck by the "vulgar talk" of the other natives, which he blamed on "the influence of the whalers." But a few things had not changed since his last visit: "The old medicine man, Egenuk, whom my wife and I had seen in this very house in 1893, sat around with his arms inside of his parka and his sleeves hanging empty, reminding me of a sleepy old bird."

On the morning of the eighteenth, with the temperature still at forty below, Lopp set off with three dogsleds for the Quaker mission at Kikiktaruk, fifteen miles north of Cape Blossom, where he expected to find further instructions from Jarvis in the hands of Lieutenant Ellsworth Bertholf, whom Jarvis and Call had left to fend for himself three days after the Overland Relief Expedition had landed at Cape Vancouver back in December. Lopp arrived at Kikiktaruk just before sunset. The American flag flew from a staff outside a half-buried log cabin.

The location of the mission had been chosen well. Unlike Cape Prince of Wales, the village of Kikiktaruk was tiny, consisting of a half-dozen houses occupied by perhaps thirty natives. But several miles to the south, toward Cape Blossom, was the site of the annual trading fair, where natives by the hundreds from as far away as Siberia rendezvoused each summer. Here the opportunities for evangelical outreach were enormous.

In July 1897, three Quaker missionaries—Robert Samms, his

wife, Carrie, and the unmarried Anna Hunnicutt—had arrived on the trading ship *Volante* to sate the "spiritual hunger" of the Alaskan natives. The Sammses were from southern California, and despite being newlyweds, they were glad for the company of Hunnicutt, who had previously taught among the Indians at a Quaker mission in southeast Alaska and had some notion of what to expect from the Eskimos.

The missionaries' one-room house made native dwellings seem capacious. "The head of Miss Hunnicutt's bunk was over the feet of Mr. and Mrs. Samms' bunk," Lopp noticed when he was invited inside. "The house was so small that there was no room to pass when the folding table was set." He politely offered to bed down with Bertholf, whom he found living in a tent not far away.

Lopp, Bertholf, and the three missionaries spent most of the day catching up on news. In August, at the time of the trading fair, Robert Samms had preached to a lively gathering of three hundred natives. After that, things had settled into a calmer routine, until George Fred Tilton surprised them on December 1.

Later that night, Lopp and Bertholf retired to Bertholf's tent for a "midnight lunch," over which the lieutenant gave a full account of his travels, from the point at which he had separated from Jarvis and Call on December 20 until his arrival at Kotzebue Sound on February 11. His experience, which would always be regarded as a sidebar to the treks of Jarvis, Call, Lopp, and the reindeer, was by no means a stroll in the park.

After saying good-bye to Jarvis and Call, Bertholf had made his way to the Yukon River and then to St. Michael, where he parted company with his two guides, Alexis Kalenin and Frederick Koltchoff. Because Jarvis and Call had taken the only tent, Bertholf had slept in native houses along the route. At St. Michael he had received instructions from Jarvis to procure a thousand pounds of supplies, including ten pounds of tobacco for Jarvis personally. By

dog team he proceeded to Norton Sound, where he managed to commandeer seven reindeer, six sleds, and two drivers from the Port
Clarence herd, which was still being held by Lapp herders near
Golovnin Bay. On February 2, he was ready to make the run across
the two-hundred-mile portage between Norton and Kotzebue sounds.
During the crossing, it was all he could do to keep his dog team from
slaughtering the reindeer. The snow was deep, and twice they had to
stop for a day to allow the sled deer to rest. Fortunately his guides
knew the trail by heart, and on February 11, nine days after leaving
Norton Sound, he arrived at the Quaker mission with his load of provisions intact.

As luck would have it, Jarvis and Call crossed the ice from Cape
Espenberg the following day and reached the mission late in the
evening. They were "relieved and overjoyed" to find Bertholf waiting for
them. "Everything at this end had turned out well," Jarvis declared in
his report, with no apologies for dividing the Overland Relief Expedition
into three parts. That night after a hearty supper, the cuttermen slept in
the same tent for the first time in fifty-four days. "The weather had
been growing colder and the light north wind made the . . . frost biting and sharp," Jarvis remarked, "but we felt much better . . . knowing
everything was in good shape."

Jarvis and Call stayed with Bertholf at the mission for two nights
before pushing on toward Point Hope. They passed through Aniyak a
day before Lopp and the herd reached the shore of the sound. By the
time Lopp arrived at Kikiktaruk, Bertholf, like Jarvis and Call, was anxious to get going. "Waiting is very tiresome in a country where one sees
nothing but an expanse of snow and ice," he confessed. He had passed
the days hauling firewood from the beach and digging his tent out of
incessant drifts.

. . .

Lopp needed little urging to resume the drive, but before leaving the

Kikiktaruk mission to rejoin the herd, he carefully quizzed the locals on the best route north. Since departing Cape Prince of Wales two weeks earlier, the expedition had traveled less than a quarter of the distance to Point Barrow. They still had at least five hundred miles to go—although it was impossible to know exactly, since government maps were incomplete. The path of least resistance, he knew, lay along the shore, passing through Point Hope and keeping to the bulging lobe of the Lisburne Peninsula. The shortest route, however, cut across the middle of the peninsula, far to the east of Point Hope. If Lopp could find a way due north—his first thought was to travel along the Noatak River and then over the western flank of the Brooks Range to Icy Cape—he could shave off at least a hundred miles, possibly more. Regrettably, few, if any, white men had explored that part of the Alaskan interior, and as Lopp soon learned, natives had only marginally more knowledge of it. Several villagers knew of others who had made the trip, but none of the people Lopp interviewed had actually been over that route. If he chose this shortcut, he would have to find his own way.

On the morning of the nineteenth, he and Bertholf packed the cache of provisions onto several dogsleds and set out for Aniyak. Bertholf had paid off the guides who had accompanied him from Norton Sound, but on Jarvis's orders, he had kept the seven reindeer, accurately predicting that they would be welcome replacements for those worn out or lost during the trip from Cape Prince of Wales. "They were splendid big fellows," Lopp noted, "[and having] had several days rest since crossing the portage, [they] therefore were in good trim."

The same could not be said for the deer that had crossed Kotzebue Sound. They were gaunt and lethargic. After talking with his herders, Lopp decided to give the deer another day's rest before resuming the drive north. And during his layover at Aniyak, he made another critical decision. There was no telling how soon the expedition would be able

to acquire more provisions—especially if they bypassed Point Hope—
and fewer men and less gear would ease the load of the overburdened
sled deer. Therefore, but with considerable misgiving, Lopp told Sokweena, Keok, and Ituk that he was sending them home. On February
21, when the herd headed north toward Point Barrow, these three lads
turned south toward Cape Prince of Wales. The choice of Sokweena
and Ituk made sense: They were the least accomplished herders. He
hated to lose Keok, who was the most capable of the bunch, but the
eighteen-year-old had been driving deer since mid-December, when
he had joined the drive from Port Clarence to Unalakleet. He was not
tired, he told Lopp, just homesick.

The team was now six: Lopp, Bertholf, Antisarlook, Ootenna,
Tautuk, and Kivyearzruk. Soon Bertholf would be gone, too. His
orders from Jarvis were to head for Point Hope, where he was to prepare for the arrival of any whalers who might make their way down
the coast from Point Barrow in the spring. Still not adept with reindeer, Bertholf continued to travel by dogsled, as did several natives
from Aniyak who had agreed to guide the expedition for the next day
or two.

Just before leaving Aniyak, someone in the group had broken the
thermometer. Perhaps it was just as well; the last reading had been
forty-three below zero. Yet ignorance of the temperature was far from
comforting, for, as Bertholf observed laconically, "Our good fortune as
to the weather now left us." On February 22, Lopp wrote in his log:
"East and northeast wind. Air thick with snow. Could see nothing
shortly after we started. Dog sleds travel behind. Deer drive badly.
Want to go with or against wind. After going six or eight miles, we
camp on the ice near a huge pile, which offered us some shelter.
Storms grew worse. . . . The flapping of the tent made our stove rock
as though it were on a ship."

In the morning the tent was drifted over, and the sleds were buried
in several feet of snow. When the herders went out to check on the

deer, they discovered that at least thirty had become separated from the main herd and presumably were lost. Trying to track them after the heavy snowfall would be fruitless.

Frustrated by the slow progress and eager to be of greater use, Bertholf volunteered to press ahead to Point Hope with his dogsleds and then return to the herd with additional supplies. If all went well, they would meet again at the Kivalina River, the halfway point between Kotzebue Sound and Point Hope. For the next two days, however, Bertholf's dogs could not outdistance the herd, and at night he pitched his tent next to Lopp and the herders. Finally on February 27, as they approached the broad delta of the Kivalina, their paths diverged. Bertholf veered toward the coast while the herd turned inland.

The Kivalina River has its headwaters on the slopes of the De Long Mountains, the westernmost spur of the Brooks Range, and claws southwestward through rugged hills before uncoiling into the Chukchi Sea. A few hours after splitting off from Bertholf, Lopp and his herders steered the deer around a low knob and paused to survey the route ahead. Off in the distance they saw a dark streak, which they guessed to be the willows and alders that grew along the banks of the Kivalina. The snow deepened as they neared the river. After a while they met a native who delivered the startling news that Jarvis and another man were camped a few miles away. Leaving his sled, Lopp hiked on foot through the deep snow until he reached Jarvis's tent, five miles downstream. The missionary and the revenue officer greeted each other with "a great handshaking and jollification," Lopp reported. In his own account of the reunion, Jarvis remarked on how badly Lopp's face had been battered by the cold in the three weeks since they were last together.

This time Jarvis was not accompanied by Call. A week earlier they had arrived at Point Hope, where they were greeted by Rustan Nelson, manager of one of the trading and whaling stations. At Point Hope, Jarvis had received word of Lopp's progress since crossing Kotzebue Sound, and on the twenty-fourth he had decided to backtrack south to rendezvous with Lopp and the reindeer herd, and perhaps with Bertholf as well, at the Kivalina. Call had stayed behind at Point Hope, and Jarvis made the trip with Nelson instead.

Jarvis and Nelson moved their tent to where Lopp and the herders had set up camp, and the next day, February 28, they were enveloped by a blizzard. "All we could do was to stay inside the tent and try to keep dry and comfortable," Jarvis griped. True to form, he found the enforced layover extremely trying, "for time was flying, and we were anxious to get the herd to its destination before the fawns began to make their appearance. We had been nearly four weeks moving the herd thus far and had fully 400 miles more of travel against the northeast wind that generally prevails in this part of the country during the winter, and only the month of March to do it in."

The days in camp were not entirely idle, however. Jarvis and Lopp pooled their knowledge, such as it was, of possible routes across the Lisburne Peninsula, and after lengthy deliberations, they decided to go up the Kivalina River and then cross the mountains to the Pit-megea River, which emerges on the coast at Cape Sabine. A number of other rivers flow north from the Brooks Range—including the Kukpowruk, Kokowlik, and Utukok—but each would require taking the herd a considerable distance inland. The route that Jarvis and Lopp chose, from the Kivalina to the Pitmegea, was a compromise; it would trim off enough of the peninsula to be helpful but not so much that the herd would be swallowed by the formidable and untracked interior. No matter which direction they went, they could not expect to find any native settlements anywhere on the Lisburne Peninsula. "This was the last great trial, to get the herd on the north side of these mountains, and had caused us much anxiety and study," Jarvis remarked in his official report. "We had canvassed and discussed with natives and whites all the routes . . . and finally after long consideration and in the light of our own experiences thus far, concluded the shortest route away from the shore was the best, and that the closer we kept to the coast the safer not only would the deer be but also the men."

While waiting out the storm, Lopp had moved into the tent occupied by Jarvis and the trader Nelson; the four herders shared the other. During "earnest discussions regarding natives and their customs," Lopp took offense at Nelson's pronouncement that "all natives were dead-beats." His regard for his tent mate did not improve the following day after two of Nelson's sled dogs got loose and chased the reindeer herd for several miles. "When the dogs started on the chase, poor Jarvis looked very much discouraged," Lopp recounted. "He seemed to think it was the end of the Overland Relief Expedition." Lopp tried to put Jarvis's mind at ease by explaining that the herd would not go very far, and as long as the deer stayed together, the dogs could do little harm. In the end, the dogs wounded a cow and calf, which the herders killed and gave to the natives.

By March 2, the weather cleared. They broke camp late in the morning, Jarvis and Nelson returning to Point Hope, Lopp and the herders turning up the Kivalina, accompanied by two other natives, Avaluk and Omruk. Avaluk was the only one in the group who had been as far as the divide where they must cross over into the Pitmegea drainage. The following day was ideal for traveling: sunny, with no wind to speak of. In his log, Lopp jotted that the temperature was "warmer," although it was still well below zero. He also noted that they were passing through "splendid moss country." However, he was feeling "unwell"—the first time he had admitted as much since leaving Cape Prince of Wales. The herd made sixteen miles that day; Lopp was too weak to walk any of it.

He was not the only one feeling poorly. As they continued up the Kivalina, deeper into the interior hills, the guide Avaluk complained of diarrhea and announced that he could go no farther. By now they were in unfamiliar territory, perhaps forty miles from the coast. Lopp had a compass but no maps—other than the ones Avaluk occasionally drew for him in the snow. Whether their guide was truly ill or simply had concocted an excuse to turn back will never be known. "We reluctantly let him go," was Lopp's only comment. From then on, he confessed uneasily, "We worried more or less about the route and were never quite sure that we were on the course which he had directed us to take."

Before quitting, Avaluk had paused at the top of a low hill and pointed to a stream that he assured Lopp was the headwaters of the Kukpuk, the next river north of the Kivalina. Throughout the rest of the day and into the next, they crossed one ridge after another, some so steep they coasted down on their sleds. Lopp became increasingly concerned as the terrain kept steering them west of north; the way to the Pitmegea lay almost due north. He wasn't exactly lost; it was just that none of the landmarks had any meaning. With each hill, the heavier sleds lagged farther and farther behind the herd.

On the morning of the sixth, after crossing yet another ridge, they reached a frozen stream, which they suspected was a branch of the Initkilly River. Lopp knew that the Initkilly, like the Kivalina and Kukpuk, drains west, not north. He grasped that if they were to stand any chance of finding the Pitmegea, they would have to veer to the northeast. More ridges, more streams—all told, they covered fourteen difficult miles that day. In his log, Lopp stated grimly, "The sleds again fall behind. The herd is very tired." And they were far beyond the country of splendid moss.

Admittedly, the land they were now crossing was not as treacherous as the ice of Kotzebue Sound, but it was more foreign and thus made them feel uneasy. The herders—Tautuk, Ootenna, Kivyearzruk, Antisarlook—were all coastal dwellers, attuned to the nuances of ice and water sky. Never in their lives had they been so far from the sea for so long. Lopp, too, had never been more than a day's walk from the coast since arriving in Alaska. It was hard to feel claustrophobic in a country as bald and barren as the interior of the Lisburne Peninsula, yet it was confining just the same. They all wanted out and as soon as possible.

On the morning of March 7, Lopp and the herders resolved that they would make a "desperate effort" to reach the north shore of Alaska by the twelfth. "We were considerably in doubt as to how far the ocean was," he admitted. "Our progress was very slow for the reason that our sled deer were very tired and weak." Yet they kept going, focusing only on the days and miles that separated them from their immediate goal.

And then suddenly, unexpectedly, they were there. At the end of the day, with the light fading, the Pitmegea basin widened into a gentle coastal plain, and in the distance they recognized the unmistakable ridge of ice grounded along the shore of Cape Sabine. "We realized that we were approaching the Arctic Ocean and were in high spirits when we sighted it," Lopp wrote. "We rejoiced at being five days ahead of our schedule."

They were now roughly three hundred miles from Point Barrow. They could expect no respite from the wind and cold—if anything, the weather would be worse—but no more mountains or ice-jammed sounds stood in the way. Their only disappointment was the unexplained absence of Jarvis, who had promised to meet them at the mouth of the Pitmegea.

. . .

After leaving the herd on March 2, Jarvis and Nelson had returned to Point Hope, a journey of about ninety miles. Bertholf likewise had headed for Point Hope after separating from the herd on February 27. At Cape Seppings, the halfway point between the Kivalina and Point Hope, Bertholf had learned from natives that Jarvis and Nelson had just passed on their way to meet Lopp and the herd at the Kivalina. He waited for Jarvis at Cape Seppings, and together they drove their dogsleds to Nelson's trading post at Point Hope, where they were reunited with Call. This was the third, and last, time the three cutter-men were together during the Overland Relief Expedition.

Also waiting at Point Hope was a man who had just arrived from Point Barrow. Ned Arey was a whaler with years in the North. Log-books indicate that he had been aboard the steam whaler *Beluga* when it left San Francisco in March 1897 and that he had expected to trans-fer to the *Mary D. Hume,* the Pacific Steam Whaling Company brig that had spent seven of the eight previous winters at Herschel Island. The *Beluga* would winter at Langton Bay, east of the Mackenzie River in the Canadian Arctic. Whether Arey ever got as far as Langton Bay, or even Herschel Island, is not clear. Somehow, though, he wound up at Point Barrow, and then in January he had departed by dogsled for Point Hope. The trip had taken him exactly a month. Naturally, Jarvis wasted no time in pumping him for every detail about the stranded whalers and the conditions at Point Barrow.

From Arey he learned that the situation had not changed drastical-ly between George Fred Tilton's departure from Point Barrow in Octo-ber and Arey's in January. Things were "bad," Arey told Jarvis, "but as yet not serious." Earlier Tilton had reported that the whalers had enough food to last until July; Arey's prediction was that the flour, bread, tea, and coffee would begin running out in the middle of May. For the time being, however, the men were in reasonably good shape. Only one man had died so far—frozen to death. Scurvy, which had killed so many sailors and polar travelers in the past, had just begun to show itself among the Point Barrow whalers. The most worrisome cases were aboard the *Belvedere.*

In 1898, scientists had not yet discovered the cause of scurvy—lack of vitamin C in the diet—but the means to prevent and cure it were widely known. Juice from lemons and limes was issued to men who spent long periods at sea, and in the Arctic, men knew to eat plenty of fresh meat. Point Barrow apparently had a sizable quantity of the latter. "Providentially," Jarvis learned, "there had come into the surrounding country large numbers of wild deer, or caribou, and native hunters, who had been sent out early in the winter, had killed and sent in enough meat to keep the crowd going."

As relieved as Jarvis was by Arey's briefing, it did nothing to curb his sense of urgency. Nowhere in his official report on the Overland Relief Expedition did he infer that his mission was now less imperative than originally believed. To be fair, he had no way of knowing for sure just how well or how poorly the whalers were doing. And he was still under orders.

He drew on other motivations as well, his sense of personal merit being far from the least. Jarvis believed that the whalers at Point Barrow were in need of relief because it gave him a reason to keep going—and also because, whether he said so or not, there was something in it for him. He was a modest, disciplined officer, but he was hardly selfless. Honor and advancement mattered to him immensely—for all the right reasons of course. Nonetheless, they had a way of informing his judgment, not to mention the story he would tell when and if he ever returned home.

And the truth was, the situation in Point Barrow was not pretty, no matter what pictures George Fred Tilton or Ned Arey had painted. Winter in the Arctic did strange things to white men.

## [ 13 ]

# Killing Time

WHAT POINT BARROW LACKED was not food—although there was no abundance of that—but discipline. And in the absence of discipline, morale declined and, inevitably, so too did the welfare of the whalers. Had Charlie Brower and Ned McIlhenny not stepped into the breach, the winter might have devolved into wretched anarchy.

The crewmen who remained on board the *Belvedere*, *Rosario*, *Newport*, *Fearless*, and *Jeanie*, as well as the other ships wintering elsewhere in the Arctic, still had to toe the line. But the law of the sea did not apply to the men whose ships had been wrecked and abandoned. The *Orca* and *Jessie H. Freeman* were not military vessels; their crews did not have to obey their officers after they had moved to the whaling station, and most of them did not. "Once they get ashore every foremast hand is as good as the captain," one of the old-timers in San Francisco explained. Nor were the officers of the whaling ships inclined to provide even the most perfunctory leadership. "As soon as their ships were wrecked, the Captains [of the *Orca* and *Freeman*] gave up all control of their men," Brower commented with equal parts astonishment and disgust. "I thought it funny [that] neither of them would try to help manage their crews. All they seemed to want was to get shut of all responsibility, which they shifted to me."

In the absence of any government presence—which in the Arctic meant the U.S. Revenue Cutter Service—Brower was the de facto quartermaster, sheriff, judge, and lord mayor of Point Barrow. Most of the natives who lived at Point Barrow worked for him or were indebted to him for something. Among the whites, he was the most capable Arctic hand. What is more, a great portion of the provisions now being doled out to the whalers belonged to him and his partners at Liebes & Company of San Francisco.

While no one—officers, crewmen, or natives—ever challenged Brower personally, the bickering and cheating that went on around him was unrelenting and for the most part inextinguishable. In October, immediately after returning from his grueling trip to inspect the ships icebound to the east of the point, Brower was confronted by a delegation of men from the bunkhouse—the crudely converted Pacific Steam Whaling Company building—accusing McIlhenny of stinting on their rations. "'He's holding out on us. So help me he is, Charlie,'" Brower recalled their spokesman saying.

Despite the belligerence of the complainants, Brower remained unmoved: "I looked the men over—a hard-bitten, ill-clad bunch—and reminded them that not every shipwrecked crew had regular food, let alone somebody to cook it for them." His solution was to give the bunkhouse one week's rations at a time and let the men divide it themselves, bringing their meals to the cook at McIlhenny's quarters as they saw fit. "After that there was no bother," Brower remarked. "If they were short that was their own fault."

But Brower was not as callous as he seemed. He might not have wanted to share his table with the crewmen, but he did not wish to see them starve, either. Likewise he felt obligated to the hundred or so natives who lived at Point Barrow, most of whom either worked for him directly or traded with him. They had to eat, too. "It was impossible that I could give them the food stuff they had been getting as part of their pay," he regretted. "Calling them all in, I explained this to them, promising to make it up to them in some other way." He then directed them to move inland for the winter to hunt and fish—for their own subsistence and also to help feed the whites at Point Barrow. The natives consented willingly, and as Ned Arey had reported to Jarvis at Point Hope, the hunting had been excellent. Within fifty miles of the whaling station, the natives had found caribou grazing by the thousands, and by mid-winter they were bringing in ten to twenty a day. "We never had so much meat," Brower exclaimed. Every icehouse was filled to capacity, and not just with caribou. McIlhenny estimated that he killed nine thousand pounds of ducks, and the natives brought in some thirty thousand pounds of fish, not counting the whales they caught in the spring.

Fuel, on the other hand, was harder to come by. The ships had enough coal to keep warm throughout the winter, but Brower worried that there was insufficient coal for the stoves on shore. As soon as the men were settled in their quarters, he and McIlhenny sent parties to collect driftwood from the beaches east of Point Barrow—wood that had floated down the Mackenzie River in the spring floods. The task was cold and backbreaking, for most of the wood was saturated with frozen salt water, and on each trip the men had to travel farther to find it. Several who volunteered for the detail were rewarded with frostbite; others refused to help out at all. On November 12, McIlhenny reported: "The fuel question is getting serious. The 'bunk house' is out of wood and the coal I allow them is hardly sufficient to keep them from freezing. I sent a gang of men out for wood today but they could not get any and got lost, and wandered several miles inland. Fortunately, they met a native sled coming in and it piloted them home."

McIlhenny was more worried than Brower about making it through the winter. In late October, a week after George Fred Tilton had departed Point Barrow on his long trek, McIlhenny had persuaded

Charles Walker, the fifth mate of the *Orca*, to make his own run, doubling the chances that word of the whalers' plight would reach the Outside. While Tilton had gone southwest toward Point Hope, Walker had gone east, toward the Mackenzie River, which he then followed inland, keeping to a well-known route that linked missions and Hudson's Bay Company posts all the way to Edmonton. The distance to civilization for both men was roughly the same—seventeen hundred miles—but Walker's route was less arduous and his journey less eventful. He and Tilton arrived in San Francisco within a few days of each other, although Walker would have arrived much earlier if he had not dawdled for two weeks at Herschel Island, drunk on stove alcohol. He too reported that the whalers' food would last only until July. By the time his news reached the appropriate authorities, the Overland Relief Expedition was more than halfway to Point Barrow.

In the meantime , McIlhenny had called off the wood-gathering forays; the job was just too dangerous, and the men's clothing was too thin and worn for working outdoors. He estimated that the coal, with careful rationing, would last until March, when he hoped that the weather would be good enough to send the men out for driftwood again.

Until then, few men were inclined to stray far from their quarters. At 11:30 A.M. on November 19, the sun inched partway above the horizon for a few minutes, then disappeared. It was not seen again until January 23. "The long Arctic night is upon us," McIlhenny's assistant Norman Buxton observed in his journal.

The men in the bunkhouse took the winter badly. Their behavior ranged from despondent to deplorable. "Last night the back of my ice house was broken and a number of ducks stolen," McIlhenny had complained in October. "It is rather early for the men to begin this sort of thing. They have been warned that the first one to be caught stealing food would be shot and we mean to stand by this decision."

But still the pilferage continued. Brower blamed himself for allowing too many men at a time in his storehouse to receive their monthly tobacco ration. "When we were finished, I looked at the shelves . . . where I kept all kinds of small articles. They were empty. Everything they could hide under their shirts was gone."

Brower was not so easily mollified when the men began robbing native graves. One day a distraught widow reported to Brower that someone had taken the mittens from her husband's body. "I told her I did not think they would do that, [but] she was sure. . . . To have her satisfied I had her go look at the corpse. Sure enough, the coffin had been opened. Not only were the mittens gone but all the clothes had been stripped from the body. It was laying naked in the box. I gave her a new outfit and had the family clothe the corpse once more, then nail the box securely. Two days later . . . they had been there again. This time they not only undressed the corpse, but rolled it out on the snow, taking the coffin for firewood. . . . Of course the men denied everything, and while I knew they were lying, I had no proof. After that the whole graveyard was gradually denuded of burial racks, broken sleds—anything made of wood."

More than a few times men got into mischief simply to relieve the boredom of their confinement. They took to walking out to greet the native sleds bringing fish to the station, offering to help carry the loads the rest of the way. "They helped all right," Brower quipped. "Each man would steal a fish or two, dropping them along the trail, stamping them in the snow. After the sleds were unloaded, back they went, dug up the fish, and carried them to the bunkhouse, cooking them . . . not because they were hungry [but] just because they did not know what else to do with them."

Killing time killed the spirit as well. "The cold you can stand and thrive under," the venerable Arctic geographer August Petermann had declared. "It is the long night that tells on body and mind." Petermann never spent a winter in the Arctic himself, but thanks in part to his armchair prognostications on the existence of an open polar sea, many others had flung themselves into the boreal unknown. Some of these early explorers had become icebound intentionally, others by accident. And even if their ships were not destroyed in the span of an Arctic winter, too often the morale and sanity of the men onboard reached the breaking point. "Oh! at times this inactivity crushes one's very soul; one's life seems as dark as the winter night outside; there is sunlight upon no part of it except the past and the far, far distant future," wrote Fridtjof Nansen, the Norwegian mariner who embedded himself in the northern ice from 1893 to 1895, hoping to drift to the North Pole. During Nansen's long (and aborted) odyssey, he longed for anything to alleviate the tedium. "I feel as if I *must* break through this deadness, this inertia, and find some outlet for my energies."

Ships that knew in advance that they would winter in the ice came prepared to create their own diversions. The British Navy, the most avid seeker of the Northwest Passage, enforced the ritual of daily inspections; its ships also carried extensive libraries, musical instruments, even costumes and props for elaborate theatrical productions. The conventional wisdom of the day held that inactivity was one of the causes of scurvy. To stave off this debilitating and often deadly condition, Dr. Elisha Kent Kane, who searched for the lost Franklin expedition and himself became icebound, prescribed a regimen of exercise for officers and crew that included "foot-ball and sliding, followed by regular games of romps, leap-frog, and tumbling in the snow."

The whalers at Point Barrow were no rompers. The officers lacked authority to rouse the crews from their indolence, and few found ways to keep busy on their own. Every now and then, a small bunch would join in a game of native football—in which one team tried to keep a sealskin ball away from another, a sort of free-for-all soccer with no boundaries. "I have seen one [native] lead for over three miles, with more than fifty following," Norman Buxton wrote in his journal. The crewmen were less intrepid in their participation. They had all heard the cautionary tale of the whalers who were caught in a sudden storm while playing baseball at Herschel Island. Four were frozen to death before they could walk the short distance back to their ships.

A few from the bunkhouse took classes from Richmond Marsh, but most of them could hardly read or write—not that there was much to read at the station anyway. (If any of the crewmen kept diaries or wrote letters during the winter of 1897–1898, none has surfaced.) Instead they played cards, swapped yarns, and with increasing frequency, carped and quarreled among themselves.

The crews of whaling ships had grown ever more polyglot since the era when Queequeg, Tashtego, and Daggoo—a South Sea Islander, a Martha's Vineyard Indian, and an African Negro—hired on to harpoon Moby-Dick. In the forecastles of Arctic steam whalers, men of different races worked, ate, and slept shoulder to shoulder with very little compunction. In the Point Barrow bunkhouse, though, the men reverted to the apartheid of landlubbers. "About two-thirds . . . were white, the others colored," Jim Allen recalled. "The whites had the northern end of the building, and the colored men"(including the Afro-European "Portuguese" from the Cape Verde Islands) "had the southern end." Allen offered no further observations on the tension in the bunkhouse, except to say, "It was a terrible place for a big bunch of men to live."

Conditions were indeed abominable. "If you happened to be passing there and the door was opened by someone going in or out, the smell would about knock you over," recalled Allen, who was lucky enough to live in the refuge station with McIlhenny. The building had no ventilation, and the heat from eighty bodies and the steam from the room's only stove formed a layer of frost on the ceiling and walls. At times the ice on the floor was a foot thick, "which in no way helped to keep the place warm," Allen commented wryly. "Probably it was just as well, however, for if the bunkhouse had been warm there might have been sickness." To ward off the chill, the men boarded up their bunks and made crude seal-oil lamps out of old fruit and tomato cans. "If you don't know how to take care of homemade seal-oil lamps they will smoke and throw off a very disagreeable odor," Allen remarked. The soot left a greasy black rime on everything and everyone in the house. "With just one stove, and that used for part of the cooking, it was impossible for that many men to melt either snow or ice enough for water to wash their hands and faces, let alone their clothes. . . . So they just had to let themselves go." White faces became black, black faces blacker. Everyone, regardless of color, grew weaker from lack of effort.

For the officers and men who remained aboard ship, conditions were slightly better. Charlie Brower had arranged a reliable shuttle service of supplies and news between the five far-flung vessels. Living in close quarters with their officers, the crews of these ships maintained better discipline and morale than did the unsupervised mob in the bunkhouse.

But not all officers were model citizens. Discord was particularly virulent aboard the *Jeanie*, the ship trapped farthest to the east and thus the most isolated. "The Captain [P.H. Mason] is a cranky sort of man and his officers have nothing in sympathy with him," Norman Buxton had been advised by the *Jeanie*'s Japanese steward, Jujiro Wada. "No two of the officers are on speaking terms, and Wada about runs the ship." The fractiousness came to a head when Mason accused First Mate J. A. Coffin of stealing from a storehouse that had been erected on shore. When Coffin tried to come aboard the ship after a trip to take inventory of supplies, the captain reportedly turned him away at gunpoint. At first it was feared that Coffin had frozen to death on the ice, but three days later he showed up at Point Barrow and was taken in by McIlhenny.

. . .

McIlhenny never did earn the affection of the whalers in the bunkhouse, but his brand of southern hospitality won over the men with whom he shared the refuge station. On Thanksgiving his cook served a feast of roast venison, rice, fried onions, peaches, and cake. The men in the bunkhouse got a ration of venison stew, rice, and plum duff, a steamed pudding that was common fare aboard ships. By McIlhenny's reckoning, the meal was better than "many a poor cuss got in the heart of civilization."

Christmas was even merrier. A month had passed since the sun had shone, and the men celebrated the solstice and the lengthening of days almost as heartily as they did the Nativity. For the occasion, the officers from the *Belvedere, Rosario, Newport, Fearless,* and *Jeanie* sledded in from their ships. On Christmas Eve, all the officers were invited to the bunkhouse for an evening of "theatricals." The curtain was made of quilts (stuffed with cotton batting originally intended for preserving McIlhenny's animal specimens). The orchestra was comprised of banjo, guitar, and accordion. There were not enough seats, so the audience sat on each other's laps. The performance included a minstrel show and a series of one-man sketches. "As a lot they could not have been much worse," McIlhenny remarked of the actors, "but the men were in earnest and showed every desire to amuse the audience." The grand finale was a boxing match between two of the crewmen. "It was some fight as long as it lasted, between a coon and one of the white sailors from the *Jessie Freeman*," Brower chronicled. "We had to separate them at last, as there was no making them quit when time was called." Concern for the well-being of the contestants was not the only reason the match ended. "The house was crowded and hot and I for one was glad to get out," McIlhenny noted in his diary.

Christmas Day festivities were somewhat more segregated. At midday, once it was light enough to see, the men played football outdoors despite a temperature of thirty-four below zero. At six o'clock, McIlhenny served a grand dinner for his seventeen guests: soup, roast venison, duck-liver stew, baked whitefish with mashed potatoes, roast ptarmigan with cranberry sauce, green peas, peach pie, and Louisiana black cake. (The menu for the bunkhouse was not recorded.) Afterward, he and his housemates were joined by the men lodged at Brower's. "A big bowl of whiskey punch was made and refilled as required," Buxton wrote, "and the evening was passed very pleasantly in singing, playing and telling stories until 2 A.M. when a lot of Roman candles were fired off to the great amusement of the natives."

Yet the greatest excitement of all occurred not at Christmastime but three weeks later when natives sighted a ship on the southwest horizon. "At first I thought I was mistaken," Brower remembered, "[but] two days later she came close to the land 12 miles south of the house." He sent several men out for a closer look. They returned to report that it was the abandoned *Navarch*, drifting along the coast about two miles offshore. The ship had already been stripped of nearly all its provisions, but its bunkers were still full of coal—some two hundred tons of it, according to Buxton. (Writing from memory, Brower estimated 80 tons.) Immediately Brower ordered every available Eskimo to begin opening a road to the ship so that sleds could haul the fuel to shore. When Buxton went aboard to help with the unloading, he discovered "much to our amusement [that] she was in perfect condition, tightly frozen in a large cake of ice, and not a drop of water in her." Over the next three weeks, a near-constant procession of sleds shuttled back and forth between Point Barrow and the ghost ship. The coal was packed in sacks, averaging one hundred pounds, each sled carrying three or four sacks; on some days, one hundred sled loads made it to shore, some pulled by dogsled, most by men in harness. At this rate, the fuel crisis would soon be over.

On January 18, the temperature hit forty below, but every day was a bit brighter than the one before. On January 23, the sun appeared for the first time since mid-November, and two nights later, the northern lights put on their most dazzling show so far. "Broad bands of silver light extended across the heavens from S.E. to N.W.," Buxton recorded in his journal, "and these were in constant and rapid motion like a bundle of long ribbons held at one end . . . and shaken in the air."

The next spectacle occurred on the morning of February 5, when a "pillar of fire" lit up the black heavens. Two crewmen from the *Orca* had gone out to the *Navarch* and set it ablaze. They claimed it was an accident, but most of the ships' officers believed that they had done it intentionally to get out of having to haul coal. The two culprits were brought before an "indignation meeting," but without proof of their guilt, they escaped punishment. "There was nothing I could do that would replace the fuel," Brower explained, "so I turned them over to the men in the bunkhouse, advising them to lick them every time they felt cold. [I told them that] I would furnish no more fuel . . . for their house, either wood or coal. If they wanted wood they could haul it themselves." Of the two hundred tons of coal on the *Navarch*, Brower's Eskimos had salvaged less than half. Adding to the inferno were 250 barrels of whale oil packed in the hold.

· · ·

Despite the waste of so much warmth and wealth, there was a growing sense among the men that winter's back had been broken. On February 22, George Washington's birthday, Norman Buxton remarked that "it's a good thing the old fellow wasn't born and bred in this frozen country for I am sure he would have died of the monotony." But with the longer days, many of the whalers—officers more so than the crew in the bunkhouse—were beginning to shake off their torpor. Brower's natives began preparing their umiaks for the spring whaling season. McIlhenny, Buxton, and their other associate, Snyder, continued to collect and preserve animal specimens, from lemmings to caribou, not to mention the bounty of birds McIlhenny had shot in the fall.

By the first of March, the amount of daylight was "about the same as December days in the Eastern States," Buxton estimated. He declared March 2 "the finest day we have experienced in the Arctic." The sun didn't set until 5:30. The next day was even balmier. The temperature rose to twenty-two above, and the men played baseball in their shirtsleeves. The only downside to the warm spell was that the layer of frost that had collected on the ceiling and walls of the bunkhouse melted, soaking the beds and forming a large puddle on the floor.

By and large, the health of the men had held up fairly well. The only fatality during the winter was the *Rosario*'s Japanese cook, Kotake, who had gone out for a walk on November 31 and frozen to death. Other than this unfortunate incident, the accidents and afflictions that befell the stranded whalers were not severe. A few toes were lost to frostbite, but no limbs were amputated. Despite the constant fear of scurvy—especially among the men living aboard ship, where the diet tended more toward salted meat—the first case did not arise until March, aboard the *Belvedere*. It was quickly ameliorated by increasing the man's ration of fresh caribou. Cold weather was brutal, but, as James Allen had observed, it also killed germs, a blessing to the men packed in the bunkhouse. The whalers were also fortunate to have the services of Dr. Richmond Marsh, who was well supplied with medicine and surgical instruments. (The medical history of the icebound whalers might be better told if Marsh left behind a record of his experiences. Nor are there any extant accounts of how his wife, Mary, spent her first winter at Point Barrow, the only white woman among more than one hundred unkempt whalers.)

In mid-March the native hunters brought in a caribou fetus, a sure harbinger of spring. On finer days, the men played baseball among themselves or football with the natives. Their renewed interest in diversion also led them down a familiar path of dissipation. Indeed, it was a commentary on the winter's tyranny that they had *not* pursued this particular offense any sooner. Pooling their rations of molasses and flour, several of the whalers set up a still in one of the native huts, bribing the residents (with hooch, no doubt) to keep mum. Brower learned of the forbidden distillery anyway and smashed it to pieces. "That was the last liquor made at Barrow," he snorted with righteous finality.

March 29 was an especially pleasant day. The sky was clear, wind calm, temperature nine above. "One can stand out of doors in shirt sleeves for some time without discomfort," Buxton noted. Later that day, a baseball game was scheduled between a team of officers and the "Hungry Nine," as the squad from the bunkhouse called itself. After breakfast, Buxton was in the refuge station, preparing another caribou skeleton for McIlhenny's collection. Suddenly Edward Akin, who had been the refuge station's final superintendent and then stayed on to work for Brower, burst in with astonishing news. "Lieutenant Jarvis and a doctor have just arrived being four months out of [Seattle] and has a herd of 400 reindeer on the way here," he blurted to Buxton.

"I heard what he said perfectly but paid no attention to him as I thought he was giving me a yarn," Buxton recalled. "He repeated what he first said. Then I looked up and as soon as I saw his face, all excitement, I knew something was up."

Yet it was not until Buxton stepped out the door and saw Jarvis and Call's sleds heading up the beach toward Brower's house that he fully grasped the significance of the occasion. "Today has brought to the white men at Point Barrow the greatest surprise that we have seen so far," Buxton declared, "and probably the greatest we will ever have."

# Last Obstacle

Upon arriving on the shore of the Chukchi Sea near the mouth of the Pitmegea River on March 7, Lopp and his herders looked about for tracks or other signs that Jarvis and Call had been there ahead of them, but they found none. Before leaving the Kivalina on March 2, they had agreed to meet at this spot, and Lopp was more glad than worried that the herd had arrived first.

After the trying traverse of the Lisburne Peninsula, men and animals were in need of rest. On the eighth, they spent the day mending their worn deerskins and sorting through their provisions. Lopp was determined to discard anything not absolutely necessary for the final push to Point Barrow. The weather was calm and beautiful, he recorded, and the next morning they were reluctant to break camp. Lopp was inclined to linger one more day in the hope that Jarvis and Call would catch up, but the herders reported that the moss nearby was too poor to sustain the herd. Before leaving the Pitmegea, they cached spare guns, ammunition, canned meat, and one sled, figuring to retrieve them on the way back. They also erected a cross made from cracker box lids that would catch the eye of Jarvis and Call. On it Lopp wrote, "Arrived here March 7, 1898. Letter between boards." That day the herd made eighteen miles, most of it on the smooth shore ice.

.  .  .

Jarvis and Call did not leave Point Hope until March 6, the day before Lopp and the herd had arrived at the Pitmegea. Before setting off, Jarvis wanted to make arrangements for the evacuation of at least some of the men from Point Barrow. Ned Arey had estimated that supplies would run out before relief ships could reach the whalers. If that proved to be the case, Jarvis intended to send one hundred of the most able men down the coast to Point Hope, where Bertholf would take charge of them until the *Bear* arrived, hopefully by early July. "If it were possible to supply the men with proper foot gear, there would be no great difficulty in carrying out this arrangement," Jarvis reasoned, though he admitted that "there was a possibility of some men [giving] out on the road." Still, he figured that it was "better to run this risk than to have them all remain at one place without sufficient food, with the consequence starvation and disorder."

Another reason for Jarvis and Call's uncharacteristically slow departure from Point Hope was that they had run into difficulty finding natives willing to guide them to Point Barrow. "None wanted to go into what seemed like a starvation camp, even though I promised to send them back to Point Hope immediately," Jarvis explained. At last they enlisted a man named Nekowrah and his wife, Shucungunga. Neither had ever been over the trail to Point Barrow, but Jarvis was confident that they would not get lost as long as they followed the shore. He mostly wanted Nekowrah to manage the dogs and sleds; Shucungunga could tend the camp and mend their clothes.

Traveling with three sleds, they were five days reaching the Pitmegea. Searching about for sign of the deer herd, one of the natives came upon the makeshift cross and Lopp's note. Jarvis tore it open anxiously and was relieved to learn that the herd had crossed the mountains in reasonably good shape. "The last great obstacle had been overcome," he cheered, "and though the cold, strong winds were hard to face it was now a straight drive over a level country, and it seemed we surely must arrive at Point Barrow before the month was out. Human nature could not accomplish more than had been done, so, pushing on until nightfall, we went into camp, feeling we had things well in hand to go to the end of the journey."

His optimism would not go untested, for the coastline now turned northeast, directly into the prevailing wind. There was hardly a day when they were not pummeled head-on by driving snow. Although Jarvis and Call had arrived at the Pitmegea River two days behind the reindeer herd, it took them a week to catch up.

· · ·

The herd had moved along admirably. Reindeer in fact prefer to travel into the wind; they can smell predators more easily, and in summer a stiff breeze helps keep the mosquitoes and flies away. Three days beyond the Pitmegea, the deer reached Kasegaluk Lagoon, a narrow band of protected water, or ice, that hugs the coast for one hundred miles to the south and north of Point Lay and Icy Cape. Traveling over the tundra had been hard work, but on the smooth lagoon, they were able to make twenty miles a day.

On the afternoon of the fourteenth, they came to a small village south of where the Kukpowruk River empties into the sea. Earlier that day, the herders had spotted wolf tracks, the first since leaving Cape Prince of Wales, but now they were concerned about a more immediate threat: dogs and their owners. Lopp sent Omruk, the native guide who had been with the herd since the Kivalina, to explain as best he could that the approaching animals were reindeer, not caribou—a difference not easily grasped by people who had never seen reindeer or by carnivorous dogs that did not care one way or the other.

Only after lengthy conversation was Omruk able to persuade the villagers to tie up their dogs and put up their rifles.

The following day was "the most severe weather of the trip," Lopp noted. Without a thermometer, he had no way of knowing the precise temperature, but his reckoning had been correct; farther down the coast, Jarvis's thermometer registered forty-five degrees below zero. Yet the cold was only half of it. "It was blowing a gale and the snow was so thick we could not see any distance," Lopp wrote in his log. "Becoming chilled, I put on a fourth parka, making in all two squirrel skin parkas and two reindeer parkas." The next morning the storm was still so fierce that he decided not to break camp. "We could find only enough wood to cook with, therefore were compelled to keep our mittens on most of the day," he stated stoically.

. . .

Jarvis and Call struggled through the same storm. Writing in his official report several months later, Jarvis made sure that his readers understood the caliber of man it took to survive such conditions. "We had been warned concerning the blizzards on this coast, and I had heard many stories of the terrible times of parties who had been caught in these storms," he commented. "One party I knew of had been storm-bound for forty-two days at a place but a few miles from where we now were, and were compelled to eat their dogs before the storm passed over. We had never allowed the darker side of the stories we had heard to trouble us, except as to make our preparations more complete, yet often during our long fight up this coast if one had dared let down we might have been left somewhere on the road."

Jarvis and Call awoke on March 17 to find their tent completely buried in a drift, as were the sleds, harness, and camp gear. Only the dogs' noses protruded from the snow. Breaking camp took more time than usual, and travel was slow. They had no reindeer to hold them back, but their sleds were heavily laden with frozen seal meat to feed to the dogs. Toward afternoon, they came to a cluster of huts, hardly a village at all, where the families were surviving on "bad walrus meat and the carcass of a whale that had drifted ashore there the previous fall." One of the natives presented Jarvis with a note from Lopp, who had passed by only hours before. Squinting northward across the level plain, Jarvis and Call could now see the herd in the distance, "like a small black cloud sweeping over the sea of intense white snow."

. . .

Lopp and his herders had had a different encounter at this bedraggled settlement. As they had arrived with the herd, they were confronted by "seven men, all the males of the village, in white snow shirts, armed with rifles, approaching to surround the 'toctoo' [caribou] . . . and kill them. . . . Had they begun the slaughter, they might have killed many of them, as reindeer do not become frightened at report of a gun. One old man who had no rifle was lashing a big butcher knife to a spear in order to assist in the slaughter." In the nick of time, Antisarlook and Ootenna were able to head them off—to the enormous disappointment of the hungry hunters.

The natives had never seen reindeer before, but to Lopp's elation, they had received some exposure to Christianity. Whether by word of mouth or through contact with a missionary, they recognized that Sunday was a special day. "One woman showed us a piece of paper and pencil," Lopp explained. "Every day she made a straight mark for week days and a cross on the seventh day for Sunday." When the natives had greeted Lopp, they had shaken his hand, which Omruk said meant they were Christians. The news boosted Lopp's spirits considerably, for he understood better than most that such progress came in small steps.

. . .

Jarvis, however, wore seven-league boots. After spying the reindeer herd in the distance, he and Call had hurried to catch up. By dark they still had not closed the gap; leaving Call and Shucungunga to set up camp, Jarvis and Nekowrah paced ahead, determined to reach Lopp that night. "It was a long chase," Jarvis wrote, "for Lopp was traveling late to make up for the time they had lost in the blizzard, and it was not until 8 in the evening that I caught up with them."

The timing of the reunion was fortunate for several reasons. Jarvis informed Lopp that he was nearly out of food for his dogs; he was down to his last seal. Lopp had plenty of food—an entire herd of food, in fact—but he had only the most general notion of where he was and how much farther he had to travel. The natives at the last village had drawn a map, but it was scarcely more sophisticated than their liturgical calendar. Jarvis, who had traveled this coast numerous times, informed him that they had just passed Point Lay and were now less than two hundred miles from Point Barrow.

That night, while Lopp and Jarvis shared a tent for the first time since the Kivalina River, a pack of wolves attacked the herd, killing an old cow and leaving behind only skin and bones. On the entire drive from Cape Prince of Wales, Lopp had never posted a night watch. He and the herders were tired enough after long days of traveling; it was too much to ask them to stay awake at night. Besides, the herd rarely wandered far. The routine was simply to round up the sled deer each morning and follow the obvious tracks to where the herd was grazing. Now, with wolves about, they would have to reconsider.

In the morning, Jarvis departed to rejoin Call, carrying with him the carcass of a lame sled deer as feed for his sled dogs. If all went well, he and Call would rendezvous with the herd again at Icy Cape, forty miles to the north. The reindeer made "fair speed" during the day, trotting over the frozen lagoon. That night, Ootenna and Tautuk stayed out with the herd, and the wolves did not attack. The next night was Kivyearzruk and Antisarlook's turn to stand watch. The northeast wind was blowing bitterly, and in the middle of the night, Antisarlook crawled into the tent, insisting there was no point in continuing his vigil. Lopp saw his point: In the dark, buffeted by the driving snow, "They could see but a few deer at a time and couldn't tell a deer from a wolf unless [they] were very close." As proof of the futility, when Tautuk went out to call in Kivyearzruk, the two became lost and would not have made it back to the tent if Antisarlook had not fired his gun in the air repeatedly.

The following morning the visibility was so poor—"thick weather," Lopp called it—that they elected to stay where they were. Each day the sled deer seemed to weaken further, and on the twenty-second, the herders were obliged to kill another, which they left in a well-marked cache on the beach. Three wolves followed them much of the day, just beyond range of their rifles. That night, Lopp offered a bounty of $20—nearly a month's pay—for each wolf killed. Ootenna and Tautuk stood watch but never got a shot. On March 23, sixteen miles past Icy Cape, they met Jarvis and Call, who had been traveling on the ocean side of the lagoon. It was the first time that Call had seen Lopp and the herders since February 7, four days after leaving Cape Prince of Wales. Point Barrow was only 140 miles away.

The worry now was not so much whether they would arrive at their destination in time but whether they would arrive with the herd intact. The presence of wolves indicated that they were coming into caribou country. Native hunters could be anywhere and armed not just with butcher knives tied to spears. Unless warned in advance, they would not hesitate to shoot as many reindeer as they had bullets. Once again, and for the last time, Jarvis and Call determined to march ahead and spread the word that the herd was coming.

The strategy worked. Over the next three days, as the herd moved steadily closer to Point Barrow, the natives gave them no trouble. As they neared Sazarzo (now spelled Sidaru, near present-day Wainwright), they came upon a dozen natives ice-fishing. "Invited them to come look at the herd," Lopp wrote in his log. "Said they did not have time. They were short of food and must fish while the fish were running." The natives' diffidence toward the herd did not hurt Lopp's feelings but rather amused him. "They had never seen reindeer," he laughed. "[P.T.] Barnum would not have made a fortune among [these] Eskimos."

The only nuisance they encountered was a dog left behind by Call. "We shot him," Lopp noted matter-of-factly.

On the twenty-sixth, Lopp spotted an old friend. From the ice-fishermen, he had learned that one of Charlie Brower's men was at Sazarzo. Leaving the herd a safe distance inland, Lopp hiked toward the village, which sits on a bluff over Wainwright Inlet. As he neared the cluster of native houses, he saw a man striding toward him. He could not make out the face, but the gait was familiar. John Grubin had been the assistant superintendent at Teller Reindeer Station during the winter of 1893–1894 when the Lopps were there. They had both traveled a long way since then, but for Lopp at least, it felt like he was finally getting somewhere. He spent the next day with Grubin, eating doughnuts and catching up.

. . .

Jarvis and Call had arrived at Sazarzo a day earlier and were already gone by the time Lopp arrived. Grubin had informed them that everything at Point Barrow was "going along all right" but that "the men in the camp were growing restless and had run down in health from their miserable way of living." Jarvis was more impatient than ever. On the morning of the twenty-sixth, he and Call hurried north, passing Point Belcher and reaching Peard Bay by noon. In the lee of Point Franklin they spotted the three bare masts of the *Belvedere*. "We drew up alongside about 4 P.M.," Jarvis wrote, "and going aboard announced ourselves and our mission, but it was some time before the first astonishment and incredulousness could wear off and a welcome be extended to us."

Jarvis was sobered by the situation aboard the *Belvedere*. Captain Martin Van Buren Millard was "a very sick man and looked as if he would hardly survive the winter." A crewman named Kelly was dying of syphilis—a "pitiable object . . . beyond help." Jarvis and Call were relieved to learn that only one of the thirty men living aboard had come down with scurvy, but provisions were "very short, and but two small meals a day was the allowance," Jarvis noted. The crew was "wholly dependent upon hunting for meat . . . but the hunting season was drawing to a close, and nearly five months had to be provided for before help could reach them from the outside." The news that the reindeer herd would soon arrive was received with "great relief," Jarvis testified, "and there was now little fear of the outcome."

Two days later, Jarvis and Call rode triumphantly into Point Barrow. To read Jarvis's account of his arrival, it was as if Stanley had found Livingstone. "March 29 was a beautiful, clear morning, cold and sharp, but with a cloudless sky and little or no wind," Jarvis wrote, "and . . . it seemed as if nature was trying to make amends at last for the hard trial she had given us." As he and Call approached Brower's post, "All the population came out to see us go by and wondered what strange out-fit it was, and when we greeted Mr. Brower and some of the officers of the wrecked vessels, whom we knew, they were stunned, and it was some time before they could realize that we were flesh and blood."

Brower remembers being stunned, but not in the way Jarvis imagined: "My first thought was that they had been wrecked and were coming for aid. As a matter of fact, it was the other way around. They were there to help *us*."

. . .

Lopp was not far behind. The herd had reached Peard Bay on the twenty-eighth, accompanied by Grubin and two dogsleds. They spotted the *Belvedere*, its sides banked with snow, but they did not go aboard. Instead they camped across the bay so that the deer could dig for moss. The next morning Lopp left the herd in the care of Tautuk, Ootenna, Kivyearzruk, and Antisarlook and continued toward Point Barrow by dogsled. March 29 was the "hardest day's traveling on the trip," he declared, not so much because of the weather or the terrain but because after two months of riding on a reindeer sled, he lacked the stamina to run all day behind a dogsled. That night, he and his driver, Quadrilla, stayed in a native house. "Having slept in tents all way along my journey, I could sleep but little . . . because of the stifling air."

On the morning of the thirtieth, Lopp made a point of washing his face before setting out for Point Barrow on foot. Soon he met up with a group of "dirty, sooty-faced sailors with guns," heading in the opposite direction. "They said they were going down the beach to see the reindeer," Lopp wrote in his log. "One walked back with me. He had been out on the ice looking for flour, etc., which had been left there months ago when the [*Navarch*] was burned." The only food Lopp had with him was a piece of frozen bread, which he shared with the whaler.

Next he came upon another group of whalers "harnessed to a sled like dogs," he noted sympathetically. "They were after wood."

At last he could see the village in the distance. "Could hardly realize that I was nearing my journey's end," he wrote. "Seemed too good to be true. Was it possible that I was about to reach the goal we had been struggling towards for two Arctic months?" As he entered the village, the natives rushed out to shake his hand. When he pulled up in front of the Presbyterian mission, Jarvis, Call, and the Marshes came out to greet him. Welcomed inside, Lopp happened to glance in the mirror for the first time since leaving home. "Certainly did not look like myself" was his stolid assessment.

# [ 15 ]

# Arctic Hole

THE GOAL OF THE Overland Relief Expedition had never been in doubt. What it accomplished is harder to calculate.

Most assuredly the journey itself was an extraordinary feat, of which the participants had every reason to be immensely proud. "We could afford to look back with a measure of satisfaction," Jarvis wrote of the fifteen-week trek from Cape Vancouver to Point Barrow. "Following the windings of the coast, as we had come, we had traveled something in the neighborhood of 1,500 miles or more. We had lived on the country, as we were directed, and had drawn from it all our means of travel, except a part of our camp gear and the small store we brought from the ship. The movements of the reindeer herd had far exceeded our expectations and were due to the extraordinary work of Mr. Lopp and his 'boys.' Our plans to overcome the many obstacles and difficulties had been carried out almost exactly as we had laid them down."

Yet getting there was only half the battle. Relief still had to be rendered, not to mention received. And the whalers were still four months and four thousand miles from home port.

The first step Jarvis took after arriving at Point Barrow was to inquire about the health of the men and the status of the food supply. "Consulting with Mr. Brower, Captains Sherman and Porter [of the wrecked *Orca* and *Jessie H. Freeman*], and E. A. McIlhenny and Dr. Marsh, I learned there had been no great suffering and that for the present there was no great need," he reported. He was informed that each man was rationed one pound of salt pork or beef four times a week, although much of this meat came from supplies left at the refuge station—old, unappetizing, and unnutritious. Additionally every man got one half-pound of frozen caribou meat one day a week; one half-pound of frozen fish one day a week; one pound of flour a day; one quarter-pound of beans on Sunday; and small allowances of coffee, tea, and sugar. "Provisions were short, very short," Jarvis remarked, "and only by the strictest economy and hard work had they been able to get along so far." The latest estimate was that the flour and meat, not counting the reindeer, would last until August.

On the day Jarvis and Call arrived at Point Barrow, they were approached by a delegation from the bunkhouse, imploring them to inspect their squalid quarters and to "do what lays in [your] power to obtain a change for us." The letter cast no specific blame other than to infer that neglect was something that could be corrected only by external intervention: "We have no facilities for keeping ourselves clean, there is one man at present under care of Dr. Marsh for scurvy, another man is confined to his bed with all the symptoms of scurvy. In justice to all we have no complaints to make, but there are evils which we cannot avoid but which you can rectify."

The following morning, Jarvis and Call entered the bunkhouse for the first time. They counted seventy-eight men living there. Once their eyes adjusted to the murky light, they could make out tiers of boxed-in bunks lining the walls. Many of the occupants did not bother to get up when the visitors entered. "The soot and smoke from [seal-oil] lamps covered everything, their clothes and bodies, with a black, greasy coating, so they were scarcely recognizable as white men," Jarvis observed with disgust. "All were in such a low demoralized condition. . . . Filth and vermin were everywhere, and those inclined to keep clean and live decently could not accomplish it in such a place and under such conditions." No wonder the bunkhouse had been nicknamed "the Arctic Hole of Calcutta."

Speaking as a physician, Call found the residents of the bunkhouse "in a most pitiable condition. . . . peer[ing] at us from their cold, dark, and frosty berths. They were in all stages of weakness, exhaustion, and despair. Four cases of scurvy had developed, two of which were in a dangerous state of the disease; others complained of dysentery, loss of appetite, and insomnia." Such symptoms are consistent with a syndrome known today as seasonal affective disorder, or SAD, which is caused by a biochemical imbalance brought on by lack of sunlight.

Jarvis and Call immediately sought remedy. "[The whalers] were much debilitated and run down," Jarvis explained, "and if something was not done quickly the weaker ones would soon die for general debility, and serious sickness attack all. . . . I determined that changes must be made at once, the men moved from their present quarters, their clothes and bodies cleaned, and proper rules of discipline, health, and exercise enforced."

What was not so obvious to Jarvis was why Brower, McIlhenny, and especially Richmond Marsh, who after all was a doctor, had not come to the same conclusion themselves and taken steps to ameliorate the deplorable conditions. Memory is often self-serving, and it was later suggested that Jarvis had cast the plight of the whalers in the most horrendous light in order to inflate his own achievement and promote his career. But at least two other sources corroborate Jarvis's description of the bunkhouse. James Allen had called it "awful . . . a terrible place." Tom Lopp described it as a "house of plagues . . . the most horrible place I was ever in." Both Allen and Lopp credit Brower for taking charge of the men once their officers washed their hands of all responsibility for their crews. "Had it not been for him," Allen wrote, "many of the shipwrecked whalers would be in Barrow yet, out where the wildflowers grow thickest." Even so, Brower had allowed the men to molder and—with scurvy beginning to set in—rot in their beds.

With the arrival of Jarvis, Brower had readily deferred to the authority of the Revenue Cutter Service; with the coming of whaling season, he was only too glad to turn over day-to-day responsibility for the icebound crews to someone else. Nevertheless, Brower was a fiercely independent man—one of the main reasons that he had come to the Arctic in the first place—and he took enormous pride in his ability to dig himself out of trouble. From his perspective, the notion that he or any of his men required "relief" would have been an insult if it were not so absurd, especially since he had, by all accounts, pulled off the astonishing feat of feeding and housing more than one hundred unexpected guests over the previous six months.

In his memoir, Brower commended Jarvis for upholding "the finest traditions of Arctic rescue work," but he also emphasized that he and the whalers would have survived just fine without the Overland Relief Expedition. As for the abominable situation in the bunkhouse, Brower insisted—rather defensively and with no small measure of revisionism—that he had been on the verge of addressing the problem himself and that Jarvis's actions were his idea in the first place. "There were several things I wanted done, that I had been unable to do," Brower explained. "One was to take the men out of the bunkhouse. . . . For some time I wanted Marsh and McIlhenny to give some of their spare room to the men. If they would take thirty each in their spare rooms, I could take the rest in an empty warehouse, fitting bunks along the sides. . . . Jarvis agreed with me." Perhaps this is the true order of events, but the fact remains that Brower had taken no steps toward moving the men until Jarvis and Call stepped in. With military firmness, Jarvis relocated the men, assigning twenty-five to the schoolhouse, twenty-five more to the former refuge station, and twenty-eight to Brower's warehouse.

While Brower was never directly criticized for the ghastly state of the bunkhouse, Ned McIlhenny did not get off so easily. Jarvis asserted that over the winter "Mr. McIlhenny refused to allow anyone but officers in his house." One of the first published accounts of the relief expedition, appearing in the *New York Sun* at the end of the summer, brought word that the whalers had leveled "charges of selfishness" at the naturalist: "[McIlhenny] was housed at the old Government refuge station at Point Barrow, and, it is alleged, refused to take in any of the 350 [*sic*] shipwrecked men, although he had ample accommodations. . . . When Lieut. Jarvis of the Government relief expedition arrived on March 29, he was very indignant over McIlhenny's conduct, and at once compelled him to open the Government house to part of the men." The *Sun* reported that resentment toward the naturalist had become so pronounced that "a number of sailors threatened to lynch McIlhenny."

McIlhenny, needless to say, saw the situation differently. "If the crews of the ships had been thrown on their own resources they would have all starved," he wrote on March 31, "but the supply of provisions in the whaling station and what I had has saved them, and although we have not had all we could eat, we have gotten through the winter safely with the loss of only one man." McIlhenny did not address the housing inequity directly, choosing instead to stress the great sacrifice he had made by accommodating those officers fortunate enough to live with him. And in his version of the story, he did the lion's share of the work: "My travels and explorations have been curtailed by my having most of the looking after of the wrecked men and much of the time of myself and men that should have been used in making collections has been given up to them."

Somehow, though, he still managed to amass "850 bird skins, 345 mammal skins, 1,100 ethnological specimens, besides small collections in other branches." Two of the specimens he chose not to mention were the skeletons of an Eskimo man and woman, which he crated and shipped home along with his skins and feathers and trinkets.

With the whalers redistributed, Jarvis ordered the bunkhouse demolished. "It was only a mass of filth and could never be used again for quarters," he reasoned. Its highest and best use now was as fuel. Concerned that the men in the bunkhouse might transfer their sloven-ly ways to their new quarters, Jarvis, in cooperation with the two doc-tors, Call and Marsh, enforced a strict regimen of cleanliness and sanitation. Bedding and clothing were aired and, as water would allow, washed. Every man was issued one pound of soap a month and expect-ed to use it. Jarvis and Call made daily inspections of the men's quar-ters and appearance. Increasing the ration of fresh meat to two and a half pounds a week eliminated worries about scurvy.

Next Jarvis had to address the delicate question of how to handle the men still living aboard the outlying ships. With the exception of the crewmen of the *Jeanie*, who had signed on for the duration of its voyage, no matter how long that voyage lasted, all of the whalers had been hired for a specific period of time, which by March had expired or was very near to expiring. In recent weeks, many of these men had begun making noises about leaving their ships and coming to Point Barrow as soon as the weather got warmer. Jarvis thought this a bad idea. Point Barrow had all the men it could handle, and discipline could be more easily maintained by keeping men in smaller groups. To head off the mass migration to shore, Jarvis made a ruling "that the vessels were caught in a position of peril through no fault of their own, but through an act of Providence, over which they had no control. As long as they remained in that position and were not wrecked, and with chances of escaping the peril, the obligation of the crew to remain by them and save them could not be broken." Accordingly, he continued, "I caused it to be known that I should hold the crews to the vessels as long as they were not wrecked, no matter when the terms of shipment expired . . . [and] that discharges could not be properly given here, in a desolate, inhospitable country, but only upon return to a proper port."

Then, having laid down the law, the peripatetic Jarvis at last gave in to the stress and fatigue of the past four months. Tonsillitis sent him to bed and rendered him virtually speechless for a week.

. . .

Unlike Jarvis, Lopp had few obligations once he arrived at Point Barrow. He did not seem disappointed that there was no urgent demand for the reindeer that he and his herders had driven up the trail. Oddly enough, in neither his log nor in any subsequent correspondence did he express any sense of anti-climax. He had done his job; the herd and herders had lived up to his expectations and proven that reindeer were the right fit for the Alaskan wilderness. Evidently this was sufficient. Lopp was never one to boast of his achievements—always putting those of the natives ahead of his own and crediting prayer, family, and the American Missionary Association for his modest successes. Where Sheldon Jackson, Harrison Thornton, David Jarvis, and Edward Avery McIlhenny were unabashedly histrionic, Lopp stood out as consistently modest.

The numbers spoke for themselves. Of 448 reindeer that had started from Cape Prince of Wales, only sixty-six had been lost or killed along the seven-hundred-mile route. The deer not butchered to feed the whalers over the next few months would become the foundation of the next important Alaskan herd—the northernmost link in the "endless chain" that Lopp and Sheldon Jackson had imagined seven years earlier. In the meantime, the reindeer were left to graze on the pond-pocked tundra thirty miles south of Point Barrow. Ootenna, Kivyearzruk, Tautuk, and Antisarlook took turns looking after them.

On the day of his arrival, Lopp was invited to dinner at the Marshes', after which he joined a prayer meeting at the schoolhouse attended by more than 130 natives. "I was called on for a few remarks," he wrote in his log. "They listened attentively with smiles at my Cape P[rince] of Wales dialect. I doubt if they understood all I tried to tell them." As usual, Lopp seemed to get as much from the natives as he gave. "They had fine faces," he noted. "In fact they were the finest looking Eskimos I had ever seen together."

At least one of those faces was familiar. Konok had been a student at Cape Prince of Wales, and she was one of the girls the Reverend Hanna had attempted to seduce. When the Cape natives began calling her "Hanna's wife," she fled to Port Clarence, where she offered herself to Captain Sherman of the *Orca*. Euphemistically her position was "seamstress," but Lopp described her more accurately as "the wife (?) [the question mark was Lopp's] of a whaling captain." From others at Point Barrow, he heard a spurious rumor that Konok was indirectly to blame for the *Orca*, *Freeman*, and *Belvedere* becoming trapped in the ice. The three ships had agreed to stick together while leaving Point Barrow in the fall of 1897. But, the scuttlebutt alleged, Captain Sherman had insisted on waiting for the supply ship *Jeanie* to arrive from Herschel Island so that he could "ship his Konok to Cape Prince of Wales." Sherman, who was heading home to his family, apparently had no further need for a seamstress. "The *Jeanie* did not come," Lopp wrote. "They waited too long for her and were caught in the ice off Sea Horse Island." In his log, he did not speculate on the veracity of this gossip, but given what he had learned about the morality of whalers, such a tale did not stretch credibility.

Nor had Sherman been the only whaler to take up with a native woman. In his tour of Point Barrow, Lopp had found "sailors in almost every house." His inference is clarified by a letter that Richmond Marsh wrote to Sheldon Jackson later in the year. "These traders"— presumably he meant Brower and his associates—"ran an open house of prostitution this winter and every officer but one of the shipwrecked men had his 'squaw.'"

Under such circumstances, Lopp did not relish the thought of spending the next few months with these men. April 3 marked exactly two months since he had left Cape Prince of Wales. "I had never been homesick for a minute while en route north," he declared. But now, with spring coming, he missed his wife and children enormously. On April 4, he started for home.

. . .

Lopp traveled by dogsled, carrying as light a load as he dared. "Small tent. Stove made of 25-pound powder can. Few cans of mutton and Boston baked beans," he recorded in his log. Flags flew outside the mission and Brower's station as he bid good-bye. "Grand handshake and we were off." Marsh and his wife had asked to accompany him as far as the reindeer herd. Before Lopp left Point Barrow, it had been agreed that any reindeer not butchered and eaten by the stranded whalers would be turned over to Marsh, as representative of the Presbyterian Church and the U.S. Bureau of Education. The ultimate distribution of the animals would await a decision by Sheldon Jackson.

Also before Lopp had left Point Barrow, Jarvis had given him a letter that he hoped would find its way to Captain Tuttle of the *Bear.* Jarvis's tone was upbeat. "There have been no accidents to the herd nor to ourselves during the entire trip," he began. "I find everything here in as good order as could be." Food, fuel, housing, and health were under control, he assured. Therefore he saw no need to "risk the men's lives sending any to Point Hope." His sole request was for clothes, for "nothing the men have ashore will be fit to take on board the *Bear.*"

Lopp and the Marshes reached the herd by lunchtime the following day. The deer were grazing easily on the tundra moss, already beginning to regain some of the weight they had lost on the long trek. The feed was not as abundant close to the coast as it was inland or on the Seward Peninsula, but there was plenty for the time being. The cows would begin calving within the next two weeks, and this was as

good a place as any to look after them. When and if the need to harvest reindeer arose, the herd would be that much stronger, larger, and
easier to move. Ootenna and Antisarlook had agreed to stay at least
through the summer, when the *Bear* arrived. They would recruit
natives from Point Barrow to help them keep tabs on the herd.

Lopp was eager to get going, so after a two-hour visit, he pushed
on, accompanied now by Tautuk, Kivyearzruk, and the guide Omruk,
who had stayed with him since the Kivalina River. By evening they had
reached the *Belvedere*, still icebound at Peard Bay. There they found
plenty of food aboard the whaling ship—Lopp and his party dined on
deer steaks, potatoes, and pie—but the mood was somewhat glum.
Shortly after Jarvis and Call had visited the *Belvedere*, Kelly, the
syphilitic man whom Call had declared incurable, had drowned himself in the hole of open water chopped around the ship's rudder. He
was only the second crewman to die since the debacle of the *Navarch*.

Leaving the *Belvedere* on the sixth, Lopp now traveled with the
single-mindedness of Odysseus. "For the return trip I had no responsibilities with reference to planning for the herd to occupy my time
and attention," he wrote. "All we had to think of was to take care of
ourselves and conserve our strength, and make the best speed possible during good weather." And the speed they made was remarkable.
"After we had been on the trail a few days we were able to trot along
thirty or forty miles a day without any great exertion," he stated.

The return trip to Cape Prince of Wales was far less challenging
than the drive north had been, yet it was more grueling than Lopp's
succinct telling suggests. Traveling twice as fast as they had done with
the herd, they reached the mouth of the Pitmegea River on the fif-
teenth, eating reindeer meat they had left in caches along the way. At
the Pitmegea they found a supply of flour, rice, bread, dried fruit,
molasses, and tea that Bertholf, on orders from Jarvis, had stored in an
abandoned house.

When the wind was favorable, they rigged a sail on one of the sleds. Mostly, though, the weather worked against them. Perversely, the worst hardship was neither wind nor cold, but the Arctic sunlight, which now shone nearly eighteen hours a day. To avert snowblindness, they traveled at night whenever possible. This, too, had its drawbacks. "Our eyes had already become affected by the glare," Lopp wrote on April 9, less than a week after leaving Point Barrow. "Started eight-fifteen P.M. It was very dark from ten until two. Could not distinguish snowdrift from level snow. Had many falls during the night."

The following day, the tenth, was a Sunday. The weather was ideal for traveling, but Lopp insisted that they lay over to observe the Sabbath. On the trip north, the urgency of getting the herd to Point Barrow had made Sunday just another day (although on three of the eight Sundays of the journey, circumstances were such that they did not break camp). But on the way home Lopp was unwavering. Sunday again became a day for rest and reflection—a measure of his own faith and his commitment to setting a good example for the herders.

They did not cut across the Lisburne Peninsula this time but kept to the coast. Rounding Cape Lisburne on the eighteenth, they encountered open water against the shore. Creeping along a narrow ledge of snow beneath the steep bluffs, they constantly wrestled with the sleds to keep them from sliding into the sea. Even so, they had one of their most productive days, advancing more than fifty miles. Only two weeks after leaving Point Barrow, they arrived at Point Hope, where they were greeted warmly by Lieutenant Bertholf, and the men of the whaling stations.

Bertholf had not been idle in the seven weeks since he had separated from the rest of the Overland Relief Expedition. In addition to ferrying supplies to the Pitmegea, he assumed the role of policeman and temperance worker. Over the winter, he broke up more than twenty stills and repeatedly lectured the natives about other villages that had been "depopulated by indulgence." The alcohol problem would never be solved, he concluded, as long as whites encouraged the manufacture of whiskey by selling natives the molasses and flour to make it and then "buying and drinking the concoction after it has been brewed." Bertholf's other assignment was to investigate several murders that had occurred near Point Hope. One of the perpetrators turned out to be Avuluk, the guide who had abandoned Lopp and the reindeer herd to find their own way across the interior of the Lisburne Peninsula.

At Point Hope Lopp was surprised to meet Keok and Ituk, whom he had sent home with Sokweena on February 21—or so he thought. While passing near Aniyak, on the north shore of Kotzebue Sound, the three herders had learned of a small group of reindeer grazing nearby. In proving their unwavering dedication and loyalty to Tomgorah, Keok and Ituk postponed their journey south and set off in search of the deer. They found thirty-four in all, the bunch that had become separated from the main herd during the blizzard of February 22–23. Sending Sokweena on to Cape Prince of Wales, Keok and Ituk stuck with the deer, eventually driving them to Point Hope. Quite by chance, they arrived two days after Lopp, Tautuk, and Kivyearzruk.

They spent five nights at Point Hope. On April 23, leaving Ituk to continue tending the reindeer and at last saying good-bye to Omruk, they pushed south toward Cape Thompson, arriving by evening at the camp of Charlie Klengenberg, a former ship's steward who had taken a native wife and turned his talents to trading. (In later years, he would add piracy and murder to his résumé, becoming one of the Arctic's most notorious scofflaws.) Lopp and his companions laid over a day with Klingenberg, honoring the Sabbath and enjoying their host's fried ptarmigan.

The run from here to Cape Krusenstern grew progressively more grueling. The wind, snow, and shortage of dog food were vexing enough. Worse still, Lopp and Kivyearzruk went blind.

Snowblindness is caused by intense exposure to ultraviolet rays, usually from sunlight reflected on snow. Besides impairing vision, snowblindness can be excrutiating. Imagine one's eyeballs balanced "on needles in sockets filled with sand," wrote a seasoned Arctic traveler. Lopp's eyes had bothered him intermittently ever since leaving Point Barrow. He and the herders were not always able to travel at night, and they had no sunglasses, not even the ingeniously slitted goggles that natives wore to reduce glare. On April 27, as the sleds were nearing the north shore of Kotzebue Sound, Lopp found he could not see at all when standing still or riding on the sled. "Only by running and perspiring could I keep my eyes open," he confessed. Crossing the sound on the ice was risky with perfect vision. To cross it blind verged on madness.

They reached Aniyak late in the early evening and were welcomed into the "hotel" where they had stayed on the way north. Lopp was overcome with "indescribable pain" as soon as he entered the house. He and Kivyearzruk blindfolded themselves and bathed their eyes in ice water. Even more soothing was a letter from Ellen. She had sent it by natives traveling up the coast, not knowing when and where it would reach her husband. In February, Lopp had sent a letter of his own via Sokweena, reassuring Ellen that he and the herders were getting along fine. While neither letter survives, they surely were two of the most comforting exchanges in the Lopps' many years of happy marriage and unwelcome times apart.

All the next day, Lopp and Kivyearzruk remained indoors, out of the sunlight. "Pain in my eyes and head almost unbearable," he wrote in his log. "Could not see the dirt around me but still had my sense of smell. A sick, wheezy dog was tied in the igloo near where I slept. . . . Stove smokes because of a faulty pipe . . . adds to our misery."

While waiting for their eyesight to recover, they quizzed the villagers about the condition of the ice on Kotzebue Sound. The news was not reassuring. "They said the ice bridge had been gone since the time we left and had just come back and that they feared in many places the ice would be too thin to hold us up," he recounted. But then their luck changed. In the evening, the wind shifted to the northwest, and the natives agreed that conditions might permit a crossing, although it would require extreme care.

The next morning, the twenty-ninth, Lopp still could not open his eyes. By afternoon, after constant application of wet towels, the pain finally began to subside, and his vision improved slightly. Not knowing how long the wind would stay in their favor, he decided that they must start across the sound that night. In exchange for three sacks of flour, a native named Owkneeruk agreed to guide them halfway.

They started onto the ice at 5:00 P.M.—Lopp, Tautuk, Kivyearzruk, Keok, Owkneeruk, and two sleds. "Kept my eyes shaded, so did not see much," Lopp wrote of the early going. The pack ice was a maze of rubble and shards, as it had been during the previous crossing. More worrisome were the frequent patches of young ice. Often they could find a way around these weak spots, but eventually they came to a span that could not be avoided. "It was certainly nerve racking to go over several miles of this rubber-like ice," Lopp recorded. "As we approach the middle it cracks and waves up and down. . . . Fearing the sled would break through I drop back a few feet behind."

Sensing that hesitation would bring disaster, the dogs picked up the pace, making it difficult for the half-blind Lopp to keep up. Finally he decided it was safer to sit on the sled than to run on his own. "The waving and cracking of this thin ice . . . recalled to me my boyhood experience on the ice of shallow ponds we would dare one another to go over . . . until one of us finally broke through," he reflected. Except that this pond was not shallow and the nearest land was more than twenty miles away.

At twilight Owkneeruk turned back. Lopp and the three herders traveled another hour on their own, at last making camp at 10:30, concerned that in the dark they might damage their sleds or fall through the thin ice.

At 5:00 the next morning, after a hasty breakfast of tea and dried salmon, they resumed their painstaking journey toward the southern shore of Kotzebue Sound. "All kinds of sledding during the day," Lopp noted in his log.

> Find some rough ice to work through. . . . Many smooth patches of new ice to cross. Depth of snow varying from two to six inches. Lunch at one o'clock on hard bread, butter, and molasses. Sight a low mountain at 3:30. Think it is Devil Mountain southeast of Cape Espenberg. Our course has been about halfway between south and southwest. Later we think we can see low land in line with the mountains. It is due south by compass. We start for this land. One dog bites another through the ankle making him useless. Long stretch of level ice covered with deep snow. There is no rough ice in sight. . . . We come to a crack in the ice, then one or two more, then patches of new ice. We go over some and around others. About five P.M. we climb a pile of very high ice and decided that we can see low land ahead and keep on south. As the sun goes down the land comes out plainer. We travel on thinking we can surely reach the land by six o'clock. For fear we shall be disappointed, I give us until seven. Ice very rough. Sleds get many hard bumps. Dogs are aggravated. They invariably stop pulling while we are trying to push the sleds over the rough places. About seven o'clock we sight a village.

. . .

Twenty-six hours after leaving Aniyak, they touched land again. The village turned out to be Kivuklouk, on Goodhope Bay, twenty-five miles south of Cape Espenberg and twenty-five miles nearer home than they thought they were. They camped a mile from the settlement. "Find wood to burn," Lopp wrote. "Have cocoa, biscuits dried fish. . . . Big sleep."

The following day, May 1, was Sunday. Lopp and his herders rested and enjoyed a hearty meal of fish, rice, and flapjacks. "We discussed many things," Lopp remarked in a rare philosophical aside. "One was the millions of things that were going on in the world at one time— deaths, births, marriages, etc." Whether his fellow travelers regarded their universe as small, large, or simply unfathomable, he did not say. Nor was there any way of knowing that on that same day, while they hunkered against a stiff northeast wind on the frozen shore of Kotzebue Sound, far across the Pacific Ocean in the Philippines, warships of the U.S. Navy were firing the opening salvo of the Spanish-American War.

From here on, they traveled "with light hearts even though the trail was heavy and the going bad." With any luck, they would reach Cape Prince of Wales in three or four days. But they were not home free yet. Passing through Kivuklouk, Lopp was approached by a native who recognized one of the dogs pulling the expedition's sleds. Lopp had gotten it from Jarvis, who apparently had gotten it from this man with the promise that it would be returned. "I gave him no encouragement, telling him we must use the dog until we reach Cape Prince of Wales," Lopp recalled. "He was rather persistent."

The man followed them all day and shared their camp that night. In the morning, Lopp again tried to placate the fellow, giving him a small amount of gunpowder. "We packed our sleds, hitched up our teams, and got ready to start," Lopp remembered. The native sat on his own sled, glaring, but did not follow them. Not until they had put several miles between themselves and their angry interloper did the herders inform Lopp that the man had been on the verge of shooting him. "They explained that he started his sled off at the same time we started ours, he going in the opposite direction, of course; that after traveling about twenty-five yards, he stopped his sled and made a motion to take hold of his gun, and drove a few yards farther, stopped again and made the same motion." They speculated that if the herders had not been in the way, Lopp might now be lying dead in the snow. "I laughed at their fears and we traveled on."

They were beyond Shishmaref, only fifty miles from Cape Prince of Wales. The trail was familiar but the snow was moist and heavy, obliging them to wear snowshoes and travel at night when the snow was firmer. "We all become worn out and tired," Lopp wrote on May 4. They continued well past sunrise, striving for a view of Cape Mountain. Soon every feature of the landscape was familiar. Looking seaward, they could make out the humps of the Diomedes in the Bering Strait. Inland, across the big lagoon, was the mouth of the Mint River. The reindeer camp was just beyond the far swales of coastal tundra. Had it been only three months since they had left?

· · ·

For Ellen Lopp, the time had passed quickly enough. Although she had joked about being "the only white adult in forty miles" (it was sixty, actually), she was hardly alone. In one of the few letters she wrote while Tom was away (to be mailed when the first ships arrived in the spring), she described a house teeming with activity and distraction: "From morning till night seven days a week I spend my time picking up things the children throw down or spill, wiping up water, changing wet clothes, getting drinks—and waiting on natives."

She did not have to do everything herself. Nora and Alice were good sitters and housekeepers. Sokweena's wife, Elubwok, and Netaxite's wife, Kongik, pitched in as well. Ellen, who was raised by a strong grandmother and mother and was one of five independent-minded sisters, seemed to thrive as the female head of a mostly female household. "I wouldn't think of such a thing as telling these people that Eve was made out of one of Adam's ribs," she wrote somewhat blasphemously to her sister Susie.

If she had worries, she expressed them in prayers, not letters. And for the thousandth time, she scoffed at the notion that the natives were in any way hostile. "Some people think these Cape people are so dangerous," she remonstrated. "They have been very pleasant to me.

Our storehouse is of half-inch boards, door of the same, and no one disturbs it." As for alcohol, she was sure that no one in the village had been drunk in over two months.

It never occurred to her to call off school. She regarded the two hours she spent teaching every day one of the "oases in a desert of undone duties and plans not carried out." Over the years, she and Tom had not taught the natives many stories from the Old Testament. But with Tom gone, she was drawn to the book of Job: "And, behold, there came a great wind from the wilderness, and smote the four corners of the house. . . ."

All winters in the Arctic demand patience and fortitude, and this one had been no exception. Sometimes simply going outside could be an immense chore. Blowing snow—the snow was always blowing— created deep drifts on the roof and along the sides of the Lopps' house. By April the front door was reached by way of a thirty-foot snow tunnel. In a letter dated April 29, she remarked, "We haven't been outdoors yet—are waiting until someone wants to get in more than we want to get out, and shovels us out." On this particular day, the shovelers were two native women, one of whom wished to trade a pound of seal meat; the other brought firewood. Once in the warm house, the visitors tended to linger, enjoying the lively company of the children and other women. Often they were content to sit and look at the illustrations in old magazines—glimpses of a world more fantastic than any Old Testament tale.

At noon, Ellen added a postscript to her letter: "The baby is taking her dinner. Sarah is crying. Dwight playing the organ and telling us what it says. Elubwok's and Nora's sisters are here, too. They hadn't been in for a few weeks, so I thought I'd let them in for a few minutes. Nora's sister held Katharine for me while I got flour for the woman with the wood. [Alice] just discovered that Dwight had a lot of loose sugar in his pocket."

Not the most tranquil home, but a happy one.

. . .

Regrettably and rather characteristically, neither Ellen nor Tom had much to say about his homecoming. "Reached the cape about eight o'clock in the morning of the 5th," Tom wrote sparely in his log. "Much excitement and rejoicing."

Ellen was even more matter-of-fact. "Tom got back yesterday morning," she wrote to her family. "Thirty-one days from Point Barrow, thirteen from Point Hope. He traveled down in just twenty days. They rested or stopped on account of the weather the eleven other days." She neglected to express her own feelings, mentioning only that two-year-old Sarah was frightened by the arrival of a stranger. "She had gone to the door to meet him, but when she saw him she ran back crying. It wasn't because he was a white man for he wasn't white at all, he was so tanned. He was darker than [Alice] Nowadluk, for she had been in the house so much she wasn't tanned." Ellen also noted that Tom's eyes were "real bad." By the next day, they were somewhat better, but "he's tired," she said.

A little snowblind and a little weary—that was all. Tom later wrote to the American Missionary Association, "So you see [Ellen] had a more difficult position, remaining here alone, than those of us who were in the expedition. It was a great trial of our faith."

Ellen shrugged off any suggestion of hardship on her part. "We got along very well while Tom was away," she declared, adding as a humble afterthought, "I mean well considering the fact that he was away." Her only regret was that he had not been around to help with school. Their star pupil, Netaxite, had endeavored to teach the younger children (while Ellen taught the older). "[H]e has some natural talent for teaching," she praised, "but he knows so very little. He hasn't been to school much since he began to herd five years ago."

Soon all was back to normal at the Cape—or as normal as things could be on the Bering Strait. In May the natives killed two whales. Ellen fried doughnuts in whale oil, boasting that they were "as good as any I ever made." With the drifts finally melting from around the house and the sun shining nearly twenty-two hours a day, Ellen contemplated planning her first garden on the sod roof—if she could only keep the dogs and children from playing on it. "The dogs had a fight up there this afternoon," she wrote her family, "and broke both panes of glass of a double skylight."

It was hard to complain when the weather was so pleasant and the kids were doing so well. The two older children, five-year-old Lucy and four-year-old Dwight, were allowed to play outdoors with the other children from the village. They were fluent in Inupiaq, but their English was still a work in progress. "Dwight's foot went to sleep the other day," Ellen laughed, "and he said it was 'curly.'"

Tom recovered quickly from his snowblindness. Without a reindeer herd to manage, he threw himself into hunting with the Cape natives. He contemplated writing a "full account" of the reindeer drive and submitting it to one of the San Francisco papers but then thought otherwise. "We are so pushed, reaping our summer harvest of walrus, that I may not attempt it," he said. The other reason he never got around to rendering a full account of the trek revealed as much about his values as his priorities. "Since we had a prominent part in the expedition," he told his father-in-law, "we feel rather modest about writing it up for the papers."

In the end, he did put together a brief travelogue, based on his log. The closest he ever came to bragging of his experience was to note the incredulity on the faces of the natives after he got home. "Many of them had prophesied that we could never travel the long distance," he wrote. "I doubt if there were ten natives in the entire village who thought we could reach Point Barrow, to say nothing of our returning to Wales the same winter. . . . Because they had never made this long journey, they reasoned that it could not be made."

# 16

# Fish in a Barrel

AT POINT BARROW, the story was still being written. In mid-April, the natives began hauling their umiaks across the shore ice to the leads through which whales would soon migrate. Then at the beginning of May, the pack ice shifted, trapping a school of belugas in a solitary hole of open water, one hundred yards long and twenty yards wide. Most likely the whales—averaging ten feet in length and weighing more than a ton apiece—were doomed anyway; there were no other openings in the ice for miles around. Still, the slaughter was orgiastic. "The number of [whales] was so great when I got there," McIlhenny recalled, "all could not rise in the hole at once and I do not think 1,000 would be a high estimate for the numbers then alive. . . . The noise made by their splashing, floundering and puffing was tremendous. For a few seconds every available inch of water space would be taken up by plunging whales; then as they got air, the numbers would gradually thin out until none were left on the surface, and they would be away so long I would think surely they had found open water and had gone for good; but back they would come with a rush at the end of a quarter of an hour or so, having stayed away from air just as long as they could, and doubtless each time they disappeared for this length of time they would swim long distances under the ice in search of open water."

It was like shooting fish in a barrel, quite literally. "At no point in the next twenty-four hours . . . [were] there less than five men shooting and at times there were ten or twelve, most of them armed with repeating rifles and the shooting was so frequent it reminded me of a skirmish line," McIlhenny wrote. Brower estimated the number of belugas shot at six hundred, but the total actually harvested was approximately half that. Unless a whale was killed instantly with a shot through the head, it sank before it could be recovered. "It was an awful waste of meat," Brower commented. "No one could stop the shooting."

If nothing else, the residents of Point Barrow could quit worrying about starvation.

Several days later, the bowhead season commenced, and many of the whalers who had been idle all winter offered to join the native crews. Jarvis would not hear of it. "The men could be of no use to the natives, would only be a burden in the boats, and make no end of confusion and trouble," he reasoned. "The natives had been able to run their own business heretofore and could do it now without the help of white men." He suspected that "this was only a subterfuge of the men to share in the natives' catch."

Jarvis had other ideas on how to keep the whalers occupied. As the snow began to melt, baseball became an even more popular pastime. "It was excellent exercise and gave all something of interest to talk about," Jarvis assured. Another occupation was duck shooting. A shooting camp had been established several miles from the station, and as the birds returned in the spring, the blinds were manned constantly. In one ten-day period, hunters killed 1,100 eider ducks. And to those whalers with bad aim or ambivalence toward baseball, Jarvis offered a third option: hike the five miles to the duck camp and carry back ten ducks.

Not everyone thrived on the regimen of fresh air and exertion. On

June 8, Phillip Mann, a crewman from the *Freeman* and a member of the delegation that had asked Jarvis to inspect the deplorable conditions in the bunkhouse, died suddenly. Curiously, Call and Marsh chose to conduct a thorough autopsy, in which they examined Mann's brain and internal organs. The cause of death, they concluded, was heart failure due to a "fatty heart."*

By the end of June, the crews of the *Belvedere, Rosario, Newport, Fearless,* and *Jeanie* began preparing for the time when they would break out of the ice that imprisoned them. Spars and rigging were refitted; temporary awnings and shelters removed from the decks; boilers cleaned and tested. Despite the harrowing winter, most of the captains expected to rejoin the whaling fleet for the summer hunt.

The *Rosario* was not so fortunate. On July 2, a storm blew from the southwest, forcing the pack ice against the battlement of ground ice that had stood to seaward of the *Rosario* all winter, protecting it from harm. This time the ridge shattered, hurling colossal chunks of shore ice toward the land. One of these shards smashed the stern of the *Rosario*, tearing away the stern post and keel, crushing the starboard bow, and thrusting the ship almost onto the beach. The demise of the *Rosario* took only a few minutes. The crew got to shore easily enough and spent the rest of the summer living in tents. The *Rosario* lay on its

---

* Also curious is the death of a fourth man, a whaler named Gray. He is not mentioned in any of the official reports filed by Call or Jarvis. Nor is Gray's death noted by McIlhenny, Buxton, Brower, or Lopp. Yet Sheldon Jackson, who was not a member of the expedition, states in his *Annual Report of the Introduction of Reindeer into Alaska* that during the winter Gray died of dropsy, known today as edema. Jackson may have mistakenly identified Gray as a crewman aboard the *Jeanie*, while a newspaper clipping pasted in Jackson's scrapbook assigns Gray to the *Jeanette*, a steam whaler that did not arrive in the Arctic until the end of the summer. The wording in the clipping is almost identical to the passage in Jackson's report that lists the fatalities at Point Barrow—strongly suggesting that the former was the source for the latter. Perhaps Jackson simply misread or miswrote *Jeanette* as *Jeanie*. This being the case, the official number of whalers who died at Point Barrow during the winter of 1897–1898 stands at three: Kotake from the *Rosario*; Kelly from the *Belvedere*; and Mann from the *Jessie H. Freeman*. Most accounts of the Overland Relief Expedition ignore the death of Point Barrow natives, of which there were several, and the death of a "Siberian" whaler, whose name, if it was ever properly recorded, has now been forgotten.

beam a few hundred yards away like a discarded toy. It would be used as firewood.

The Fourth of July was a more cheerful day. A large crowd turned out to watch the baseball games, and Jarvis authorized an extra allowance of meat and flour. The highlight of the festivities was a pie-eating contest between two black crewmen. "Each had his hands tied behind and was furnished a dried apple pie," Brower chronicled. "They sat at a table out on the sand. One had a prehensile lip. He could reach it over the pie, drawing it into his mouth, biting off great pieces. The other had a mouth almost from ear to ear. He just went down on the pie and there was no pie in sight." The officers who shared Brower's table that evening enjoyed a feast of roast swan, goose, and crane.

By mid-July, having grown impatient waiting for the ice to clear, Jarvis sent out an umiak skippered by Captain Albert Sherman, formerly of the *Orca*, and crewed by six whalers, two natives, and Brower's man, Fred Hopson. Following the narrow margin of open water along the shore, they made their way two hundred miles down the coast to Point Lay, where they hoped to find the *Bear* and update Captain Tuttle on the situation at Point Barrow. Jarvis's latest estimate was that supplies would last until August 20. Because the *Belvedere* lay sixty miles to the southwest and that much closer to relief, Jarvis allotted it only enough food to last until August 1.

So long as the supply of caribou and fish—not to mention the belugas—was abundant, Jarvis insisted that the slaughter of reindeer be kept to a minimum. The deer were still gaunt after their long trek; the more time they were allowed to recover, the better. During the spring, 190 fawns had been born, and Jarvis was pleased with how well the herd was adapting to its new range. Like Jackson and Lopp, he was a strong believer in reindeer for Alaska. "At first the reindeer were regarded with curiosity by the natives [near Point Barrow]," he wrote in his official report, "but later they began to see the great usefulness of the animals, and wonder how they could be secured. I was constantly asked by the better class of the people if the reindeer were to be left there after we had used all we needed."

Just how much reindeer meat was "needed" is still debated. As the supply of wild caribou began to dwindle in the spring, Jarvis permitted more reindeer to be killed and eaten—especially by the crew of the *Belvedere*. All told, 180 deer were slaughtered, providing more than twelve thousand pounds of fresh meat. "The addition of this when most needed," Jarvis asserted, "made it possible to bring the men through without extreme suffering and sickness."

Others begged to differ. On the day the Overland Relief Expedition arrived at Point Barrow, Norman Buxton, an otherwise reliable taxonomist, had dismissed reindeer as a "white elephant," concluding that "there is no feed for them here and we have no pressing need for them." Charlie Brower was no less harsh in his assessment of reindeer as meat-on-the-hoof. "No one ever ate any of the meat," he insisted. "One day Mac [McIlhenny] and I were talking about the condition of the deer, saying that it was a shame to kill any of them, being unfit for food. . . . Mac said that if they killed none, there would be no chance to say how [the expedition] arrived just in time to prevent starvation. In a joke I reported this to Jarvis. It was the only time I saw him mad."

Brower was somewhat kinder toward Tom Lopp, admiring him for the extraordinary feat of bringing the herd through to Point Barrow. "But perhaps it was just as well that Lopp started back to Wales with the dog team almost at once," Brower offered sympathetically. "Had he stayed around longer he might have realized that he'd really been driving 'coals to Newcastle.'"

. . .

Needy or not, the ships were still bottled up at Point Barrow, and the summer was half over. By mid-July, the *Newport* and *Fearless* had managed to work their way free of the ice that had immobilized them side by side for the past nine months. They inched carefully westward to within thirty miles of Point Barrow before again coming up against the impenetrable pack ice. They were stalled near Cooper Island when the *Jeanie* caught up with them several days later. Both the *Jeanie* and the *Newport* had developed nagging leaks that required the constant attention of pumps.

Meanwhile, the *Bear* was having its own difficulties. After enduring a dull winter at Dutch Harbor, Captain Tuttle had steamed north on June 19, anxious to gather whatever information he could on the Overland Relief Expedition. Anchoring off of Cape Prince of Wales on the twenty-third, Tuttle went ashore and was gratified to learn from Tom Lopp that "the overland expedition had been entirely successful." The Lopps were glad to have letters from home so early in the season. The most recent newspapers were checkered with stories of the war with Spain and the gold rush to Alaska.

During the next three weeks, the *Bear* also called at St. Michael, Port Clarence, and Kotzebue Sound, performing its various duties of search and supply and biding its time until the ice along the northern coast receded enough to permit passage to Point Barrow. On July 15, the cutter reached Point Hope, where Bertholf was welcomed aboard. Exactly seven months had passed since he had been put ashore at Cape Vancouver with Jarvis and Call.

Picking its way through drifting ice floes, the *Bear* stood off of Point Lay on July 18. The following morning an umiak was sighted, threading through the shore ice—Captain Sherman and the crewmen from Point Barrow. Sherman carried a letter from Jarvis, informing Tuttle that "there was no danger of any distress [at Point Barrow] but we will be in urgent need should the ship not arrive by August 1." If the *Bear* did not get through by that date, Jarvis added, he would begin sending men down the coast. Neither he nor Tuttle needed to be reminded of the years when the *Bear* was not able to reach Point Barrow at all.

On the twentieth, the *Bear* tried to nudge its way northeastward, only to be turned back by heavy ice. The next day was no better. Finally on the twenty-second, the cutter crept as far as Icy Cape, sixty miles closer to its goal. There it stalled once more, this time for three uneasy days, constantly shifting anchorages to evade the onslaught of broken ice. On July 27, the *Bear* crept past Point Belcher, past Point Franklin. Squinting into the midnight sun, the watch on deck could make out the *Belvedere*, tucked behind the Sea Horse Islands, ten miles away. Tuttle sent a party ashore with several hundred pounds of flour, beans, and tinned beef. And then he continued on.

The chaos of drifting ice was unrelenting, but at last the *Bear* sighted the whaling station at Point Barrow at 5:00 A.M. on July 28. A hulking ridge of ice, thirty feet thick in places, was grounded a mile offshore, holding the *Bear* at bay. Tuttle ordered the ship to make fast to the outside of the ice barrier.

By 5:15, everyone at Point Barrow was awake and rushing outdoors. Jarvis, who had worked so diligently to keep the men active, now could not contain them. As he hurried across the ice to the ship he had served on for the better part of a decade and had not set foot on for seven months, he was followed by a procession of whalers, ecstatic to greet their liberators. Their long ordeal was over. The *Bear* promised better food, clean clothes, mail from home . . . escape.

Or did it? Just because the *Bear* could get in did not guarantee that it could get out.

Shortly after arriving at Point Barrow and conferring with Jarvis, Tuttle ordered the crew members from the wrecked *Orca*, *Freeman*, and *Rosario* to move aboard the *Bear*. Somehow he found space for one hundred rumpled and redolent whalers, many of them dressed in the same clothes they had worn (and slept in) since abandoning their ships ten months earlier. The *Bear* did not have enough bunks to sleep everyone at once, so the men were divided into three watches, each apportioned eight hours of rack time. A ship that normally carried fifty officers and crewmen now accommodated three times that number of passengers.

As dearly as Tuttle would have liked to put on steam and make for home with his disheveled cargo, he dared not leave until he was sure that the other ships were safe. The one ship that he did not have to worry about was the *Belvedere*. The landing party that had delivered supplies to the *Belvedere* reported that the ship was in good condition and nearly clear of the ice. Captain Millard informed Tuttle that he would sail for Port Clarence as soon as possible. And as proof of Millard's Yankee grit, he announced that the *Belvedere* would resume whaling as soon as its coal was replenished.

The *Newport*, *Fearless*, and *Jeanie* were another matter. Until the pack ice receded northward, these ships could not get beyond the tip of Point Barrow. And the *Bear*, it soon became evident, was hardly better off. A day after the cutter had fastened itself to the ice off of the whaling station, it was joined by the steam brig *Jeanette*, the vanguard of the summer whaling fleet probing eastward from the Bering Sea. For the next four days, the *Bear* and *Jeanette* were harassed by drifting ice; the only refuge was a small niche—"indentation," Jarvis called it—in the ground ice. All went well until the wind shifted to the south.

The indentation sheltered the *Bear* and *Jeanette* from the northern pack ice, but it could not deflect assault from the opposite direction. At first Tuttle was not so concerned. For two days slabs of loose ice encased the *Bear* with only "trifling pressure." Then on the afternoon of August 3, the vise tightened. With the ship's port side pressed hard against a hummock of ground ice, the pack ice bore down from starboard. The *Bear* had been designed to break ice with its reinforced bow, but now the brunt came amidships, where the cross-bracing was weakest. A ledge of ice pressed against the port side. The groaning of timbers was demonic. The pressure was so great that it buckled the metal plates on the floor of the engine room, lifting them six inches from the deck. Tuttle hastily ordered crewmen over the side with ice chisels to hack away the offending ledge of pack ice. "As soon as the ice was removed the pressure at that point ceased and the floor plates dropped back into place," he reported with enormous relief. He was certain that if the ship had been made of iron, rather than wood, which was more pliant, it would have been "jammed to pieces." Charlie Brower reckoned that "it was as close a shave as [the *Bear*] ever had in the north."

Even then the *Bear* was not out of trouble. Tuttle worried that if another southwest gale riled the pack ice, "nothing could save the vessel." As a precaution, he ordered a quantity of provisions, along with the ship's papers and logbook, placed on deck where they could be quickly passed to the ice. "From the 3d until the 14th of August we remained in suspense," he wrote. All the while, the *Jeanette* was nipped just as firmly, though thankfully it did not come as near to being crushed as the *Bear*.

Tuttle decided that he could not wait for the pack ice to retreat, and on the seventh he ordered the crew to begin blasting a channel through the ridge of ground ice to the open water that lay between it and the beach. But 150 pounds of powder had no effect on the mammoth reef of ice. The only good news was that the *Newport*, *Fearless*, and *Jeanie* had managed to slip around Point Barrow and were now anchored in open water close to shore.

Finally on the fourteenth the pack began to retreat, and a lead appeared in the ground ice within a few hundred yards of the *Bear* and *Jeanette*. This time well-placed charges cleared the way. Over the next two days, the ships fought their way south to open water, which, while not completely ice-free, was at least navigable. By the afternoon of August 17, the *Bear*, *Jeanette*, *Newport*, *Fearless*, and *Jeanie* had left Point Barrow well astern and were approaching the Sea Horse Islands. As the fog cleared, they beheld a heartening sight. Lying at anchor just offshore was the Arctic whaling fleet: the *Alexander*, *Bowhead*, *Karluk*, *William Baylies*, and, most gratifying of all, the *Belvedere*, seemingly no worse off after nearly a year of icy incarceration.

The next day was devoted to gamming and a considerable shuffling of crews. The *Fearless* had spent the past four winters in the Arctic—three intentionally, one against its will. Its captain, James McKenna, planned to finish out the summer in the North; quite understandably, many in his crew were less than eager to work another season. They gladly gave their places to men from the shipwrecked *Orca* and *Freeman* who hoped to accrue at least a small lay before returning to San Francisco. Similar exchanges among the other ships continued throughout the day. The ill and indifferent were allowed to remain aboard the *Bear*. Tuttle did not tolerate slackers, however. When several able-bodied whalers refused to turn out for work during the trip south, he ordered them put into irons.

There were three other passengers of note aboard the *Bear*. Charlie Brower, who had sacrificed his supplies, his livelihood, and quite nearly his life to aid the icebound whalers, had wisely decided to present his bill for reimbursement to the ship owners and the government in person. And at last Ootenna and Antisarlook were going home. They had stayed with the reindeer throughout the spring and summer at a salary of $30 a month. On August 4, Captain Tuttle had officially transferred ownership of 378 deer to Richmond Marsh on behalf of the Presbyterian Church. With that, the Overland Relief Expedition, or at least the delivery phase, was officially concluded. It seemed only fair that the herders who had stayed in the North the longest be granted the easiest trip south. Ituk, who had been minding the reindeer at Point Hope, came aboard the *Bear* when it put in there.

As for McIlhenny and his two assistants, they took passage aboard the supply ship *Jeanie*. Their collection of zoological and ethnological specimens, including two Eskimo corpses embalmed in formaldehyde, fit into forty-five packing cases weighing eleven tons. Their year at Point Barrow was not a complete loss.

Even with a surfeit of passengers, and despite having been at sea for nine months, the *Bear* did not hurry home. At Point Hope it came upon the schooner *Louise J. Kenney*, which had dragged its anchor and wrecked in the surf. With great difficulty, a boat from the *Bear* succeeded in rescuing the captain and eight crewmen from the beach, further crowding the revenue cutter.

Yet nothing compared with the mass of humanity awaiting the *Bear* when it called at Kotzebue Sound. Earlier that year, rumors of a gold strike on the Kobuk and Selawik rivers had sparked a stampede that mimicked but in no way diminished the ongoing rush to the Yukon. By the time the *Bear* arrived, more than a thousand prospectors were camped on the beaches, most of them with inadequate provisions or experience. Not one had struck gold. With winter looming, most of them had recognized their folly and were desperate to get out. Several ships were anchored at Point Blossom, taking on passengers, when the *Bear* appeared. Despite pleas to participate in the evacuation, Tuttle held firm, insisting that his vessel was already overcrowded.

The *Bear* anchored at Cape Prince of Wales late in the evening of August 23. Tom Lopp wasted no time coming aboard, where he was embraced by Jarvis, Bertholf, and Call—the first and only time the four were in one place at one time. He was equally thrilled to greet his trail mates, Antisarlook, Ootenna, and Ituk. The latter two disembarked at the Cape; Antisarlook would remain onboard until the *Bear* delivered him to his wife and village on Norton Sound later in the month.

As pleased as Lopp was to see familiar faces, he also had a bone to pick. Back in January, Jarvis had promised to repay him 432 deer—representing the 292 appropriated for the relief expedition plus an estimated increase of 140 fawns. Instead, Sheldon Jackson's most recent excursion of the Siberian coast had procured fewer than half that number. In August, just before the *Bear* arrived, two Lapps had driven a herd of 159 reindeer over the mountains from Port Clarence. "Four died on the way from P[ort] C[larence], about ten are so sick they are likely to die, and all of the rest that are not fawns are so old or bad that they are not worth much," Ellen wrote to her family, making little effort to hide her disappointment. But as few and as poor as the new herd was, it was better than no deer at all—which is precisely what Antisarlook could expect when he got home.

Lopp remained aboard the *Bear* overnight. By the time the ship weighed anchor at six the following morning, he had extracted fresh assurances from Tuttle, as captain of the *Bear*, and Jarvis, as commander of the Overland Relief Expedition, that they would make every effort to ensure that the government honored its commitment to pay him and the herders all that was owed them. "Mr. Lopp said that by the terms of his agreement with Lieutenant Jarvis the Treasury was responsible for the return of the deer he drove to Point Barrow," Tuttle wrote dutifully in his official report. "If Lieutenant Jarvis had not made this agreement [Lopp] would not have given up the deer or gone with them. Without the reindeer and the assistance of Mr. Lopp the relief expedition would have gone no farther."

Tuttle persisted in his advocacy. In a letter to the secretary of the Treasury, he urged, "W.T. Lopp and Charlie A[n]tisarlook, who gave up their herd[s] of reindeer, left their families, and accompanied the expedition to Point Barrow, are deserving of substantial rewards for the sacrifices they made and the hardships they endured."

What their compensation, if anything, might be depended a great deal on how the Overland Relief Expedition was regarded by the Outside. As missionaries and teachers, Tom and Ellen Lopp had often felt like voices crying in the wilderness. Now more than ever they recognized that their patch of wilderness had very little voice of its own. "Faith in the government won't procure deer," Ellen observed bitterly. And in one of her final letters home that fall, she confessed, "It's a miserable business all around, the taking north of the deer for the Expedition. I suppose it is for the best some way, but we can't see it yet."

# 17

# Real Deermen

THE ARRIVAL OF THE *Bear* on September 13 drew a crowd to the Seattle docks, but the welcome was less than tumultuous. For one thing, news of the success of the Overland Relief Expedition had reached the States two months earlier, passed along by Tom Lopp. It hadn't made a big splash. The nation was still preoccupied with the Spanish-American War. Throughout the spring and summer, the headlines had been spectacular, beginning with Commodore Dewey's stunning victory at Manila, followed by the trouncing of the Spanish fleet at Santiago and the Rough Riders' bully charge up San Juan Hill. By August, Spain had folded, relinquishing Cuba, Puerto Rico, Guam, and the Philippines. That same month, President McKinley had annexed Hawaii, expanding the nation's global grasp farther still. In the autumn of 1898, America was a different country—grander, mightier, more full of itself—than it had been when the *Bear* had embarked from Seattle nine months earlier. Derring-do was now de rigueur.

Other distractions stole the *Bear*'s thunder as well. Gold fever was more rampant than ever, and the tales of dashed dreams seeping from the Yukon and Kotzebue Sound did nothing to diminish the allure of the North as a land of providence and plenty. In the coming months, the stampede would gain new momentum, as word of a bonanza near Cape Nome reached the Outside. To a public accustomed to the pomp and patriotism of homecoming parades and the frenzied exodus of Alaska-bound fortune-seekers, the appearance of a hundred bedraggled whalers on the Seattle waterfront stirred only passing curiosity.

. . .

There was yet another reason why the Overland Relief Expedition did not rivet the attention of a grateful nation. The combined exploits of the U.S. Revenue Cutter Service, a self-effacing missionary, and seven Eskimos had been upstaged by another reindeer "rescue"—and this one had proven to be a fiasco.

The Overland Relief Expedition's last contact with the Port Clarence reindeer herd had been on January 12, near Golovnin Bay. The deer in Albert Kittilsen's care were originally headed for Unalakleet, where Sheldon Jackson was planning a new reindeer station to be colonized by Lapps. But before Kittilsen could deliver the deer to Unalakleet, the Army ordered that they be made available to transport supplies to "starving" miners on the upper Yukon.

This change of plans was fine by Jackson. Indeed, the shifting circumstances seemed to play into his hands rather niftily. On his trip to the Yukon in the summer of 1897, he had foreseen the food crisis in the Klondike, and when he had arrived in Washington later that fall, he was in an ideal position to advise the cabinet and Congress on how best to aid the Yukon miners. Then, when word came from San Francisco that eight ships were icebound near Point Barrow, Jackson was again on hand to offer informed counsel. His reputation, his connections, and his considerable gift of persuasion had made a big difference.

As always, the panacea he proffered was reindeer. But with two relief expeditions under way, a new problem had emerged. Although the herds of the American Missionary Association and Charlie Antisarlook might be adequate to save the whalers at Point Barrow, even Jackson had to acknowledge that the herd eastbound from Port Clarence did not include enough reindeer broken to harness to establish a thousand-mile supply line between St. Michael and Circle City, on the upper Yukon.

Jackson was not flummoxed for long. By marvelous coincidence, he already had a man in Norway recruiting Lapp herders. Why not authorize William Kjellmann to purchase a herd of reindeer, ship it to Alaska, and drive it inland to Circle City? To be sure, the proposition was far-fetched, but no more so than the overland expedition already being undertaken by the Revenue Cutter Service. In Congress, charity—and the impulse for action—overcame perspicacity. On December 18, 1897—the same day that Jarvis, Call, and Bertholf set off by dogsled from the rocky shore of Cape Vancouver—the House of Representatives appropriated $200,000 for the War Department to "purchase and import reindeer . . . and bring into the country reindeer drivers or herders not citizens of the United States" for the purpose of transporting "subsistence stores, supplies, and materials for the relief of people who are in the Yukon river country." (The Senate had passed identical legislation two days earlier.)

Jackson did not wait around for President McKinley's signature on the bill. By Christmas, he was on his way to Norway as a special agent of the War Department. Somehow Jackson had to purchase a herd of five hundred *trained* deer and persuade sixty or so herders to give up home and country on a few days' notice. Next he had to hire a ship and load the deer, along with enough moss to keep the animals alive not only during a wintertime crossing of the North Atlantic but also during the subsequent three-thousand-mile rail journey across the American continent and then aboard ship, again, for however many days or weeks it took to reach southeast Alaska. All this was mere prologue to the far more daunting task of harnessing and driving the deer overland—a thousand miles at least, carrying packs or pulling sleds—to the upper Yukon, where, God willing, the miners would not yet have succumbed to scurvy and famine.

To Jackson, who until now had never been given more than a few thousand dollars to spend on reindeer, such obstacles added up to an embarrassment of riches. Evidently it never occurred to him that his reach might have exceeded his grasp.

Amazingly, he almost succeeded. In mid-January, Jackson caught up with Kjellmann in the Norwegian port of Alta, three hundred miles above the Arctic Circle. Over the next three weeks, despite a relentless blizzard, they managed to procure 539 reindeer, 418 sleds, and 511 sets of harness. They also recruited 113 emigrants—68 men, 19 women, and 26 children, most of them Lapps, the others Norwegians and Finns. Many had responded to notices in the local paper advertising passage to "Goldland Klondyke." For two years' service, they were offered $500, plus housing, food, clothing, medical services, and schooling for their children.

The reindeer were driven to the harbor of Altafjord and ferried in large rowboats to a barge, where they were first dehorned and then prodded up gangplanks into pens on the deck of the steamer *Manitoban*. The hold was filled with 500 tons of reindeer moss. The herders were relegated to steerage, with hardly more room to move than the reindeer. They staggered aboard, still drunk from all-night farewell parties ashore. Seasickness replaced hangovers once the ship was under way.

The crossing was hellacious. Southwest of Iceland, snow began to fall, and the wind gained hurricane force. The storm lasted nine days. One of the lifeboats was dashed from its davits, and waves ripped the figurehead from the *Manitoban*'s bow. "The danger of being swept overboard was so great," Jackson wrote in his journal, "that none of the herders were allowed outside & the 130 deer on the hurricane deck [were] drenched in salt water as wave after wave broke over . . . their pens." Even under such miserable conditions, Jackson reported, the deer "proved to be good sea travelers, learning to balance themselves with the rolling of the ship, and to rest by lying down as if they had been on their native pasture."

The herders had a harder go. The bucking of the ship, foul quarters, and fouler food churned stomachs and sapped the vigor of the normally hardy Scandinavians. By the time the ship reached the docks at Jersey City on February 28, half a dozen had come down with measles.

The train trip across the country took a week, allowing the herders a chance to see America and for Americans to gawk at the curiously dressed foreigners at every stop. William Kjellmann had accompanied the train, while Sheldon Jackson had hurried to Washington, where he was handed the worst possible news. On March 1, only hours before the reindeer had departed the Pennsylvania Railroad yards, the War Department had announced that it was abandoning the Yukon Relief Expedition. "[N]o necessity exists for it," secretary of War Russell Alger had declared with military bluntness. Rumors of starvation that had circulated so frantically in the press and been corroborated by the unimpeachable Sheldon Jackson had proven to be greatly exaggerated. Citing his own sources, Secretary Alger had assured Congress that "the miners are in no danger of suffering." He proposed that the reindeer be sold as soon as they arrived in Seattle.

Once again, Jackson had to act fast. With his consummate talent for bending authority to his own designs, he got the War Department to allow the deer to continue on their way to Alaska for relief of the miners and also as reimbursement for the deer appropriated from Cape Prince of Wales and Charlie Antisarlook. With that, Jackson boarded a train and raced for the Northwest.

In Seattle, the reindeer and their herders were creating quite a spectacle. While waiting for a ship to transport them north, the deer were driven to Woodland Park, north of the city center. To conserve the remaining supply of reindeer moss, the Army officer in charge had pastured the herd on the park's green grass. William Kjellmann, who knew better, was apparently given no say in the matter. Reindeer would not eat the grass, and over the next seven days they began to die from hunger. The Lapps, meanwhile, spent the week merrily soaking up the attentions of Seattle society and getting drunk. On Sunday, March 13, several thousand picnickers crowded Woodland Park to gaze at the stricken deer and frolic with the rosy-cheeked herders.

The revelry ceased once Jackson arrived on March 16. The following day, he had the deer and herders aboard the three-masted *Seminole*, bound for Alaska.

The trip north presented a new set of problems. Lacking engines, the *Seminole* had to be towed most of the way by tugboat. It was eleven days reaching Haines, the jumping off point for the Dawson Trail, which followed the Chilkat River to Chilkat Pass and finally to the upper Yukon. With the reindeer moss brought from Norway now completely gone, the deer were fed a poor grade of hay, which not even cattle would eat, much less reindeer. Every day more deer died. In desperation, the herd was driven inland. By the time the herders located a source of moss, 374 reindeer had perished. The rest were so weak that there was no point in driving them farther. All summer they were kept near the headwaters of the Thleheena River, a tributary of the Chilkat. When the drive to Circle City resumed on September 1, only 144 of the original 539 reindeer purchased in Norway remained. Most of these eventually reached their intended destination of Circle City, but not until January 1899, a full year after Sheldon Jackson had purchased them. Without question, the reindeer spent a hungrier winter than the miners did.

. . .

So went the first "reindeer rescue." When Sheldon Jackson arrived back in Seattle on September 3, 1898—ten days before the battered *Bear* returned from Point Barrow—he was given less than a hero's reception. The Seattle correspondent for the *San Francisco Examiner*—a paper whose endorsement of the Overland Relief Expedition had been desultory—referred to Jackson snidely as "the father of Alger's Lapland reindeer Klondike relief expedition, which collapsed with a loss of upward of a hundred thousand dollars to the Government." The *Examiner* also ridiculed Jackson for failing to obtain the eight hundred reindeer he had pledged to procure in Siberia that summer. "The United States, not the roving divine, is again the loser," the paper clucked, "for Mr. Jackson was undertaking, in the name of the Federal Government, another of his pet schemes, involving transportation of reindeer from Siberia to Western Alaska." The headline above the story scolded: "Another of the Reverend Jackson's Plans Fails."

But he had not failed entirely. Notwithstanding the fact that the Yukon Relief Expedition was proving to be worse than ineffectual and that the Overland Relief Expedition had not been of life-or-death urgency, Jackson nonetheless had accomplished his ulterior objectives. "In my estimation," he wrote to Secretary Alger shortly after learning that the Yukon expedition had been canceled, "next to the discovery of gold the most important event, commercially, in the history of Alaska during this year will be the importation of this colony of Lapps. Experience is rapidly demonstrating that the only possible efficient transportation service in Alaska must be through expert drivers of reindeer among partially civilized Lapps and Finns. The 68 men brought over by this expedition . . . hope ultimately to have herds of their own. . . . Their success will naturally attract others of their people and render permanent the establishment of the reindeer industry in Alaska."

If so, Jackson had no reason to be disappointed. In the fall of 1898, most of the herders whom he had brought from Norway—with the exception of the small group that was still driving the reindeer herd to Circle City—had settled at the Eaton Reindeer Station at Unalakleet (named for John Eaton, a past commissioner of Education and one of Jackson's early supporters). The herd that Albert Kittilsen had started from Port Clarence in December arrived at the new station at about the same time. The newspapers could second-guess all they wanted, but Jackson had at last established the hub from which he figured to extend a vast network of reindeer herds and "express" routes. The Teller station at Port Clarence had been a worthy start, but the Eaton station at Unalakleet was centrally located; the hills were well timbered, the ground less boggy, the moss more plentiful.

.  .  .

At Cape Prince of Wales, Tom Lopp had a different take on the Lapp invasion. "The landing of so many Laplanders to look after the small Government herd at Unalakleet or colonize this part of Alaska is much ridiculed here," he wrote in the July 1898 edition of the *Eskimo Bulletin*, the plucky newspaper printed on the mission's crude press. "The 500 deer with which they started from Lapland are reported to have starved to death in S.E. Alaska. According to the papers, these people, on account of their intemperate habits, have given the Gov[ernment] officer no little annoyance."

Lopp's displeasure spilled over onto another page of the *Bulletin*. "What the U.S. Bureau of Education expects to accomplish by bringing so many Laplanders to Arctic Alaska is an enigma to all who are personally acquainted with the destitution, need and possibilities of the Eskimo race," he fumed. "There is already an excess of trained herders, and experience has demonstrated that it is easier to increase their number than the number of herds."

Lopp had good reason to feel betrayed. In his view, Sheldon Jackson had turned the reindeer program on its head. The idea that drew Lopp to reindeer in the first place was to educate, empower, and elevate natives, not lower their ranking on the totem pole, as Jackson now seemed to be doing. To keep the Lapps happy, Jackson was proposing a series of incentives that far exceeded any offered to the

Eskimos. In addition to providing salary, food, clothing, and shelter, he also recommended that Lapps be loaned herds and allowed to keep 10 percent of the annual increase—all of which stood in stark contrast to the rewards promised (but not necessarily delivered) to native apprentices.

Over the winter, the inequity cut even deeper. "Driving the herd to Point Barrow was a valuable experience to our herders," Lopp stated in his annual report, "but . . . [it] was rather discouraging to begin the winter with but 1 sled deer and but few deer for breaking and none for butchering." Indeed, the timing of the shortfall could not have been worse. The native herders, whom Lopp had recruited in 1894, were completing their fifth year of apprenticeship and looking forward to becoming "real deermen," he pointed out. By the terms of the original agreement with the government, they were entitled to their own animals to use as they wished—for sleds, breeding, or, as circumstances now demanded, food. The seal and walrus hunting had been poor that winter; but instead of being able to fall back on reindeer, as Sheldon Jackson had originally envisioned, the Cape herders had to survive on flour, molasses, and tea, "a very unsatisfactory diet," Lopp noted with unbridled scorn. The Cape Prince of Wales natives, who had delivered their herd intact and on time, were barely getting by. Meanwhile, the Lapps, who had participated in a wasteful wild goose chase, were comparatively well cared for and well compensated. In addition, most of the Lapps were assured American citizenship, a distinction still not available to native Alaskans.

More irritating still, many of the Scandinavians had no desire to herd reindeer. At the earliest opportunity, several had taken leave of the station to prospect for gold. One of them, Jafet Lindeberg, struck it rich at Anvil Creek, west of Cape Nome, just six months after arriving in Alaska. His discovery would launch the biggest gold rush since the California stampede of 1849. Within a year of Lindeberg's lucky strike, five thousand impatient prospectors were digging for gold along the beaches and creeks of Norton Sound. By 1900, the population of Nome, as the bonanza's new boomtown was called, approached twenty thousand.

. . .

It was only a matter of time before this wave of unwelcome change broke upon the shore of Cape Prince of Wales. The summer of the Nome gold strike, the entire Lopp family came down with what Ellen described as a "cold" but was more likely influenza. The Lopps recovered, but eighteen villagers died. The natives speculated that the bug had originated in Siberia, but the steady influx of whites heightened the Eskimos' exposure to outside diseases.

The Lopps felt about miners the way they felt about whalers: They were venal and vulgar, a source of corruption and disease. Commercial whaling in the Arctic appeared to be on the ebb after the great calamity at Point Barrow in 1897–1898, but the rapid spread of prospectors promised only "new anxiety and greater work" for the missionaries. Those who passed through the Cape, usually en route from the aborted boom at Kotzebue Sound to the better bet at Cape Nome, proved to be a great burden on the Lopps' time and resources. "We have had miners here part of every day for a week and I am tired of them," Ellen wrote to her family. Some of them offered to pay for meals and lodging, "but no money could pay me to keep a miner's hotel," she declared.

Still, it was getting harder to look the other way. Several missionaries, including Toleef Brevig and two Swedish Evangelicals from Golovnin Bay, had filed mining claims. So had the reindeer superintendents, William Kjellmann and Albert Kittilsen. "They say they have found gold in quite a number of places south of here," Ellen wrote in January 1899. "The latest is a place where they have found $8 to the pan." She insisted that she and Tom would not give in to gold fever, but two months later her tone softened somewhat. "I hope they will find gold near enough to us that we can take claims," Ellen confided to her brother. "I shouldn't want Tom to neglect his work here, as a teacher south of us did. [She probably meant Brevig.] Of course, Tom doesn't want to, but it may be so near next summer that we can spend our summer vacation that way."

For the time being, Tom focused on a more spiritual prize. "[T]he business [of a missionary] is to plant churches, in well-chosen parts of his field," Rufus Anderson had directed in *Foreign Missions*, "committing them as soon as possible to the care of native pastors." Accordingly, Tom erected a small mission house at Mitletok, twenty-five miles to the north, in which he installed his best pupil, Sokweena, and wife, Elubwok, as teachers. "There are sixteen children of school age there and eight or ten young men and women who will take an interest in trying to learn to read, and I think all the old ones will attend the Sunday service," Tom reported optimistically to the American Missionary Association. He also added two rooms to his own house at the Cape. Ellen was expecting their fifth child in September.

Finally, though, Tom took his mining "vacation." Rather than join the parade to Nome, he decided to explore the creeks near Cape York, an area on Norton Sound he knew well from his many trips to nearby Point Clarence. He returned from his first forays with only a few dollars in gold dust. Feeling a twinge of guilt, he hastened to clarify that he was not prospecting for personal gain only. "Should these claims turn out well the American Missionary Association will not be forgotten," he assured.

Gold, he reasoned, would pay for many needed improvements at the Cape, including salaries for more teachers and perhaps a doctor and a medical clinic. But until he hit the jackpot, the best hope for the future remained reindeer. The government had finally managed to replenish the Cape herd, albeit a year late—some of the animals coming from Siberia, the rest from government herds. By the end of 1899, the Cape herd exceeded seven hundred, twice the number on hand at the start of the Overland Relief Expedition. The government had at last made good on its pledge to Charlie Antisarlook as well; his herd now totaled 328.

Although Lopp himself was now a miner, he could not warm to them. Like Ellen, he did not want to be near them or be asked to provide for them. But he did not mind taking their money. He estimated that if the government had restocked the Cape herd in 1898 as promised, he and his herders could have earned at least $3,000 hauling supplies from Kotzebue Sound to Cape Nome. Looking ahead, he sketched plans for two experimental reindeer carts, with "pneumatic" (rubber) tires that could carry three hundred pounds of provisions across the soft summer tundra.

By the end of 1899, three thousand reindeer were spread among nine different herds, from Point Barrow to the upper Yukon. In the camps at Nome and along Norton Sound, hungry newcomers were paying a dollar a pound for reindeer meat. Yet Jackson and Lopp's scheme to use reindeer to deliver mail and supplies throughout the region did not succeed as well as they hoped. A contract to carry mail along the Yukon had failed to materialize, and another plan to carry mail from the ice-free port of Valdez to Circle City also fell through. So far, the only reindeer mail routes were between St. Michael, Eaton Reindeer Station, Golovnin Bay, Kotzebue Sound, and Cape Nome. The Army and various miners occasionally hired reindeer to haul supplies, but the demand was erratic.

Nevertheless, Jackson kept making his case for reindeer as the camels of the Arctic, and he found at least one convert in the territorial governor, John G. Brady. "When editors and writers raise the cry of 'failure' and 'fad' they simply show that they are not acquainted with the facts," Brady wrote in defense of reindeer. "Since the excitement at Cape Nome began the whites are beginning to understand what utility there is in a reindeer. . . . How can it be possible for the Government to make a mistake in fostering and encouraging such an enterprise?"

. . .

The Lopps' final two years at Cape Prince of Wales made the previous ten seem serene by comparison. In the fall of 1899, Tom filed a mining claim on Buhner Creek, near Cape York, west of Port Clarence. "No one knows whether or not there is a foot of land worth working in the district, but indications are good," Ellen wrote to her family. York, however, did not prove to be the next Nome. There was no stampede this time and not much gold, either. Over the winter, Lopp initiated a reindeer mail and supply express between the new district and Nome but had to shut it down after two trips for lack of customers. The little money he made that season came from his job as recorder for the district.

One good thing did come out of the Cape York venture. Ever since the first gold strikes in the Yukon had captured the world's attention, Ellen's father, Charles "C.B." Kittredge, had yearned to come to Alaska. At fifty-nine, he had lost little of the wanderlust that had drawn him west to Minnesota from New England. When Ellen and Tom mentioned that they needed help with their claim at Cape York, C.B. jumped at the chance. Although his wife, Katharine, prudently stayed in Minnesota, two of their children decided to make the trip. From time to time over the years, Ellen had urged her sisters to join her at Cape Prince of Wales, to teach and help with her expanding family. Sister Frances, now twenty-six, was the one who finally answered the dare, accepting a teaching job at the Cape that Tom and Ellen had arranged through Sheldon Jackson. She left the States a month after C.B., chaperoned by her eighteen-year-old brother Charlie.

C.B. arrived at Cape Prince of Wales in late June, then moved to Cape York to work Tom's mining claim. Frances and Charlie arrived at the end of July. Over Tom and Ellen's protests, Charlie spent the summer digging for gold with his father. "I don't believe it is a good thing for a young man to be in a mining camp," Ellen had written before his arrival. "Not that I think that you would take to gambling and swearing and such, but I think a young man at that age . . . should be careful not to put himself into a bad environment where he would become familiar with the sight of vice and constantly be with people, the majority of whom have lower ideals than his own."

All in all, however, Tom and Ellen were overjoyed to have family members close by. They could use all the help they could get as one illness after another punished the Cape: first scarlet fever, then mumps, and, worst of all, measles. Ellen and Tom were so busy caring for themselves and their children that they could do little for the natives. On July 12, Ellen reported that twenty Cape natives had died so far, including the two children of Sokweena and Elubwok. The house girls, Nora and Alice, had come down with measles, as had several of the herders. All of them eventually recovered; one sad exception was Charlie Antisarlook, who died at Cape Rodney on July 15. An obituary in the Nome newspaper called him "the Richest Eskimo in Northern Alaska." His widow, Mary, eventually became known as the "the Reindeer Queen."

By mid-August another thirty Cape natives had succumbed from either measles or the influenza that followed. "Hardly any Eskimos over fifty years old and only a few under five are left," Frances wrote to her mother in October. "There is hardly a family where someone is not gone. . . . During the worst of the epidemic, the Natives were constantly coming to the Lopps for medicine and food. Many of the sick ones simply could not eat the pickled walrus meat which was most of the food that they had. The sickness came at the time the Eskimos would have been hunting walrus. Thus they were unable either to get them for a present supply of food, or to store to use during the coming year. . . . There are so many times, Ellen says, when sick Natives reach the place where, in story books, the doctor says, 'Now, with good care, he will pull through.' But here they never can have the good care, including food and fresh air, so time and again they reach this point, then slowly die away."

The tragic gauntlet was not quite finished. In the fall, nearly all the Lopp children came down with whooping cough, including one-year-old "Baby," who would not be called by her proper name—Weyana—until a younger sister, Irene, was born the following summer.

To accommodate a growing family, Tom built another addition onto the house, which now included four bedrooms and a sitting room for natives. Ellen had covered the living room walls with floral wallpaper, but she decorated the kitchen with pages from *Sunday School Times*, *Youth's Companion*, *Ladies' Home Journal*, and old newspapers. "I keep stopping my work to read from the walls," she wrote, laughing at herself, "but don't find anything to make me so homesick as an advertisement [for] 'Yakima Burbank potatoes, sixty cents for a hundred pounds.' Our potatoes have been gone since the last of January."

The house was warm enough, but too much warmth created its own discomfort. "This is the fourth day of a hard south wind," Frances wrote in mid-February. "We have dreaded a thaw, knowing what a deluge we will have in the house. All the moisture in the air . . . has risen to the ceiling and frozen there. This all has to come down. It commenced Sunday night. . . . All Monday it rained . . . in one end of the sitting room and a part of the kitchen."

Nothing in Ellen's letters had prepared Frances for the amount of toil it took to keep the house and mission going. Tom was gone constantly, either tending the reindeer herd or working the mining claim at Cape York. Ellen never had a moment's rest, Frances observed: "There are perpetual interruptions from Natives, of course, who come for everything from having a 'box' made for someone who has died and cut fingers to bandage, to trading for food and supplies."

Shortly after Frances arrived at the Cape, Nora and Alice both married—Nora to Ootenna, Alice to Kivyearzruk—leaving Ellen short-handed. "There are some things we do not have to do here, which we would have to do at home," Frances quipped, endeavoring to make light of mission life. "[D]usting for instance—as we live in such small space that nothing is left alone long enough so it can gather dust." On the other hand, she groused, "There are a great many more things which we would not have at home. For instance . . . stranded miners who have sailed about without being able to reach their destination. . . . There are two such parties camping here now, and both are a great bother."

The Lopp mining venture was not going well, either. On their best day, C.B. and Charlie sluiced $15 from their claim, but that was a rarity. In September, Charlie moved back to the Cape, where, with Sheldon Jackson's approval, he was given a nine-month contract to assist with the teaching. C.B. elected to stay on at Cape York for the winter.

Father and son enjoyed their Alaskan adventures thoroughly, but one year was plenty. Both left at the end of the second summer, rich in experiences but no wealthier otherwise. The Lopps, too, were nearing the end of their tether. Whether they admitted it or not, the years had taken their toll. "Since I came here," Frances noted, "there have always been several in the family who were not really well even if they were not really sick." She was especially concerned about her sister's health. "Ellen is very tired," she commented. Nursing one baby after the next, Ellen was chronically tormented by painful mastitis.

Even when the family was healthy, there was concern over what sort of education the children were receiving. "The Lopp children have such queer ways of expressing themselves," Frances remarked. "Yesterday I told Ellen that if I heard them talking in another room and did not know who they were, I would not dream that their parents were Americans. They have mixed a great deal of the Eskimos' broken English with the usual odd things children say, making the results very interesting." Once when Frances was trying to teach the children about American Indians, she asked them, "What people live in tents?" They answered quite sensibly, "Miners."

Tom and Ellen had always known that sooner or later they would leave Cape Prince of Wales, but when it came to picking a date, they were profoundly torn. By all measures, their accomplishments had been extraordinary. In 1890, when Tom had first landed in Alaska, many doubted he could survive the first winter. But he had. And after the murder of Harrison Thornton, no one would have faulted him for not returning to the Cape with Ellen and two young children. But they had returned. And they had made converts and built a foundation of education and industry that they hoped would sustain the natives through the vicissitudes of the coming century and beyond. Nonetheless, they were the first to admit that their work was just a beginning. The Lopps' biggest fear was that their hard-won achievements would erode after they left. For years they had hoped they would be joined by other missionaries who shared their faith and resolve. But first with Thornton and then with Hanna, they had been darkly disappointed.

Nor were they sanguine about the latest wave of outside influence. Charles Ryder, corresponding secretary of the American Missionary Association, once wrote to the commissioner of education that "an isolated people is generally an undeveloped people. Contact with others, especially those of higher civilization, is the important factor in race development." Ten or even five years earlier, Tom and Ellen Lopp might have agreed with this principle, but civilization now meant something completely different. It endangered not only the health of the native populace, but threatened its soul as well. The growing pains of one culture might well be the mortal wounds of another.

In the spring of 1901, the Lopps announced that they would stay at least one more year. But even then they waffled. "Ellen said today she not for anything would go down to the States next year," Frances wrote to Margie, the youngest of the Kittredge sisters. "It would be too dreadful to leave the Natives. A host of bad influences will come with the miners. Even if the Natives had all but been converted and reformed (and it would be a wonder if they were), they would have to be better than white people to hold out and stay good if left alone. Since they are stepping over from old ways to new, if they have not something to help them to the new side, the combination of old ideas and superstitions, temptations (some of which are connected with whaling ships), and some new ones (temptations which are connected with some of the miners) would pull many of the Natives back until conditions became worse than before. And since the Lopps have worked so hard and have succeeded so much as they have with the young people especially, they feel simply obliged to continue their work."

· · ·

Yet by summer Ellen was once again leaning toward leaving. "I have felt, with two exceptions of a few days relapse, that I was certainly going home next year, though I haven't been able to get my courage up to say so to anyone," she wrote to her mother at the end of May. Two months later, she asked her mother to send clothes to wear on the trip home. She had not been to the Outside in six years, and her old dresses were shabby and out of fashion. Her decision to return to the States became that much easier with the birth of Irene on July 30. As with all of her other children, Ellen delivered without a doctor's assistance.

The final year at the Cape presented further trials. In October, Sheldon Jackson sent a teacher to replace Charlie Kittredge. Susan Bernardi had grown up in Valley City, Indiana, Tom Lopp's hometown, and, like Ellen, she had taught for a number of years in the South. She came to Alaska with two brothers, who were prospecting for gold near the Teller Reindeer Station at Port Clarence. She was given her own room in the Lopp house and was assigned to teach the older native children, who spoke the best English. At first she impressed everyone with her spunk, and she adjusted quite well to the peculiar confines of the mission and Lopp family. But by March—with the house buried so deeply in snow that only the chimney was visible— the thirty-three-year-old Bernardi developed a severe case of cabin fever and departed for Teller, where her brothers—and a sizable population of single men—were living. Frances and Ellen were obliged to take charge of her class.

By spring of 1902, the Lopps' decision to leave was firm. Ellen began packing in mid-June, not knowing when the revenue cutter would arrive to take them south. The last letter written from the Cape was by Frances to Mrs. Kittredge on July 7: "We are ready to go. Four trunks are locked and the fifth mostly packed and waiting for the last things. . . . There are still things we are sewing but which we could get through without." The children, meanwhile, had chosen this inopportune time to get sick. "It seems almost as if an epidemic of severe colds had begun in the village. . . . Nellie has had a terrible cold for weeks. . . . For a week and a half we have washed every other day so as to have things clean and ready to leave suddenly."

In twelve years—ten for Ellen—the Lopps had formed a deep bond with the people of Cape Prince of Wales. They had taught the villagers to read and write English, but unlike teachers at Indian schools in the States—and despite the early urging of Sheldon Jackson—they had not forbidden the natives to speak their own language. The Lopps had taught the Bible with patience and passion; they had led the natives in prayers and hymns. But mostly their approach to proselytizing had been to set an example of Christian virtue—temperance, tolerance, courage, courtesy, honesty, charity, trust, and faith. More than teachers or preachers, they had been friends and neighbors to the natives. They had striven to learn the Inupiaq language; indeed, few white men spoke it better than Tom-gorah. In no sense had they gone "native" while at Cape Prince of Wales; inevitably, though, they had struck a cultural balance, out of respect as well as necessity. They had hunted and fished with the Eskimos; they had shared each other's food, adopted each other's dress, and acknowledged each other's humanity. Saying good-bye, as Ellen had predicted, was bittersweet in the extreme. They still had no idea who, if anyone, would take their place.

When the Lopps and Frances left the Cape on July 15, they could not picture circumstances that would allow them to return to Alaska. One thing was obvious: With six children, Tom and Ellen would never live as missionaries again. Nor would they return to Minnesota or Indiana. C.B. Kittredge, after leaving Alaska, had settled in Seattle and brought his wife west. Seattle would be the Lopps' home as well—for the rest of their lives, as it turned out.

The ship that stopped for them at Cape Prince of Wales was the revenue cutter *Thetis*, an older, frowsier sister to the *Bear*. By pleasant coincidence, its captain was the reinstated Michael Healy, who was making only his second trip North since being court-martialed seven years earlier. At Nome the Lopps transferred to the steamer *Ohio*, which delivered them without incident to Seattle eight days later. "It seems as if the best thing was to succumb gracefully to the inevitable," Frances wrote upon their arrival.

Yet re-entry was not so easy. The most basic amenities made them feel spoiled at first. The simplicity of daily life at the Cape had eclipsed the grime and uncertainty of their years there, and not surprisingly they were slow to embrace the profane clatter of the modern age. In one of the letters Ellen wrote from the Cape, she had done her best to articulate how she and her family had come to find contentment in the midst of so much hardship: "People talk about how dreadful it must be. They don't know how it is to be here. The sacrifice would be in leaving. I was trying to think of how to explain our being willing to go it alone, without things, all the way from fresh milk and bicycle rides to not seeing our friends, or even the daily papers, and in my reading I came across the expression, 'We limit our wants to the things we are likely to get.'"

# Epilogue

ON JUNE 28, 1902, while the Lopps were in the midst of packing to leave Cape Prince of Wales, Congress voted—belatedly—to honor the heroes of the Overland Relief Expedition. In the previous 126 years, congressional Gold Medals had been awarded on only forty-three occasions. The list of recipients included George Washington, John Paul Jones, Andrew Jackson, and Ulysses S. Grant. Now were added three more: First Lieutenant David H. Jarvis, Second Lieutenant Ellsworth P. Bertholf, and Dr. Samuel J. Call.

The medals had been in the works for some time, although none was ever officially considered for Tom Lopp or any of the Eskimo herders who gave so much to making the reindeer drive a success. Upon landing in Seattle, Captain Tuttle of the *Bear* had done his best to ensure that proper tribute was paid to all of the participants in the expedition, at the same time admitting that such acclaim might be hard to muster. "The skill and the courage which made the expedition a success and saved the lives of the imprisoned whalers have robbed the incident of sensationalism," Tuttle acknowledged, "but it should not be permitted to rob those who are emphatically entitled to recognition and reward." Responding to Tuttle's

prompting, the *San Francisco Examiner* on September 17, 1898, anticipated that Jarvis, Bertholf, and Call would be given medals shortly after
their arrival in San Francisco. The promise was premature.

Yet it was not forgotten. Four months later, on January 6, 1899,
President McKinley drafted a letter to the Senate and House of Representatives, singling out the three cuttermen:

> The hardships and perils encountered by the members of the
> Overland Expedition in their great journey, facing death itself
> every day for nearly four months, through an almost uninhabited
> region, a barren waste of ice and snow, over a route never before
> traveled by white men, with no refuge but at the end of the jour-
> ney, carrying relief and cheer to two hundred and seventy-five dis-
> tressed citizens of our country, reflecting, by their heroic and
> gallant struggles, the highest credit to the Service to which they
> belong, all to the honor and glory of the nation, commend the per-
> sonnel of this great Relief Expedition to the highest consideration
> of Congress and the American people.

Specifically, the president recommended that Congress give an
official vote of thanks to Captain Francis Tuttle for guiding the *Bear*
through such treacherous seas and that "gold medals of honor, of
appropriate design" be awarded to Jarvis, Bertholf, and Call. Furthermore, McKinley proposed that "the sum of twenty-five hundred dollars . . . be appropriated to be disbursed by the Secretary of the
Treasury in bestowing rewards upon W. T. Lopp, A[n]tisarlook and
native herders who rendered material aid to the Relief Expedition."

On the upper corner of McKinley's letter, someone, presumably the
president's secretary, George Cortelyou, scrawled in black ink: "Killed."
The reason for the rejection is hinted at in the letter itself. "The year
just closed has been a fruitful one . . . in the field of war," McKinley
reasoned, "and while I have commended to your high consideration the

names of heroes who have shed luster upon the American name in val-
orous contests and battles by land and sea, it is a pleasure to invite your
attention to a victory of peace."

As a young soldier in the Civil War, McKinley had been decorated
for delivering hot coffee to Union troops at Antietam. Evidently Congress did not yet share the president's sentiment toward bravery of a
non-belligerent nature.

It took another three years for the medals to be approved, and they
were not actually minted until 1904. By then McKinley was long dead—
assassinated in Buffalo—and the notion of rewarding or even recognizing Lopp and the native herders had fallen by the wayside.

In the meantime, all three of the Revenue Cutter Service men had
returned to Alaska. In the spring of 1899, Jarvis was given command of
the *Bear* in place of an ailing Captain Tuttle; Bertholf took Jarvis's former position as executive officer; Call was once again the ship's surgeon.
They spent the summer purchasing reindeer in Siberia, policing the
Nome gold rush, and evacuating luckless miners. It was the last time the
celebrated heroes of the Overland Relief Expedition served together.

In 1899 Call resigned from his position as contract surgeon and
threw himself into the bedlam of miners at Nome, serving first as city
health officer for the burgeoning, disease-plagued outpost and then as
collector and inspector of customs. His own health deteriorated, and
after rejoining the Revenue Cutter Service for a couple of years, he
died in California at the age of fifty-one.

Bertholf flourished under the extreme rigors of the North. In the
winter of 1900, he volunteered to journey across Russia from west to
east in order to purchase yet another herd of Siberian reindeer. This,
his second overland odyssey, took almost a year, much of the distance
covered by sled. Seven years later, it was Bertholf's turn to command
the *Bear*. As its skipper, he spent three summers patrolling the Bering
Sea. Climbing steadily up the masthead, he was promoted in 1911 to
captain-commandant of the Revenue Cutter Service, its highest rank-

ing officer. When the Revenue Cutter Service was merged with the Life Saving Service in 1915 to form the U.S. Coast Guard, Bertholf became its first commandant—just in time to guide the fledging service through the World War I. He retired shortly thereafter and died in New York at the age of fifty-five.

Jarvis, who was certainly no less able or ambitious than Bertholf, wound up following a more mottled path. His exemplary service in Alaska had won the admiration of the new president, Theodore Roosevelt, a man of similarly restless energy. In 1900 Roosevelt appointed Jarvis customs collector for Alaska, and five years later the president tried to persuade him to accept the position of governor of the territory. Jarvis had other ideas. In his years in Alaska, he had watched men of lesser ability reap considerable fortunes. Now it was his turn. He became a principal in a Seattle salmon cannery. Next he became involved in a New York–based syndicate that was developing railroads and copper claims in Alaska. During the donnybrooks of territorial commerce and politics, he was accused of a variety of shady dealings, including bid-rigging and bribery. The ignominy finally got to him, and on June 23, 1911, he shot himself in his room at the Seattle Athletic Club. His suicide note read simply, "Tired and worn out." He was fifty-eight years old.

Ellsworth Bertholf, by then a captain in the Revenue Cutter Service, offered a note of reserved condolence for his fellow traveler: "I lived with him in the same tent, was his comrade in times of hardship and danger." Yet, Bertholf added, "Not many people really knew him, for he was a silent man. . . . Ever conscious of rectitude in his own actions, he seldom defended himself when criticized by those who misunderstood him."

In the end, the Coast Guard chose to understand Jarvis not for his ethical indiscretions, none of which were ever proven, but for his well-documented acts of courage, duty, and determination. Today one of the Coast Guard's most prestigious honors is the Jarvis Award, given for "inspirational leadership." And in 1972 the Coast Guard commissioned the *Jarvis*, a 378-foot cutter homeported in Honolulu, where the waters are much more hospitable than any Jarvis sailed aboard the rugged *Bear*.

Jarvis is not the only Alaska hand to have a vessel named after him. Michael Healy managed only three more trips north after his humiliating court-martial in 1895. On one of them, he too attempted suicide but was saved by alert crewmen. He died in 1904 of "a failing heart and a general breaking down of what was generally a robust constitution," the San Francisco *Call* reported. A century later, his name remains a proud presence in the North. In 1999 the Coast Guard commissioned the 420-foot, 16,000-ton *Healy*, the largest icebreaker in its fleet. Like its namesake, who pushed himself beyond all limits—breaking ice (loudly) and the color barrier (quietly)—the *Healy* has thrust its reinforced steel bow through the once impassable Northwest Passage. Even more daringly, in 2001 it attained the ultimate grail of Arctic navigation, the North Pole—and got home safe and sound.

As for the *Bear*, it lived a longer life than any of its skippers. Although the market for whalebone had collapsed by 1910 (fashions changed, lightweight spring steel was cheaper) and the Arctic whaling fleet had shrunk to almost nothing, the *Bear* continued patrolling Alaskan waters well into the 1920s. Still fit for ice duty, it later made voyages to Antarctica and Greenland. In 1963, the *Bear* was being towed from Nova Scotia to Philadelphia, where its latest owner intended to turn it into a floating restaurant. The venerable cutter was spared a toothless retirement when it suddenly parted its towline, broached, and disappeared beneath the North Atlantic.

. . .

Tom Lopp's legacy is less conspicuous but arguably more remarkable. His life, already so full, was only half over when he and the family moved to Seattle. They lived in a rambling bungalow a few blocks from the University of Washington campus. Ellen bore two more children and ultimately was blessed with fourteen grandchildren. She remained active in the Congregational Church; she took classes at the university; and she was a welcome addition to the local chapter of the Women's Christian Temperance Union. She never went back to Alaska.

In some respects, Tom never left. In 1904 he was put in charge of native schools and the reindeer program for northern Alaska, serving as a not-so-compliant lieutenant to the aging Sheldon Jackson. Whereas Jackson had faithfully supported Lopp during his years at Cape Prince of Wales, the sentiment was no longer mutual. Lopp had been outspoken in his opposition to Jackson's advocacy of non-native, particularly Lapp, ownership of reindeer. Lopp's goal, as always, was to enable natives to own their own herds.

Despite the demonstrable successes of the Cape Prince of Wales program and the continuing growth of the Antisarlook herd, Jackson— ever the patriarch—continued to insist that native herds have a non-native supervisor, preferably one of the Lapps brought from Norway. The conflict between Lopp and Jackson came to a head in 1905, when Jackson directed Lopp to hire a Lapp to take charge of a reindeer herd to be delivered to a new Quaker mission at Deering, on Kotzebue Sound. Instead, Lopp recruited James Keok and Stanley Kivyearzruk, two of the original Quints from Cape Prince of Wales, and together they drove a herd of 365 reindeer from the Cape to Deering. The 180-mile trek went smoothly, and Keok and Kivyearzruk proved their competence once again.

Lopp did not have to worry about the Lapp problem for long, and Sheldon Jackson was on his last legs as well. In 1906 the Interior Department issued a scathing report on the reindeer program and its interconnection with the mission schools in Alaska. While generally complimentary of the original motives for introducing reindeer, the report's author, a former Indian agent named Frank Churchill, chastised Sheldon Jackson for "mixing up church and government matters" in an "arbitrary and high-handed way." The marriage of church and state, once regarded as the mortar and pestle for "civilizing" natives, was now frowned upon. In passing, Churchill noted that even while reindeer were valued as a source of food, they had never established themselves as a means of transportation, even during the height of the gold rushes. The report's gravest criticism, however, was that "after many years the number of natives having deer is not very considerable." The solution to this shortcoming, Churchill concluded, "is to gradually get the deer into the hands of the natives, and, so far as possible, to allow no white men, under any pretext, to buy or control female deer."

Within a year of the Churchill report's publication, Sheldon Jackson had resigned, ostensibly for health reasons. Two years later, he died at the age of seventy-five and his job as head of the Alaska Division of the U.S. Bureau of Education was given to the man universally regarded as the most trustworthy and knowledgeable authority on reindeer in Alaska: Tom Lopp.

The change was dramatic, to say the least. Under Lopp's guidance, a new set of rules was implemented for reindeer herding. As the Churchill report had recommended, sale of female deer was forbidden, except to other natives. The intent was to prevent Lapps and other non-natives from acquiring breeding stock and increasing their share of Alaska's reindeer industry. "It was a lucky break for the Eskimos that [Jackson] was prevented from carrying out all his plans [to provide deer to Lapps]," Lopp reflected many years later. "He did, however, succeed in loaning 800 reindeer to 8 Laplanders in lieu of part of their wages. If the other 40 or 50 Lapps to whom he had promised loans had not quit the Reindeer Service to join the Nome Gold Rush, about 5,000 more deer would have been added to the ownership of the colonists, and today the Lapps would own most of Alaska's reindeer."

Another effect of the 1907 regulation was that it diluted the apprentice program. Under Tom Lopp, the number of reindeer stations increased, several with native superintendents, but apprenticeship was no longer the only path natives could take to gain ownership of reindeer. Now they could buy deer, trade for them, receive them as a gift from another native owner, or pass them from one generation to the next.

The long-term consequences were both good and bad. Churchill and Lopp's goal of increasing the number of native herders was achieved. Between 1906 and 1916, Eskimos who owned deer went from fewer than one hundred to more than one thousand. Formerly the majority of the reindeer in Alaska had been owned by missions, the government, or individual Lapps; now natives owned two thirds of the total.

On the other hand, with the shift of control and ownership from whites to natives, the size of individual herds shrank drastically and the approach to herding, and training herders, grew lax. In the first decade of Lopp's management of the reindeer program, the number of deer in Alaska increased from ten thousand to more than seventy thousand, yet the typical native herder owned fewer than one hundred deer.

Such calculus was harmfully cockeyed. With so many deer in Alaska, the market became saturated, especially as the gold rush subsided; deer meat and hides were readily available and cheap. And because small herds were more difficult to manage, owners forsook the close-herding regimen passed down from the Chukchi and the Lapps. Eskimos who owned reindeer, beginning with Charlie Antisarlook, had always been coastal dwellers who traditionally hunteed whales, seals, and walruses; the notion of traipsing across the tundra to tend a reindeer herd went against the cultural grain. The result was that native reindeer tended to run wild, and the vocation of reindeer husbandry—lassoing, breaking to harness, sled-driving, selective breeding—eroded even as "ownership" increased.

Over the years, Lopp worked tirelessly to keep the reindeer program on firm footing. Endeavoring to expand the market for reindeer products, in 1911 he arranged to ship 18,000 pounds of reindeer meat from Nome to Seattle. In 1915 he convened the first reindeer fair, in which reindeer herders from throughout the Seward Peninsula came together for a week of contests that tested their skills at lassoing, harnessing, and sled-racing. Through the reindeer fairs, Bureau of Education employees urged individual herders to form reindeer associations, to make it easier for deer to be herded cooperatively, under stricter supervision. One by one, all of these measures failed. The market for meat was spotty at best; the influenza epidemic of 1918 ended the reindeer fairs; and the reindeer cooperatives collapsed due to lack of cooperation—too many owners, too few willing to take charge.

The biggest blow to native reindeer herding came from a single family. Gudbrand Lomen and his sons were Norwegian-Americans who landed in Nome during the gold rush of 1900. Soon they had their fingers in a wide variety of pots; they acquired mining interests, a drugstore, and a photography studio. The senior Lomen became the federal judge for the district, allowing him inclusion and invulnerability in all the affairs of northern Alaska. In 1914 the family formed Lomen & Company, and with the financial backing of Jafet Lindeberg, the Norwegian herder who had made millions in the Nome stampede, they purchased 1,200 reindeer from Alfred Nilima, a Lapp who had started a herd at Kotzebue Sound (using deer provided by the U.S. government). The following year, the Lomens bought the mission herds at Golovnin Bay and Teller. These transactions blatantly violated government regulations, but no one, including Tom Lopp, had the clout to thwart the new "reindeer kings." Within ten years, they owned nearly forty thousand reindeer.

Over the years, the Lomens would be called many things—bullies, liars, swindlers, usurers—but no one ever said they lacked nerve. They invested hundreds of thousands of dollars in corrals and slaughterhouses. They dug cold storage plants in the permafrost. (Eskimos had been preserving meat this way for millennia.) They bought tugs and barges to carry reindeer carcasses to the ships that would transport them to the States. And they owned the ships, too.

Their largest hurdle was figuring a way to stimulate the world's appetite for reindeer. The Lomens had declared from the beginning that they had no intention of selling reindeer meat to Alaskans. They would leave that market to the natives. Besides, it was far too small for what the Lomens had in mind. They envisioned turning reindeer into a commodity as popular and lucrative as salmon. Through exhaustive promotion, they succeeded in placing reindeer steaks and chops on the menus of prominent hotels and two different transcontinental railroads. They published cookbooks with recipes for Swiss steak of reindeer and boned reindeer rib roast with apple stuffing. (The American housewife was assured that the flavor of reindeer is "gamy but not strong.") In 1926, Lomen publicists talked New York City Mayor Jimmie Walker into declaring April 5–10 New York Reindeer Week.

The Lomens' most visible spokesperson, however, was Santa Claus. In 1927, they enlisted the help of department stores and newspapers around the country to arrange appearances by Santa and his reindeer at Christmastime. How this would incite people to eat more reindeer was explained in a letter from Carl Lomen to syndicated columnist Heywood Broun: "Hit by the high cost of living, Santa Claus—whose herds in Alaska have increased to more than 325,000 animals—is now placing some of his choicest animals on the market, to secure funds to buy gifts for his sack, and also to supply the good people of these United States with an additional and welcome food product."

Reindeer never caught on in the United States, not to the extent that the Lomens had dreamed of. Several states blocked sale of reindeer meat, insisting that, as wild game, it had sidestepped meat-inspection regulations. Cattlemen pressured railroads not to accept reindeer meat as freight. In the best year, the Lomens sold only 14,000 carcasses—much of it winding up in dog food—and once the Depression tightened the nation's belt in 1929, shipments plummeted.

As poorly as reindeer were received in the States, the reputation of the Lomens among their fellow Alaskans, particularly native Alaskans, was far worse. Separate from the question of whether the Lomens had a legal right to own reindeer was their behavior once they thrust themselves into the industry. Lomen herds soon occupied the best grazing range, from Kotzebue Sound to Unalakleet. When natives lapsed from "close herding" to "open herding" of their deer, their stock had a way of merging with Lomen herds. Evidence suggested that this intermingling was abetted by Lomen herders, and once the assimilation had occurred, the Lomens gave little effort to sorting native deer from Lomen deer.

The Lomen monopoly rolled on. Natives who sold deer to the Lomens were given credit at Lomen-owned trading posts; somehow the natives always seemed to owe more than they were paid. Government officials who called attention to the Lomens' transgressions were intimidated or removed. Judge Lomen and his sons had friends in high places. Appearing before a congressional committee, Carl Lomen scoffed at the authority of the Bureau of Education, which still oversaw the reindeer program in Alaska. "We have a million reindeer in Alaska governed by a group of schoolteachers," he testified. "Take it in your own state, as in Wyoming and Montana, [if] the cattle and sheep industries [were] conducted by federal schoolteachers who have gone out there to teach the Indians. . . . That is the situation in Alaska today."

Tom Lopp did his best to keep native herders—and the reindeer program that he had fostered—from being trampled by the Lomens. He helped set up native stores as an alternative to Lomen trading posts. He organized native stock companies and enabled the *Boxer*, the government-owned ship that carried supplies to Alaska schools each summer, to transport native-owned reindeer meat on the return trip. And he was never shy about expressing his disdain for his enemies, the Lomens, labeling them "robbers" and "racketeers."

But while Lopp had all of native Alaska on his side, the Lomens had the ear of the Harding administration—whose wheeler-dealer Interior secretary, Albert Fall, had already earned a place in history, if not in prison, for his hand in the colossal Teapot Dome scandal. At first, the higher-ups in Interior tried to force Lopp to resign, reducing his authority and then transferring him to Anchorage for a time. Finally, in January 1925, three months before Harding and his cronies left office, Lopp received a telegram notifying him that his position had been abolished. "You can guess who influenced Washington to retire me," Lopp wrote to a native friend at Cape Prince of Wales. "They"— the Lomens—"knew that I was in their way, would oppose them when they were ready to force their 'merging' policy upon you people. My securing the *Boxer* for the natives was the last straw. My head must come off."

For the first time in thirty-five years, Lopp had no official position in the education of Alaskan natives and the management of Alaskan reindeer. Yet he never considered giving up. Though he was sixty-one years old in 1925, he was quite robust, his hair thick and dark, his constitution as hardy as ever. His grandchildren thought it queer that he stuffed grass in his boots, Eskimo fashion, to keep his feet dry and warm. He learned to drive an automobile, but he would have preferred  driving a sled. Despite his rude dismissal in 1925, he continued to be regarded as a preeminent expert on reindeer management. Needing work, he accepted a job from the Hudson's Bay Company to inspect its reindeer herd on Baffin Island in the eastern Canadian Arctic. The trip also took him to England and the reindeer country of northern Norway, Sweden, and Finland. He was away from home for more than a year. By then, all of the Lopp children were finished college; most of them were married and living in the Seattle area. The one exception was Lucy Alaska Lopp, who had died, as she was born—prematurely, in 1909.

Upon his return, Lopp continued to lobby for reform of the reindeer program, working through the Philadelphia-based Indian Rights

Association and corresponding frequently with friends in Alaska. "I am sending a word to you concerning the Lomen[s] and the Reindeer trouble," George Ootenna wrote to him from Cape Prince of Wales, which was now known simply as Wales. "I am only telling you that . . . if the Lomen herd is taken away from the midst of Eskimo herds things would turn to the better. It is true the Lomens are causing trouble." Reports like this both touched and riled Lopp. In 1890, when he had first met Ootenna, the young Eskimo could not read or write. Since then, and thanks in no small part to Tom Lopp, Ootenna had become quite well educated; he was a Christian, a leader in his community, and the owner of a sizable reindeer herd. That such an exemplary man of such sterling accomplishments would be threatened by the Lomens went against everything Lopp stood for. He wanted the Lomens out of the reindeer business, entirely and everlastingly.

Even without the hounding of native-rights activists, the Lomens were in serious trouble. By the mid–1930s, shipment of Lomen reindeer to the States had shrunk to nearly nil, while the estimated number of reindeer in Alaska had grown to more than half a million. The Lomens' reindeer company claimed assets of $4 million, yet they had never made a dime of profit from their enterprise. Investors finally lost patience and shut off their credit. The Lomens' only chance, however slight, was a lifeline from the federal government. Ironically, it was their detractors, Tom Lopp included, who helped to make such a bailout possible.

Pressured relentlessly by the Indian Rights Association and its newsletter, *Indian Truth*, the Interior Department dispatched a series of investigators to sort out "the reindeer controversy." One of the most compelling studies pronounced: "The Alaska reindeer enterprise . . . should be regarded as essentially a *developmental* and educational enterprise primarily intended for the benefit of the natives. . . . This fundamental principle has been almost completely overlooked in recent handling of reindeer matters."

The report was far from kind to the Lomens: "It is impossible to read the testimony of the Lomens themselves without coming to the conclusion that here is a group that [was] determined by hook or by crook to get possession of native deer; that defied and denounced government representatives engaged in protecting the interests of natives; that would go to almost any lengths to achieve their particular brand of business success. It is important to be fair to this group, but it is necessary to recognize it for what it is—an aggressive, domineering, cynical outfit, made bitter by the partial thwarting of its grandiose schemes."

The consensus in Washington was that the federal government ought to re-assert its control over the reindeer program and put all of Alaska's reindeer back into the hands of natives. To do this required buying out the Lomens—a proposal not authored by the Lomens directly but which pleased them greatly. The figure tossed around was $2 million. As much as Lopp wanted the Lomens gone, it sickened him to think that they would be rewarded in any way for their reprehensible conduct. "Think of it, . . . to buy off Reindeer Rustlers and Pasture Poachers!" he railed to a friend at the Indian Rights Association. "How can the old Interior Department . . . admit they can only protect their 'wards' [natives] by buying off these wild-catters who should be serving time behind prison bars?"

In the end, the wildcatters were bought off. Despite sarcastic jibes from the floor of Congress that the government was jumping into the role of Santa Claus, the so-called Reindeer Act of 1937 authorized the Interior secretary to purchase all of the Lomens' reindeer, warehouses, slaughterhouses, cold storage plants, and other reindeer-related equipment. The same went for the property of all other white reindeer herders in Alaska, including Lapps. Henceforth, only natives could own reindeer. Although Congress had originally appropriated $2 million, the Lomens wound up receiving one-tenth of that amount. When the herds were counted, the government tallied only 42,000 reindeer, not the 260,000 the Lomens claimed.

For the Lomens, anything was better than nothing. For Alaskan natives and their allies, the Reindeer Act of 1937 was a resounding victory. Yet it was hardly the final solution. "With our withdrawal from the industry," Carl Lomen wrote caustically, "we could think only that it would be interesting, and doubtless not a little heart-rending, to sit back and watch how the Government would deal with the problem."

When Franklin Roosevelt's Interior secretary, Harold Ickes, cast about for someone to implement the reforms of the Reindeer Act, the name most often mentioned was Tom Lopp. "I wish I was in the field to help, as a teacher, local superintendent, or in any other position which would give me opportunity to get the deer industry out of the big snowdrift which seems to have engulfed it," Lopp wrote to one of the native herders. But Lopp was seventy-three in 1937. He had not held a job in ten years. In 1934, when the Territory of Alaska's delegate to Congress, Anthony Dimond, invited him to Washington to share his ideas on reindeer, Lopp had to decline; he couldn't afford to pay his own way.

Since leaving the Bureau of Education, he had returned to Alaska only once, in 1936, sponsored by the Indian Rights Association. Among his stops was a bittersweet visit to Cape Prince of Wales. The school had been sustained, and the mission was now in the hands of the Presbyterians. Several dozen natives had converted to Christianity; but so far none had assumed the position of pastor. So many familiar faces were gone—from age, accident, and the influenza epidemic of 1918—and he had found the reindeer herders in Alaska in disarray. "They are finding it more and more difficult to round up their deer," he wrote with deep regret.

Lopp stayed in the fight until the end. "Some people think [reinvigorating the reindeer program] too hopeless for even the Government to undertake," he wrote in *Indian Truth* shortly after his 1936 trip. But Lopp had a plan by which "a worthy and patient people will be helped and their confidence restored." The future, he declared, lay in returning to the practices of the past. Old style herding ("O-S-H," he called it) must replace new style herding ("N-S-H"). The new style, in which reindeer ran free over large areas for long periods was essentially a "no-herding" system. "Surely it has been demonstrated beyond any doubt that the big cattle ranch idea foisted on the reindeer country of Alaska has been a miserable and threatening failure," he wrote in his report to the Indian Rights Association. By contrast, the merits of old style herding, in which "deermen wander with the herd and see part or all of it daily" were myriad. To create a new generation of herders, Lopp called for a renewed commitment to "outdoor vocational herding schools" similar to the ones he had developed during his years at Cape Prince of Wales and as superintendent of the reindeer program.

"O-S-H has been OK in northern Europe and Asia for hundreds of years," he reminded. "It is the only system that will make real deermen out of part of the native hunters; the only kind of herding that will keep the native's body and mind working 12 months of the year; the only system that will insure him and his children against food-famines and the lack of clothing." To continue with laissez-faire new style herding, Lopp warned, would eventually turn the natives "towards the old caribou round-ups and drives of their forefathers, when thousands of caribou were driven into lakes and crude corrals for slaughter— back to the old 'FEAST AND FAMINE DAYS.'"

It wasn't that Lopp wanted the natives of Alaska to go backward. Rather, he wanted them to begin again. He spoke from experience, and although he never admitted as much, surely he spoke from nostalgia as well. If only the natives would recommit themselves, beginning at the point where he had started with them.

But there was no starting over—not for the Eskimos and not for William Thomas Lopp. On April 10, 1939, nineteen months after passage of the Reindeer Act, he suffered a stroke at his home in Seattle and died in hospital later that day.

Obituaries called Lopp a "pioneer" and an "authority" on reindeer. Yet some of the best eulogies had been composed many years earlier, at the time he was so rudely dismissed from government service. "Mr. Lopp," vouched Elmer Ellsworth Brown, chancellor of New York University and a former commissioner of Education, "is of exceptional character, devoted to the interests of backward people, rich in experience of their ways, with a lively insight into the workings of their minds and a sense of both the humor and tragedy of their lot."

F. J. Birkett, a lieutenant commander in the Coast Guard, had testified that "Lopp's initiative and practicability [were] directed along not the lines of least resistance but what he knew to be right. Scrupulously honest, untiring in his efforts, far-sighted and guided by a love for his fellow man, he has unselfishly blazed the most difficult trails, has overcome conditions seemingly [i]nsurmountable, and will go down in Alaskan history as her Lincoln. Had he been out for commercial gain instead of a servant toward idealism he could now be a wealthy man."

Laconic to the end, Lopp never reflected deeply on his philosophy or accomplishments. The closest he came, perhaps, was in a children's book he wrote in 1927. *White Sox* chronicles a young reindeer's coming of age. In the final chapter, White Sox at last discerns the difference between his fellow reindeer and their ancestors, the wild caribou: "And man . . . did us a better turn when he taught us to serve him,'" White Sox reasons. "'Mother, if I am to live to a ripe old age and die a natural death, I must make myself so useful to man that my services will be of greater value than my flesh and skin. Isn't that right, mother?'

"'That's the whole lesson, my son,'" Mother Reindeer responds.

Ellen Lopp outlived her husband by eight years, surrounded by her children and grandchildren. She died in 1947 at the age of seventy-nine.

More than a century has passed since Ellen and Tom Lopp built a life together at Cape Prince of Wales. Alaska finally became a state in 1959. The Alaska Native Claims Settlement Act of 1971 gave Alaskan natives a greater chance for self-determination, not to mention a steady stream of royalties from the development of oil and minerals on the state's federal lands. Alcoholism and diseases such as diabetes still ravage native families, but Eskimos are in some ways better off than Native Americans in the lower forty-eight states. They were never defeated in war. They were never forcibly evicted from their homeland.

The village of Wales still hunkers in the lee of Cape Mountain, reachable now by airplane, weather permitting. Of the 150 residents, many are descendants of families who have lived at the Cape for hundreds of years. Today they dwell in "American" houses—that is, above ground—and get around by snow machines in winter and all-terrain vehicles during the short summer. Yet not all of the boats on the beach are aluminum; some natives maintain traditional walrus-skin umiaks. Reindeer, offspring of the original herd brought from Siberia, still graze on the moss-covered hills. Not many Eskimos eat reindeer with any regularity—they never did. They much prefer walrus, whale, and fish—or the brand-name groceries advertised on satellite television and available in the village store.

Tom Lopp did not live long enough to witness the full devolution of the reindeer industry. The Reindeer Act of 1937 endures—only natives can own deer—but Lopp's plea for a vigorous recommitment to Old Style herding was never embraced. New Style herding, as he had cautioned, was tantamount to "no herding," and today the owners of reindeer herds live in villages and round up their animals once a year, mostly to harvest the horns. Reindeer antlers, especially antlers covered in velvet, are said to boost male sexual performance. Koreans bought them by the thousands—until Viagra came along. Since then the price of reindeer horns has collapsed.

There is yet another element to the "reindeer crisis." The original impetus for importing Siberian deer to Alaska was as replacements for the caribou that had disappeared from the Seward Peninsula. Today, due to natural shifts in migration, Alaska's native caribou have drifted back to their old grazing grounds. Every year more and more reindeer "go caribou," eloping and interbreeding. The total number of reindeer in Alaska is now around twenty thousand and declining rapidly.

Gazing from the vantage point of the twenty-first century, it is difficult to regard Alaskan history as anything other than a bold, continuous line of settlement, development, extraction, and exploitation. And yet if there is such a thing as coming full circle, the story of reindeer and caribou may be it.

# Acknowledgments

I first happened upon an account of the Overland Relief Expedition while perusing papers on the presidency of William McKinley in the Library of Congress. I thought I had already read my share of ice sagas—Shackleton's spectacular survival in the Antarctic, Peary and Cook's neck-and-neck race to the North Pole—but here was a tale that took me by surprise. At first I considered writing a book that focused strictly on the military angle of the expedition—the courageous feat of the U.S. Revenue Cutter Service men dispatched by McKinley. But as I dug deeper, I found a much richer and, dare I say, warmer story in the lives of Ellen and Tom Lopp.

The achievements of the Revenue Cutter Service men are enshrined in the archives of the Revenue Cutter Service and in the *Report of the Cruise of the U.S. Revenue Cutter Bear and the Overland Expedition for the Relief of the Whalers in the Arctic Ocean, from November 27, 1897, to September 13, 1898*, published by the Treasury Department in 1899. Yet the extraordinary experiences of the Lopps would have been lost to history had it not been for the conservatorial impulses of their family members and descendants, most especially Kathleen Lopp Smith, daughter of Dwight Lopp and granddaughter of Tom and

Ellen. Kathleen devoted a great deal of her life to collecting the letters, photographs, and mementos of her grandparents. Her dedication finally bore delectable fruit in 2001 with the publication of *Ice Window: Letters from a Bering Strait Village, 1892–1902*, which she edited with her husband, Verbeck Smith.

Shortly after reading *Ice Window*, I tried to call Kathleen Lopp Smith. Sadly, I never reached her. Verbeck answered the phone and informed me that Kathleen had died a few weeks earlier. I regret that I never got the chance to thank her in person for pursuing and preserving her grandparents' story. The best I can do now is to infuse these pages with profound gratitude and admiration. Without Kathleen, I could not have undertaken *In a Far Country*. Now the memory of her grandparents endures, and so too does Kathleen, a Lopp in grace and grit if there ever was one.

One person I have been able to thank in person is Verbeck Smith. Shelving his own despondency, he welcomed my inquiry as a validation of Kathleen's work. He invited me to his home in Seattle, where he offered me complete access to the originals of the letters that had appeared in edited form in *Ice Window*, plus hundreds of pages of family papers, including those of Frances Kittredge, accumulated by Kathleen but not included in the book. When it came time for me to visit Cape Prince of Wales in the summer of 2004, Verbeck gave me a list of who to see and alerted them to expect me. And once I had finished my manuscript, he gave it a thoughtful and thorough review. He did all these things as a way to honor Kathleen and Tom and Ellen Lopp, but also as a favor to me directly. "By works was faith made perfect" is a verse that fits Verbeck Smith very aptly.

Shortly after my attention was drawn to the Lopps, I had another serendipitous encounter—this time as I waited for a librarian to show me the one other important collection of Lopp papers, housed at the University of Oregon in Eugene. Dennis L. Noble is a preeminent authority on the Coast Guard. His numerous articles and books include the essential *Alaska and the U.S. Revenue Cutter Service, 1867–1915*, co-authored with Truman R. Strobridge. Once Dennis and I recovered from the shock of bumping into another author keen to examine the Lopp papers, we became friends and fellow travelers. (Dennis, I was relieved to learn, was researching a biography of Michael Healy.) With kindness and patience, he coached me in the historiography of the Revenue Cutter Service. Throughout my research and writing, he fed me valuable morsels of fact and wisdom and steered me away from gaffes of scholarship and seamanship. It was Dennis's impetus that got me aboard the icebreaker *Healy* for a patrol of the Bering, Chukchi, and Beaufort seas in October 2004. Luckier still, he was my congenial roommate for this three-week crash course in the nature and un-niceties of Arctic ice.

Now, too, is the time to thank the officers and crew of the *Healy* and the oceanographers, led by Larry Mayer, director of the Center for Coastal and Ocean Mapping, NOAA-UNH Joint Hydrographic Center, University of New Hampshire, for allowing me to join their team on this fantastic voyage of icebreaking and undersea mapping. No less hospitable were reindeer herd owner Tom Gray, veterinarian and state senator Donny Olsen, and Greg Finstad, program manager of the Reindeer Research Program at the University of Alaska, who made it possible for me to observe (and hopefully not disrupt) the all-day, all-night roundup of Gray's reindeer herd at White Mountain in July 2004.

My research took me to more than a few far-flung places, not the least of which was Avery Island, Louisiana, home of the esteemed McIlhenny family and headquarters of the sauce of sauces, Tabasco. Shane Bernard, historian and archivist for Tabasco (and a font of Cajun lore), introduced me to the affairs and affinities of Edward Avery (Ned) McIlhenny, who in 1897 took a wild notion to trade the hurricanes and bayous of the Gulf Coast for the blizzards and ice of Point Barrow. The diaries of McIlhenny, along with those of his two assistants, Norman

Buxton and Will Snyder, also within the McIlhenny collection, offer a vital vantage point on the ordeal of the trapped whalers. Without McIlhenny's records, my tale would be far less flavorful.

Many others helped me on my journey. In Nome: Hunter Mikelbrink, Kirk and Dana Scofield, Mary Knodel, Rose Atuk Fosdick, and the staff of the Nome library and Carrie M. McClain Memorial Museum. At the University of Alaska Fairbanks: archivist Caroline Atuk-Derrick (sister of Rose Atuk Fosdick, their family originally from Wales) at the Rasmuson Library and oral historians William Schneider and Karen Brewster. In Montana: the staff of the Livingston Public Library, who cheerfully suffered my interlibrary-loan requests. In Austin: Cyndi Hughes, deft advocate and considerate reader.

And finally, cheers and thanks to my editor, Kate Darnton, for her nurturing and to my agent, Esther Newberg, for her nudging. Or vice versa.

· · ·

All of the photographs in this book are from the Kathleen Lopp Smith Collection, University of Alaska Fairbanks, with two exceptions: The portrait of Tom Gordon, Fred Hopson, and Charles Brower is courtesy of the New Bedford Whaling Museum; and the portrait of Edward Avery McIlhenny is courtesy of the E.A. McIlhenny Collection, Avery Island, Louisana.

# Bibliographic Notes

## Introduction

It is difficult to find two sources that agree on the spelling of Inupiaq words, so I mostly relied on Russell Tabbert, *Dictionary of Alaskan English* (1991). Rather than risk confusing readers with the plural of Inupiaq words (e.g., umiak, s.; umiat, pl.), I have gone with an anglicized plural (umiak . . . umiaks). With proper names of people and places, I have sought the most recent spelling wherever possible.

## *1 · Beyond the Pale*

My knowledge of Lopp family history comes from an undated typescript, "The Lopps of Harrison County," and other papers in the Kathleen Lopp Smith Collection, now in the archives of the University of Alaska Fairbanks.

The American Missionary Association is now part of the United Church Board for Homeland Missionaries. The AMA archives are housed in the Amistad Research Center at Tulane University in New Orleans.

Sheldon Jackson cut a wide swath, and his path is readily traced. The artifacts he collected during his annual trips to Alaska were given their own museum on the campus of Sheldon Jackson College, which Jackson originally founded as a school for natives, in Sitka, Alaska. See Rosemary Carlton, *Sheldon Jackson, the Collector* (1999) and Peter L. Corey, ed., *Faces, Voices & Dreams: A Celebration of the Centennial of the Sheldon Jackson Museum*

(1987). Most of Jackson's correspondence, diaries, speeches, and other writing, as well as scrapbooks of news clippings relating to his life and interests, are in the safekeeping of the Presbyterian Historical Society in Philadelphia. Other Jackson material is at the Princeton Theological Seminary, Princeton, New Jersey.

It's a gross understatement to say that Jackson published prolifically. Most pertinent to my study are Jackson, *Alaska and the Missions on the North Pacific Coast* (1880) and his annual contributions to two government publications: *Report of the Commissioner of Education*, titled variously "Report of the General Agent of Education for Alaska" and "Report on Education in Alaska," beginning in 1886; and the "Report on Introduction of Domestic Reindeer into Alaska" (hereafter the Reindeer Report or Reindeer Reports), submitted each year to the U.S. Senate, beginning in 1892.

Numerous books and articles have examined Jackson's record and influence, including: Robert Laird Stewart, *Sheldon Jackson: Pathfinder and Prospector of the Missionary Vanguard in the Rocky Mountains and Alaska* (1908); J. Arthur Lazell, *Alaskan Apostle: The Life Story of Sheldon Jackson* (1960); Norman J. Bender, *Winning the West for Christ: Sheldon Jackson and Presbyterianism on the Rocky Mountain Frontier, 1869–1880* (1996); John Eaton, "Sheldon Jackson, Alaska's Apostle and Pioneer," *Review of Reviews* 13:6 (June 1896), 691–696; Karl Ward, "A Study of the Introduction of Reindeer into Alaska," *Journal of the Presbyterian Historical Society* 33:4 (December 1955), 229–237; Ward, "A Study of the Introduction of Reindeer into Alaska—II," *Journal of the Presbyterian Historical Society* 34:4 (December 1956), 245–256; Jackson, "Exploring for Reindeer in Alaska: Being the Journal of the Cruise of the U.S. Revenue Steamer *Bear*," introduction by Charles A. Anderson, *Journal of the Presbyterian Historical Society* 31:1 (March 1953), 1–24; Jackson, "Exploring for Reindeer in Alaska: Being the Journal of the Cruise of the U.S. Revenue Steamer *Bear* (Second Installment)," introduction by Charles A. Anderson, *Journal of the Presbyterian Historical Society* 31:2 (June 1953), 87–112; Theodore Charles Hinckley, Jr., "The Alaska Labors of Sheldon Jackson, 1877–1890," Ph.D. dissertation, University of Indiana, 1961; Ted C. Hinckley, "Sheldon Jackson and Benjamin Harrison: Presbyterians and the Administration of Alaska," *Pacific Northwest Quarterly* 54:2 (April 1963), 66–74; Hinckley, "Sheldon Jackson as Preserver of Alaska's Native Culture," *Pacific Historical Review* 33:4 (November 1964), 411–424; Hinckley, "Publicist of the Forgotten Frontier," *Journal of the West* 4:1 (January 1965),

27–40; Hinckley, "The Presbyterian Leadership in Pioneer Alaska," *Journal of American History* 52:4 (March 1966), 742–756; Hinckley, *The Americanization of Alaska, 1867–1897* (1972); Dorothy Jean Ray, "Sheldon Jackson and the Reindeer Industry of Alaska," *Journal of Presbyterian History* 43:2 (June 1965), 71–99; Ray, *The Eskimos of Bering Strait, 1650–1898* (1975); Glenn Smith, "Education for the Natives of Alaska: The Work of the United States Bureau of Education, 1884–1931," *Journal of the West* 6:3 (July 1967), 440–450; Stephen W. Haycox, "Sheldon Jackson in Historical Perspective: Alaska Native Schools and Mission Contracts, 1885–1894," *Pacific Historian* 28:1 (Spring 1984), 18–28; and Donald Craig Mitchell, *Sold American: The Story of Alaska Natives and Their Land, 1867–1959* (1997).

America's treatment of its natives is outlined in Paul A. Prucha, *American Indian Policy in Crisis: Christian Reformers and the Indian, 1865–1900* (1976), and distilled even more trenchantly in Prucha, *The Great Father: The United States Government and the American Indians*, vols. 1-2; (1984; combined ed. 1995). Also of interest are Michael C. Coleman, *Presbyterian Missionary Attitudes toward American Indians, 1837–1893* (1985); and Prucha, *Americanizing the American Indians: Writings by the "Friends of the Indian," 1880–1900* (1978).

The 1890 voyage to Alaska and Lopp and Thornton's first days at Cape Prince of Wales are recounted in the Jackson papers in Philadelphia; the annual *Report to the Commissioner of Education*; and submissions by Lopp and Thornton to the *American Missionary*, published monthly by the American Missionary Association. Biographical information on Leander Stevenson was provided by the Presbyterian Historical Society; John Driggs's life and bona fides are confirmed in the Archives of the Episcopal Church in Austin, Texas.

The most vivid description of the Gilley Affair is found in Herbert L. Aldrich, *Arctic Alaska and Siberia, or Eight Months with the Arctic Whalemen* (1889; reprint 1937). Tom Lopp tells a slightly different version of the tragedy—this one more sympathetic to the natives—in an undated manuscript, "Gilley Affair," collected in the Kathleen Lopp Smith papers. Lopp's records list thirteen Eskimos killed.

## 2 · *The High Place*

For my portrayal of Cape Prince of Wales, I have drawn on my visit in July 2004. To gain a sense of the Cape before the arrival of the missionaries, I relied on Roger K. Harritt, "Re-Examining Wales' Role in Bering Strait Pre-history: Some Preliminary Results of Recent Work," in Allen P. McCartney, ed., *Indigenous Ways to the Present: Native Whaling in the Western Arctic* (2003), 25–67; Harritt, "A Preliminary Reevaluation of the Pinuk-Thule Inter-face at Wales, Alaska," *Arctic Anthropology* 41:2 (2004), 163–176; Dorothy Jean Ray, "Nineteenth Century Settlement and Subsistence Patterns in Bering Strait," *Arctic Anthropology* 2:2 (1964), 61–94; Ray, *The Eskimos of Bering Strait, 1650–1898*; Edward William Nelson, *The Eskimo about Bering Strait* (1899; reprint 1983); Frederick W. Beechey, *Narrative of a Voyage to the Pacif-ic and Beering's Strait to Co-operate with the Polar Expeditions*, vol. 1 (1831; reprint 1968); Henry Trollope, "Journal Kept by Commander Henry Trollope, during a trip from H. M. Sloop Rattlesnake in Port Clarence to King-a-ghee, a village of four or five miles round Cape Prince of Wales, January 9, 1854–January 27, 1854," enclosure to "Proceedings of Her Majesty's Discovery Ship 'Rattlesnake,'" in *Further Papers Relative to the Recent Arctic Expeditions in Search of Sir John Franklin and the Crews of H. M. S. "Erebus" and "Terror,"* 35:1898 (1855), 861–881. Also see J. R. Bockstoce, *Eskimos of Northwest Alas-ka in the Early Nineteenth Century* (1977).

My favorite field guide to the plants and wildlife of northern Alaska is E. C. Pielou, *A Naturalist's Guide to the Arctic* (1994).

Of the long list of sources that I consulted on Eskimo ethnology, those by Ray and Nelson, cited above, are among the most valuable. Others include, in no particular priority: William W. Fitzhugh and Aron Crowell, eds., *Crossroads of Continents: Cultures of Siberia and Alaska* (1988); David Damas, ed., *Arctic*, vol. 5 of *Handbook of North American Indians* (1984); Kaj Birket-Smith, *Eski-mos* (1935; reprint 1971); Ernest S. Burch, Jr., *The Eskimos* (1988); Burch, *The Inupiaq Eskimo Nations of Northwest Alaska* (1998); Burch, *The Traditional Eskimo Hunters of Point Hope, Alaska, 1800–1875* (1981); Burch, "Modes of Exchange in North-west Alaska," in Tim Ingold et al., *Hunters and Gatherers 2: Property, Power, and Ideology* (1988), 95–109; Burch, "The Eskimo Trading Partnership in Northern Alaska," *Anthropological Papers of the University of Alaska* 15:1 (November 1970), 49–80; Ray, "Early Maritime Trade with the Eskimo of Bering Strait and the Introduction of Firearms," *Arctic Anthropol-ogy* 12:1 (1975), 1–9; Ray, "Land Tenure and Polity of the Bering Strait Eski-mos," *Journal of the West* 6:3 (July 1967), 371–394; Ray, *Artists of the Tundra and the Sea* (1961); Ray, *Eskimo Art: Tradition and Innovation in Northern Alas-ka* (1977); J. C. H. King et al., eds., *Arctic Clothing of North America–Alaska*,

*Canada, and Greenland* (2005); John Murdoch, *Ethnological Results of the Point Barrow Expedition* (1892; reprint 1988); Wendell H. Oswalt, *Eskimos and Explorers* (1979); Clark M. Garber, *Stories and Legends of the Bering Strait Eskimos* (1940); Edward L. Keithahn, *Alaskan Igloo Tales* (1958); Margaret Lantis, "The Religion of the Eskimos," in Vergilius Ferm, ed., *Ancient Religions* (1950); Lantis, *Alaskan Eskimo Ceremonialism* (1947); Middleton Smith, "Superstitions of the Eskimo," in Rudolf Kersting, comp., *The White World: Life and Adventures within the Arctic Circle Portrayed by Famous Living Explorers* (1902); Diamond Jenness, *Dawn in Arctic Alaska* (1957); Knud Rasmussen, *Across Arctic America: Narrative of the Fifth Thule Expedition* (1927; reprint 1999); Richard K. Nelson, *Hunters of the Northern Ice* (1969); and David Boeri, *People of the Ice Whale: Eskimos, White Men, and the Whale* (1983).

Harrison Thornton reveals himself in his posthumously published book, *Among the Eskimos of Wales, Alaska, 1890–93*, edited by Neda S. Thornton and William M. Thornton Jr. (1931). Thornton also wrote regularly to the *American Missionary*, sometimes sharing a byline with Tom Lopp. Lopp's papers at the University of Oregon and the University of Alaska Fairbanks and Sheldon Jackson's papers in Philadelphia provide insights into Thornton; so does Maurice R. Montgomery, "An Arctic Murder: A Cultural History of the Congregational Mission at Cape Prince of Wales, Alaska, 1890–1893," master's thesis, University of Oregon, 1963.

I am grateful to Dennis Noble for guiding my characterization of Michael A. Healy. I have also relied on Gerald O. Williams, "Michael J. [*sic*] Healy and the Alaska Maritime Frontier, 1880–1902," master's thesis, University of Oregon, 1987; James M. O'Toole, *Passing for White: Race, Religion, and the Healy Family, 1820–1920* (2002); O'Toole, "Racial Identity and the Case of Captain Michael Healy, USRCS," *Prologue* 29:3 (Fall 1997), 191–201; Mary and Albert Cocke, "Hell Roaring Mike: A Fall from Grace in the Frozen North," *Smithsonian* 13:1 (February 1983), 119–137; Jane Apostol, "Sailing with the Ruler of the Arctic Sea," *Pacific Northwest Quarterly* 72:4 (October 1981), 146–156; John F. Murphy, "Portrait of Captain Michael A. Healy," *U.S. Coast Guard Academy Alumni Bulletin* 41:1 (January/February 1979), 14–18; Paul H. Johnson, "Portrait of Captain Michael A. Healy, Part III," *U.S. Coast Guard Academy Alumni Bulletin* 41:3 (May/June 1979), 3–30; and Gary C. Stein, "A Desperate and Dangerous Man: Captain Michael A. Healy's Arctic Cruise of 1900," *Arctic Journal* 15:2 (Spring 1985), 39–45. Healy family papers, including those of his wife, Mary, are collected at the Huntington Library, San Marino,

California; I viewed microfilm of many of these papers in the archives of the University of Alaska Fairbanks. Also of interest was *The Odyssey of Captain Healy,* a film by Maria Brooks, 1999. Healy's brothers are profiled in Albert S. Foley, *God's Men of Color: The Colored Catholic Priests of the United States, 1854–1954* (1955).

The logbooks of the revenue cutter *Bear* are at the National Archives, Washington, D.C. A far richer resource—not just on Healy and the *Bear* but also on matters relating to the Alaska missions, Sheldon Jackson, Tom Lopp, Harrison Thornton, Eskimos, reindeer, whalers, traders, gold rushes, and the entire history of Alaska—are the hundreds of letters written to and by officers of the Revenue Cutter Service, known collectively as the "Alaska File of the Revenue Cutter Service, 1867–1914" (hereafter the Alaska Files), yet another of the splendid treasures retrievable from the National Archives. For more on the *Bear* in particular and the Revenue Cutter Service in general, I consulted William Bixby, *Track of the* Bear (1965); Frank Wead, *Gales, Ice and Men: A Biography of the Steam Barkentine* Bear (1937); Stella Rapaport, *The Bear: Ship of Many Lives* (1962); Strobridge and Noble, *Alaska and the U.S. Revenue Cutter Service, 1867–1915*; Noble and Strobridge, "Early Cuttermen in Alaskan Waters," *Pacific Northwest Quarterly* 78:3 (July 1987), 74–82; Noble, "Fog, Men, and Cutters: A Short History of the Bering Sea Patrol," 1979, www.uscg.mil/hq/g-cp/history/BeringSea.html; Stephen H. Evans, *The United States Coast Guard, 1790–1915: A Definitive History* (1949); and Irving H. King, *The Coast Guard Expands, 1865–1915: New Roles, New Frontiers* (1996).

### 3 · A Race Worth Saving

Today more is known about Mary Antisarlook than about her husband, Charlie (sometimes spelled Charley). She survived him by nearly fifty years, stirring the avarice and admiration of the whites who settled around her. Charlie appears in the diaries, letters, and reports of Sheldon Jackson and in various Revenue Cutter Service documents, and he is profiled briefly by Tom Lopp in his undated typescript, "Eskimo Boys on Drive of 1898." The best articles on the Antisarlooks are Ray, "Sinrock Mary: From Eskimo Wife to Reindeer Queen," *Pacific Northwest Quarterly* 75:3 (July 1984), 98–107; and a manuscript entitled "Story of Sinrock Mary," attributed (by Ray) to Esther Oliver and found in the Lopp papers at the University of Oregon.

The starvation on St. Lawrence Island is related in Captain C. L. Hooper, *Report of the Cruise of the U.S. Revenue-Steamer Corwin in the Arctic Ocean* (1881). The naturalist John Muir was aboard the *Corwin* for its Arctic cruise the following summer and essentially repeats the story of starvation in Muir, *The Cruise of the* Corwin (1917; reprint 1993). Of those who doubt that drinking was to blame, one of the most outspoken is Ray.

Alaska Governor Swineford's comments on to the superiority of Eskimo (over Indians) were reprinted in Jackson, "Report on Education in Alaska," in the *Report of the Commissioner of Education* (1886).

Charles Townsend first suggested that reindeer might make a viable replacement for Alaskan caribou in Townsend, "Notes on the Natural History and Ethnology of Northern Alaska," in Capt. M. A. Healy, *Report of the Cruise of the Revenue Marine Steamer Corwin in the Arctic Ocean in the Year 1885* (1887).

The acquisition of Siberian reindeer and their transport and introduction to Alaska are documented in Sheldon Jackson's Reindeer Reports; in his journals and letters; and elsewhere throughout his papers. The letters of Mary Healy add detail and color to this extraordinary experiment, as do the logbooks of the *Bear* and the Alaska Files of the Revenue Cutter Service.

George Kennan observes the reluctance of the Chukchi to part with live reindeer in *Tent Life in Siberia and Adventures among the Koraks and Other Tribes in Kamchatka and Northern Asia* (1870; reprint 1910). My knowledge of the Chukchi, their region, and their neighbors was enriched by Waldemar Bogoras, *The Chukchee* (1909); Bogoras, *Chukchee Mythology* (1910); Anthony Leeds, "Reindeer Herding and Chukchi Social Institutions," in Leeds et al., eds., *Men, Culture, and Animals: The Role of Animals in Human Ecological Adjustments* (1965); Fitzhugh and Crowell, eds., *Crossroads of Continents*; Anna M. Kerttula, *Antlers on the Sea: The Yup'ik and Chukchi of the Russian Far East* (2000); Yuri Slezkine, *Arctic Mirrors: Russia and the Small Peoples of the North* (1994); Harold U. Sverdrup, *Among the Tundra People* (1938; first English translation 1939; reprint 1978); James Forsyth, *A History of the Peoples of Siberia: Russia's North Asian Colony, 1581–1990* (1992); Anna Reid, *The Shaman's Coat: A Native History of Siberia* (2002); Igor Krupnik, *Arctic Adaptations: Native Whalers and Reindeer Herders of Northern Eurasia* (1993); Piers Vitebsky, *The Reindeer People: Living with Animals and Spirits in Siberia* (2005); Richard J. Bush, *Reindeer, Dogs, and Snow-Shoes: A Journal of Siberian Travel and Explorations Made in the Years 1865, 1866, and 1867* (1871); and

C. Daryll Forde, "The Northern Tungus and Other Reindeer Herders of Siberia," in Forde, *Habitat, Economy and Society* (1934).

No two authorities seem to agree on when caribou were first domesticated, which makes the vast library of research on the biology, husbandry, and culture of reindeer, first in Asia and then in Alaska, that much more absorbing. Some sources of note: Bertholf Laufer, "The Reindeer and Its Domestication," *Memoirs of the American Anthropological Association* 4 (1917), 91–147; Gudmund Hatt, "Notes on Reindeer Nomadism," *Memoirs of the American Anthropological Association* 6 (1919), 75–133; Ronald Oliver Skoog, "Ecology of the Caribou (*Rangifer tarandus granti*) in Alaska," Ph.D. dissertation, University of California, Berkeley, 1968; James Johnson Koffroth Simon, "Twentieth Century Inupiaq Eskimo Reindeer Herding on Northern Seward Peninsula, Alaska," Ph.D. dissertation, University of Alaska Fairbanks, 1968; Simon and Craig Gerlach, "Reindeer Herding, Subsistence, and Alaskan Native Land Use in the Bering Land Bridge National Preserve: A Review of the Impact of Reindeer Herding on Community Relationships and Land Use in the Early Twentieth Century," National Park Service, 1992; Dean Francis Olson, *Alaskan Reindeer Herdsmen: A Study of Native Management in Transition* (1969); Richard O. Stern, Edward L. Arobio, Larry L. Naylor, and Wayne C. Thomas, *Socio-Economic Evaluation of Reindeer Herding in Relation to Proposed National Interest (d)2 Lands in Northwest Alaska* (1977), revised as *Eskimos, Reindeer, and Land* (1980); Ward, "A Study of the Introduction of Reindeer into Alaska"; Ray, "Sheldon Jackson and Reindeer Industry of Alaska"; J. Sonnenfeld, "An Arctic Reindeer Industry: Growth and Decline," *Geographical Review* 49:1 (January 1959), 76–94; Lantis, "The Reindeer Industry in Alaska," *Arctic* 3:1 (April 1950), 27–44; Lantis, "Eskimo Herdsmen: Introduction of Reindeer Herding to the Natives of Alaska," in Edward H. Spicer, ed., *Human Problems in Technological Change: A Casebook* (1952); Burch, "The Caribou/Wild Reindeer as Human Resource," *American Antiquity* 37:3 (July 1972), 339–368; Seymour Hadwen and Lawrence J. Palmer, "Reindeer in Alaska," United States Department of Agriculture Bulletin no. 1089 (1922); Palmer, "Raising Reindeer in Alaska," United States Department of Agriculture Miscellaneous Publication no. 207 (1934); Gilbert H. Grosvenor, "Reindeer in Alaska," *National Geographic* 14:4 (April 1903), 127–148; Clarence L. Andrews, *The Eskimo and His Reindeer in Alaska* (1939); Andrews, "Reindeer in Alaska,"

*Washington Historical Quarterly* 10:3 (July 1919), 171–176; Andrews, "Reindeer in the Arctic," *Washington Historical Quarterly* 17 (1926), 14–17; Andrews, "Driving Reindeer in Alaska," *Washington Historical Quarterly* 26 (1935), 90–93; and Alice Postell, *Where Did the Reindeer Come From?* (1990). Other useful information can be found through the website of the Reindeer Research Program at the University of Alaska Fairbanks (http://reindeer.salrm.uaf.edu).

### 4 · *Just the One for the Place*

Life at the Cape Prince of Wales mission is stitched from sources already mentioned: the Lopp papers, both in Oregon and in Alaska; Lopp and Thornton's contributions to the *American Missionary*; the Jackson papers; Sheldon Jackson's annual reports to the commissioner of education; the Alaska Files of the Revenue Cutter Service; and Thornton's *Among the Eskimos of Wales Alaska, 1890–93*. With the appearance of Ellen Kittredge in 1892, the narrative is enriched by her wonderful letters, published as Kathleen Lopp Smith and Verbeck Smith, eds., *Ice Window: Letters from a Bering Strait Village, 1892–1902* (2001). These letters and many more are among the Kathleen Lopp Smith papers in the archives of the University of Alaska Fairbanks. The log of Tom and Ellen's sled journey from Cape Prince of Wales to Point Hope in the winter of 1893 is another of the gems of the Kathleen Lopp Smith papers. In as few instances as possible, I have modified punctuation and capitalization to improve clarity.

I first learned about the missionary influence of Rufus Anderson in William R. Hutchinson, *Errand to the World: American Protestant Thought and Foreign Missions* (1987).

John Driggs recounts his experiences at Point Hope, including the unexpected visit by the Lopps, in Driggs, "The Latest News from the Alaskan Mission," *Spirit of Missions* 56:12 (December 1891), 473–475; Driggs, "Dr. Driggs' Work at Point Hope, Alaska," *Spirit of Missions* 57:3 (March 1892), 99–104; and Driggs, "Dr. Driggs's Work at Point Hope, Alaska, in 1892–93," *Spirit of Missions* 59:1 (January 1894), 15–18. Driggs also published a small book on his missionary endeavors, *Mission Life at Point Hope* (1900). For a broader view of Point Hope, see James V. Vanstone, *Point Hope: An Eskimo Village in Transition* (1962); and Burch, *The Traditional Eskimo Hunters of Point Hope, Alaska: 1800–1875*.

### 5 · Not So Much to Be Pitied

Editions of the *Eskimo Bulletin* are preserved with the Kathleen Lopp Smith papers in Alaska and Oregon.

Miner Bruce published his own book, *Alaska: Its Resources, Gold Fields, Routes and Scenery* (1895).

The sources chronicling Thornton's decline and fall have already been cited.

My introduction into Lapp (now Saami) reindeer-herding culture was provided by Bjorn Collinder, *The Lapps* (1949); Roberto Bosi, *The Lapps* (1960); and John Tauri, "The Story of the Reindeer Lapps," in Carleton S. Coon, ed., *A Reader in General Anthropology* (1948).

### 6 · Good Faith

Toleef Brevig's missionary experience in Alaska is recounted in J. Walter John-shoy, *Apaurak in Alaska: Social Pioneering among the Eskimos, Translated and Compiled from the Records of the Reverend T. L. Brevig, Pioneer Missionary to the Eskimos of Alaska from 1894 to 1917* (1944); and Henriette Lund, *Of Eskimos and Missionaries: Lutheran Eskimo Missions in Alaska, 1894–1973* (1974). Vene and Nellie Gambell's years on St. Lawrence Island are recounted in V. C. Gambell, *The Schoolhouse Farthest West: St. Lawrence Island, Alaska* (1910). Sheldon Jackson's papers, diaries, and official reports help piece together the Gambells' story. For more on the natives of St. Lawrence, see Jane M. Hughes, *An Eskimo Village in the Modern World* (1960); and Carol Zane Jolles, *Faith, Food, and Family in a Yupik Whaling Community* (2002).

### 7 · Camels of the Far North

William Kjellmann's diary of the two-thousand-mile trip by reindeer sled is excerpted in the seventh Reindeer Report (1898).

The best rendering of the Yukon gold rush is still Pierre Berton, *Klondike: The Last Great Gold Rush, 1896–1899* (1958; revised 1972). I also drew upon Barry C. Anderson, *Lifeline to the Yukon: A History of Yukon River Navigation* (1983); Melody Webb, *Yukon: The Last Frontier* (1985); William R. Hunt, *North of 53: The Wild Days of the Alaska-Yukon Mining Frontier, 1870–1914* (1974); Kathryn Morse, *The Nature of Gold: An Environmental History of the Klondike Gold Rush* (2003); Sam C. Dunham, "The Alaskan Gold Fields and the Opportunities They Offer for Capital and Labor," *Bulletin of the*

*Department of Labor* 16 (May 1898; reprint 1983), 297–425; and P. H. Ray and W. P. Richardson, "Relief of the Destitute in Gold Fields," in *Compilations of Narratives of Explorations of Alaska* (1900; reprint 1964).

Tom Lopp's initial refusal to sell reindeer to Andrew Kittilsen is confirmed by Kittilsen, "Annual Report of the Eaton Reindeer Station for 1898," in the eighth Reindeer Report (1898). Kittilsen's reindeer drive to Golovnin Bay and his encounter with Jarvis and Call on January 10, 1898, is described in the same report; and also by Jarvis in "Report of First Lieut. D. H. Jarvis" in the *Report of the Cruise of the U.S. Revenue Cutter* Bear *and the Overland Relief Expedition for the Relief of the Whalers in the Arctic Ocean, from November 27, 1897, to September 13, 1898* (hereafter the ORE Report).

## 8 · Floe Monsters

The most indispensable text on whaling in Alaska is John R. Bockstoce, *Whales, Ice, and Men: the History of Whaling in the Western Arctic* (1986). Yet no single book could cover the waterfront completely. My hunt for a deeper view of whaling led me to: Alexander Starbuck, *History of the American Whale Fishery from Its Inception to the Year 1876* (1878; reprint 1964); J. Ross Browne, *Etchings of a Whaling Cruise* (1846; reprint 1968); Elmo Paul Hohman, *The American Whaleman: A Study of Life and Labor in the Whaling Industry* (1928; reprint 1970); Margaret S. Creighton, *Rites and Passages: The Experience of American Whaling, 1830–1870* (1995); Robert Lloyd Webb, *On the Northwest: Commercial Whaling in the Pacific Northwest, 1790–1967* (1988); Bockstoce, *Steam Whaling in the Western Arctic* (1977); Aldrich, *Arctic Alaska and Siberia, or Eight Months with the Arctic Whalemen*; Arthur James Allen, *A Whaler and Trader in the Arctic, 1895 to 1944* (1978); Everett S. Allen, *Children of the Light: The Rise and Fall of New Bedford Whaling and the Death of the Arctic Fleet* (1973); Harston H. Bodfish, *Chasing the Bowhead* (1936); Walter Noble Burns, *A Year with a Whaler* (1913); John A. Cook, *Pursuing the Whale: A Quarter-Century of Whaling in the Arctic* (1926); Lloyd C. M. Hare, *Salted Tories: The Story of the Whaling Fleets of San Francisco* (1960); Don Charles Foote, "American Whalemen in Northwestern Arctic Alaska," *Arctic Anthropology* 2:2 (1964), 16–20; Howard I. Kushner, "'Hellships': Yankee Whaling along the Coasts of Russian-America, 1835–1952," *New England Quarterly* 45:1 (March 1972), 81–95; Jack Hadley, "Whaling off the Alaskan Coast," *Bulletin of the American Geographical Society* 47:12 (1915), 905–921; and the granddaddy of them all, Herman Melville, *Moby-Dick; or, The Whale* (1851; reprint 1988).

Roald Amundsen's protest against the use of baleen for corset stays is quoted in Roland Huntford, *The Last Place on Earth* (originally *Scott and Amundsen*, 1979; reprint 1999), 107–108. The bible on bowheads is John J. Burns et al., eds., *The Bowhead* (1993). Further articles on bowhead and baleen appear in *Marine Fisheries Review* 42:9–10 (September-October 1980), including: Michael A. Tillman, "Introduction: A Scientific Perspective on the Bowhead Whale Problem," 2–5; Willman M. Marquette and Bockstoce, "Historical Shore-Based Catch of Bowhead Whales in the Bering, Chukchi, and Beaufort Seas," 5–19; Bockstoce, "A Preliminary Estimate of the Reduction of the Western Arctic Bowhead Whale Population by Pelagic Whaling Industry: 1848–1915," 20–27; and Howard W. Braham et al., "Spring Migration of the Western Arctic Population of Bowhead Whales," 36–46.

Elisha Kent Kane's "floe-monsters" and other icy imagery are evoked in Kane, *The U.S. Grinnell Expedition in Search of Sir John Franklin: A Personal Narrative* (1854). Ice is serious business, and over the years, navigators have attempted to codify a lexicon of terms so that others might benefit from their experiences. See, for example: William Scoresby, *An Account of the Arctic Regions, with a History and Description of the Northern Whale-Fishery* (1820); Edward Simpson, *Ice and Ice Movements in Bering Sea and the Arctic Basin* (1890); Terence Armstrong et al., *Illustrated Glossary of Snow and Ice* (1973); and Mariana Gosnell, *Ice: the Nature, the History, and the Uses of an Astonishing Substance* (2005).

Richard Henry Dana's comparison of the life of a sailor to that of a dog appears in his classic, *Two Years Before the Mast* (1840; reprint 1981).

I am inspired by two marvelous histories of Arctic exploration: Berton, *The Arctic Grail: The Quest for the Northwest Passage and the North Pole, 1818–1909* (1988; reprint 2000); and Fergus Fleming, *Ninety Degrees North: The Quest for the North Pole* (2000).

Whaling and wintering at Herschel Island are described by Bockstoce, *Whales, Ice, and Men*; Bockstoce, "The Consumption of Caribou by Whalemen at Herschel Island, Yukon Territory, 1890 to 1908," *Arctic and Alpine Research* 12:3 (1980), 381–384; Iris Warner, "Herschel Island," *Alaska Journal* 3:3 (Summer 1973), 130–143; and Paul Fenimore Cooper Jr., "Herschel Island and the History of the Western Arctic," in Shirley Milligan et al., eds., *Living Explorers of the Canadian Arctic: The Historic Symposium of Arctic Scientists,*

*Explorers, and Adventurers* (1986), 245–254.

Leander Stevenson's disgust for whalers is expressed in the Sheldon Jackson papers. Gilbert Borden reveals his bigotry toward Eskimos in "The Wanton Esquimaux," *Evening Standard* (New Bedford, Massachusetts), 4 January 1893 and in his journals in the Yale Collection of Western Americana, Beinecke Rare Book and Manuscript Library, Yale University. The troubles of Borden at the Point Barrow Refuge Station are dissected in Bockstoce, *Whales, Ice, and Men*; Bockstoce, "Arctic Castaway: The Stormy History of the Point Barrow Refuge Station," *Prologue* 11:3 (Fall 1979), 153–169; and correspondence pertaining to the refuge station in the National Archives.

Biographical information on H. Richmond Marsh was provided by the Presbyterian Historical Society. Edward Avery McIlhenny comes to life courtesy of the invaluable E. A. McIlhenny Collection, Avery Island, Louisiana. His first trip to the Arctic in 1894 is documented in Henry Collins Walsh, *The Last Cruise of the Miranda: A Record of Arctic Adventure* (1895).

Charles Brower remains a larger-than-life figure, thanks in no small part to his autobiography, the initial (unpublished) draft of which he titled "The Northernmost American," (n.d.). The original remains in the Rauner Special Collections, Dartmouth College Library, Hanover, New Hampshire; I read a photocopy at the University of Alaska Fairbanks. Drastically edited and with many passages totally rewritten, "Northernmost American" was finally published as *Fifty Years Below Zero: A Lifetime of Adventure in the Far North* (1942).

The logbooks of the *Alexander, Navarch, Belvedere,* and *Orca* survive in the Kendall Institute and Library of the New Bedford Whaling Museum, New Bedford, Massachusetts. My telling of the *Navarch* disaster jibes with Bockstoce's in *Whales, Ice, and Men.* The *Alexander's* close call and escape is related by Michael McKinnon in the *Call* (San Francisco), 4 November 1897. James Allen makes his allegations of the whaling captains' blithe drinking spree in Allen, *A Whaler & Trader in the Arctic.*

For depictions of Eskimo whaling, I have consulted Boeri, *People of the Ice Whale*; Nelson, *Hunters of the Northern Ice*; Bill Hess, *Gift of the Whale: The Inupiat Bowhead Hunt, A Sacred Tradition* (1999); Helge Larsen and Froelich Rainey, *Ipiutak and the Arctic Whale Hunting Culture* (1948); Karen Brewster, ed., *The Whales, They Give Themselves: Conversations with Harry Brower, Sr.* (2004); Rosita Worl, "The North Slope Inupiat Whaling Complex," in Yoshinobu Kotani and William B. Workman, eds., *Alaskan Native Culture and History* (papers presented at the Second International Symposium, National Museum of Ethnology, Osaka, Japan, August 1978) (1979), 305–320; and Mark Shannon Cassell, "'If They Did Not Work at the Station, They Were in Bad Luck': Commercial Shore Whaling and Inupiat Eskimo Labor in Late 19th and Early 20th Century North Alaska," Ph.D. dissertation, Binghamton University, 2000.

## 9 · *Godspeed*

Deliberations over the plight of the whalers and the formation of the Overland Relief Expedition are chronicled in the *Call* and other newspapers of the day, including the *Examiner* and *Chronicle* of San Francisco, the *Post-Intelligencer* and *Daily Times* of Seattle, the *Oregonian* of Portland, the *New York Times*, and the *Star* and *Post* of Washington, D.C. Other pertinent materials are found in the Alaska Files of the Revenue Cutter Service and among clippings in the Sheldon Jackson papers. The most vital record of the expedition remains the ORE Report. For shorter summaries of the expedition, see Paul H. Johnson, "The Overland Expedition: A Coast Guard Triumph," *U.S. Coast Guard Academy Alumni Bulletin* 34:5 (September/October 1972), 63–71; "The Incredible Alaska Overland Rescue," Naval Historical Foundation 2:9 (January 1, 1968); William L. Boyd, "Jarvis and the Alaska Reindeer Caper," *Arctic* 25:2 (June 1972), 75–82; and A. W. Greely, *True Tales of Arctic Heroism in the New World* (1912). More recently, another slim history of the relief expedition has appeared: Shawn Shallow, *Rescue at the Top of the World: The True Story of the Most Daring Arctic Rescue in History* (2005).

I thank Dennis Noble for digging the service record of Francis Tuttle from the archives of the U.S. Coast Guard. Tuttle is also profiled and interviewed in several articles in the *Call*. Ellsworth Bertholf comes to life in C. Douglas Kroll, *Commodore Ellsworth P. Bertholf: First Commandant of the Coast Guard* (2002). In addition to the "Report of Second Lieut. E. P. Bertholf, R.C.S.," in the ORE Report, Bertholf also wrote his own account of the relief expedition, "The Rescue of the Whalers," *Harper's New Monthly Magazine* 99:589 (June 1899), 3–24. David Jarvis's career is assessed in Elizabeth A. Tower, "Captain David Henry Jarvis: Alaska's Tragic Hero—Wickersham's Victim," *Alaska History* 5:1 (Spring 1990), 1–21, and again in Tower, *Icebound Empire: Industry and Politics on the Last Frontier, 1898–1938* (1996). The "Report of First Lieut. D. H. Jarvis" commands center stage in the ORE Report. Samuel Call is given somewhat slighter recognition, most notably in Albert K. Cocke, "Dr. Samuel J. Call," *Alaska Journal* 4:3 (Summer 1974), 181–188. Call is the reason why I refer to Jarvis, Bertholf, and Call collectively as "Revenue Cutter Service men" or "cuttermen" and not as "officers." Call, while he wore a uniform, was a contract surgeon and not a true officer of the service.

Jarvis and Call's chance meeting with George Fred Tilton is recounted not only in the ORE Report, but also in George Fred Tilton, *"Cap'n George Fred" Himself* (1969); Cooper Gaw, "Capt. George Fred Tilton Tablet Dedication at the Seaman's Bethel, Johnny Cake Hill, July 16, 1933: Tilton's Walk and Whaling Tradition," *Old Dartmouth Historical Sketches*, vol. 3, pt. 2, no. 62 (n.d.), 503–525; and in accounts in San Francisco papers: the *Call*, 9 and 11 April 1898, and the *Examiner*, 8 April 1898.

### *10 · Sorry-Looking Bunch*

The misfortunes of the Arctic whaling fleet are related by Brower, "The Northernmost American" and *Fifty Years Below Zero*; the ORE Report; diaries of McIlhenny and his two assistants, Norman Buxton and Will Snyder; the logbooks of the stranded ships; Allen, *A Whaler & Trader in the Arctic*; Tilton, *"Cap'n George Fred" Himself*; Bockstoce, *Whales, Ice, and Men*; and Bockstoce, "The Arctic Whaling Disaster of 1897," *Prologue* 9:1 (Spring 1977), 27–41. The map showing the positions of the icebound ships is adapted from Bockstoce, *Whales, Ice, and Men*.

The discovery of gold near Cape Nome is explored by Terrence Michael Cole, "A History of the Nome Gold Rush: The Poor Man's Paradise," Ph.D. dissertation, University of Washington, 1983; Cole, "Nome: 'City of the Golden Beaches,'" *Alaska Geographic* 11:1 (1984); H. L. Blake, "History of the Discovery of Gold at Cape Nome," Senate Document 441, 56th Congress, 1st Session, June 5, 1900; and T. H. Carlson, "The Discovery of Gold at Nome, Alaska," *Pacific Historical Review* 15:3 (September 1946), 259–278.

### *11 · Errand of Mercy*

The arrival of Jarvis at Cape Prince of Wales is recorded in the ORE Report; the *Report of the Commissioner of Education for the Year 1898–99* (1900); and the Lopp letters in Fairbanks. Typescripts of Lopp, "Log of the Overland Relief Expedition" and "Story of the Relief Expedition" are in the Lopp papers in Eugene. Like Jarvis and Bertholf, Call authored a separate account of the ordeal in the ORE Report. He published a similar recap of the expedition in the San Francisco *Examiner*, 21 July 1898.

The native herders are sketched by Lopp in "Eskimo Boys on Drive of 1898," a brief typescript in the Lopp papers in Eugene.

## 12 · Labyrinth

For information on Carrie and Robert Samms and Anna Hunnicutt, I am grateful to the Evangelical Friends Church Southwest, Whittier, California, keeper of valuable records related to the Quaker mission on Kotzebue Sound. This archive includes a journal of Carrie Samms, 9 June 1897 to 30 June 1898, and an undated booklet by Anna H[unnicutt] Foster, "California Friends Church—Forty Years of Missions in Alaska, 1897–1937." Also see Arthur O. Roberts, *Tomorrow Is Growing Old: Stories of the Quakers in Alaska* (1978).

Scurvy is diagnosed in Stephen R. Bown, *Scurvy: How a Surgeon, a Mariner, and a Gentleman Solved the Greatest Medical Mystery of the Age of Sail* (2004); Kenneth J. Carpenter, *The History of Scurvy and Vitamin C* (1986); Alfred F. Hess, *Scurvy Past and Present* (1920); and Robert E. Feeney, *Polar Journeys: The Role of Food and Nutrition in Early Exploration* (1997).

## 13 · Killing Time

The long winter at Point Barrow is chronicled in the diaries of McIlhenny, Buxton, and Snyder; Brower's narratives, "The Northernmost American" and *Fifty Years Below Zero*; and Allen, *A Whaler & Trader in the Arctic.*

I came upon August Petermann's remonstrations against the long Arctic night in Leonard F. Guttridge, *Icebound: The* Jeannette *Expedition's Quest for the North Pole* (1986). Fridtjof Nansen describes souls crushed by inactivity in Nansen, *Farthest North* (1897; reprint 1999). Elisha Kent Kane's prescription of exercise appears in Kane, *The U.S. Grinnell Expedition.*

## 14 · Last Obstacle

As ever, the tracks of Jarvis, Call, Lopp, and the herders are traced through the ORE Report, the Alaska Files of the Revenue Cutter Service, and Lopp's log and "Story of the Relief Expedition."

## 15 · Arctic Hole

Charges of selfishness against McIlhenny appear in the New York *Sun*, 30 July 1898. These allegations are declared "unjust" by a writer identified only as "J. S. C." of Philadelphia, in the *Sun*, 15 August 1898 (clipping in the E. A. McIlhenny Collection).

Another damning allegation—that the traders at Point Barrow ran "an open house of prostitution"—was lodged by Richmond Marsh in a letter dated 12 August 1898 to Sheldon Jackson, included among the Jackson papers in Philadelphia.

Snowblindness makes one's eyeballs feel as if they are balanced "on needles in sockets filled with sand"—this on the eloquent and unimpeachable authority of Barry Lopez, *Arctic Dreams: Imagination and Desire in a Northern Landscape* (1986).

## 16 · *Fish in a Barrel*

The voyage of the *Bear* from Dutch Harbor to Point Barrow and then south to Seattle is recorded in Captain Tuttle's "Movements of the *Bear* Since June 23, 1898," in the ORE Report. Tuttle elaborated on the *Bear*'s ordeal in the ice at Point Barrow in interviews that appeared in the *Seattle Post-Intelligencer* and the *Call* and *Examiner* of San Francisco.

## 17 · *Real Deermen*

The incredible saga of the acquisition of reindeer and herders from Norway and their preposterous journey halfway around the world to Alaska is detailed in Sheldon Jackson's diary, correspondence, and clippings; and in Jackson, "Commission to Lapland," included in his eighth Reindeer Report (1898). In addition to news accounts published at the time, several books and articles also track the odyssey: V. R. Rausch and D. L. Baldwin, *The Yukon Relief Expedition and the Journal of Carl Johan Sakariassen* (2002); Keith A. Murray, *Reindeer and Gold* (1988); Murray, "Doctor Jackson and the Dawson Reindeer," *Idaho Yesterdays* 2:1 (Spring 1958), 8–15, 34; Peter M. Rinaldo, *The Great Reindeer Caper: The Missionary and the Miners* (1997); and Sverre Arestad, "Reindeer in Alaska," *Pacific Northwest Quarterly* 42:3 (July 1951), 211–223.

Alaska Governor John H. Brady's defense of reindeer is quoted in the ninth Reindeer Report (1900).

Charles Ryder's observations on "race development" appear in Ryder, "Congregational Missions in Alaska," in the *Report of the Commissioner of Education for the Year 1898–99* (1900).

The illnesses that ravaged the native population of Alaska are discussed in Robert Fortuine, *Chills and Fever: Health and Disease in the Early History of Alaska* (1989).

## Epilogue

The recipients of the Congressional Gold Medal are listed on the website of the Office of the Clerk of the U.S. House of Representatives: www.clerk.house.gov. A draft of McKinley's letter to Congress on behalf of the heroes of the Overland Relief Expedition reposes among the papers of the president's secretary, George Cortelyou, in the Library of Congress.

The further adventures of Jarvis, Call, Bertholf, Healy, and the *Bear* are recorded in sources already cited for Chapter 9.

Tom Lopp's faithful efforts on behalf of Alaskan natives and reindeer, including his lengthy and bitter conflict with the Lomens and their partisans, are related in his reports on education in Alaska, published annually in the *Report of the Commissioner of Education*; the annual Reindeer Reports; and the Lopp papers at the University of Oregon and University of Alaska Fairbanks. The Lomen family's campaign to establish a reindeer empire in Alaska is described in Carl J. Lomen, *Fifty Years in Alaska* (1954); and the Lomen Family Papers at the University of Alaska Fairbanks. The Lomens' protracted struggle with the federal government and the ongoing ups and downs of the reindeer industry are rendered in rancorous detail in the Lopp and Lomen papers and also in the papers of Anthony J. Dimond at the University of Alaska Fairbanks. The Dimond papers include a number of significant letters written by Lopp, and they also contain many of the primary documents relating to the government's efforts to come to grips with the Lomens and the reindeer problem.

# Index

PublicAffairs is a publishing house founded in 1997. It is a tribute to the standards, values, and flair of three persons who have served as mentors to countless reporters, writers, editors, and book people of all kinds, including me.

I.F. STONE, proprietor of *I. F. Stone's Weekly*, combined a commitment to the First Amendment with entrepreneurial zeal and reporting skill and became one of the great independent journalists in American history. At the age of eighty, Izzy published *The Trial of Socrates,* which was a national bestseller. He wrote the book after he taught himself ancient Greek.

BENJAMIN C. BRADLEE was for nearly thirty years the charismatic editorial leader of *The Washington Post.* It was Ben who gave the *Post* the range and courage to pursue such historic issues as Watergate. He supported his reporters with a tenacity that made them fearless and it is no accident that so many became authors of influential, best-selling books.

ROBERT L. BERNSTEIN, the chief executive of Random House for more than a quarter century, guided one of the nation's premier publishing houses. Bob was personally responsible for many books of political dissent and argument that challenged tyranny around the globe. He is also the founder and longtime chair of Human Rights Watch, one of the most respected human rights organizations in the world.

. . .

For fifty years, the banner of Public Affairs Press was carried by its owner Morris B. Schnapper, who published Gandhi, Nasser, Toynbee, Truman, and about 1,500 other authors. In 1983, Schnapper was described by *The Washington Post* as "a redoubtable gadfly." His legacy will endure in the books to come.

Peter Osnos, *Founder and Editor-at-Large*